The Merchant Taylors' Company of London:
Court Minutes, 1486–1493

Publications of the

RICHARD III & YORKIST HISTORY TRUST

THE
MERCHANT TAYLORS'
COMPANY OF LONDON:
COURT MINUTES,
1486–1493

Edited and Introduced by

MATTHEW DAVIES

RICHARD III AND YORKIST HISTORY TRUST

in association with

PAUL WATKINS

STAMFORD

2 0 0 0

Published by the
RICHARD III AND YORKIST HISTORY TRUST

in asssociation with

'PAUL WATKINS'
(an imprint of Shaun Tyas)
18 Adelaide Street
Stamford
Lincolnshire
PE9 2EN

ISBN
1 900289 36 9

Printed and bound in the United Kingdom by the Alden Group, Oxford

CONTENTS

LIST OF ILLUSTRATIONS, TABLES AND MAPS

Cover: Detail from the earlier of the two funeral palls (*c.*1490 x 1520) belonging to the Merchant Taylors' Company. On the right an angel carries the head of St. John the Baptist, patron saint of the Company, on a silver platter. To the left are two symbols closely associated with tailoring: the scissors represent the task of cutting out cloth, while the pavilion is probably a direct reference to John de Yakesley, Edward III's tent-maker, who in 1332 acquired the site of what later became Merchant Taylors' Hall. (By permission of the Merchant Taylors' Company)

ACKNOWLEDGMENTS

I should like to thanks all those from whose help I have benefited in preparing this edition. As general editor for the book for the Richard III and Yorkist History Trust, Anne Sutton has been unfailing in her advice and encouragement as the book progressed towards publication. Caroline Barron and Ian Archer both generously read the entire manuscript and made a number of valuable suggestions, particularly concerning form and content. I am grateful to Fiona Kisby, Hannes Kleineke, Penny Tucker, Stephanie Hovland, Jessica Freeman and Eleanor Quinton for information about some of the people and subjects mentioned in the text. The translation of some of the more obscure Latin words and phrases has been much improved by the help of Stephen O'Connor. An early version of the Introduction was read as a paper to the seminar on Medieval and Tudor London at the Institute of Historical Research in June 1998, and my thanks go to all those who contributed their ideas and opinions. I am also grateful to the librarians and archivists of the Corporation of London Record Office, the Goldsmiths' Company and the Public Record Office, whose records I have drawn on extensively in the footnotes and appendices. Since 1996 the archive of the Merchant Taylors' Company has been in the possession of the Guildhall Library, and I owe a particular debt to the Keeper of Manuscripts, Stephen Freeth, and his staff for assisting with access to the manuscript and with the photography. I am pleased to thank the Clerk and Court of the Merchant Taylors' Company for their long-standing support of my work on the Company's history, and to the Richard III and Yorkist History Trust for accepting this volume for publication. Finally, this book could not have been written without the support and encouragement of my wife, Jane.

History of Parliament Trust, London

LIST OF ABBREVIATIONS

Accounts, I, II, III	Guildhall Library, London, Merchant Taylors' Company, Accounts, vols I (1398–1445), II (1453–69), III (1469–84).
Beaven, *Aldermen*	A. B. Beaven, *The Aldermen of the City of London*, 2 vols (London, 1908–13).
BL	British Library.
Bolton (ed.), *Alien Communities*	J. L. Bolton (ed.), *Alien Communities in the Fifteenth Century: The Subsidy Rolls of 1440 and 1483–4* (Richard III and Yorkist History Trust/Stamford, 1998).
Cal. Letter Bk. A, B etc.	*Calendar of the Letter Books preserved among the Archives of the Corporation of the City of London*, ed. R.R. Sharpe, 11 vols A–L (London, 1899–1912).
Clode, *Early History*	C. M. Clode, *The Early History of the Guild of Merchant Taylors of the Fraternity of St. John the Baptist, London*, 2 vols (London, 1888).
Clode, *Memorials*	C. M. Clode (ed.), *Memorials of the Merchant Taylors' Company* (London, 1875).
CLRO	Corporation of London Records Office.
Cobb (ed.), *Overseas Trade*	*The Overseas Trade of London: Exchequer Customs Accounts 1480–1*, ed. H. S. Cobb, London Record Society, 27 (1990).
Coro. Richard III ed. Sutton and Hammond	A. F. Sutton and P. W. Hammond (eds.), *The Coronation of Richard III: the Extant Documents* (Gloucester, 1983).
CWCH	*Calendar of Wills Proved and Enrolled in the Court of Hustings, London, 1258–1688*, ed. R. R. Sharpe, 2 vols (London, 1889–90).

Davies, 'Artisans, Guilds and Government'	M. Davies, 'Artisans, Guilds and Government in London', in R. H. Britnell (ed.), *Daily Life in the Late Middle Ages* (Stroud, 1998), pp. 125–50.
Davies, 'Charity'	M. Davies, 'The Tailors of London: Corporate Charity in the Late-Medieval Town', in *Crown, Government and People in the Fifteenth Century*, ed. R. E. Archer (Stroud, 1995), pp. 161–90.
Davies, thesis	M. P. Davies, 'The Tailors of London and their Guild, c.1300–1500', unpublished D.Phil. thesis, University of Oxford (1994).
GL	Guildhall Library, London.
Lobel (ed.), *Atlas*	M. D. Lobel (ed.), *The British Atlas of Historic Towns, III, The City of London to c.1520* (Oxford, 1989).
P&P	*Past and Present.*
PCC	Prerogative Court of Canterbury.
PRO	Public Record Office.
Stow, *Survey*	J. Stow, *A Survey of London*, ed. C. L. Kingsford, 2 vols (Oxford, 1908).
Thrupp, *Merchant Class*	S. L. Thrupp, *The Merchant Class of Medieval London* (Chicago, 1948; repr. Ann Arbor, MI, 1962).

INTRODUCTION:
THE MERCHANT TAYLORS' COMPANY
AND ITS COURT IN THE
LATE FIFTEENTH CENTURY

In September 1492 the master of the guild of London tailors, Walter Povey, came before the governing body of the craft, the court of assistants, and claimed that 'the councelles and secretes of the said crafte by som persones beforetyme have ben disclosed and discovered out of the said crafte wherby grete inconvenyences have ensued'. To try and prevent further disclosures all members of the court were required to appear at the company's hall in Bradestrete (now Threadneedle Street) to swear their oaths of office again.[1] Although nothing is known of the nature of any indiscretions, or the identities of the alleged culprits, this entry from the surviving minutes of the court provides a striking illustration of the central place which this body had come to occupy in the life of the company by the close of the fifteenth century. The Tailors, soon to become 'Merchant Taylors', were not alone, for an increasing number of the city's other livery companies also possessed formal courts of this kind for the transaction of business relating to their respective crafts. As studies of the companies in the early modern period have demonstrated, court minutes are especially valuable as an ongoing record of decision-making processes, the resolution of disputes and the evolution of policies affecting the crafts and their relationships with each other and with the City government.[2] For the pre-Reformation period, however, fewer court records survive in the archives of the London livery companies. The most significant are those belonging to the Goldsmiths, Mercers and Merchant Taylors, all three of which were well-established companies with a long tradition of record-keeping. There are, however, certain important differences in the form and content of these records which should be borne in mind when considering their value for historians. In the case of the Goldsmiths, for instance, the main series of 'minute books' compiled in the fifteenth century is far from being a complete record of the proceedings of the court as the name would seem to imply. These books in fact contain what amounts to a series of 'annual

---

[1]   Below, pp. 203–4.
[2]   See esp. I. W. Archer, *The Pursuit of Stability: Social Relations in Elizabethan London* (Cambridge, 1991) and S. Rappaport, *Worlds Within Worlds: Structures of Life in Sixteenth-Century London* (Cambridge, 1989).

reports' which included selected details of expenditure and income and only what were perceived as the most important proceedings of the company's court for each year. In 1492 a new minute book was begun which ran in tandem with the main series until 1499. Though it too was compiled annually, many more proceedings were included and for two of the six years it appears that most, if not all, of the court's meetings were written up in some form. The annual compilation of these books suggests that the Goldsmiths' clerks had at their disposal some kind of ongoing, draft account of the proceedings of each court meeting that was used to construct a more limited formal record of the court's activities and decisions. By contrast, the formal records of the Mercers' and Merchant Taylors' Companies continued to be compiled on a meeting-by-meeting basis, a practice which, though still open to editorial changes, resulted in the inclusion of a greater quantity and variety of court proceedings. In the case of the Mercers, however, the medieval records of their court of assistants, covering the period 1453–1527, survive in the form of a much edited sixteenth-century transcript, along with records of the Merchant Adventurers. It is likely, therefore, that the copyist omitted or heavily edited proceedings which he regarded as less noteworthy.[3] The surviving fifteenth-century court minutes of the Merchant Taylors' Company are thus unique as a record of the day-to-day governance of a London livery company in this period. Though covering just seven years in the life of the company, from April 1486 to August 1493, they contain proceedings of more than four hundred meetings held in the presence of the master and wardens alone, or else with a larger body of 'assistants' in attendance. Like the governing body of any large organisation, the Tailors' court discussed a wide range of issues, from relatively mundane administrative matters, such as the payment of officers and almsmen, to economic concerns and the company's often tense relations with other companies and with the City government. The proceedings of the court, now deposited in Guildhall Library with the rest of the company's archive, are thus a rare and fertile source for this period of London's history and have been edited here for the first time.[4]

---

[3] *Acts of Court of the Mercers' Company 1453–1527*, eds L. L. Lyell and F. D. Watney (Cambridge, 1936); A. F. Sutton and P. W. Hammond, 'The Problems of Dating and the Dangers of Re-dating: The Acts of Court of the Mercers' Company, 1453–1527', *Jnl. of the Society of Archivists*, 6 (1978), pp. 87–9. Goldsmiths' Company, London, Minute Books A (1–2) and B. See also T. F. Reddaway and L. E. M. Walker, *The Early History of the Goldsmiths' Company, 1327–1509* (London, 1975), pp. 32–5, 187.

[4] Subject to re-cataloguing by Guildhall Library, the minutes are currently filed as Merchant Taylors' Co., Ancient MS. Bk. 37. The only historian to have used the Merchant Taylors' court minutes extensively is Prof. Sylvia Thrupp, who drew upon them in her study of London's merchant class in the later middle ages, first published in 1948: Thrupp, *Merchant Class*.

I. THE ORIGINS AND DEVELOPMENT OF THE COURTS OF THE LONDON LIVERY COMPANIES

Before examining in more detail the subject matter contained in the minutes, it is important to place them in the context of the development of the London livery companies in the middle ages. In common with most of the 'Great Twelve' companies, those who stood at the apex of the city's craft hierarchy, the origins of the Merchant Taylors' Company can be traced back to the late thirteenth and early fourteenth centuries, a period when organisations of various kinds emerged within London's crafts. By 1300, according to John Stow, the City's tailors were said to have founded a fraternity dedicated to St. John the Baptist, which was then governed by a master, Henry de Ryall, known as the *peregrinus* or 'pilgrim', and four wardens known as 'purveyors of alms'.[5] Like the similar organisations founded by the goldsmiths (St. Dunstan) and the skinners (Corpus Christi), the fraternity of St. John the Baptist was an elite association which catered for the social and spiritual needs of the most prominent freemen of the craft. Livery robes and hoods were commonly worn by fraternity members on feast days and during civic processions, and in due course the term 'liveryman' was used to denote membership of these exclusive associations. Other occupational groups in London, notably the Vintners and Mercers, never developed formally constituted 'fraternities', but despite this most used liveries as a means to distinguish, and to draw together, their wealthier freemen into an identifiable group at the head of the craft.[6] In addition to their social and religious functions, many of these elite associations were also beginning to develop a regulatory role within the craft as a whole, one which stemmed from the fact that the wardens of the exclusive craft fraternities were increasingly being recognised by the City and by the Crown as the officials to whom the governance of the craft as a whole (i.e. all the freemen, their wives and apprentices) could be entrusted. It is this latter development that seems to provide the key to understanding the emergence of other formal structures, particularly the establishment of 'courts' for the transaction of business

---

[5] Stow, *Survey*, vol. 1, p. 181. Henry de Ryall, tailor, appears in a number of sources between 1300 and 1305 as a prominent common councilman: *Cal. Letter Bk. B*, p. 185; ibid. *C*, pp. 67-8; *Calendar of Early Mayor's Court Rolls AD 1298-1307*, ed. A. H. Thomas (Cambridge, 1924), p. 180. The Palmers' guild in Ludlow was headed by a 'pilgrim': see C. Liddy, 'The Palmers' Gild Window, St. Lawrence's Church, Ludlow: a Study of the Construction of Gild Identity in Medieval Stained Glass', *Transactions of the Shropshire Archaeological and Historical Society*, 72 (1997), pp. 28, 30.

[6] See E. M. Veale, 'The "Great Twelve": Mistery and Fraternity in Thirteenth-Century London', *Historical Research*, 64 (1991), pp. 237-63.

affecting both the fraternities and the crafts they headed. In the late thirteenth and early fourteenth centuries a number of changes took place within the government of the City of London which placed greater reliance upon representatives of the misteries. As Dr. Anne Sutton has described, a period of confrontation in the 1260s and 1270s gave way to a recognition by the city authorities, and indeed by the Crown, that the misteries could usefully be involved in the process of government, to bolster the traditional powers of the aldermen in the wards in the maintenance of public order. To this end in 1282 and 1294 the 'better and more discreet' men of the misteries were ordered to present the names of their masters, servants and apprentices.[7] The evolution of regulations concerning the freedom of the City reflected these developments, and the formal relationship between the misteries and access to the franchise was enshrined in the royal charter granted to the City in 1319. Alongside these developments came a clarification of the means by which access to the freedom through the crafts should be regulated, and, more importantly, by whom. This can be seen in an entry in Letter Book E from November 1328 when lists were drawn up of men who were to be responsible for governing twenty-four of the city's crafts. Each mistery appears to have had a group of governors in proportion to its size: the Tailors, already among the largest of the crafts, were to have twenty such governors, a number exceeded only by the twenty-one men who were to supervise the fishmongers and the twenty-four for the butchers. At the other end of the scale the cappers, girdlers and painters were to have four each.[8] These men did not take the place of wardens or other officials recorded elsewhere, such as those named in the Tailors' first charter, acquired by them in 1327. Rather, these lists of prominent citizens from each craft suggest that the principle of drawing upon senior craftsmen to help in the regulation of the misteries was becoming well established. In 1340, for instance, the Tailors were the subject of another mayoral ordinance which specified that 6 out of a named group of 24 men were to assess the fitness of those who sought the freedom through the craft.[9] In this period, however, there is little to suggest that these groups were meeting together regularly as formal 'courts' to transact business relating to the internal affairs of the crafts or the guilds founded within them. Though doubtless regarded as the natural representatives of the crafts, their primary role was still to assist the wardens as delegates of the City government.

The evolution of more formally constituted bodies occurred gradually over the course of the fourteenth century and well into the fifteenth. It is a difficult movement to trace, partly because of the patchy nature of many guild records and partly because the need for such formal governing bodies was by

---

[7]   A. F. Sutton, 'The Silent Years of London Guild History before 1300: the Case of the Mercers', *Historical Research*, 71 no. 175 (1998), pp. 121–41.

[8]   *Cal. Letter Bk. E*, pp. 231–4.

[9]   *Cal. Letter Bk. F*, pp. 52–3.

no means widespread. City records continue to refer to the 'good men' of particular crafts, such as those who appeared before the mayor to submit their ordinances for scrutiny in line with a Statute passed in 1437, but the place of these groups in the structures established within the crafts is often unclear.[10] It may, for instance, have been assumed that wardens would seek the advice and opinions of senior members of their craft when necessary, but, until these bodies met together regularly, such discussions would not have generated records. The move towards a more formal basis for consultation is indicated in the Grocers' Company accounts which for 1376 show that a body of six men was chosen for 'helpyng and counsellyng of the wardens' for the coming year. In the early fifteenth century this body, known as the 'fellowship associated', met quarterly, its numbers fluctuating between 6 and 10.[11] The need for regular consultation was partly a consequence of the ever more complex internal operations of the crafts themselves, which placed additional burdens on the masters and wardens. By the end of the fourteenth century a growing number of the guilds, including the Goldsmiths, Tailors and Skinners, had acquired premises of their own, as well as other property holdings and had developed a range of other services such as the administration of chantries and assistance for their poor and sick members.[12] The proliferation of paid officials such as clerks, beadles and rent collectors was a symptom of these changes, and in many cases they were not merely doing the bidding of the wardens of the crafts but also implementing the decisions reached at regular meetings of men known as 'assistants'.

Ordinances that describe the methods of choosing assistants are one indication of the formalisation of these bodies. Annual elections were adopted by some crafts: the Shearmen in 1452 agreed an ordinance for the election by all the liverymen 'of twelve persons discrete and well avised ... for to assist and counsel the said wardens'.[13] In practice these bodies may not have changed much from year to year: continuity was provided by the prominence of elder statesmen, particularly former masters and wardens, who often dominated the membership. This was certainly the case with the Tailors in the first half of the fifteenth century: some surviving folios from an ordinance book record a series of regulations agreed in 1436 by the master and wardens 'and bi wyse

---

[10]   *Statutes of the Realm* (1101–1713) eds A. Luders, T. E. Tomlin, A. France, W. E. Taunton and J. Raithby, 11 vols, Record Commission (London 1810–28), IV, p. 507.

[11]   *Facsimile of the First Volume of the MS. Archives of the Worshipful Company of Grocers of the City of London, AD 1345–1463*, ed. J. A. Kingdon, 2 vols (London, 1883–6), vol. 1, p. 21; P. Nightingale, *A Medieval Mercantile Community: The Grocers' Company and the Politics and Trade of London, 1000–1485* (New Haven, 1995), pp. 249, 380.

[12]   See Veale '"Great Twelve"', pp. 237–63; Davies, 'Charity', pp. 164–80.

[13]   G. Unwin, *The Guilds and Companies of London* (London, 1908), p. 218.

discrecions and good avyse' of sixteen liverymen, a list headed by 'Master Rauf Holand alderman'.[14] Nine of these men, including Holand, were former masters of the craft while two others were shortly to hold that office. The prominence of such elder statesmen was of course nothing new and one can revisit the lists of 1328 to see a similar pattern among the governors of the crafts appointed by the City. The main differences stem from the regularity with which some of these bodies were meeting in the mid to late fifteenth century, and the clarification of the size and nature of their membership, marking their transition from informal advisory bodies to formally constituted courts that initiated policy and discussed all manner of matters affecting both craft and guild. In 1442, for instance, the Tailors' assistants were described for the first time as the 'xxiiij men', and although no proceedings survive it is almost certain that they were meeting together on a regular basis.[15]

II. THE COURT MINUTES, 1486–1493

The Construction of Ancient MS Book 37

The production of documents relating to meetings of the assistants was a natural next step for some crafts, although others probably continued to record the proceedings second-hand, so to speak, in the form of entries in account books and collections of ordinances. The surviving proceedings of the Tailors' court are contained in two volumes, together making up Merchant Taylors' Company, Ancient MS Book 37, now deposited in Guildhall Library. The bulk of these entries relate to ordinary meetings of the court, which were normally held on Mondays and Fridays, interspersed with entries for quarter-days. Both volumes are written on watermarked paper measuring 216mm x 395mm (approx.). From an examination of the two volumes it is apparent that they comprise the remnants of a much longer series of court proceedings, the bulk of which has not survived. Volume I originally contained 257 folios of which folios 1–227 and 235–44 have been lost, leaving a total of 20 folios covering the periods 7 April–18 December 1486, and 12 November 1487–24 June 1488. These remaining pages have been bound up with other later material (see below) and renumbered as ff. 1–22. The second volume follows on from the first, beginning with an entry describing the election of William Buck as master on 24 June 1488. It contains 75 folios and covers the period up to and including 9 August 1493. It is almost certain that the minutes continued after this date, but once again the folios have been lost. The best internal evidence of the original state of the minutes can therefore be

---

14   GL, Merchant Taylors' Company, Misc. Docs. A.2 (Early Ordinances 1429–55), f. 8.
15   Ibid., f. 9v.

found in volume I, where the missing 227 folios may represent records dating back as far as the early 1460s, or even earlier. While no actual minutes survive from that period, a clue to the original coverage of the volume can be found on the last two folios (now ff. 21–22v) which seem to have been used by the clerk to record documents that related to particular meetings held by the court in those years but which may have been considered too lengthy for inclusion with the minutes for a particular meeting. Of particular interest is a series of documents relating to the transfer of a tailoring business from Stephen Piers to his son, John, which took place between 1467 and 1470, a rare example from late-medieval London of a *pre-mortem* contract.[16] As well as this earlier material, however, volume I also contains two folios that provide evidence of the minutes lost from the period after 1493, confirming that volume II similarly covered a longer period. The material on these folios mainly comprises incomplete jottings, which probably related to more formal proceedings, but among them are two assessments made of the membership of the company for the purpose of raising revenue, one of which is dated 30 May 1494. When volume I was re-bound and re-foliated, probably in the nineteenth century, the two pages concerned were placed at the front and so were numbered ff. 1–2v, even though they post-date the rest of the volume.

A clearer picture of the original state of the manuscript, and indeed of the company's archive as a whole, is provided by two seventeenth-century inventories. The first of these, compiled in 1609, describes the company's minute books as: 'Nyne books severally marked with these severall letters viz A, B, C, D, E, F, G, H and I ... the Booke A begynnyng in the xxviiith yere of K. Edw. the First Anno Domini 1299 and the Booke I endyng the xxiiiith day of January 1574'. Of this remarkable series, only Book I survives intact as the first volume (1562–74) of the company's extensive run of court minutes which continues with only a few gaps up to the present day. By 1689, however, most of volumes A–H had apparently been lost, for an inventory taken in that year recorded just two early minute books, one commencing in March 1404, now also lost, and a second, which, significantly, covered the period 37 Henry VI (1458–9) to 3 Henry VII (1487–8). The end date corresponds exactly with that of the first volume of Ancient MS Book 37 (24 June 1488) while the start date of 1458–9 is entirely consistent with the volume as it must have appeared before the loss of the first 227 folios. Less clear, however, is the original size and coverage of the subsequent volume, not mentioned in 1689. At some point after this inventory was compiled, the first 75 folios reappeared and were bound together as volume II of the present Ancient MS Book 37.[17]

---

[16]   The majority of these were first printed in Clode, *Early History*, vol.1, pp. 367–70. The full contents of ff. 21–22v are included here as Appendix II.

[17]   GL, Merchant Taylors' Company, Ancient MS Bks. 12, f. 14; 13, p. 3; H. L. Hopkinson, *Report on the Ancient Records in the Possession of the Guild of Merchant Taylors of the Fraternity of St. John the Baptist in the City of London* (London, 1915),

The reference in the 1609 inventory to a series of books stretching back to 1299 is striking, but does not necessarily mean that the Tailors' court and its records can be traced back to that date. It is probable that the very early books contained a mixture of financial records, ordinances, and other documents connected with the fraternity of St. John the Baptist in the period during which it acquired the site of its Hall and the first of its many royal charters. One is perhaps on safer ground in assuming that by the fifteenth century they had grown into specialised records pertaining to the court which complemented the account books of the company, which survive from 1398, and other records. As the inventories of 1609 and 1689 suggest, other books were also lost in the eighteenth and nineteenth centuries, including 'one other auntient book in paper contaynyng the names of all the M[aste]rs and the Wardens of this company sithence the yere Anno Domini 1300 being the xxviiith yere of the raigne of King Edward the First'. According to Charles Clode, master in 1873-4, this 'invaluable book' was produced by the clerk in 1865 but had vanished from the archives ten years later when Clode compiled his *Memorials* of the company. The manuscript was almost certainly the source for Stow's account of the fraternity's origins and his identification of the master of 1300 as Henry de Ryall.[18]

Authorship
The period covered by the surviving court minutes saw three men occupy the position of clerk of the company. The first of these, Thomas Kirton, spent the first half of his career as a clerk in the mayor's court in London, but he had already established links with the Tailors by the late-1450s when he was one of a team of attorneys employed by the company to represent their interests in a dispute with the church of St. Katherine Cree. His appointment as clerk of the fraternity of St. John the Baptist in the autumn of 1464 reflected a growing demand on the part of the livery companies for clerks who, as well as being competent administrators, also possessed valuable legal skills. These were particularly important in the quasi-judicial context of a company court where bonds and other contracts were regularly entered into by their freemen, and where law-suits with other institutions and individuals were discussed.[19] The date of Kirton's appointment means that he was responsible

---

pp. 99–101.

18 Hopkinson, *Ancient Records*, pp. 3, 105; Clode, *Memorials*, p. 2n. For Henry de Ryall see above, n. 5.

19 Accounts, II, ff. 137, 177v, 259. Kirton was active as an attorney in the city from about 1443 until his appointment as the Tailors' clerk, see for instance CLRO, Journals, 5, f. 210; 6, f. 24. I am grateful to Dr Penny Tucker for these and all subsequent references to Kirton's career in London. For London's law courts see idem, 'London's Courts of Law in the Fifteenth Century', in *Communities and Courts in Britain 1500–1900*, ed. C. Brooks and M. Lobban (London, 1997), pp.

for approximately 80 per cent of the original volume of court minutes that had been begun by his predecessor in 1458-9, as well as the material from 1467-75 written into the back of volume I. However, of his entries only those for the period 7 April 1486 to 18 December 1487 survive. Records for the following 11 months (original folios 235-44) are missing, a period which coincided with Kirton's retirement, probably in August 1487.[20] Kirton's minutes are written in a mixture of Latin and English, the choice of language being related to the nature of the entry concerned. Apprentice enrolments, for instance, were written up in Latin, reflecting the formal legal contract that was entered into by both master and apprentice in front of the assembled court. These were normally followed, however, by entries in English recording the payment of the enrolment fee (normally 40d. for each apprentice). Kirton's retirement may well have been prompted by ill health, for on 30 July 1487 he drew up his will, describing himself as 'Thomas Kyrton of London, gentleman' and asking to be buried in the church of St. Olave Silver Street. Among his bequests was the sum of 13s. 4d. 'to the maister and brethren of the fraternite of Seint John Baptist of Taylors of London to thentent that they shalhave me in ther speciall remembraunce at the quarterdayes among them holden'. In the event, however, Kirton survived for at least another two and a half years, and his will was finally proved in October 1490.[21] His successor was William Duryvale, who was paid wages of 12s. for half a quarter ending on the feast of St. Michael (29 September) 1487, suggesting that he had succeeded Kirton in August the same year. What little is recorded of him elsewhere suggests a legal background of sorts, for in January 1488 he took the oath of admission to the fraternity of the London Scriveners. Two years later another entry in the Scriveners' Common Paper lists him with a servant.[22] Unlike his predecessor, Duryvale wrote almost entirely in Latin, employing English only for quotations and for the more unusual entries, such as that for 7 February 1488 when the theft of 'a peyre of Rostyng Rakkes' by John Watertoft, the mayor's chief cook, was discussed by the court.[23] His tenure of the office lasted for just under five years: he was responsible for the entry of 10 September 1492 but had clearly departed by 12 October when his final quarterly wages of 25s. were noted by his successor, Henry Mayour.

25-42.

[20] Below, pp. 81-2

[21] PRO, PROB 11/9, f. 63. In the meantime (Lent term 1486/7) Kirton had been specially admitted to Lincoln's Inn where he was permitted to 'have a clerk at the commons as Benchers have'. He was still alive in the autumn of 1489 when he was elected as escheator of the Inn. *The Records of the Honourable Society of Lincoln's Inn, Black Books*, 5 vols (Lincoln's Inn, 1847-1968) vol. 1, pp. 86, 90.

[22] F. W. Steer (ed.), *Scriveners' Company Common Paper 1357-1628, with a Continuation to 1678*, London Record Society, 4 (1968), pp. 13, 23.

[23] See below, pp. 92-3.

Although responsible for all the entries from 10 October onwards, Mayour did not officially take over as clerk until the new year, as his first quarterly wages were not paid until 3 March 1493. The list of officials to be paid their quarterly wages on 22 December 1492 does not include a payment to anyone serving as clerk, and it seems clear that the post of clerk was vacant for some three months from mid-September onwards. An initial attempt was made to continue the official record of the court's proceedings during the interregnum, but this was abandoned after just two meetings (17 September and 3 October 1492), whose proceedings were written up by an unknown hand. Mayour's first task on taking office in January 1493, therefore, was to write up a three month backlog of entries, presumably from notes taken by one of the members of the court. As a result the minutes for October to December 1492 differ slightly from the usual pattern in that entries for the meetings are interspersed with a complete list of the anniversaries celebrated by the company throughout the year, details of all those who paid fines to open shops and a list of the annual quit-rents paid by the company. Normally such payments and receipts were noted individually as and when they occurred. Like his predecessor, Mayour was a long-standing member of the Scriveners' Company: he was apprenticed at an unknown date to a Robert Legett and his oath of admission to their fraternity, written in his own hand, was recorded in the Common Paper on 24 November 1481.[24] Five years later, on 26 October 1486, Mayour was appointed to the joint offices of clerk and beadle of the Goldsmiths' Company, posts he was to hold for just under six years. He took over the task of writing up brief annual lists of payments and receipts, together with selected proceedings of the company's court: the first to be written in his distinctive hand is thus the account for the year to the feast of St. Dunstan, 2 Henry VII (19 May 1487) which included the entry recording that he had been 'sworen and admytted clerk of this feliship'.[25] The limited nature of these annual records gave Mayour relatively little scope for innovation in terms of presentation or content, and it appears that, for the most part, he continued the matter-of fact approach of his predecessors by including only certain proceedings of the company's court with lists of fines received and payments made. Nevertheless, it is likely that his service as both clerk and beadle of the Goldsmiths provided him with a valuable insight into the day-to-day operation of an important city company, and the fact that the company's records were written in English probably helped him to develop the distinctive style of writing which pervades his entries in the Tailors' minutes. His departure from the Goldsmiths in the summer of 1492 remains

---

[24] *Scriveners' Common Paper*, ed. Steer, p. 23. For a general overview of the legal profession, including the many attorneys who were not members of the inns of court and had received no formal training, see J. H. Baker, *The Legal Profession and the Common Law* (London, 1986), esp. pp. 87–8.

[25] Goldsmiths' Company, London, Minute Book A (vol. 2), p. 268.

something of a mystery. At a well-attended meeting of the Goldsmith's court on 20 July those present 'were accorded and aggreed and there dismyssed Harry Mayowre of his office that is to saye both of clerkeshipp & also of Bedilshippe'. There is no indication that he had committed any particular offence, but his removal may well have been connected with a reorganisation of the Goldsmiths' administration that was put into effect once he had left.[26]

Less than six months later Mayour succeeded William Duryvale as clerk of the Tailors' Company. He held the post of clerk until at least 1512 when he compiled a detailed inventory of the Hall and its contents, and was still alive in 1515 when he was left a small bequest by an Essex clergyman.[27] His standing within the company was doubtless enhanced by the fact that, like many scriveners, he possessed legal skills which could be used to good effect in the drafting of contracts, arbitration awards and leases. In March 1493, in a rare reference to his own position, Mayour described himself as 'notary and clerk of this worshipful company', and six years later, in the will of John Povey, a former warden, he was described as a 'notary papall'. In the light of these descriptions it is not difficult to see why he was chosen as an executor by both Povey and another prominent tailor, Thomas Howdan (d.1512), and why his services were particularly valued by the company itself.[28] Of the three men responsible for the surviving court minutes it is Mayour's remarkable contribution that stands out most clearly. His entries, written almost exclusively in English, are characterised by a fluency and an appreciation of language and narrative which are particularly in evidence in his accounts of the numerous disputes and debates which were heard before the court. They provide a wonderfully vivid insight into the life of the court and the issues it dealt with in this period. Perhaps the best example of his approach is his 1,500 word account of a dispute involving a former master of the craft, John Heed, whose refusal to submit to the will of the court in the summer of 1492 eventually resulted in his imprisonment by the mayor. This

---

[26]   Goldsmiths' Company, London, Minute Book B, p. 1. The offices of clerk and beadle were separated and Mayour's successor as clerk began to compile a separate 'minute book' of court proceedings which, though still selective, ran in parallel with the main series of records.

[27]   I. Darlington (ed.) *London Consistory Court Wills 1492–1547*, London Record Society, 3 (1967), p. 32. The 1512 inventory is printed in Clode, *Memorials*, pp. 84–91.

[28]   See entry for 15 March 1493, below p. 239. For the wills of Povey and Howdan see Appendix IV. The precise meaning of the term 'notary papall' in this period is uncertain. It originally denoted officials of the papal chancery, men who were generally distinct from 'notaries public'. By the late 15th century, however, the term 'notary' was frequently used in connection with men such as Mayour whose legal skills had been acquired through his training as a scrivener. See esp. C. R. Cheney, *Notaries Public in England in the Thirteenth and Fourteenth Centuries* (Oxford, 1972).

drastic step was taken in the aftermath of a dramatic show-down with the current master of the company, Walter Povey, who, in a final attempt to secure Heed's obedience, read out some of the ordinances of the craft and asked him if he would obey them. Heed's answer as recorded by Mayour was unequivocal: 'Sir, I know thise ordynaunces as well as ye do but I wole not abide nor fulfill theym'. This left the master with no choice but to refer the matter to the mayor who promptly imprisoned Heed for five days. Following his release Heed appeared before another meeting of the court when, in the words of the clerk, he 'humbly submytted hym self to the maister and wardeyns hertily desiryng theym to be good Maister and frendes unto hym for he knewe well that he had mysse used hym self in brekyng of the ordynaunces wherfore he was penitent.'[29] Most striking about Mayour's account is that it refers to events which took place before his appointment as clerk, and which had been noted by his predecessors in the form of terse entries for 15 August, 10 and 17 September, and 3 October 1492. Mayour's appointment seems to have coincided with a decision to have a more detailed account of the dispute written up, and it is clear that this was a task he was well suited for. His use of reported speech, in particular, suggests that he was keen to make use of testimony, whether written or oral, in order to present an accurate and vivid account of proceedings. This freedom of expression was possible partly because of Mayour's preference for English, and partly because proceedings of the court were written up meeting-by-meeting with no apparent pressure on him to keep the entries concise. As a result no fewer than twenty-four of the seventy-five folios (i.e. thirty-two per cent) surviving in volume II were written by Mayour, even though he was clerk for only seven of the sixty-two months covered by this volume.

In late June 1493 Mayour ceased to be responsible for writing up the proceedings of the court which, for the remaining six folios, were compiled by an unknown author. The form and presentation of the minutes followed the pattern set by Mayour, suggesting that he was supervising the work.

III. MEMBERSHIP OF THE COURT

Despite the changes in authorship, the proceedings of the court continued to be recorded in more or less the same manner, concentrating upon entries for each of the ordinary meetings of the court, normally held on Mondays or Fridays, and the quarter-days. Meetings were held frequently: in the six-and-a-half years covered by the surviving minutes there are entries for no fewer than 405 meetings, an average of just over five a month. Clearly, therefore, attendance at each and every meeting would have been an onerous burden for

---

[29] Below, pp. 207–10.

many members of the court, particularly those who were also members of the court of aldermen. It is striking, therefore, that only ninety-five of the meetings are accompanied by lists of the assistants who were present. The majority of headings just refer to the date of the meeting, often noting that it was held in the presence of the master and wardens. While some of these headings are misleading, judging from subsequent references to others present, it seems probable that most meetings of the court were indeed held before just the master and wardens, the elected officials of the company who were responsible for the day-to-day administration of the affairs of the craft. This is perhaps not surprising given the frequency with which meetings were held: it seems unlikely that assistants would have been expected to attend five meetings of the court every month when much of what was transacted could be dealt with by the master and wardens, the annually elected officers responsible for the day-to-day affairs of both craft and guild. Full meetings of the court were probably convened once or possibly twice a month, as well as on quarter-days, as a means of reviewing the progress of important issues. These larger gatherings were clearly important occasions, the most significant being the meeting held on the eve of the feast of the Nativity of St. John the Baptist (24 June) at which the election of the master and wardens took place. Even so, the attendance lists reveal that the burdens of court membership were not shared equally. For a start, these meetings of the court were attended, on average, by only 11 of the 24 assistants, a statistic which barely improves when the quarter-days alone are considered. Furthermore, as Table 1 demonstrates, some individuals were far more active as court members than others, with men such as Hugh Pemberton, John Percyvale and Robert Duplage among those who attended more than fifty of the eighty-two meetings for which attendance lists survive.[30] Several others attended more than forty of these meetings. These men provided the core of the court in a period when a total of thirty-six different men served as assistants at one time or another. In terms of its social composition, the court of the late 1480s and early 1490s bears remarkable similarities to its predecessor of 1435: the table shows that all but three of those attending more than twenty meetings served as master of the company at some point during their careers. Three men, Stephen Jenyns, Walter Povey and John Spencer were elected to that office during the period covered by the minutes, while Owen Boughton was the only individual to be elected subsequently, in 1495–6. As in 1435, therefore, the court was dominated by former masters, with the remaining places largely being filled by those destined for high office. Consequently the members of the court were a vastly experienced group: those who were assistants in 1435 had been liverymen for, on average, twenty-two years, with their

---

30 This period has been chosen for analysis because it contains an unbroken run of minutes. It does not, therefore, include the 13 attendance lists from the period 7 Apr. to 18 Dec. 1486 which are followed by a gap of some 11 months.

counterparts of 1488 having averaged twenty-four years each.[31]

Table 1. Attendance at the Court, November 1487–August 1493

Maximum number of meetings = 82

1.	Hugh Pemberton *M, A*	67	12. Stephen Jenyns *M*	36
2.	John Percyvale *M, A*	58	13. Alan Hoberd	31
3.	Robert Duplage *M*	57	14. John Stodard *M*	29
4.	Richard West *M*[32]	53	15. Richard Adyff *W*	27
5.	John Lee *M*	52	16. John Swan *M, A*	27
6.	William Galle *M*	47	17. Walter Povey *M*	26
7.	John Heed *M*	39	18. Roger Tego *M*	26
8.	William Buck *M*	39	19. John Spencer *M*	25
9.	Gilbert Keyes *M*	39	20. Owen Boughton *M*	22
10.	Roger Barlowe *M*	39	21. Thomas Randall *M*	21
11.	James Fitte	38		

Note: only those who attended more than 20 meetings are listed here.

M – denotes those elected to the mastership during their careers
A – denotes those who were aldermen in the period 1486–93
W – Adyff served as warden in 1473–4 and may have served as master in 1484–5.

One important change revealed by the attendance lists is the growing significance of mercantile interests among court members.[33] In 1435 trading activity among the court members was mostly confined to the supplying of cloth to noble households and the Great Wardrobe, but by the late 1480s several men were regularly concerned in overseas trade: Pemberton, Percyvale, Richard West, Gilbert Keyes and Stephen Jenyns were among a number of court members who were engaged in regular trade with the continent, involving a range of commodities in addition to cloth. John Percyvale, for instance, exported corn and imported wine from Gascony and also had dealings with a Spanish iron merchant.[34] This shift had little effect

---

[31] Figures compiled using the lists of those admitted to the livery contained in the company's account books. A working list of the members of the Court from 1488 survives on one of the unfoliated fly-leaves which were bound with volume II of the minutes, see below, pp. 263–4.

[32] That West was a former master is clear from his description as 'M. West'. He probably served in 1478–9 as his name is usually listed before that of the master of 1479–80, Roger Barlowe. The company's accounts for the late 1470s and early 1480s are badly damaged.

[33] For the biographies of all the men who served on the court in this period see Appendix IV.

[34] See Appendix IV. For Percyvale's career see Clode, *Early History*, vol. 2, pp. 8–21 and M. Davies, 'Dame Thomasine Percyvale, "The Maid of Week" (d.1512)', in

upon the everyday activities of the court, many of whose members in any case continued to be involved at some level in the tailoring industry. In the political arena, however, the prominence of wealthy merchants could serve to advance the interests of the Tailors in the City as a whole. In 1498, at the fourth attempt, John Percyvale was elected as the Tailors' first mayor: the author of the Great Chronicle (Robert Fabyan, a draper) put down his earlier failures to the 'hote apetyte' he had for the office, while the Tailors themselves blamed the Drapers for blocking his election.[35] The ambitions of the Tailors carried them further in 1503 when, after negotiations with the Crown, they secured a charter allowing them to call themselves Merchant Taylors; the charter claimed that members of the craft had 'from time immemorial in many parts and realms of the world frequented, occupied and exercised all and singular kinds of merchandise', a statement which conveniently glossed over the fact that only a relatively small, albeit particularly visible, section of the craft was involved in commerce on such a scale.[36]

IV. THE COURT AND ITS FUNCTIONS

The Fraternity of St. John the Baptist

One of the court's main functions was to administer the affairs of the fraternity of St. John the Baptist. Like the Goldsmiths' fraternity of St. Dunstan and the Corpus Christi fraternity established by the Skinners, this was an exclusive association established for the most prominent and wealthy freemen who, because of the livery robes worn on ceremonial occasions, were known as 'liverymen'.[37] As the public face of the craft, the fraternity's image in the city was an important consideration for the court and consequently it played a key role in the selection of those freemen who were to become members of this exclusive 'club'. While not being the only criterion for admission, the possession of wealth was viewed as an essential precondition and one which the court was determined to maintain. At a quarter-day held on 5 May 1490 it was reported that 'sum persones have bene admitted in to the fraternytie have bene in substaunce of goodes as it hath bene supposed

Medieval London Widows, 1300–1500, ed. C. M. Barron and A. F. Sutton (London, 1994), pp. 194–5.

[35] CLRO, Journals, 9, f. 239; *The Great Chronicle of London*, ed. A. H. Thomas and I. D. Thornley (London, 1938), pp. 245–6.

[36] *The Charters of the Merchant Taylors' Company* ed. F. M. Fry and R. T. D. Sayle (London, 1937), p. 38. For the furore caused by the Merchant Taylors' charter of January 1503 see H. Miller, 'London and Parliament in the Reign of Henry VIII', *Bulletin of the Institute of Historical Research*, 35 (1962), pp. 128–49.

[37] For discussion of the fraternity see Davies, 'Charity', pp. 161–8.

wherby they have lytely fallen into the almes of this fraternytie to the grete charge of the same fraternytie'. Although the court refrained from introducing a property qualification, as some other guilds had done, it was decided that admission to the livery should take place less frequently. An exception was made for any tailor who married the widow of a former master or warden of the craft 'or that he be promoted by maryage of eny other woman oute of the felasship'. The behaviour of those who were successful in gaining admission to the livery was also a matter of concern. At the same quarter-day it was agreed that members should no longer be allowed to pay their annual alms in the cloistered courtyard of the Hall because 'sum persones goyng there forth have spoken and sayde sum wordes soundyng rather to dishonour than to worship'. Instead they were to pay their dues 'in this place and not in the said cloystre', probably referring to the parlour, a small room next to the common hall where the new master and wardens were formally installed.[38] Misbehaviour in public was viewed even more seriously by the court. At a meeting held on 3 February 1490 those present heard that 'a grete cryme and defamacion renneth upon this fraternytie by cause that sum persones of this felaship excede in ther behavour and demeanyng amonges men of worship and other honest persones and namely at Blakwellhall'. As the city's principal centre for dealing in woollen cloth, Blackwell Hall was important for those tailors who were involved in the cloth trade, and so the court immediately required the two culprits to enter into bonds of £10 each for their future good behaviour.[39]

The importance of social standing and appropriate behaviour was also emphasised in the court's deliberations over the internal rituals of the fraternity, particularly those which accompanied the annual elections of the master and wardens on the feast of the Nativity of St. John the Baptist (24 June). Although elected to govern the craft as a whole (i.e. all the freemen, their wives, apprentices and servants), the master and wardens, like the mayor, were chosen by a carefully defined electorate. On 4 June 1490, for instance, the court determined that the new master 'shall be named and chosen by them that have ben Maisters in the parlour on midsomer even before dyner'. Typically this meant that, in any one year, only around a dozen men were entitled to choose the next master of what was probably the largest of London's crafts.[40] A further glimpse of the fraternity's ritual life is afforded by an entry for 5 July 1493 which described the installation of the new master and his wardens:

---

[38] Below, p. 158.

[39] Below, p. 150. For another incident at Blackwell Hall see below, pp. 227–8.

[40] Below, p. 161. On 26 May 1486 William Marchall made a donation towards repairs to the roof of the Hall and in return was 'discharged of one of the vj persones to be warned to be Maister of the craft', below, p. 58.

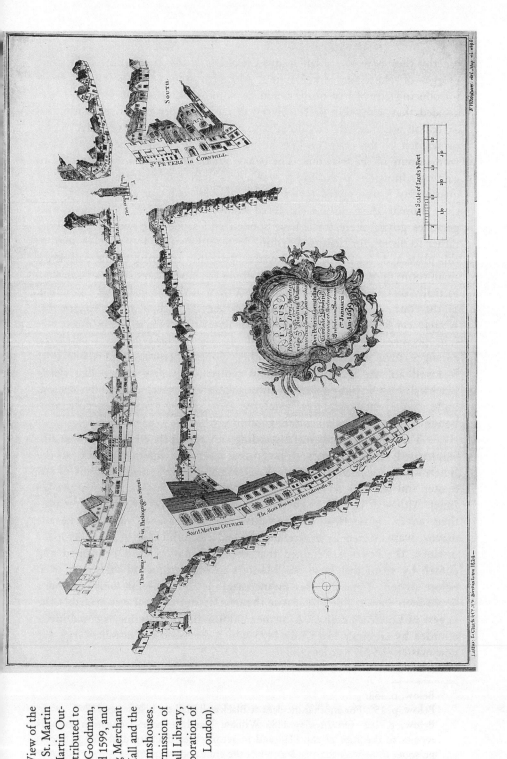

Plate 1: View of the parish of St. Martin of St. Martin Outwich, attributed to William Goodman, dated 1599, and showing Merchant Taylors' Hall and the almshouses. (By permission of Guildhall Library, Corporation of London).

The same daye the forenamed maister and the iiij wardeyns sworen in the daye of Nativitee of Seint John Baptist last passed and his next predecessour Maister Povey and the iiij wardeyns late with the same M. Povey within the chapell perteignyng to this present place herd their Masse of tholy goste and after Masse don and seyde the new M. and the iiij wardeyns to hym electe came into this parlour and were sette in their romes and places by their said next predecessours...

The Administration of the Tailors' Estates

The fraternity of St. John the Baptist was a formal association whose status was consolidated at various points in its history through the acquisition of royal charters, documents which also confirmed the jurisdiction of its master and wardens over the craft as a whole. As such the fraternity was able to acquire and hold property on behalf of the craft, the income from which could be used to fund its many other activities such as distributions of alms, participation in ceremonial occasions and the payment of its priests, clerks and other officials. By the late fifteenth century the fraternity's income from its estates, all of which at this stage were in London, was typically in excess of £150 *per annum*, and thus a second major task of the court was to ensure that these were administered efficiently. The management of the estates themselves was often a subject for discussion by the court. Particularly important, of course, was the Hall itself in Bradestrete, much of which was built in the mid to late fourteenth century.[41] On 14 June 1493 the rent collector, Richard Gryston, alarmed the master and wardens by reporting that the chimney in the King's chamber at the west end of the Hall 'is so ruynouse and feble that it may in no wyse long stand and every daye is in all lyklyhode to fall down to the grete perill and jeopardye to the good man of the Cok his gestes, servauntes and bestes'.[42] The court duly authorised the demolition of the chimney and its replacement with a more robust structure. The rebuilding of the Saracen's Head in Friday Street, a property acquired by the fraternity from trustees in 1401, was another matter of concern to the court, for in November 1489 it was said to be in 'a great state of ruin'. Nothing further was recorded in the minutes until the following May when the court was told that the master had entered into a contract with two carpenters who were to 'bylde newe the Saresyns Hede accordyng to a patron therof to be made by endentours'. The carpenters were to receive £200 for labour and materials. In November that year a 'sub-committee' of the court was established in order to co-ordinate the building work which may not yet have got under way. By December 1491, however, the project seems to have been near completion,

---

[41] H. L. Hopkinson, *The History of Merchant Taylors' Hall* (Cambridge, 1931), esp. pp. 16–24; J. Schofield, *The Building of London from the Conquest to the Great Fire*, rev. edn. (London, 1993), pp. 99, 116–7.

[42] Below, p. 250.

18

but at a meeting held on the 12th it transpired that no funds had been raised to pay for the work and that 'bycause of shortnesse of tyme that a sessyng coude not be had and made in the crafte before the feest of Cristemas next comyng'. To save the scheme, three prominent members of the court, John Percyvale, Hugh Pemberton and Roger Barlowe, agreed to lend their fraternity a total of £40 to pay the workmen until a levy could be organised. A list of sixty-five liverymen subsequently assessed for the 'new bieldyng in Fridaye strete' survives and was added to the beginning of the first volume of minutes with other miscellaneous jottings (see Appendix I). Work on the building was certainly finished by August 1492 when the court ruled that the master and wardens could now let the Saracen's Head to tenants 'so alwey that they lete it for v *li.* or above'.[43]

The identity of the fraternity's tenants was always of concern to the court. At a quarter-day held on 17 October 1486 it was agreed to allow one of its tenants, Richard Derby, to sub-let his recently refurbished tenement 'to what man he will excepte to a pewterer, fuller, sherman, blaksmyth or founder'.[44] As well as letting their properties to individuals the Tailors were also landlords to one of their fellow crafts, the Pinners. The relationship between the two guilds can be traced back to at least 1443–4 when the repairs to the Tailors' properties included money spent on the 'pynners hous', the location of which is unclear from the surviving accounts. This was 18 years before the Pinners acquired their first charter. As their fifteenth-century account book shows, the Pinners subsequently took up residence for a time in the halls of the Girdlers and Armourers before, in 1480, taking out a lease on a hall of their own from a London carpenter, Thomas Payne.[45] This tenement, located in Adlane (Adelstrete) in the parish of St. Alban Wood Street, was in fact one of several properties in the area which belonged to the Tailors, and had been bequeathed to them by the London embroiderer, Thomas Carleton (d. 1389). Payne began renting it from the Tailors at some point between 1476 and 1479, before sub-letting it to the Pinners at a rent of 20s. p.a. from 1480 onwards. This state of affairs continued until 1492 when Payne seems to have decided to give up his lease. At a meeting of the court held on 16 August 'a communicacion was had for the mater bytwene this crafte and Thomas Payne, carpenter, for the lece of the house in Adlane'. The outcome of these discussions was made known on the 31st when it was agreed that Payne

---

43 Below, pp. 144, 160, 173, 191–2, 202.
44 Below, p. 74. These crafts were deemed to be particularly anti-social because of the noise and waste products they generated.
45 Payne was admitted to the freedom of the city by redemption in 1455, for which he paid 4 marks to the Carpenters' company. He served as warden of the Carpenters for 1468–9 and 1481–2. *Records of the Worshipful Company of Carpenters*, ed. B. Marsh, J. Ainsworth and A. M. Millard, 7 vols (Oxford, 1914–68), vol. 2, pp. 18, 42, 61, 260–1.

INTRODUCTION

should surrender the lease in exchange for that of another property in
Lymestrete which he could rent for 10s. p.a. This allowed the sub-tenants to
become head-tenants of the Tailors in their own right, and indeed later that
year they began paying rent of 5s. a quarter directly to the master and
wardens. The relationship between the two guilds continued even after the
1497 merger of the Pinners with the Wiremongers to form a new company,
the Wiresellers. Their lack of significant common funds prevented them from
buying premises of their own, and in 1511 the Wiresellers even had difficulty
in meeting their rental payments to the Tailors.[46]

Religious and Charitable Activities
The Tailors' extensive estates were mainly acquired as a result of bequests
from deceased liverymen, many of whom requested their fraternity to make
arrangements for the celebration of Masses for their souls in one of London's
parish churches. These arrangements typically took the form of a chantry,
where a priest celebrated Mass daily either in perpetuity or for a specified
number of years, or an obit, a Mass celebrated on the anniversary of the
deceased's death. By the time of the Reformation the company was funding
no fewer than thirteen chantries and twenty-seven obits at a cost of more than
£120 *per annum*.[47] Although eight of these chantries were established after the
period covered by the minutes it is significant that the remaining five were all
perpetual chantries, founded before 1415 through substantial bequests of
property in London to the Tailors' fraternity. These provided a significant
boost to the funds of the Tailors and thus to the prestige of the company in
London as a whole. Four of the five chantries were administered directly by
the Tailors while the fifth, founded by John Buke (d.1422), was maintained by
the rector and wardens of All Hallows Lombard Street using revenues paid
over to them by the Tailors each year.[48] Consequently the only chantries
recorded in the minutes are those of Thomas Carleton (d.1389) in the Tailors'
chapel in St. Paul's cathedral, Peter Mason (d.1412) in St. Peter Cornhill, John
Churchman (d.1412) in St. Martin Outwich, and Lady Beatrice de Roos
(d.1414), also in St. Paul's. Particularly striking is the chantry of Beatrice de

---

[46]　Below, pp. 130, 202–3, 214, 251; Accounts, I, f. 380v, III. ff. 86, 124; BL, Egerton
MS 1142 (Pinners' Company account book), ff. 28–30v, 32, 33v, 35v, 38, 40v–41v,
48v; *Cal. Letter Bk. L*, p. 319. Prior to these events the only indication from the
minutes that the Tailors had any connection with the Pinners was a payment of
16s. 8d. received from the latter in March 1489 for cleaning a latrine: below, p.
130.

[47]　PRO, E301/34, m. 37d. For the London companies in general see C. J. Kitching
(ed.), *London and Middlesex Chantry Certificate 1548*, London Record Society, 16
(1980), pp. 81–95. For the administration of *post obit* arrangements by the Tailors
see Davies, thesis, pp. 48–66.

[48]　For the chantry priests see Appendix III. A document relating to Buke's chantry
is transcribed and translated in Appendix II.

Roos, one of the many hundreds of men and women who joined the fraternity of St. John the Baptist as 'honorary' members in the fourteenth and fifteenth centuries.[49] She was the widow of Maurice, earl of Desmond (d.1358), Thomas, Lord Roos (d.1384) and Sir Richard de Burley (d.1387). The date of her admission to the Tailors' fraternity is not known, but in 1409 she conveyed property in Lymestrete to the Tailors, in return for which they agreed to pay the salary of a chantry priest in St. Paul's cathedral. The priest himself was to be chosen by her descendants, but his appointment was also noted by the court: on 21 July 1489, for instance, 'Harry Chesshire prest of Powlys' was admitted as a liveryman following his appointment as chaplain. One of his successors, Thomas Roos, was almost certainly a member of the family.[50] The acquisition of property was therefore inextricably linked with the development of the spiritual dimension to the activities of the fraternity of St. John the Baptist, the body which held property on behalf of the craft. Consequently the court of assistants played an important role in ensuring that the wishes of benefactors were carried out, whether it be the payment of chantry chaplains, the distribution of coals to poor householders, or the funding of anniversary services on the correct day each year. The clerk of the company was also responsible for reading out the wills of particular benefactors once a year at a meeting of the court.[51] The salaries of the chantry priests were paid quarterly and were noted regularly in the minutes of the court along with the wages of other officials such as the clerk, the beadle (responsible for the hall premises and the garden) and the rent collector.[52] The minutes also contain details of the arrangements made for the celebration of the fourteen anniversaries or 'obits' which had been founded by 1486, events which typically required payments for several chaplains, wax for candles, alms given to the poor, as well as the purchase of bread, ale and cheese for those who attended. The costs of such events varied according to the terms of each bequest. The most elaborate was the obit of John Stone (a former master and sheriff who died in 1474) which cost a total of 26s. 8d. each year, a sum which included payments to three priests and to the master, wardens, clerk and beadle of the Tailors as well as alms to poor men and children and food and

---

[49] For the 1,200 non-tailors who joined the fraternity between 1398 and 1473 see Davies, 'Charity', pp. 166–71.

[50] Below, p. 66. For the agreement between Beatrice de Roos and the Tailors see Davies, thesis, p. 56 and W. Dugdale. *The History of St. Paul's Cathedral*, ed. H. Ellis (London, 1818), pp. 354–7. Beatrice was the daughter of Ralph, 1st earl of Stafford, by his wife Margaret, daughter of Hugh, earl of Gloucester: see 'Roos/Ros of Helmsley', *The Complete Peerage*, ed. G. E. Cokayne, 13 vols (London, 1910–40). Her will is printed in *Testamenta Eboracensia I*, Surtees Soc., 4 (1836), pp. 375–6. The chantry priests are listed in Appendix III.

[51] For example see below p. 73.

[52] For the names and dates of these officials see Appendix III.

drink for those present. The least expensive, at 2s. 4d., was that of William and Alice Jawderell.[53] As the list of obits compiled by Henry Mayour in late 1492 shows, October was a busy month for the Tailors with anniversary services for John Halygate (a mercer, d.1432) and his wife Idonea (d.1451) held on the 20th, John Stone on the 24th, and William Jawderell and his wife on the 26th. The anniversaries funded during this period were celebrated in seven different parish churches: three were held in St. Mary Abchurch and a further five were celebrated in the nearby church of St. Martin Outwich. The relationship with St. Martin's was particularly close: the advowson of the church was granted to the company by John Churchman, a grocer and alderman, in 1405 and it had subsequently become the Tailors' principal place of worship away from the small chapel in their own hall. They maintained Churchman's chantry there and in addition paid half the stipend of another priest who celebrated Mass for the souls of John and William Oteswich who substantially rebuilt the church in the fourteenth century.[54] A number of prominent members of the company were buried in the church including Hugh Pemberton (d.1500), whose tomb was moved to St. Helen's Bishopsgate following the demolition of St. Martin's in 1874. Many tailors also left bequests to the church: Stephen Trappys, as well as leaving £10 'toward the ledyng of the roof of the comon hall' of the Tailors, left £3 to the fabric of St. Martin's and 20s. for repairs to the window over the high altar in his will proved in October 1485.[55]

In the meantime the court also had to respond to further bequests that came the fraternity's way, some of which involved the establishment of new anniversaries and chantries. In July 1493, following the death of John Swan, master of the craft for 1470-1, his widow Rose approached the court through one of its members, Nicholas Nynes, with a view to establishing two temporary chantries and an obit for her late husband out of the large sum of 1,015 marks (£659 15s.) which she intended giving to the Tailors for this purpose. This was more than enough to pay for the post obit arrangements specified by Rose which together were to cost £149. Even allowing for the need to increase the stipends of the chantry priests and other miscellaneous expenses, such as the sums allocated to the master and wardens who attended, this still represented a substantial boost to the fraternity's coffers.[56] A number of those who left bequests of money or property to the Tailors also specified that distributions of money or coals should be made to the almsmen of the

---

53   Below, p. 75.
54   Davies, thesis, pp. 55–6.
55   GL, MS 9171/7, ff. 33v–35. For Trappys see also below, p. 56. A biography of Pemberton is included in Appendix IV.
56   Below, p. 257. Almost all the property given to the livery companies for what the chantry commissioners termed 'superstitious purposes' yielded a 'profit' over and above the costs of the priests and other services: see Davies, 'Charity', p. 171.

company. These contributions augmented the quarterly payments which members had to make to the common box of the fraternity of St. John the Baptist, funds which were intended to provide financial support to fellow liverymen and their families who had fallen upon hard times. In addition, an almshouse next to the Hall, built in 1413 on land given to the company by John Churchman, provided accommodation for up to seven tailors and their wives.[57] The court's responsibility was to ensure that, like the salaries of the chaplains and officials, the almsmen received assistance regularly and at an appropriate level. The minutes show that a clear distinction was made between those who lived in the almshouse and those who lived elsewhere. The inmates of the almshouse received a lesser stipend, presumably because they did not have to pay rent. The minimum for a resident was 20s. *per annum*, paid quarterly, but it is clear that the court was prepared to listen to requests for greater assistance and to act when necessary. On 8 Oct. 1488, for instance, the court agreed to increase Geoffrey atte Welle's alms to 26s. 8d. starting from the following 24 June. Not content with this he petitioned the court again on 26 February 1488/9 asking for a further increase of 13s. 4d. *per annum* and this too was granted. Over the next four years atte Welle made two subsequent requests 'humbly beseeching' the court for 'sufficient alms', with the result that by July 1492 he had improved his annual stipend to £2 13s. 4d., more than double the alms he had received in 1488.[58] In looking after those who were not residents of the almshouse it was necessary to adopt a different approach, characterised by a higher level of financial assistance combined with more frequent payment. During the period covered by the minutes only two men were in this category, but both Robert Walthew and Thomas Robyns were paid 2s. 10d. every fortnight. This equated to a stipend of 16d. a week or £3 6s. 4d. a year, which compared favourably with the alms paid by most of the other London companies with the exception of the Mercers whose almsmen received 14d. a week as well as accommodation in Whittington's almshouse.[59]

The Bachelors' Company

By the later fifteenth century the Grocers, Skinners, Tailors, and a number of other crafts, had established separate, but dependent associations for the majority of freemen who were not members of the livery. The names given to these freemen – 'yeomen' or 'bachelors' – reflected the fact that many of them were at a relatively early stage in their careers and as such doubtless hoped one

---

[57]   For a detailed study of the provision made by the Tailors for their poor members in the fifteenth century see Davies, 'Charity', pp. 161–90. The almshouse was described by Stow as built around 'a proper quadrant or squared court': Stow, *Survey*, vol. 1, p. 181.

[58]   See below, pp. 118–19, 127–8, 200, 246.

[59]   J. Imray, *The Charity of Richard Whittington* (London, 1968), Appendix I, p. 118.

day to be admitted to the livery. In reality, of course, the exclusiveness of the Tailors' fraternity of St. John the Baptist and the Goldsmiths' fraternity of St. Dunstan meant that only a small proportion of freemen could hope for such advancement. The nature of these associations of 'yeomen' or 'bachelors' varied, although in a number of cases, notably the Skinners and Tailors, there was a clear attempt to create junior fraternities which, though subordinate to the fraternities for the liverymen, had many of the same characteristics. Thus those freemen of the Skinners who were not members of the Corpus Christ fraternity were members of a fraternity dedicated to the feast of the Assumption of the Virgin. The yeomen tailors, by contrast, adopted the same patron saint, St. John the Baptist, as the liverymen, but in their case chose to celebrate the feast of the saint's Decollation (29 August) rather than his Nativity (24 June). By the 1490s the fraternity of yeomen tailors had become an integral part of the structure of what would later be known as the Merchant Taylors' Company, acting both as a stage in the *cursus honorum* for those freemen destined for promotion to the senior fraternity and as a means to support those who were never able to reap the benefits of membership of the livery.[60] The approach adopted by the court of assistants to the yeomen tailors reflected its recognition of the important role it played as a focus for the interests of the wider body of freemen, many of whom were young men who had recently emerged from their apprenticeships. For the court it was essential to have firm control of the junior fraternity's activities: as early as 1436, for instance, it had allowed the yeomen to celebrate their feast as long as the jollifications at St. John's Clerkenwell, well away from Tailors' Hall, were conducted 'under the rule and governaunce of the maister and wardens of the Fraternite of Seint John Baptist of taillours of London'. They were then to attend dinner at the Hall where four wardens were chosen for the coming year.[61] The establishment of a degree of control over the activities of the yeomen allowed the rulers of the craft to make use of its structure and organisation in order to assist with the difficult job of enforcing the rules and regulations of the craft among the freemen. As well as employing the wardens of the yeomen to gather revenues, the court also had dealings in November 1486 with a body known as the 'five', which received 20*d*. for assisting the master and wardens. Two years later, perhaps in recognition of its growing importance, the court agreed to allow the yeomen tailors formally to change their association's name to the 'Bachelor's company', while in August 1489 William Brownyng was sworn as one of the 'sixteen men' appointed to

---

60 For the development of associations of 'yeomen' or 'bachelors' in 14th and 15th century London see Davies, 'Charity', pp. 175–6 and idem, 'Artisans, Guilds and Government', pp. 127–30. The relationship between livery and yeomanry in the 16th-century companies is discussed in Archer, *Pursuit of Stability*, pp. 108–12 and Rappaport, *Worlds Within Worlds*, pp. 219–32,

61 GL, Merchant Taylors' Company, Misc. Docs. A.2, ff. 8v–9.

govern it.[62] The nature of the relationship between the Bachelors and the court is difficult to assess. While on one level the officers of the Bachelors were drawn upon to assist the master and wardens, which would presumably increase their own chances of gaining admission to the livery, it is also clear from the minutes that they actively sought to represent the interests of the freemen in discussions with the livery. In May 1489, for instance, the subject was their annual feast, while in the summer of 1493 'iij actes conteyned in the Bachelers bill', the contents of which are not recorded, were ratified by the court. Such dialogues undoubtedly had the potential both for creating rifts between the court and the Bachelors and for resolving problems, although the minutes are notably silent about any disagreements that did take place. Indeed, one of the court's main duties was to maintain its control over the junior association: on 25 June 1493, for instance, 'with licence of the M[aister]. and wardeyns' the Bachelors held their quarter-day. Their subordinate position within the craft was underlined when 'divers ordynaunces were redd unto the said company by Henry Mayour, clerk of the M[aisters] clothyng [i.e. the livery]'.[63]

Arbitration and the Settlement of Disputes

Central to the successful operation of the court was an insistence upon submission to its will, not least because of the importance of creating and maintaining a favourable image of the craft in the city at large. In many of the entries there is an emphasis upon the need for discipline and appropriate behaviour on the part of members of the craft, and on the importance of dealing with disputes internally as far as possible. In February 1493, for instance, a breach of the City's apprenticeship regulations was deemed so serious by the master that he feared the 'grete infamy that of lyklyhode myght have growen in tyme to com to the hoole body of the feliship ... if the said matier shuld be publisshed and com to lyght affore the Chambreleyn of this citee and ferther ... affore the mair and aldremen of the same citee'. The culprit himself risked public humiliation by being 'openly shamed with a paper over his hede as untrue citezein'.[64] The court relied heavily upon principles of hierarchy and deference to authority in order to enforce its will. As well as fines and other sanctions, the master and court employed symbolism in order to ensure that judgements were obeyed. One method designed to instil a sense of awe was the public reading of the craft's ordinances, to remind the culprit of the power of custom and tradition. In

---

62   Below, pp. 76, 115, 137.
63   Below, pp. 132, 258–9. Evidence from the records of the Skinners' Company suggests that the subordination of the yeomen skinners to the livery also appears to have been tightened towards the end of the 15th century: E. M. Veale, *The English Fur Trade in the Later Middle Ages* (Oxford, 1966), p. 114.
64   Below, p. 237.

December 1492 a William Barton was accused of verbally abusing a member of the court, John Lee, and his wife. At first Barton displayed a certain arrogance, 'not regardyng this place nor having reverence unto such persones as have ben governours and rulers of this worshipfull craft'. The master, seeing his 'firy heet and brennyng rancour ... caused certeyn ordinances to be redd, the same William heryng thextremitees and penalties set upon such transgressours and brekers of thordynaunces sobred hymself and humbly submytted hym to the good rules of this crafte'. Barton escaped with a fine of 6s. 8d. although he was forced to go to John Lee's house and, in the presence of two of the wardens, 'there to aske forgyfnesse of Maistres Lee'.[65] Barton was one of several individuals who appear to have made a habit of causing problems for the governors of the craft. In March 1493 he appeared once again, accused this time of not enrolling an apprentice within a year of the date on the indenture. Barton replied that his apprentice had long since abandoned him and that 'he had litell joy to enroll hym'. Once again the master asked him to calm down, but he refused and said 'with grete violence and a fiery agony that he had never right in this present place and also he seyde that M. Jenyns served hym lyke a falsse Judas whan he was M. of the felishyp'. Personal animosities of this kind often underlay proceedings of the court and such outbursts were frequently entered into the written record, especially by Henry Mayour, suggesting that in a limited way the court could function as a forum for the articulation of grievances. The master at the time of Barton's outburst, Walter Povey, was himself a target of abuse: in July 1493 William Gerveys was asked to withdraw a suit he had taken out against a fellow tailor. Povey was one of two court members present alongside the newly elected master, Thomas Randall, and Gerveys decided not to waste this opportunity. He asserted that 'the same M. Povey dyd unto hym whan he was ruler of this worshipfull fraternitee open wrong', adding that 'M. Povey was the covetouse man that ever was in his dayes gouvernour of the said company. And he had lever forswere Englond for vij yeres rather than the said M. Povey shuld be ruler of the said company ayeyn'.[66]

The fact that few of these acts of rebellion appear to have undermined in any serious way the authority of the court seems to reflect the important position it had attained within the craft. Primarily this was a consequence of the gulf in status between the majority of those who were brought before the court and those who sat in judgement upon them. The same principles applied to the use of arbitration as a means to resolve disputes that arose between members of the craft. Arbitration had a number of advantages over other means of resolving disputes which meant that in the later middle ages it was as widely employed in the towns as it was among gentry communities, if not

---

[65] Below, p. 217–18
[66] Below, p. 239.

more so given the desirability of a speedy solution to commercial disputes that would otherwise drag on for months if not years. Apart from the desirability of keeping matters away from the law courts, arbiters appointed by the guilds in particular also had the technical knowledge to deal with craft-based disputes.[67] The advantages of speed, cheapness and flexibility were perceived clearly by the guilds, and the Tailors' minutes contain numerous examples of disputes that were submitted to the arbitration of fellow freemen. On 14 October 1491, for instance, a dispute between Rowland Hymeson and his covenanted servant, John Langryk, was put to arbitration, after Langryk had left his master before the end of his one year contract. The award was to be made by the feast of Saints Simon and Jude (28 October), and was eventually delivered to the court on the 31st by the arbiters, Richard Adyff and John Doket, both of whom were members of the court. In their award they acknowledged that the covenant had irretrievably broken down, and made arrangements for the servant to recover his possessions from Hymeson's house on condition that Langyk returned a pair of shears which he had taken from a stall belonging to his former master and paid 10s. compensation for leaving his service early. Both parties were to share the costs of making the award, and Hymeson was to withdraw the suits he had taken out against Langryk.[68] The language used on such occasions was designed to promote reconciliation, or at least avoid further conflict: in February 1490 Thomas Ethell and John Copelond were required to 'take the other of them by the hande and to desyre that good love may be had bytwene them from hensforth'. In case parties were tempted to take arbitration less than seriously, every effort was made to stamp the authority of the court upon judgements and to heighten the solemnity of proceedings at the Hall and elsewhere. On one occasion, for instance, the parties were required to go to the church of St. Thomas of Acre between eight and nine in the morning to put their cases to the arbiters, a tactic often employed to impart a religious dimension to the arbitration process.[69]

The challenge posed by John Heed to the court in the summer 1492, described so vividly by Henry Mayour, reveals the limitations of its authority. The court's helplessness in dealing with Heed's refusal to submit to arbitration was compounded by its mistake in appointing Richard Hill and Alan Hoberd as arbiters in the dispute between him and John Darby. Both men were newcomers to the court and neither had served as master of the craft, points that would not have been lost on a man who had been elected to

---

[67]   See esp. C. Rawcliffe, "'That Kindliness Should be Cherished More, and Discord Driven Out": the Settlement of Commercial Disputes by Arbitration in Later Medieval England', in J. Kermode (ed.) *Enterprise and Individuals in Fifteenth-Century England* (Gloucester, 1991). pp. 99–117.

[68]   Below, pp. 189–90.

[69]   Below, pp. 191, 207.

that office in 1483. Matters were made worse by a personal grudge Heed bore towards Stephen Jenyns, who was appointed to oversee a second attempt at arbitration, and who, he alleged, 'had caused hym to lose xxxvij li. [£37]'. The only option was for the master, Walter Povey, to take over the role himself, and to this end he announced 'Sir I most be your juge this yere'. Heed, alluding to his own period in office, responded by making 'grete comparisons with the Maister as beyng charge in the crafte and other thinges without regardyng or reverencyng his office or the place'. At this point Povey seems to have lost his temper, and declared that it was a pity that Heed had ever been chosen as master; Heed retorted that Povey himself was far from being a popular choice. The referral of Heed's case to the mayor was a tacit admission that the limits of the court's authority to control one of its own members had been reached. It may have been small comfort that, following his spell in prison, Heed returned to the court to beg its forgiveness on his knees.[70] This case is unique among those contained in the minutes. No other dispute of this kind had to be referred to the mayor, which partly explains the full treatment given to the Heed case by the clerk, Henry Mayour. Most cases, even those involving court members, were brought to a swift conclusion through the efficient implementation of the arbitration process. One such dispute, sent to arbitration in January 1490/1, concerned Walter Povey, whom both Heed and William Gerveys were later to denounce as unfit for the office of master after his election in June 1492. During the course of an altercation with a London draper, John Stokes, Povey was alleged to have hit his opponent and knocked out two of his teeth. Both Povey and Stokes agreed to abide by the arbitration of two senior court members, John Lee and William Buk, and in due course Povey was found to be the main culprit and required to pay 10s. damages.[71] Any assessment of the success rate of arbitration is bound to be impressionistic at best, as it is difficult in most cases to determine how permanent the settlements were. All that can be said from the evidence of the Tailors' court minutes is that very few disputes appear to have flared up again in the lifetime of the surviving records.

The Enforcement of Ordinances

Although the wardens and other officials had the primary responsibility for regulating and supervising the economic activities of the city's tailors, many of those who had been caught in breach of the craft's ordinances were brought

---

[70]   Below, p. 207–10.

[71]   Below, p. 177. In 1493 Stokes was listed as one of 123 drapers who did not wear the livery of the craft: A. H. Johnson, *The History of the Worshipful Company of the Drapers of London*, 6 vols (Oxford, 1914–22), vol. 1, p. 366. His willingness to submit to the arbitration of members of another craft suggests that he felt confident of securing a settlement in his favour, despite Povey's status within the Tailors' Company.

before the court for punishment. The nature of the fines recorded in the minutes seems to confirm that, despite the broad span of most legislation enacted by the guilds and by the city government, in practice it seems that the wardens were content to concentrate upon certain key areas.[72] Apprenticeship was the most important of these, and the fines extracted for the non-enrolment of apprentices, or for other breaches of regulations, was a reflection of the court's concern to supervise access to the craft. Another important area was competition from strangers to the city, particularly (but not exclusively) aliens who had arrived in London from northern Europe. As well as lobbying the City government (see below) the Tailors were also active in enforcing their own controls. During the period covered by the minutes fines were regularly extracted from members of the craft employing aliens. Enforcement moved up a gear in late 1492, however, when, following the passing of a new ordinance, a meeting held on 22 December listed fines received from 'those persones that sette foreyns awerke contrary to thordynaunces made therfore'. A total of 14 men were fined, a significant statement of intent by the wardens, and, for good measure, 'a foreign' named Peter was himself fined 8d. for making a doublet. In contrast to the effort expended on fining those who breached apprenticeship regulations or who employed foreigns illegally, there are very few instances of the court dealing directly with issues connected to the manufacture or sale of clothing. Quality control or problems of over-charging for materials are not prominent among the topics discussed by the court, and fines are rarely recorded for such matters. That is not to say that the court was not interested in preserving the reputation of the craft, and there were occasions when accusations of malpractice provoked a strong reaction. On 27 April 1493 the court was informed of a sermon given by a preacher at St. Thomas of Acre, who

> shewed openly affore a grete audience that many and divers taillours of this citee occupiyng shapyng and makyng of garmentes bene worsse extorcioners than they that lye in a wayte by a high wey side in robbyng and spoillyng the kynges liege people that passen furth by

This charge has echoes of those made by writers such as the author of 'Richard the Redeles', who alleged that tailors working for the royal court were charging twenty times the cost of the cloth they were using.[73] The court was clearly worried about the impact of such accusations, particularly when delivered in a sermon, and decided to send the master himself, along with two of the wardens and two court members to see the preacher at Greenwich.[74]

---

[72] See Davies, thesis, pp. 163–80. For the relationship between guilds and municipal authorities see esp. G. Rosser, 'Crafts, Guilds and the Negotiation of Work in the Medieval Town', P&P, 154 (1997), pp. 3–31.

[73] Mum and the Sothsegger, ed. M. Day and R. Steele, EETS, 199 (1936), p. 17, lines 167–9.

[74] The first house of Friars Observants (Grey Friars) had been founded at

This could be seen as an indictment of the court's seemingly relaxed approach to the regulation of 'consumer issues' such as charging excessive prices for materials. The preacher's allegations certainly touched a nerve and the response of the court suggest that the craft had a poor image in the City which was unlikely to be improved by a lack or action by the guild responsible.

A central problem for all the City's crafts was the practical enforcement of the legislative framework drawn up by their governing bodies or imposed on them by the City. Even by prioritising certain issues it was by no means clear that the wardens would succeed in implementing ordinances passed to deal with them. Many of these ordinances were themselves a response to the difficulties of locating and scrutinising the work of craftsmen. A number of guilds, including the Tailors, introduced regulations designed to prevent freemen from working in alleyways, in attic rooms or in other places where they were prone to work in order to avoid scrutiny. Other problems were caused by jurisdictional disputes over monastic and ecclesiastical precincts, as well as by the numbers of freemen who set up businesses in places such as Southwark, outside the city's boundaries.[75] The fines recorded in account books or in sources such as the Tailors' court minutes must therefore be viewed in the context of these problems: the fact that so many fines were extracted testifies to the zeal and persistence of the wardens. One particular example illustrates the dangers that could be faced by those who sought to extract fines from offenders. At a meeting of the court held in December 1492 it was reported that the company beadle, Thomas Grysell, had gone to the house of one William Tetford to seize goods to the value of a fine imposed on him for employing an alien craftsman, contrary to the recently introduced ordinances. Tetford refused to allow the beadle to come in and threatened to 'sette his heres on the poste at his shop dore ... if the said Bedell toke any distresse there'. Following a complaint by the beadle, Tetford's behaviour was immediately brought to the attention of the mayor who had him arrested and imprisoned.[76]

Greenwich by Edward IV in 1482, and confirmation of this foundation, for a warden and at least 12 friars, was obtained from Henry VII in 1485: D. Knowles and R. N. Hadcock, *Medieval Religious Houses in England and Wales* (London, 1971), pp. 230–1.

[75]   For these issues see G. Rosser, 'London and Westminster: The Suburb in the Urban Economy in the Later Middle Ages', in *Towns and Townspeople in the Fifteenth Century*, ed. J. A. F. Thomson (Gloucester, 1988), pp. 45–61; M. Carlin, *Medieval Southwark* (London, 1996), pp. 119–27, 157–62. For the enforcement of ordinances by the Tailors and other guilds see Davies, 'Artisans, Guilds and Government', pp. 145–9.

[76]   Below, pp. 229–30.

Apprenticeship

Central to the activities of the court was the regulation of apprenticeship, the route by which the vast majority of individuals obtained the freedom of the City. This formed part of the overall task of controlling access to the various stages of the *cursus honorum* within the craft, a route which, for the most successful tailors, would ideally include admission as a shop-holder, election as an officer of the Bachelors' Company, entry to the senior fraternity of St. John the Baptist, service on the court of assistants and eventually, perhaps, election as a warden and then as master of the craft. Entry to each stage was carefully regulated, but it was apprenticeship which, because of the numbers involved and its importance as a route to the freedom, took up most of the court's time. As well as being formally enrolled before the chamberlain of the city, the apprentices of the city's tailors were presented at meetings of the court by their new masters, who would pay a fee for each one they took on. The level of the fee paid was in itself a means to regulate access to apprenticeship and could be raised or lowered according to economic circumstances. For most of the fifteenth century the Tailors had demanded a fee of 3s. 4d. for each apprentice, but at some point between 1482 and the commencement of the court minutes in April 1486 new arrangements were introduced which raised the enrolment fees to 10s. for liverymen and 20s. for all other freemen, a sum which on several occasions was broken down to include 10s. to be paid to the wardens of the Bachelors.[77] The reason for the change is unclear, but it may well have been aimed at restricting recruitment to the craft in response to increased immigration into London at the end of the fifteenth century. Whatever the reason, it is likely that the decision proved unpopular, for by November 1487 the fee had reverted to its former level of 3s. 4d. Several enrolments recorded over the subsequent months referred to a 'new ordinance', although the details of this do not survive.[78]

Altogether the court minutes contain a total of 297 apprentice enrolments, of which 291 took place between 9 April 1486 and 24 June 1491. After this date only six enrolments are recorded, reflecting an apparent change in policy which, conversely, may have been responsible for a sharp increase in the number of licenses to open a shop that were noted by the clerks. This underlines the fact that many of the financial transactions recorded in the minutes would also have appeared in an abbreviated form in the account books of the company, and that other books may also have been used for recording apprentices and shop-holders.[79] Nevertheless, taking into account the gap in the minutes covering 18 December 1486 to 12 November 1487, it seems that, on average, sixty-eight apprentices were enrolled each year before

---

[77] For example see p. 84.

[78] For discussion of enrolment fees and other methods of restricting the recruitment of apprentices see Davies, thesis, pp. 186–7.

[79] The account books covering the period 1484–1545 have, however, been lost.

such enrolments ceased to be recorded in July 1491. This figure can be compared with those for the longer period from 1425 to 1469 when a total of 2,552 apprentices were enrolled by London tailors. During that period the craft as a whole expanded significantly so that the average number of apprentices taken on each year rose from fifty-eight in the late 1420s to eighty-five in the 1460s. The figures for 1486–91 suggests that this expansion may have come to an end, or at least that the Tailors, perhaps with the help of the temporary increase in enrolment fees, had succeeded in introducing stricter controls upon recruitment to their craft.[80]

Central to the effectiveness of the apprenticeship system was the indenture, a document which contained clauses relating to the respective obligations of the master and his apprentice, as well as specifying the length of the term to be served and the date on which it was to commence. While the minutes do not contain full details of the indentures themselves, the formal enrolment clauses, especially those written by Thomas Kirton and William Duryvale, occasionally make a point of including other information. Particularly valuable are the seventy-eight enrolments (26 per cent of the total) where the apprentice's father is named, along with his place of residence. The inclusion of these details was a reflection of the role played by an apprentice's family in the negotiations that often preceded the drawing up of the indentures. Sometimes this resulted in a payment being made to the master for food and clothing for the apprentice, an arrangement which could also form part of an attempt to secure a placement with a particularly influential member of the craft. Equally a payment of some kind might lead to the apprentice being bound for seven or eight years, rather than for a longer term. The geographical origins of the apprentices (see Map, overleaf) are especially useful as an insight into migration into London in the late fifteenth century, albeit from the perspective of one craft and over a very short period. Particularly striking are the large numbers of young men who were recruited from the Midlands and the North of England, a pattern similar to that which emerges from analysis of the roughly contemporary Skinners' Company records. Recent research seems to confirm that lesser companies, with few of the advantages of wealth and social status possessed by the Great Twelve, recruited from less far afield, with the Home Counties and London together supplying just over half of their apprentices.[81]

---

[80] For an analysis of the apprentices enrolled between 1425 and 1469 see Davies, thesis, pp. 183–95.

[81] Using a cohort of 316 apprentices from a variety of mostly printed sources from 1313 to 1482 Jenny Ryan found that just under 24% of the 214 apprentices, whose origins are recorded, were London born, with another 28% from the Home Counties: Jenny T. Ryan, 'Apprenticeship in Later Medieval London, 1200–1500', unpublished M.A. thesis, University of London (1992) pp. 1–3, 14–18. Many of the issues touched on here are to be explored more fully by Stephanie Hovland in

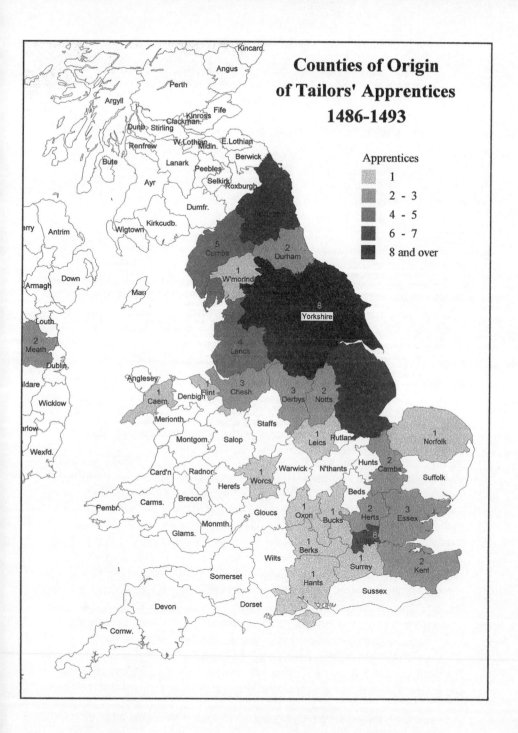

Counties of Origin of Tailors' Apprentices 1486-1493

Apprentices
1
2 - 3
4 - 5
6 - 7
8 and over

33

Table 2. Occupations of Apprentices' Fathers

Occupation	Number	%
Tailors	6	10.2
Other artisans	15	25.4
Merchants	2	3.3
Gentlemen	5	8.5
Yeomen	25	42.4
Husbandmen	5	8.5
Other	1	1.7
Total	59	100

In fifty-nine of the enrolments contained in the court minutes the father's occupation is also given (see Table 2).[82] Most numerous were the twenty-five men (42.4 per cent) who were described as 'yeomen', a description which, by this time, indicated the possession of a small amount of income-yielding land. Most were from rural areas, although some, such as William Casteley of York, were from urban centres. The next largest group (twenty-one or 35.6 per cent) were the sons of craftsmen, most of whom were from other towns and cities. Although six of them were themselves from tailoring backgrounds the overall pattern suggests that the vast majority were following trades different to those followed by their fathers. This was even the case with those apprentices who came from London itself: the six fathers whose occupations are recorded included a haberdasher, two brewers, a barber and a waterman, but only a solitary tailor. In some instances, however, a connection with the cloth and clothing industries may have been a factor in their choice: two enrolments concerned the sons of shearmen (from Newcastle-upon-Tyne and Wirral) and a third involved the son of a weaver from Lacton in Yorkshire. Given that most members of the craft were still concerned with the manufacture of clothing, rather than with trade, it is perhaps not surprising that only two merchants sent their sons to be apprenticed to London tailors. One of these was a merchant of the Staple, John Hennyng, from Boston in Lincolnshire, while the other was a mercer from Liverpool. On the other hand there is some evidence from these enrolments that individuals higher up the social scale were not averse to securing placements for their sons with some of the more influential members of the company. Five apprentices (8.5 per cent) were the sons of men described as 'gentlemen', all of whom appear to have been from the middle to lower ranks of the gentry

---

her forthcoming London University Ph.D. thesis, 'Apprenticeship in London c.1450–c.1520'.
[82] Map 1 and Table 2 correct errors and omissions from Sylvia Thrupp's analysis of apprentices' social and geographical origins: Thrupp, *Merchant Class*, pp. 389–92.

in their respective counties. One of the most prominent families was that of Thomas Leek of Granby in Nottinghamshire, whose father managed to secure him an eight year apprenticeship with one of the leading members of the company, Stephen Jenyns, in June 1486. Jenyns was chosen as master of the craft three years later, became an alderman in 1491 and was mayor of London in 1508–9 when he represented the City at the coronation of Henry VIII.[83] Leek's choice of master gave him an immediate advantage over most of his peers, particularly those who were not able to secure apprenticeships with members of the livery. Indeed, other evidence suggests that those who were apprenticed to liverymen were twice as likely to end up as members of the fraternity of St. John the Baptist themselves than those who were not.[84]

A final feature of the enrolment clauses recorded in the court minutes was the length of the term which each apprentice had to serve. In London a minimum term of seven years had been adopted by the City by the close of the thirteenth century, although this did not prevent crafts from introducing longer minimum terms or allowing their masters the freedom to vary the length of the apprenticeship.[85] The term to be entered on the indenture might depend on a number of factors relevant to each case, such as the wealth and influence of the apprentice's family or the age and experience of the apprentice. Despite this, half of the eighty-two apprentices whose terms are recorded in the minutes were bound to their masters for the minimum seven years, while a further 42.7 per cent were to serve for eight or nine years (see Table 4). Only four apprentices were enrolled for longer terms, the most striking of whom was the unfortunately-named Rowland Lytillskyll, son of John Lytillskyll of Hexham, who was bound to William Huelette in July 1486 for twelve years.

Table 3. Length of Terms of Tailors' Apprentices, 1486–93

Years	Number	%
7	41	50
8	21	25.6
9	14	17.1
10	3	3.7
12	2	2.4
14	1	1.2
Total	82	100.0

Average term = 7.9 years.

---

[83] For Jenyns's career see Clode, *Early History*, vol. 2, pp. 22–38 and below, Appendix IV.

[84] For quantification of this 'sponsored mobility' see Davies, 'Artisans, Guilds and Government', pp. 137–8.

[85] For the City custom regarding apprenticeship see *CPMR 1364–81*, pp. xxx–xlvii.

The role of the court was not confined to the mechanical recording of apprentice enrolments. One of its central functions was to monitor the way in which apprenticeships operated in practice, and to deal with breaches of the conditions of the indentures and offences against the rules and regulations laid down by the City and the guild. Inevitably, therefore, the minutes have much to say about the breakdown of the master/apprentice relationship and relatively little about the positive aspects of apprenticeship as, for instance, a means of assimilating immigrants into London society and providing a stable environment for the acquisition of highly prized skills. On the other hand, the surviving proceedings do suggest that the court itself could play a constructive role, beyond merely apportioning blame for a failed apprenticeship or fining those who broke ordinances. An example of this approach was an endorsement of the part that women, particularly widows, could play in the training of apprentices. Few references survive in the minutes, principally because the transfer of an existing apprentice to a widow did not need to be recorded formally in guild records. However, a rare example does survive of a widow who appeared before the court to enrol an apprentice in her own right. Joan Geffrey's enrolment of Richard Bonde as her apprentice followed the death of her husband, Richard, the intended master, in the early summer of 1491. As no indentures had been entered into by her husband (who also died intestate), Joan appears to have made a positive decision to rescue Bonde's apprenticeship. More common in the records of the court, however, are transfers of the terms of apprentices to other freemen, particularly after the death of a master.[86] In December 1489 William Bryan successfully petitioned the court for a transfer to a new master after his own master, Roger Shavelock had committed suicide; this exceptional event was noted by the author of the Great Chronicle who recorded that Shavelock had cut his own throat, leaving behind a shop in Ludgate 'well storid with drapery' including cloth and other goods said to be worth nearly a thousand marks.[87]

Apprentices were also transferred to new masters in the aftermath of disputes with their masters, many of which were heard before the court. On those occasions when the master was found to be at fault the court tried to ensure that the apprentice was able to continued his training with another freeman. In January 1491, for instance, William Devenish petitioned the court after his master, Hugh Stokes, simply refused to train him. The court agreed that Devenish should be placed with another tailor, John Shemell, until he had completed the term specified in the indenture. During the period covered by the minutes the court dealt with numerous disputes between masters and

---

[86] Apprentices themselves were not chattels and could not be bought and sold or transferred to other citizens. Thus it was the term of apprenticeship that was, legally speaking, the subject of these transactions.

[87] *Great Chronicle*, eds Thomas and Thornley, pp. 243–4.

their apprentices, many of which resulted in the termination of the contract between them. Such evidence, though anecdotal, is invaluable in helping to assess some of the reasons for the failure of up to two-thirds of apprenticeships in late medieval London.[88] The court did not deal with cases of apprentices who absconded before the end of their terms – perhaps because there was little that either the master or the guild could do about such cases. The extent of the problem is difficult to quantify, particularly in a period which was beginning to see increased immigration into the capital and the expansion of the pool of labour available to masters.[89] The concern of the court was generally only with disputes where a settlement of some kind was at least a possibility, or where offenders against the craft's ordinances could be punished. As a result it was common for both master and apprentice to be required to appear before the court in order that each could give his version of events. In February 1493, for example, the court heard conflicting stories from William Ashby and his apprentice, John Hebblethwaite. Ashby alleged that his apprentice would not be ruled by him and that 'he used the company of a woman which was to his grete losse and hynderyng for asmoch as he was so affectionate and resorted dailly unto hyr'. The frequent clauses against fornication in surviving apprenticeship indentures provided this charge with a legal as well as a moral foundation, but it was one that was disputed by Hebblethwaite. The apprentice instead alleged that Ashby himself had broken one of the regulations concerning apprenticeship by inducing him to enter into an illegal contract in which he was to receive 32s. a year in wages. The breach between them occurred after Hebblethwaite tried to claim his first quarterly payment of 8s. The apprentice's version of events was backed up by two witnesses, a shearman and a dyer, testimony which led the master and wardens to end the apprenticeship and force Ashby to drop his actions against Hebblethwaite. This was one of several occasions when contradictory versions of events were given to the court by the parties. On 4 June 1492 Robert Archer was charged with a catalogue of breaches of his duties as a master: as well as failing to provide Thomas Godfrey with food and clothing,

---

[88] An estimated 65% of tailor apprentice failed to become freemen, compared with 50% of those apprenticed to mercers in the period 1390–1464: see Davies, 'Artisans, Guilds and Government', pp. 137–9; idem, thesis, pp. 194–5; Imray, '"Les Bones Gentes de la Mercerye de Londres": a Study of the Membership of the Medieval Mercers' Company', in *Studies in London History Presented to P.E. Jones*, ed. A. E. J. Hollaender and W. Kellaway (London, 1969), p. 168. These figures are similar to those compiled by Dr. Rappaport for the companies in the later 16th century: Rappaport, *Worlds Within Worlds*, Appendix 2, Table A2.1 pp. 394–5.

[89] By contrast, the labour shortage in the decades following the plagues of 1348–9 had doubtless been partly responsible for the 48 letters sent by the mayor and corporation to a number of towns and cities requesting the return of runaway apprentices: *Calendar of Letters from the Mayor and Corporation of the City of London c.1350–1370*, ed. R. R. Sharpe (London, 1885), *passim*.

he had failed to 'find the apprentice to school', a requirement of the indentures entered into by both parties on this occasion. At first, however, the court accepted Archer's protestations of innocence, and sent Godfrey away. He returned a few days later but once again the master and wardens 'not gevyng credence unto the same apprentice commaunded hym ayen to doo his master service as he was bound to doo'. Some time after this he came before the court for a third time 'piteously complaynyng' of his 'undue chastesyng' at the hands of Archer who had beaten him about the head with a rod described as a 'mete yerd', an iron yardstick used to measure cloth. He also described the vermin-infested conditions in which he was forced to live. Finally the court believed him and 'having respecte to the tendre age of the said apprentice, beyng faderles and moderles, and also of the undue and unreasonable kepyng of the same apprentice' ended the apprenticeship and placed the matter before the mayor and chamberlain who briefly imprisoned Archer.[90] In another case the court heard that 'John Bowman gave unto his said apprentice unlefull and without reason chastisyng as well with wepyns defensyve as with lak of mete, drynke, vitailles and apparaill'. Bowman refused to cooperate with an investigation into his behaviour, asserting that 'he wolde be maister over his own apprentice', and his violent reaction prompted the master and wardens to take the unusual decision to send the unnamed apprentice to live with John Doget, upper warden of the guild. The provision of a 'safe house' for the apprentice indicates that the charges against Bowman were taken seriously and that guild officials could intervene effectively away from the formal surroundings of the Hall. In this case, however, the choice of the house of a warden did not prevent Bowman from having his apprentice arrested there, a move which landed him in further trouble with the court.[91]

Relations with the City Government and other Companies
As well as its disciplinary and supervisory roles, the Tailors' court was also an important forum for discussing wider issues, particularly those that involved its relations with the other crafts and with the city government. Financial matters figure prominently in the minutes, not surprisingly given the increasing extent to which the guilds were drawn upon by the city government for defence and loans to the Crown.[92] On 18 July 1490, for example, the court met to make arrangements for the raising of £193 6s. 8d., part of a loan of £2,000 made by the city to the Crown. This was one of a number of 'loans' that were levied on the crafts in the early years of Henry VII's reign, and had been agreed by the common council seven days earlier. To raise the money the Tailors' court selected ten men to act as assessors with

90 Below, pp. 197–8.
91 Below, pp. 228–9.
92 See Davies, 'Artisans, Guilds and Government', pp. 140–1.

four others appointed to collect the levy.[93] Other requests for money were
dealt with on a less formal basis. In late July 1493 the court requested that 'the
M. and wardeyns shuld attempte and take knowlege what every persone of
the clothyng of his good will and benyvolence wole gyfe toward the new
makyng of thest ende of this hall and the celyng of the Guyhald of London
which was moved by my lord the Mayre of this citee'. This may have been
additional work carried out after the installation of 2 louvred windows in the
Guildhall roof, paid for by a bequest made by William Heryot, a former
mayor. Heryot died in 1485 but, according to one source, the work was not
completed until the seventh year of Henry VII's reign (1491–2).[94]

As well as financial matters the court also discussed important
economic issues affecting the craft. One such issue was an ongoing debate in
the City concerning provincial fairs and the rights of citizens to buy and sell
there. Prominent in this debate were the Mercers and Grocers of London
who, in 1376 and 1420 respectively, had forbidden their freemen to attend
fairs or send their goods to be sold there. These ordinances, designed to
encourage country chapmen and merchants to come to London for their
supplies, were very much a reflection of the self-confidence of the City's
merchants and of the growing importance of the City as a market-place for
goods. By the late 1470s, however, the Mercers were becoming concerned
about the activities of other crafts, notably the Haberdashers, whose freemen
were not subject to a similar ban on attending fairs and who were encroaching
on their business with the provinces. In 1477, as a result of lobbying by the
Mercers, the mayor tried to achieve a consensus on this issue, but in the event
only seventeen crafts were prepared to stay away from fairs while another
eleven 'in no wise would be therto greable'. This left the Mercers with no
choice but to abandon their century-old policy, but they continued to make
representations to the City for a general agreement among the crafts, and
eventually, in February 1487, the City imposed a seven year ban on freemen
sending their goods to fairs.[95] The Tailors' position prior to this ordinance is
unclear, but the court of assistants subsequently discussed the issue on two
occasions later that same year. In April it considered a request from the
Drapers that both crafts should agree to forbid members to 'rede into the
contre for to by any woollyn clothis'. The court agreed to send six senior
assistants to meet with the Drapers at Blackwell Hall. The outcome of the

---

93   Below, pp. 162–3; CLRO, Journals, 9, f. 251v.
94   Barron, *Guildhall*, p. 32; Stow, *Survey*, vol. 1, p. 272; *The Chronicle of the Grey Friars of London*, ed. J. G. Nichols (Camden Society, 1852), p. 25.
95   For a full discussion of this issue see S. L. Thrupp, 'The Grocers of London, a Study of Distributive Trade', in *Studies in English Trade in the Fifteenth Century*, eds E. Power and M. M. Postan (London, 1933), pp. 273–6. The role of the Haberdashers is described in I. W. Archer, *The History of the Haberdashers' Company* (Chichester, 1991), p. 31.

meeting is not known, although it does indicate a willingness on the part of the Tailors and Drapers to co-operate on issues that affected both their crafts, despite the intense rivalry that existed between members of these companies who were involved in the domestic cloth trade. In the event, the only decision recorded in the minutes later that year was to comply with the city government's ban on sending goods to sell at fairs. The ban was short lived, however, and was annulled by the Parliament which met in November 1487 in response to a Commons petition protesting at the damage that was being inflicted on the fairs by the city's ordinance. The debate in Parliament may have been acrimonious, for at a meeting of the Tailors' court held in March 1488 it was reported that 'divers controversies are pending between William Gerveys and certain others of the Commons lately held etc.'. Gerveys, as we have seen, went on to gain a reputation as a trouble-maker and it is possible that, on this occasion, he had become involved in a dispute with some of those MPs from towns which were most directly affected by London's ban on citizens attending fairs. The Tailors may have had particular reason to feel embarrassed by Gerveys, for one of the MP's chosen to represent London was Hugh Pemberton, master of the company in 1482–3, and a future alderman, who was the first tailor to represent the City in Parliament.[96]

A second issue that occupied both the Tailors' court and the court of aldermen in this period was the employment of aliens and other immigrants to London, men and women who were generally referred to as 'foreigns'. Attitudes towards these men and their families had changed over the course of the fifteenth century as crafts that had been large scale employers of foreigns, including the Tailors, became ever more concerned that opportunities for their freemen were being threatened by increased immigration into London.[97] By the late fifteenth century, as the minutes testify, the Tailors were actively involved in a campaign to have restrictions introduced on the employment of foreigns. Delegations were sent to the mayor on three occasions, in September 1489, July 1492 and in April 1493 when their purpose was to propose a bill 'for the reformacion of all foreyns that they hereafter worke with no freman and citezein of this citee'. This was in keeping with the renewed vigour with which the court was punishing those freemen tailors who were employing 'foreyns', many of whose fines are recorded in the minutes from the late autumn of 1492 onwards. The aim of the petition submitted to the city government, like those presented by a number of other crafts in these years, was to turn this policy into a city wide ordinance that would ensure that newly qualified apprentices had the means to earn a living as covenanted servants before setting up shop on their own.[98]

[96] CLRO, Letter Book L, ff. 226–226v, 232, 236; *Statutes of the Realm*, vol. 2, pp. 157–8. For Pemberton see Appendix IV.
[97] See Davies, 'Artisans, Guilds and Government', pp. 146–7.
[98] *Cal. Letter Bk. L*, pp. 2, 10–11, 254, 256–7, 295, 302. For the alien community in

Civic and Royal Ceremonial

By the later fifteenth century ceremonial had become an important dimension of the lives of the livery companies, and the Tailors' court played an important role in co-ordinating the participation of the craft in events which ranged from mayoral processions to royal entries. From the mid 1450s, for instance, the election of the mayor on 13 October was followed by a water-borne procession to Westminster where he was presented to the King. The Tailors, like many of their fellow crafts, were required to provide a barge for their senior members on this occasion: on 21 October 1488, for instance, the court noted payments of 13s. 4d. to 'John Heth bargeman for a barge for the presentation of the mayor' and another 12d. for the boatmen.[99] Of particular significance for the Tailors' Company, however, was its role in hosting the annual feast which was held by the new mayor following his election. Prior to the construction of new kitchens and other facilities at Guildhall between 1501 and 1505 the mayoral feast was, according to John Stow, held either at the hall of the Tailors or that of the Grocers.[100] Few details of the feasts held at Tailors' Hall are contained in the minutes, presumably because the cost would have been borne by the mayor himself or by his own company, but there are occasional references to freemen being fined for attending without permission. An exception is the entry for a meeting held in February 1488, which was attended by 17 of the 24 court members. Here it was reported that after the mayoral feast held at the hall the previous October, John Watertoft, chief cook of the new mayor, William Horn, a salter, had stolen two roasting racks from the Tailors' kitchen. When confronted with his alleged crime Watertoft gave 'croked and ungodley answere', admitting his guilt but refusing to compensate the Tailors. The fact that it took almost four months for the matter to be dealt with by the court suggests that it was a sensitive issue, presumably because the company would not have wanted to jeopardise future feasts at the Hall by pursuing Watertoft through the courts. Their decision reflected this: although Watertoft was banned from catering at the Hall, an exception could be made if a special licence was obtained on his behalf from the court.[101]

Occasions for the Tailors and the other companies to participate in lavish royal ceremonial were plentiful in the early years of Henry VII's reign, a time when royal entries and other events were being used to create a

---

[99] London in this period see Bolton (ed.), *Alien Communities*, esp. pp. 1–40, 134–40.
See below p. 121.

[100] Barron, *Guildhall*, p. 32; Stow, *Survey*, vol. 1, p. 273.

[101] Below, pp. 92–3. William Horn, citizen and salter, became an alderman in 1480 and was knighted on his election as mayor in October 1487. He died in 1496 and in his will required his executors to paint a window in the church of Snailwell in Cambridgeshire with images of his parents, their 24 children, himself and his wife and their 12 children: Beaven, *Aldermen*, II, p. 16; Thrupp, *Merchant Class*, p. 350.

favourable image for the new dynasty. The Tailors participated in a number of these events during the period covered by the minutes, and indeed it is striking that, unlike the contemporary records of the Mercers' court, the Tailors' minutes focus almost entirely upon the ceremonial relations between the Crown and London's crafts. The Mercers, by contrast, were equally concerned to record details of their negotiations with the Crown over economic matters, such as the level of the subsidy.[102] The first royal occasion noted in the surviving Tailors' minutes was the welcome given to Henry on his return from a royal tour of towns and cities across England undertaken in the spring of 1486. By 5 June he was back at Sheen and from there journeyed by water to Westminster and was met at Putney by the mayor and aldermen of the City and the guilds 'in a great Multitude of Barges, garnyshed with Banners, Penounces, Standers, and Pensells'. The Tailors paid 14s. for their barge 'to fette in the kyng Harry the viith' and hired organs and a choir of children under the direction of a 'Master Crane'.[103] More barges were hired on 23 November 1487 when the livery companies assembled at Greenwich to accompany Henry's bride, Elizabeth of York, to the Tower from where she departed for her coronation two days later.[104] Similarly, the creation of the young Prince Arthur as prince of Wales in November 1489 was preceded by a welcoming party of representatives of the crafts, together with the mayor and aldermen, who assembled their barges at Chelsea. A meeting of the Tailors' court on 7 December recorded the payment of 13s. 4d. to 'Hassok bargeman' for the hire of a barge for the encounter.[105] The participation of the companies in such events was normally co-ordinated by the City government. In November 1492, for instance, the court received a letter from the mayor requesting the master and wardens of the craft to provide 'xxx persones on horssebak in gownes of violet accordyng to the sample herunto annexed to meete with the kyng our soveraigne lord at his next comyng to London from the parties of beyond the see'. The occasion was the imminent return of

---

[102] *Acts of Court*, ed. Lyell and Watney, pp. 116–30.

[103] Below, p. 60; S. Anglo, *Spectacle, Pageantry and Early Tudor Policy* (Oxford, 1969), p. 33; L. Attreed, 'The Politics of Welcome: Ceremonies and Constitutional Development in Later Medieval English Towns', in *City and Spectacle in Medieval Europe*, eds. B. A. Hanawalt and K. L. Reyerson (Minneapolis, 1994), pp. 220–5. A William Crane was a gentleman of the Chapel Royal by 1509 and became master of the children of the chapel in 1523: this could either be a reference to him or to a relative, perhaps his father, who may also have served in the Chapel: see F. Kisby, 'The Royal Household Chapel in Early-Tudor London, 1485–1547', unpublished Ph.D. thesis, University of London (1996), pp. 389–91 and App. I. I am grateful to Dr. Kisby for providing me with details of Crane's career.

[104] Below, p. 83; Anglo, *Spectacle*, p. 49. For a description of these events see John Leland, *De Rebus Britannicis Collectanea...*, 6 vols, ed. T. Hearne (London, 1770), vol. IV, pp. 216–33.

[105] Below, p. 146; Anglo, *Spectacle*, p. 52.

Henry VII from France following the concluding of a peace treaty with Charles VIII of France at Etaples on 3 November, the news of which was communicated to the mayor and aldermen six days later. Letters to the city's companies were sent out on 16 November when, according to an entry in the Goldsmiths' records, the common council met and agreed that each craft should provide 'certeyn persones' to ride to meet the King at Blackheath. The precise number was related to the size and prominence of the craft concerned: the Goldsmiths were asked to provide twenty-four riders compared with the thirty who were to represent the Tailors and the Mercers. The Tailors responded to the mayor's letter by drawing up a list of riders, and it was agreed that each man would receive expenses of 10s., with former masters of the craft being allocated 13s. 4d. This cost was offset by a special levy that was raised from all members of the livery according to their wealth and standing. The King eventually landed at Dover on 17 December, from where he proceeded to Greenwich, and on Saturday 22 December, according to the author of the Great Chronicle, he was met at Blackheath by the mayor and aldermen, clothed in scarlet, and 'a competent numbyr of the Comoners clothid In vyolet' who together escorted him into the city to St. Paul's Cathedral and, following services held there, on to Westminster.[106]

---

[106]   Below, p. 221; *Acts of Court* eds Lyell and Watney, pp. 229–30; Goldsmiths' Company, London, Minute Book B, p. 5; *Great Chronicle*, pp. 247–8. For the treaty, concluded after Henry had besieged the town of Boulogne, see A. F. Pollard, *The Reign of Henry VII from Contemporary Sources*, 3 vols (London 1914), vol. 3, pp. 7–25.

THE TEXT

EDITORIAL METHOD

Foliation
The first 227 folios of volume I have been lost, and the remaining 22 folios are foliated as ff. 1–22. Volume II retains its original foliation (ff. 1–75).

Translation and Transcription
The text is made up of entries in Latin and Middle English, with the two languages sometimes used interchangeably, depending on the nature of the entry. The exception is the period from October 1492 to August 1493 for which the minutes are almost exclusively in English. The aim of this edition is to reproduce as faithfully as possible the original tone and content of the minutes, while making them accessible to a modern audience.

1. Latin Entries
All entries in Latin have been translated into English and indented to distinguish them from those in the original language. Latin text, apart from the headings for the meetings (for which see 'Dating'), has only been included where it provides a useful illustration of the vocabulary or formulae being employed. In the case of a complete entry or paragraph, the medieval Latin (not indented) is followed by a translation (indented). Where particular words or phrases are of interest they have been included as *italicized* text in round brackets. Throughout the text all Latin contractions and abbreviations have been extended, and punctuation modernised. Calendaring has been kept to a minimum, except in the case of lengthy, repetitive formulae or where the clarity of a particular entry can be significantly improved.

2. Middle English Entries
All entries in Middle English have been included here uncalendared and unaltered, although in many cases the punctuation has been modernised to improve the sense of particular sentences and paragraphs.

Dating
The headings for the meetings of the court have been included unaltered from the original Latin or Middle English. Ordinary meetings of the court were

normally held on a Monday (*Lune*) or a Friday (*Veneris*), while quarter-days were frequently held on a Wednesday (*Mercurii*). Explanations of these, and other dating methods, are given in the Glossary.

Dates in the text from 1 January to 24 March are given in the form 24 March 1488/9 to reflect the common use of the feast of the Assumption (25 March) as the beginning of the year of grace. Dates from 25 March to 31 December follow the normal form, i.e. 25 March 1489.

Errors in dating made by the clerks have not been corrected in the text, although the correct day and/or date has been noted in the footnotes.

Dating using saints' days and festivals was frequently employed by the clerks. To assist the reader the correct day and month has been added in square brackets, while a full list of the fixed feasts used by the clerks is given in the Glossary.

Marginalia
Text written into the margins of volumes I and II has been included here only in those cases where additional information is provided about the entry to which it relates. All other marginal material has either been omitted or referred to in the footnotes. Where marginal text has been included it is <u>underlined</u>.

Capitalization
Capitalization of the entries in Middle English has not been modernized.

All titles have been left uncapitalized except for those instances where the minutes refer to a former or current master of the craft using the style 'Master Percyvale', 'Master Povy' etc. The same applies to references to the wives of masters, referred to as 'Mistress Swan' etc.

Abbreviations
All abbreviations of names and titles in the original Latin or Middle English have been included unchanged. The most common is the use of 'M.' to denote 'Magister' or 'Maister' when referring to the master of the craft, or occasionally to 'Maistres' for the wife of a master. The abbreviation for a master was later corrupted to become 'M[aiste]r' or Mr. in the company's records.

Biographical Material
Biographies of all those who attended meetings of the court and of those who were elected as master or warden of the company have been included in Appendix IV. Information about other prominent individuals is contained in the footnotes. In the cases of individuals whose names occur frequently in the text, such as those whose anniversaries were celebrated by the company, a

biographical note has been inserted after the first occurrence; references in the Index to the pages containing such notes are given in **bold text**.

< > denotes interlined text
[ ] denotes an editorial insertion
... denotes a gap in the text
~~denotes text that has been struck out in the original~~

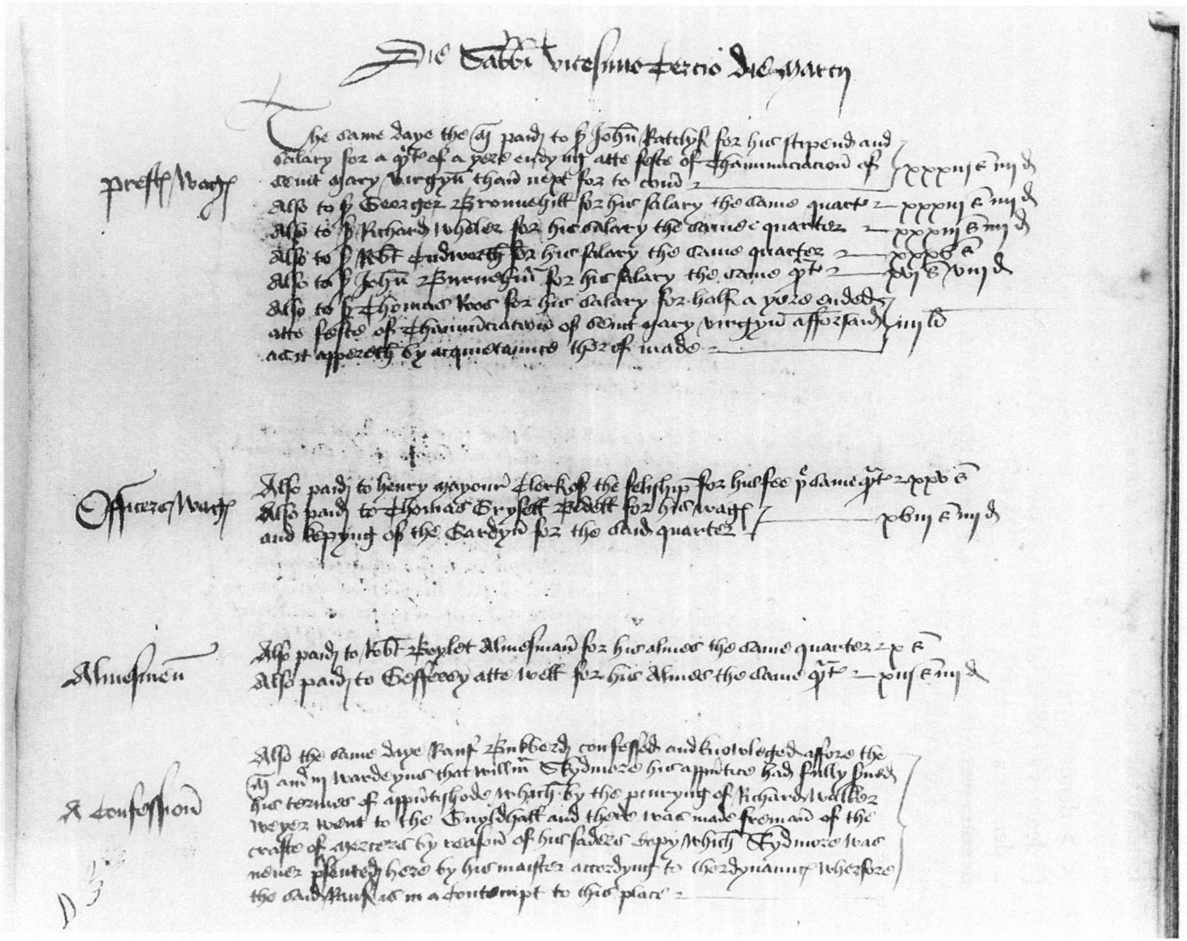

Plate 2: Proceedings of a meeting of the court held on 23 March 1493. The entry shows quarterly payments to priests, officers and almsmen, as well as a 'confession' by a member of the court whose apprentice had joined the Mercers' Company: volume II, f. 63).
(By permission of the Guildhall Library, Corporation of London, and the Merchant Taylors' Company).

VOLUME I: 7 APRIL 1486—24 JUNE 1488

[f. 3][1] Percyvale[2]

Veneris vij° die mensis Aprilis[3] in presencia Magistri et custodum.

This day the Maister resceyved of Richard Quykrell for John Humfrey apprentice for the maisters parte xs.

> The same day James Shirwode came here and presented William Mortimer, son of John Mortimer of Thaxted in the county of Essex, yeoman. And the said William bound himself as an apprentice to the aforesaid James from the feast of Easter last [26 Mar.] for seven years.

And the said James promysseth to pay accordyng to the ordinaunce.

This day the Maister resceyved of Thomas Randall for William West apprentice xxs.
This day the Maister resceyved of Thomas Warton for Thomas Penycoke prentice in party of paiment of xs. vjs. viijd.
~~Item resceyved of Richard Quykrell for John Humfrey apprentice xs.~~
Item resceyved of William Brownyng for Thomas Humfrey apprentice vjs. viijd.
Item resceyved of Thomas Cartwryght for his ffredome xxs.

This day Thomas Randall presented William West his apprentise the son of Richard West citizen and Tailour of London ffro the fest of candilmas [2 Feb.] last passed unto thend of viij yere.

---

[1] Following the loss of the first 227 folios of the original volume of minutes, the remaining folios, together with two pages of miscellaneous jottings from the mid-1490s (Appendix I), were bound together and renumbered. Thus f. 3 corresponds to the original f. 228. The original composition of the Minute Books of the company is discussed in the Introduction, above pp. 6–8.

[2] The headings on each page refer to the master for the current year, in this case Sir John Percyvale for whom see Appendix IV. This format is similar to that adopted in the city's journals and may reflect the fact that the current clerk of the company, Thomas Kirton, was city-trained.

[3] 7 April 1486.

This day Richard Quykrell presented Thomas Hennyng the son of John Hennyng[4] of Bostone in the counte of Lyncolne Marchaunt of the Stapull apprentise to the sayd Richard Quykrell fro the fest of Candilmas last passed [2 Feb.] un to thend of vij yer

And the said Richard browght in a peire of indenturs of John Humfrey his apprentise for the wich prentice he paid to the Maister for the maisters part acording to the ordinaunce xs. for the wych he is alowed the tone apprentize for the tother.

Lune x die mensis Aprilis in presencia Magistri et custodum, Stodard, West, Materdale, Duplage, Pemberton.[5]

This day the Maister rescyeved of William Newpord in parti of paiment out of his prentise Robert Gray for Ester payment vjs. viijd.

This day Richard Bate is admitted in to the liberte of this crafte for the summa of iijli. accordyng to the ordinaunce that is to say he paid to the Maister this same day xxs. an at lamas nex comyng xxs. and at mydsomer come xij moneth xxs. for the wich Roger Clay and John Lewes be suerte for the pament of the same and promyseth to bynd them to the Maister and wardeins by obligacion undir this condicion that the said Richard Bate fortune to dissece within the said terme, as God defend, that than the said obligacions shall stond voide of no effecte.

This day the Maister resceyved of Thomas Wardall for full paiment of his alowance vs.

Veneris xiiij die mensis Aprilis in presencia magistri et custodum, M. Swanne shreve,[6] Tego, Stodard, Gall, Cays, Materdale, Duplage, Pemberton, Lee, Hede, Bukks, Hobard, Spencer, Povey, Martyne, Fytte.[7]

This day Robert[8] presented John Pattason the son of William Pattason of Anwyke in the counte of Northumbr' yeman apprentice to the same Robert fro the first day of May unto thend of vij yer.

---

[4]   For references to Hennyng see, for example, *CCR 1476–85*, p. 390; *CPR 1485–94*, pp. 349, 493.

[5]   For John Stodard, Richard West, John Materdale, Robert Duplage, and Hugh Pemberton: see Appendix IV.

[6]   John Swan: see Appendix IV.

[7]   For biographies of Roger Tego, William Galle, Gilbert Keys, John Lee, John Heed, William Buck, Alan Hoberd, John Spencer, Walter Povey, Thomas Martyn and James Fitte: see Appendix IV.

And the said Robert presented the indenture of prentizod of John Humfrey the son of Thomas Humfrey of Brabam[9] in the comitie of Cambrygg fro the fest of Penticost [14 May] unto vij yer for the wich the said Robert paid to Maister Stalworth accordyng to the ordinaunce vjs. viijd. for the wich old prentize he is graunted the said newe apprentice accordyng to the ordinaunce.

This day James Shirwode presented here William Mortimer, son of John Mortimer of Thaxted in the county of Essex, yeoman, and the said William bound himself as an apprentice to the aforesaid James from the feast of Easter last [26 Mar.] for seven years.

And the said James promiseth to pay to the Maister accordyng to the ordinaunce xxs. that is to sey at midsomer next comyng

[f. 3v] Percyvale.

Lune xvij die Aprilis in presencia Magistri et custodum, Tego, Stodard, Cays, Lee, Bukke, Povey, Boughton,[10] Spencer, Crosby.[11]

The same day John Burgh came here and presented Thomas King, son of Richard King of Hayes in Middlesex, yeoman.[12] And the said Thomas bound himself as an apprentice to the aforesaid John from the feast of Easter last [26 Mar.] for eight years.

And the forsaid John Burgh promiseth to pay for the said apprentice xxs. accordyng to the ordinaunce at the sealyng of the sayd indenturs.

This day[13] it was shewed by the Maister that there as the Drapers wold that they and the ffelaship of this ffraternitie shuld make an acte by the auctoryte of the Maire and his brethren that neyther non of the felashippe of Drapers nor none of this felashippe shuld not ryde in to the contre for to by any wollyn clothis etc. For the wich ther be chosen to commyn with the Drapers first for the shettyng in of Blakwell hall[14] tyll it be one of the cloke every markert day they to comen with the said Drapers for the brech of the same and of none other mater these persons folowyng[15]

---

8   A marginal annotation gives his surname as Hall.
9   Perhaps Braham or Brame in the Isle of Ely, Cambs.
10   Owen (or Ewen) Boughton: see Appendix IV.
11   William Crosby: see Appendix IV.
12   In 1443 a man of this name leased the manor of Edgware from All Souls College, Oxford: VCH, *Middlesex*, IV (1971), pp. 28, 156.
13   The margin has a small drawing of a hand pointing at this entry.
14   Blackwell Hall, from 1396 the city's principal marketplace for woollen cloth: Lobel (ed.), *Atlas*, p. 66.
15   For biographies of these court members see Appendix IV.

Maister Gall
Maister Pemberton
Maister Lee
William Bukke
Stephyn Janyns
John Hardyng

Veneris xxj die mensis Aprilis in presenci Magistri et custodum.

The same day William Swanston came here and presented William
Hugh, son of Hugh Hugh of Carnarvon in Wales. And the said William
bound himself as an apprentice to the aforesaid William from the feast
of Easter [26 Mar.] last for seven years.
And the forsaid William Swanston paid to the Maister for the same apprentis
in parti of paiment for the maisters part vjs. viijd. at Midsomer [24 June] iijs.
iiijd.

This day the Maister paid to William Wrasam, Maister of the Ospitall of Seint
Katerins[16] for a quiterent goyng out of a Tenement of maistres Langwith in
Seint Marie Abchurch for a hole yere in the tyme of Maister Lee[17] xs.
This day the Maister paid to the priores of Kylborn[18] for a quiterent goyng
out of a Tenement in the same parissh of Maistres Langwith for halfe a yer
viijs. vjd.
Item this day the Maister [paid] for xiij quarters colis for the bequest of
Maistres Langwith vs. vjd.
This day the Maister payd to Robert Walthew and Thomas Robyns,
Almesmen, for a fortnyght passed vs. viijd.
This day the Maister resceyved of John Baynard for occupieng of a freman of
a nother craft to hym unknowyng vjd.
Whereof paid to the vewears of the yemen felaship for theyr labur in that be
halfe for presentyng of the same iiijd.
Item the Maister resceyved of William Swanston for occupyeng[19] of a prentis
not presented ijd.

---

16 The hospital of St. Katharine by the Tower, founded 1148 and refounded 1273:
    Lobel, Atlas, p. 88; VCH, *London*, I (1909), pp. 525–30. See also C. Jamison, *The
    History of the Royal Hospital of St. Katharine* (London, 1952).
17 John Lee was master of the company in 1483–4: see Appendix IV.
18 For Kilburn and other London nunneries see C. Paxton, 'The Nunneries of
    London and its environs in the Later Middle Ages', unpublished D.Phil. thesis,
    University of Oxford (1992).
19 See Glossary for 'occupy'.

The same day Robert Bette presented here David Thomson, son of Thomas Thomson of Wandsworth in Middlesex, yeoman. And the said William bound himself as an apprentice to the aforesaid James from the feast of St. Michael the Archangel last [29 Sept.] for seven years.

And the said Robert paid to the Maister the same day in parti of pament for the maisters party iijs. iiijd., at Witson tyde [14 May] iijs. iiijd., at Midsomer [24 June] than next iijs. iiijd.

Henry Brewster and John Harreson, citizens and tailors, submitted themselves to the rule and judgement of Geoffrey Here and William Hewelet, citizens and tailors, arbitrators impartially chosen to determine all actions pending between them. A judgement is to be reached by the Octave of Pentecost [21 May].

Lune xxiiij die Aprilis in presencia Magistri et custodum.

This day Harry Grene was admitted in translating of his fredome from the craft of wevers to this craft for the sum of xxs. of the wych he paid in party of paiment vjs. viijd. And at Lammas next comyng [1 Aug.] xiijs. iiijd.[20]

This day John Brown made a fyne for ocupieng of a foren ijs.
Wherof the Maister paid to the vewers of the yemen ...

This day the Maister paid to the Maister of Burton[21] for a quiterent goyng out of a tenement of Elen Langwyth[22] in the parissh of our lady Abchurch for halfe a yere passed at Ester xiijs.

[f. 4] Percyvale

Veneris xxviij die Aprilis in presencia Magistri et custodum.[23]

---

[20] The margin has a small drawing of a hand pointing to this entry.

[21] The leper hospital of St. Giles-in-the-Fields became a cell of the house of Burton Lazars in Leicestershire in 1299, the headquarters of the Order of St. Lazarus of Jerusalem in England. Thereafter the master of Burton Lazars was also *ex officio* master of St Giles's: M. B. Honeybourne, 'The Leper Hospitals of the London area', *Transactions of the London and Middlesex Archaeological Society*, XXI (1963–7), pp. 20–31.

[22] For the obit celebrated for John and Elene Langwith see below p. 65.

[23] No entries are included under this heading.

Veneris in presencia Magistri et custodum, quinto die Maii, Tego, Pemberton.

The same day Thomas Petyt presented here Thomas Elys, son of William Elys of the parish of Horton in Kent, deceased.[24] And the said William bound himself as an apprentice to the aforesaid Thomas from the feast of Pentecost [14 May] last for nine years.

And the said Thomas Petite paid for the same apprentize accordyng to the ordinaunce xxs.

This day the Maister resceyved of William Warton for Jeram Smyth apprentize and bounde to the craft of Skynners to his wyfis other husband and for consederacion that he was inrolled to the same craft of Skynners it was also concedered that the Skynners had for the same apprentize accordyng to theire ordinaunce xxs. ther for the Maister agreed and the Maisters above wrytten that the same indenturs bound to Skynners crafte shall be cancellyd and the seyd apprentice to be bound to this craft and for the concederacions a bove he shall pay for the prentize new bound to this crafte xs. and no more.

This day John Warner made a ffyne for John Tailour not jurato [i.e. sworn] iiijd.

This day John Kynder made a ffyne for ocupyeng and not juratus ijd.

The Maister resceyved of Robert Kyllam for Harry Bysshop apprentice xxs.

This day the Maister resceyved of William Hall[25] for ocupieng of a childe not bound ijd.

This day the Maister resceyved of Maister Pemberton for the full contentacion of such dettes as Maister Nayler alderman owght to the craft of Taylours by the sentens and determinacion of M. Gall and M. Pemberton iiijli. xiijs. iiijd.

The same day Nicholas Somer, son of William Somer, citizen of London, was presented here and [he] bound himself as an apprentice to Richard Elys, citizen and tailor of London, for ten years from the feast of Pentecost 2 Ric. III [22 May 1485].

For wich prentyze Katerine Ellys promeseth to pai to the Maister according to the ordinaunce on Monday next xxs.

---

[24] Possible references to Elys include *CCR 1476–85*, p. 92; *CPR 1485–94*, p. 136.

[25] This may well be the William Hall who was appointed as a yeoman tailor of the Great Wardrobe in 1467 with the usual wages of 6d. a day. He rented a tenement in the parish of St. Audoen from the Bridge House Estates from 1470–1502 at 40s. p.a. and died two years later: see *Coro. Richard III* ed. Sutton and Hammond, p. 352.

The Maister resceyved of John Colette for ocupyeng without lycence iiij*d*.
The Maister paid to Robert Walthow and Thomas Robyns almesmen for a
fortnyght passed the first day of May *vs*. viij*d*.

> The same day Thomas Rotherham, son of John Rotherham of
> Newcastle upon Tyne, yeoman, was presented here and [he] bound
> himself as an apprentice to John Wolstone, citizen and tailor of
> London, from the feast of Pentecost [14 May] coming for seven years.

And the said John Wolstone promiseth to pay for the same apprentyze
accordyng to the ordynaunce for the maisters parte at the sealyng of the
indenturs *vs*. at lamas [1 Aug.] *vs*.

> The same day John Sparrow, son of Thomas Sparrow of Reading in
> Berkshire, yeoman, was presented here and [he] bound himself as an
> apprentice to John Campinotte,[26] citizen and tailor of London, from the
> feast of Pentecost coming [14 May] for twelve years.

And the said John Campynotte promiseth to pay to the Maister for the same
apprentice accordyng to the ordinaunce xx*s*. that is to say ...

**Lune viij die mensi Maii in presencia Magistri et custodum, Tego,
Stodard, Phillipe,[27] Cais, West, Materdale, Pemberton, Stalworth,[28]
Duplage, Cotton,[29] Hede, Bukke, Spencer, Boughton, Povey, Lewes,[30]
Ffytte, Martyne, Adyf.[31]**

> The same day William Warton came here and presented Jeremy Smyth,
> son of Henry Smyth of Ely in Cambridgeshire, gentleman. And the said
> Jeremy bound himself as an apprentice to the aforesaid William from
> the feast of the Nativity of St. John the Baptist coming [24 June] for
> eight years.
> The same day the said William presented here William Edmond, son of
> John Edmond of Watford in Hertfordshire, yeoman. And the said
> William Edmond bound himself as an apprentice to the aforesaid
> William from the feast of Pentecost [14 May] for seven years.

---

26 Perhaps of French origin. He died in late 1488 leaving John Sparrow 20*s*. and releasing him from the last two years of his apprenticeship: GL, MS 9171/7, ff. 140v–141.
27 Probably John Philip: see Appendix IV.
28 Walter Stalworth: see Appendix IV.
29 Thomas Cotton: see Appendix IV.
30 John Lewes: see Appendix IV.
31 Richard Adyff: see Appendix IV.

This day the Maister reseceyeved of ... for ocupieng with in this citie xiij*d*.
Item resceyved of William Irysely for ocupyeng of a fforen contrary to the ordinaunce xij*d*.

[f. 4v] Percyvale

The obit of Ralph Basset[32] held on 9 May in the church of St. Martin Outwich. For bread 7*d*., for ale 10*d*., for cheese 6*d*., to 5 chaplains 20*d*., to the rector of the church 6*d*., for offerings 2*d*., for alms 13*d*., to a child 2*d*., for wax 12*d*., to the clerk of the church 6*d*.
[Total] 7*s*.

Lune xij die mensis Maii in presencia Magistri et custodum.

The same day Lawrence Bardeney[33] presented here John Charnall, son of Adam Charnall of Moulton in Lincolnshire, yeoman. And the said John bound himself as an apprentice to the aforesaid Lawrence from the feast of Pentecost [14 May] next for seven years.

This [day] the Maister resceyved of Richard Ellys wyfe for Nicholas Semer in full paiment xx*s*.
Item the Maister resceyved of John Combys for Percyvall Danyell for the maisters parte x*s*.
Item the Maister resceyved of Richard Bothom for ... apprentize v*s*.
Item the Maister resceyved of Laurence Bardoney for John Charnell apprentize in party of pay for the maisters parte v*s*. at Witteson tyde [14 May] v*s*.
Item resceyved of the said Laurence for ocupieng of a foren iiij*d*.

---

[32] Sir Ralph Basset of Drayton (d. 1352). The Tailors acquired an interest in Bassett's Inn in St. Mary Aldermanbury from Sir Gerard Braybroke (d. 1429) in 1418–19 which resulted in an income of 40s. p.a. from the property. This was used to fund the obits of Basset and Braybrooke, along with that of Basset's nephew Sir Hugh Shirley (d. 1403), in St. Martin Outwich from that year onwards. The inn itself was finally acquired by the Tailors following the death of Ralph Holland (Master 1419-20) in 1452; from 1454 onwards the fraternity's income from the property was £6 3s. 4d. p.a. *CWCH*, vol. 2, p. 525; Accounts, I, f. 111v, II, f. 27; Lobel, *Atlas*, p. 65. For Braybrooke and Shirley see *The History of Parliament: The Commons 1386-1421*, eds J. S. Roskell, C. Rawcliffe and L. Clark, 4 vols (Gloucester, 1992), vol. 2, pp. 346–9, vol.4, pp. 364–6.

[33] Bardeney was employed by the Great Wardrobe to work on robes for Richard III's coronation in 1483: *Coro. Richard III* ed. Sutton and Hammond, p. 307.

Veneris xix die mensis Maii in presencia Magistri et custodum.

This day Crystofer Wodehouse the son of William Wodehouse, grocer, is admitted to the liberte of this craft for the sum of xxs. that is to say he paid to the Maister the same day xs. and at Lammas [1 Aug.] next xs. and his openyng to be alowyd for the same xxs.

This day John Harryson came here and presented John Lenard, son of Thomas Lenard of Athboy (*Aboy*)[34] in Ireland, gentleman, and the same John bound himself as an apprentice of the aforesaid John Haresson from the feast of Christmas for eight years.

And the said John Harreson promiseth to pay for the same apprentice accordyng to the ordinaunce xxs. that is to say he payd forth with iijs. iiijd., at Midsomer [24 June] iijs. iiijd., at Lammas [1 Aug.] iijs. iiijd., and to the yemen felashippe xs.[35]

The obyte [of] Hugh Talbot[36] holden the Fryday next a fore Trenete Sonday [19 May] holden at Seint Martyn Otwych In Brede iijd., in Ale vjd., to the parson vjd., to v prestes xxd., to the clarke vjd., to a childe ijd., in offeryng ijd., to the waxchandlers xijd.

[Total] iiijs. ixd.

This day the Maister paid to Robert Walthow and Thomas Robyns almesmen for a fortnyght passed on Monday last passed vs. viijd.

Lune xxij die mensis Maii in presencia Magistri et custodum.

Quarter-day held on the 24th day of May in the presence of the master and wardens and Stodard, Materdale, West, Pemberton, Barlowe, Lee, Stalworth, Philip, Cotton, Buke, Hobard, Spencer, Povey, Lewes, Boughton and the whole commonalty.

This day William Grene that hathe wedded the wyfe of Stephen Trappes[37] brought in to the Maister in to Tailours hall xli. sterlynges accordyng to the Bequest of the said Stephyn Trappys toward the ledyng of Taylours halle.

---

34 County Meath.
35 The margin is annotated with 'John Harreson John Lenard at Ledynhall apprentice'.
36 Hugh Talbot, cit. and tailor (d. 1395). For his will see GL, MS 9171/1, f. 367.
37 Stephen Trappys, citizen and tailor, was apprenticed to William Marchall (for whom see Appendix IV) in 1463–4 and entered the livery of the craft himself in 1474–5. He drew up his will on 24 Sept. 1485 in which he left £10 towards 'the

This day was graunted to Crystofer Kyrke by his humble supplicacion of the almes over his xiijs. iiijd. to hym graunte a ffore by the ffelashippe other xiijs. iiijd. by yere that is to say the hole graunt by yere is xxvjs. viijd.

The same day the wills of Master Stone,[38] Master Benton[39] and Hugh Champernon[40] were read out.

The same day the following persons were admitted and sworn into the fraternity of this craft:

James Willefort[41] 20s.
Richard Geffrey 20s.
Richard Hille[42] 20s.
Paten Paterson 20s.
John Sperman 20s.

---

ledyng of the roof of the comon hall' of the Tailors, a bequest made on condition that the project was completed within two years. This time-scale also applied to a bequest of £5 made to the church of All Hallows the Great for 'makyng and the gildyng of a table for the high altar ... in honour of the blissed sacrament so that the said table be made within the spas of ij yeres'. His other bequests to the Tailors' fraternity included £2 to the common box and 20s. to the almsmen of the fraternity of yeomen tailors. The clerk and beadle received bequests of 13s. 4d. and 6s. 8d. respectively. He left various sums of money and items of clothing to members of his family, his servants and his apprentices and left his son, Reynold, and daughter, Elizabeth, £100 each. His widow, Ellen, was bequeathed a life interest in all his lands in Essex and his 'grete place' in the parish of St. Giles Cripplegate, London. The will was proved on 15 Oct. the same year. Accounts, II, f. 239v; III, f. 74v; GL, MS 9171/7, ff. 33v–35. For Grene see Appendix IV.

[38] John Stone served as warden of the Tailors for 1439–40 and was chosen as master for 1449–50. He was chosen as sheriff of the city in September 1464. He made his will 10 Oct. 1474 leaving the Tailors' fraternity money resulting from the sale of his property in Southwark to fund his obit for 100 years. The obit was celebrated on 24 Oct. (see below). *Cal. Letter Bk. L*, p. 55; Hopkinson, *Ancient Records*, p. 111; GL, Merchant Taylors' Co., Ancient MS Bk. 9, p. 30; PRO, Prerogative Court of Canterbury, Reg. 17 Wattys.

[39] Richard Benton was admitted to the livery in 1425–26 and probably served as master in 1447–8. He died in 1456 but his obit (22 Mar.) was not celebrated for the first time until 1463–4, by which time his wife Agnes had also died: Accounts, I, f. 160; II, f. 245v; Hopkinson, *Ancient Records*, p. 111; PRO, PROB 11/4, ff. 62v–63.

[40] Champernoun was admitted to the livery of the Tailors for 1437–38, but did not serve as master of the craft. In his will dated 8 Dec. 1463 he left bequests to the fraternity of yeomen tailors and to the almsmen in the almshouse next to the hall. Accounts, I, f. 294v; GL, MS 9171/5, f. 350.

[41] For Wilford see Appendix IV.

[42] For Hill See Appendix IV.

Robert Hertishorn 20s.
John Flye 20s.
John Staunton 20s.
Alexander Carnavell 20s.
Hugh Acton[43]

Veneris xxvij^{o44} die mensis Maii in presencia Magistri et custodum.

The same day Richard Toft, citizen and tailor of London, presented here John Watson, son of John Watson of Hexham in the county of Hexham,[45] and the said John bound himself as an apprentice to the said Richard from the feast of Pentecost last [14 May] for eight years.

This day William Marchall[46] hath graunted toward the ledyng of the hall at the grete instaunce of the Maister and wardeins xxs. And at the grete praire and instaunce of the said William Marchall he is discharged of one of the vj persones to be warned to be Maister of the craft.

This day John Flemyng presented here Robert Knight, son of Miles Knight, late of Radwell[47] in Yorkshire, yeoman, and the said Robert bound himself as an apprentice to the said John from the feast of Pentecost last [14 May] for seven years.
And the said John Flemyng promyseth to pay accordyng to the ordinaunce for the maisters part xs. wherof paid to the Maister the same day iijs. iiijd. and to the yemen on Monday com vjs. viijd.

[f. 5] Percyvale

Lune xxix die mensis Maii in presencia Magistri et custodum, Stodard, Duplage, Pemberton.

This day the master paid to Robert Walthow and Thomas Robyns, almsmen of this fraternity, for 15 days 5s. 8d.

---

43   Acton was warden in 1498-9 and 1502-3, and may have served as master for 1508-9. Hopkinson, *Ancient Records*, pp. 115, 120.

44   An error for 'xxvj'.

45   A John Watson was a tenant of Hexham Priory in 1479: see A. B. Hinds, *A History of Northumberland* (London and Newcastle, 1896), vol. 3 (1), p. 149.

46   For a brief biography of Marchall see Appendix IV.

47   Possibly Radwell End, or Rothwell (both W. Riding), see *The Place-names of the West Riding of Yorkshire* (English Place-name Society, XXXI), pt. 2, pp. 143-4; *ibid.* pt. 3, p. 176.

Veneris iij° die mensis Junii in presencia Magistri et custodum, Tego, West, Materdale, Duplage, Pemberton, Stodard.

This day Richard Adyff and Owen Bowghton were chosen as arbiters between Richard Bedyll and Edward Molenes, citizens and tailors of London, and an award to be made by the feast of St. Peter's Chains [1 Aug.] next.

This day Robert Raby, son of Robert Raby of the parish of St. Mary Whitechapel in the suburbs of London, was presented as an apprentice, and the said Robert the son bound himself as an apprentice to George Bolton, citizen and tailor of London, from the feast of the Nativity of St. John the Baptist [24 June] next for seven years.

And the said [George] paid to the Maister for the same prentice accordyng to the ordinaunce xxs.

This day the Maister resceyved of the wardeins of the craft in the tyme of Maister Lee[48] Maister of this fraternite of there gadderyng of the serche as it is accustumyd to theym due and paid by the hand of the said Maister Lee xxxvijs. xd. The wych the said wardeins gave toward the ledyng of the hall.[49]

Thomas Martyn and Ewen Boughton were chosen as arbiters between John Hede and William Stone, each bound in 100s., and an award to be made by the 17th day of June.

Item resceyved vjd. of Richard Bedyll for Charles Sharpe apprentice.

The obit of Thomas Reymond[50] held on the 8th day of June. To the tavern 20d., to the rector 6d., for 4 priests 16d., to the clerk 8d., for the offering 2d., for wax 12d., in alms [4s. 8d.]
[Total] 10s.

Veneris x[51] die mensis Junii in presencia Magistri et custodum.

This day John Smyth presented here John Wakelyn, son of William Wakelyn late of Dunmow in Essex, and the said John Wakelyn bound

---

48 John Lee, master 1483–4: see Appendix IV.
49 No accounts survive to show the full extent of this building work, although an earlier meeting of the court (24 May) had recorded a bequest of £10 for the project (see above).
50 Thomas Reymond, master 1446–7. Died in 1464 and established an obit in the church of St. Thomas the Apostle to be administered by the Tailors for 40 years. Accounts, II, f. 260; GL, MS 9171/3, f. 518v.
51 An error for 'ix'.

himself as an apprentice to the said John Smyth from the feast of St. John the Baptist next [24 June] for nine years.

And the said John Smyth promiseth the Maister to pay accordyng to the ordinaunce xxs. that is to sey the Friday after Midsomer day [30 June] vs., and at Lammas next [1 Aug.] vs., and to the yemen felashippe xs.

Lune xij° die mensis Junii in presencia Magistri et custodum.

This day the master paid to Robert Walthew and Thomas Robyns, almsmen of this fraternity, for 15 days [5s. 8d.]

Item paid for hyryng of a barge to fette in the Kyng Harry the vij[the] xiiijs.[52]
Item paid to Crane for hym his childryn and his orgyns for the same barge iiijs. viijd.
Item for a kylderkyn of Bere and Brede ijs. ijd.
Item to a Taberet the same tyme iiijs.
Item a nother Taberet xxijd.
Item for bote hyre ijd.

The obit of Hugh Cavendish[53] held in the church of St. Martin Outwich on the 12th day of June. For bread 6d., for ale 13d., for cheese 5d., to the parson 6d., for 5 chaplains 20d., to the clerk of the parish 8d., for offerings 4d., in wax 12d., to a child 2d.
Item to the Maister, wardens, Clarke and Bedyll accordyng to his wyll xjs. viijd.

---

[52] Henry VII embarked upon a royal tour in March 1486, during which he visited a number of towns and cities where he was welcomed with pageants and other celebrations. He was in Bristol from 20 May, but by early June had returned to the royal palace at Sheen. On Monday 5 June he journeyed by water to Westminster bridge. The royal barge was met at Putney by the mayor and aldermen of the City and the guilds 'in a great Multitude of Barges, garnyshed with Banners, Penounces, Standers, and Pensells'. After disembarking, the royal procession made its way to Westminster Abbey: S. Anglo, *Spectacle, Pageantry and Early Tudor Policy* (Oxford, 1969), p. 33; Attreed, 'The Politics of Welcome', pp. 220–25.

[53] Cavendish was related to John C. an embroiderer who was master of the Tailors company for 1413–14. Hugh was admitted to the livery of the Tailors in 1429–30. Shortly before his death in 1454 he conveyed family properties in Walbrook and Fenchurch Street to fellow tailor Richard Tolle (d. 1460) who, in turn, bequeathed them to the Tailors on condition that they were used to fund Cavendish's obit in St. Martin Outwich and a quarterly distribution of coals to the residents of the almshouse next to Tailors' Hall. Accounts, I, f. 205; II, f. 246; GL, Merchant Taylors' Co., Ancient MS Bk. 8, pp. 97–9; PRO, PROB 11/1, f. 78v; Clode, *Memorials*, pp. 106, 279; idem, *Early History*, vol. 2, p. 411.

Martis xiij⁵⁴ die mensi Junii in presencia Magistri et custodum et xxiij^pr, Tego, Cays, Barlow, Duplage, Pemberton, Lee, Stalworth, Cotton, Hede, Bukke, Adyffe, Crosby, Povey, Martyn.

This day it was graunted by all the Maisters above wrytten that George Brodehurst is admitted to the liberte of this craft for xx*s*.

Also it is condecendyd by all the Maisters above wryttyn to take out of tresoure chest for the ledyng of the halle and other reparacion of the same xx*li*.
And the said   xx*li*. to be delyvered in to the hands of Maister Hugh Pemberton.

Paid to Robert Walthow and Thomas Robyns almesmen for a fortnyght past the xij day of Junii *vs. viijd.*

Veneris xvj die mensis Junii in presencia Magistri

The obit of Ralph Holand⁵⁵ held on the 18th day of June in the church of St. Mary Aldermary, in accordance with his will 13*s*. 4*d*.

Lune xix die mensis Junii in presencia Magistri et custodum et xxiij^pr, ..., Cays, West, Materdale, Barlow, Duplage, Lee, Hede, Hoberd, Bowghton.

This day it was shewyd by the Maister that where as an ordinaunce is made afore tyme that the Maister at the quarter day afore Mydsomer day shuld ax lycence of the body of the ffelaship for dyner of mydsomer the morn after mydsomer day [24 June] in payn of xx*li*. it was not axid at the quarter day wherof the Maister axid a pardon of the xxiiij accordyng to the ordinaunce.

[f. 5v] Percyvale

Eodem die xix° die presentis mensis in presencia predicti Magistri et custodum et xxiij^or.

This day it is graunted to Margery Spekyngton wedowe the Tenement Inne of the Sarsyn hede in Frydaystrete⁵⁶ the wych she dwellyth in where as she had

---

54   An error for 'xiv' or 'xiiij'.
55   Master of the company 1419–20 and alderman 1435–44. For his controversial career see C. M. Barron, 'Ralph Holland and the London Radicals, 1438–1444', in R. Holt and G. Rosser (eds), *The Medieval Town: A Reader in English Urban History 1200–1540* (London, 1990), pp. 160–83.

by lese the said Tenement with ij Tenementes by the said grete Tenement payng by yere for all the hole xiiij marke where as she by her peticion dysyred to be dischargyd of the said ij tenuantrees and so it is to her grauntd payng yerly for the said grete tenement inne x marke duryng her lyfe tyme and so she to be dischargyd of the said ij tenementes and her terme to begyn at the ffest of Midsomer next comyng [24 June].

John Clarke, son of Geoffrey Clarke of Cambridge, vintner, bound himself as an apprentice to William Grene, citizen and tailor of London from the feast of Pentecost last [14 May] for seven years.

John Haryyng, son of Robert Haryyng of Hoxton in the parish of Shoreditch in Middlesex, 'coynour',[57] bound himself as an apprentice to William Grene, citizen and tailor of London, from the feast of Christmas last for nine years.

Thomas Leke, son of Thomas Leke of Granby in Nottinghamshire, gentleman,[58] bound himself as an apprentice to Stephen Jenyns, citizen and tailor of London, from the feast of St. George the Martyr last [23 Apr.] for eight years.

Robert Mountenay, son of Thomas Mountenay[59] of Willoughby in Norfolk, gentleman, bound himself as an apprentice to Oliver Warner,

---

[56] The Saracen's Head, along with two shops in Friday Street, was acquired by the Tailors between 1398 and March 1401, when a licence to alienate in mortmain was obtained by a group of feoffees which included several prominent members of the company. The properties together yielded an income of £8 p.a., a figure which had risen to £9 6s. 8d by 1468. Margery was the widow of Thomas Spekyngton, a liveryman of the company, who leased the Saracen's Head from 1461 until after 1478. Accounts, I, ff. 4–5; II, ff. 204v, 326; III, f. 111; *CPR 1399–1401*, p. 455.

[57] For the will of Robert Heryonge of Hoxton, coiner (d. 1500) see PRO, PCC 17 Moore (PROB 11/12, ff. 131v–132). His executors were his widow and two of his sons, Richard and William, who received bequests of silver vessels as well as lands in Shoreditch, Islington and Tottenham. John did not receive any bequests himself, although his own son, Henry, benefited from bequests of lands and goods. I am grateful to Jessica Freeman for this reference.

[58] Several branches of the Leek family were active in late 15th-century Nottinghamshire. It is possible that Thomas may be identified as the member of the Kirkton branch of the family who was a prominent commissioner and J.P. during the 1480s and 1490s: see *CPR 1476–85*, pp. 395, 400, 489, 569, *1485–94*, pp. 241, 396, 496; *Inquisitiones Post Mortem Relating to Nottinghamshire 1437–1485*, ed. M. A. Renshaw (Thoroton Society Rec. Ser. XVII, 1956), pp. 49, 76, 78.

[59] A Thomas Mountenay was one of the lords of the manor of Beckhall in Norfolk in 1505: F. Blomefield, *A History of Norfolk*, 12 vols (1805), vol. 1, p. 363.

citizen and tailor of London, from the feast of St. Michael the Archangel [29 Sept.] for eight years.

Item paid for oyle for the lampe in Seint Martyn Otiswyche church for thys yere vij*s*.

Sabbati viginti quatuor die mensis Junii anno regni regis Henrici septimi post conquestum primo Thomas Cotton electus est in magistrum istius fraternitatis in festo Nativitatis Sancti Johannis Baptiste.

[translation] On Saturday 24 June 1 Hen. VII [1486] Thomas Cotton was chosen as master of this fraternity on the feast of St. John the Baptist

John Gardyner, deceased[60]
Thomas Randell
George Lufkyn, sworn   wardens
~~Thomas Randolfe sworn~~
William Grene, sworn
~~John Barnard~~

Thomas Randell
John Barnard sworn   wardens[61]
William Grene sworn
George Lufkyn sworn

Lune tercio die mensis Julii in presencia Magistri et custodum.

This day the master paid to Robert Walthew and Thomas Robyns almsmen of this fraternity, for the 15 days before the 27th of June 5*s*. 8*d*.

---

[60] The date of Gardyner's death is uncertain. He drew up his will on 17 Mar. 1483/4 requesting burial in St. Margaret's Bridge Street and leaving family property in Sawbridgeworth, Herts. to his eldest son, John. No date of probate is given, but from its position in the register it was probably proved in May 1487, nearly a year after this election. PRO, PROB 11/8, ff. 9v–10v.

[61] The circumstances of this election are not recorded, although it appears that Gardyner's death was followed by the removal of Randolfe from office. It may have been the second of these events which prompted the clerk to draw up a revised list of wardens. For biographies of those elected see Appendix IV.

<u>Admyssion John Aleyton operandum shopam per Seint M. Patens.</u> This day the Maister rescyved of John Aleyton in party of payment of his admissyon vs.

Lune x die Julii in presencia Magistri et custodum.

John Crowe, son of Thomas Crow, citizen and haberdasher of London, bound himself as an apprentice to Richard Croft,[62] citizen and tailor of London, from the feast of St. Michael the Archangel next [29 Sept.] for eight years.

And the said Richard payde the Maister in party of payment for the same vs.

This day the master paid Robert Walthew and Thomas Robyns, almsmen of this fraternity, for the past 15 days 5s. 8d.

Veneris xiiij die Julii in presencia Magistri et custodum.

This day William Tailour browght in to the Maister xxs. as he was commaunded by the Maister and wardeins the wych xxs. is in the hand of the Maister wardeyn.

This day the Maister warden hath resceyved of John Lytton in party of payment of his admissyon vs.

This day the Maister wardein resceyved of Robert Grevys and of Thomas Bedford of every of them xls. by the commaundement of the Maister and wardens.

This day Thomas Bedford and Robert Grevys submitted themselves, on a bond of £20 each, to the rule and judgement of Walter Povey and Ewen Boughton, arbiters, and an award to be made between them by the feast of the Assumption of the Blessed Virgin Mary [15 Aug.]

This day Robert Clay made a fyne for ocupyeng of a fforen viijd.

This day the Maister resceyved of Richard Croft for ocupyeng of a fforen iiijd.

This day John Kyng the wich was prentice with William Berd is admitted by redempcion for xxvjs. viijd. to be paid.

---

62 Richard Croft worked 19 days in the Great Wardrobe prior to Richard III's coronation. Among the bequests in his will (dated 17 June 1493 and proved 18 July the same year) was 40s. to 'the childe that my wyff goyth with all nowe'. He asked to be buried before the image of the Holy Trinity in church of St. Laurence Jewry. *Coro. Richard III* ed. Sutton and Hammond, p. 329; GL, MS 9171/8, f. 56v.

[f. 6] Cotton.

Lune xvij die Julii in presencia M. et custodum.

This day John Broughton and William Taylour submitted themselves, on a bond of £10 each, to the rule and judgement of Robert Byllyngham and Dionisius Burton, arbiters, and an award to be made between them by the feast of the Assumption of the Blessed Virgin Mary next [15 Aug.]

<u>Admissio Roberti Bolton operandum shopam Estchepe end.</u>
This day Robert Bolton was granted licence to open a shop.
And the said Robert payd the same day in party of payment vs. at Crystmas and vs.

This day Richard Swanne presented here William Lache, son of James Lache of Liverpool in Lancashire, mercer, and the said William bound himself as an apprentice to the said Richard from the feast of the Nativity of St. John the Baptist [24 June] next for eight years.
And the said Richard Swanne paid to the Maister for the same apprentize in party of paiment iijs. iiijd. at Mighelmas iijs. iiijd. at Crystmas iijs. iiijd.
The Maister resceyved of the said Richard Swanne for the same apprentice not presented vjd.

The obit of John Langwith and Elene his wife,[63] held in the church of St. Mary Abchurch. For bread, wine etc. and 6 chaplains, parish clerk, offerings, wax and alms 10s.
And paid to the master, wardens, clerk and beadle for their labour, according to the last will of Elene 6s. 8d.

Veneris xxj° die mensis Julii in presencia M. et custodum.

This day William Bysshop and John Laddysdale submitted themselves, on a bond of 40s. each, to the arbitration of Christopher Banks, tailor, and an award to be made by the feast of St. Peter's Chains next [1 Aug.]

---

63 John Langwith was master of the Tailors in 1444-5. He died in 1467 but the obit, funded out of property left to the Tailors in Candlewick Street and Shirbourne Lane, was not celebrated until after the death of Elene, a successful silkwoman, in 1480. For their wills see PRO, PROB 11/5, f. 153v, 7, ff. 19v–20v; *CWCH*, vol. 2, p. 585. A short study of the Langwiths by the present author and Dr. Caroline Barron is currently in preparation.

This [day] Sir[64] Harry Chesshire prest of Powlys to syng for my lady Roos[65] is admitted and sworn a Brother of this fraternite
And the said Harry graunteth to paie accordyng as a brother xxs.

Lune xxiiij die mensis Julii in presencia M. et custodum.

This day the master paid to Robert Walthew and Thomas Robyns, almsmen of this fraternity, for the last quindene 5s. 8d.

This day John Spencer and William Danby, tailors, submitted themselves, on a bond of ..., to the arbitration and judgement of William Crosby and Richard Adyff, citizens and tailors, and an award to be made by the feast of the Assumption of the Virgin next [15 Aug.]

Veneris xxviij° die mensis Julii in presencia M. et custodum.

This day William Casteley, son of John Casteley of the city of York, yeoman, bound himself as an apprentice to John Lewys, citizen and tailor of London, from the feast of the Nativity of Saint John the Baptist last [24 June].
And the said John Lewes promyseth to pay the Maister accordyng to the ordinaunce xxs. that is to say at the selyng of the indenturs vs. rec[eyved], at Alhalowyn tyde [1 Nov.] vs., and to the yemen xs.

Lune ultimo die mensis Julii in presencia M. et custodum.

This day the Maister rescyeved of Walter White in parte of paiment of his admission and openyng vs. and at   xs.
This day the Maister resceyved of Robert Baker in party of pament of his admission and of his openyng iijs. iiijd. per J. Hede

---

64   See Glossary.
65   Lady Beatrice de Roos (d. 1414), widow of Maurice, Earl of Desmond (d. 1358), Thomas, Lord Roos (d. 1384) and Sir Richard de Burley (d. 1387), drew up an agreement with the Tailors in April 1409 for the foundation of her chantry in St. Paul's which was to be funded out of the revenues from property in Lymestrete conveyed to the Tailors. Her heirs were to select the chaplains, while the Tailors were responsible for paying his salary of 12 marks p.a. See Davies, thesis, pp. 56–7 and W. Dugdale, *The History of St. Paul's Cathedral* (London, 1818), pp. 354–7.

[f. 6v] Cotton.

Veneris iiij° die Augusti in presencia M. et custodum.

Lune vij die Julii[66] in presencia M. et custodum M. Percyvale,[67] Stodard, Gall, Cays, Materdale, Pemberton, Lee, Hede, Hoberd, Jenyns,[68] Spencer, Adyff, Fytte.

This day Rowland Lytillskyll, son of John Lytylskyll of Hexham in the county of Hexham,[69] bound himself as an apprentice to William Hulette, citizen and tailor of London, from the feast of St. Michael the Archangel next [29 Sept.] for twelve years.
And the said William Hulette promyseth to pay accordyng to the ordinaunce xxs. that is to say resceyved the same day iijs. iiijd. at the sealyng of the indenturs xxd. at Alhalowyntyde [1 Nov.] vs.

This day the Maister payd to Robert Walthow and Thomas Robyns almesmen for xv dies elapsum vs. viijd.

This day the Maister resceyved of William Irysley for ocupyeng of a foren ijs.

This day ... was admitted into ...

Die Veneris xj die Augusti in presencia M. et custodum.

This day John Kyng was admitted into the freedom of this craft for 26s. 8d.
Item received the same day by the master in part payment for the terms of Christmas, Easter, the Nativity of St. John the Baptist [24 June] 6s. 8d.

Item 6s. 8d. was received from William Wase for his redemption in part payment of 26s. 8d. Of the remainder, 6s. 8d. is to be paid at Christmas next, 6s. 8d. at Easter following [15 Apr. 1487], and 6s. 8d. at the feast of the Nativity of St. John the Baptist following [24 June 1487].

---

66 An error for 'Augusti'.
67 For a brief biography of John Percyvale see Appendix IV.
68 For Stephen Jenyns see Appendix IV.
69 Members of this family are recorded in Hexham in the 16th and 17th centuries: Hinds, *Northumberland*, vol. 3 (1), pp. 79, 81, 102.

Lune xiiij die mensis Augusti in presencia M. et custodum.

<u>Admissio Roberti Berker per M. Duplage</u>. This day Robert Berker was admitted as a shop-holder and paid to the master 3s. 4d. with 6s. 8d. payable at the feast of St. Michael the Archangel next [29 Sept.]

This day Thomas Hoggeson bound himself as an apprentice to John Bolton, from the feast of Assumption of the Blessed Virgin Mary next [15 Aug.] for seven years.

Veneris xviij die mensis Augusti in presencia M. et custodum.

This day the Maister [paid] to Richard Bette draper for a quiterent goyng in the parissh of Halhalowyn in Bredstrete for this yere passed at the fest of the Nativite of Seint John Baptiste [24 June] vjs. viijd.

Lune xxj day of August in presencia M. et custodum.

This day the master paid to Robert Walthew and Thomas Robyns, almsmen of this fraternity, for the past 15 days 5s. 8d.

This day the Maister rescyved of John Browghton for a fyne for an accion takyn and wrownfully a restyng of a Brother contrary to the ordinaunce iijs. iiijd.

The obyte of Barnard Dakers[70] holden at Freer Austyne accordyng to the compocision vjs. viijd.

William Shotteswell presented here Christopher Brandley, son of Christopher Brandley of the city of Lincoln, tailor, [and the said Christopher] bound himself as an apprentice to the said William from the feast of the Assumption of the Blessed Virgin Mary next [15 Aug.] for seven years.

And the sayd William Shotiswall promiseth to pai the Maister for the same apprentise xs. that is to sey at the fest of Seint Michell next comyng [29 Sept.] iijs. iiijd. and at the fest of Cristmas than next folowyng vjs. viijd.

---

[70] Little is recorded of Dakers whose obit is first recorded in the company's accounts for 1480-1, just ten years after he was admitted to the freedom of the city by redemption. He may well, however, have been related to Richard Dacres, a London tailor who died in 1495: Accounts, III, ff. 19v, 139; GL, MS 9171/8, f. 100.

[f. 7] Cotton.

The same day William Hall presented here Thomas Alye, son of Roger Alye of Watford in Hertfordshire, brewer, and the said Thomas bound himself as an apprentice to the said William from the feast of the Nativity of the Blessed Virgin Mary next [8 Sept.] for eight years.
And the said William Hall ...

This day Richard West presented here William Nicholson, son of Thomas Nicholson of Biggesworth[71] in Northumberland, yeoman, as his apprentice from the feast of St. Bartholomew the Apostle next [24 Aug.] for eight years.
        And the said Richard West ...

Lune xxviij day of August in presencia [M.] et custodum.

This day the master paid to the abbot of Bermondsey[72] for a quit-rent arising from tenements in the parish of St. Mary Abchurch for a whole year from the feast of the Nativity of St. John the Baptist 1 Hen. VII [24 June 1486] 2s. 6d.

Paid and spent on the eve and day of Seint Bartilmew [24 Aug.] in the serche of the ffaire ther ijs.[73]

Item resceyved of John Tailour for his admission and openyng xs. per Frydaystrete

---

[71]   Unidentified, although possibly connected with Bigges Quarter, 6 miles north of Morpeth.

[72]   Bermondsey abbey, a Cluniac foundation established 1082: VCH, *Surrey*, II (1905), pp. 64–72.

[73]   St. Bartholomew's fair was an important annual cloth fair held for three days around 24 August. The Drapers' Company had traditionally exercised rights of 'search' (i.e. scrutiny) of the cloth bought and sold there, but by the 1430s the Tailors were claiming the right to search the workshops of the increasing number of its freemen who were involved in the retailing of trade. For the resulting dispute between the two companies see Barron, 'Ralph Holland', esp. pp. 165–9, 179.

Veneris primo die mensis Septembris in presencia M. et custodum.

This day John Getforth was admitted as a shop-holder[74] and paid in part-payment 3s. 4d., at Christmas 3s. 4d., at Easter next [15 Apr. 1487] 3s. 4s.

This day John Clarke presented here Tristram Farnworth, son of Elias Farnworth of Buxbury[75] in Lancashire, yeoman, as an apprentice of the said John Clarke from the feast of the Nativity of St. John the Baptist [24 June], for seven years.

And presented here the same day was William Walton, son of Robert Walton of Kirkham in Lancashire, yeoman, from the feast of St. John the Baptist last [24 June] for seven years.

And the said John Clarke paid the Maister in parti of paiment of bothe prentizes vs. and the xix day of Octobre vs.

On the feast of the Decollation of St. John the Baptist [29 Aug.] the following were elected and sworn as wardens of the yeomen tailors
mort' Stephen Cotford
Robert Serle
<John Stoyle>
John Morten
Thomas Hoby

Lune iiij die mensis Septembris in presencia M. et custodum.

This day the master paid to Robert Walthew and Thomas Robyns, almsmen of this fraternity, for the last 15 days 5s. 8d.

Lune xj die mensis Septembris in presencia M. et custodum.

This day the Maister resceyved of Dayvth John for his admission and openyng xs.
This day the Maister rescyeved of William Tailour for his admission in party of payment iijs. iiijd.

---

74 Those who obtained the freedom were required to pay an additional sum of 10s. to the company if they wished to open a shop.
75 Perhaps Bucks, Lancs.

This day the Maister resceyved of Davith John for ocupieng of a foren ij*s.* viij*d.*

This day the Maister paid for xij quarters colys delyvered in the almeshowse accordyng to the wille of Hugh Caundyssh[76] at Lammas [1 Aug.] v*s.*

Willelmus Gybson Ricardi May apprenticie per Byllyngsgate

    This day William Gybson presented here Richard May, son of Simon May, citizen and brewer of London, as his apprentice from the feast of the Nativity of the Blessed Virgin Mary [8 Sept.] for seven years.

Resceyved of the same William Gybson in party of payment of the same apprentize iij*s.* iiij*d.*, at Crystmas iij*s.* iiij*d.*, at Ester [15 Apr. 1487] iij*s.* iiij*d.*

[f. 7v] Cotton.

Veneris xv die mensis Septembris in presencia M. et custodum.

    This day Ralph Traford presented here Hugh Wilson, son of Adam Wilson of the Episcopate of Durham, yeoman, as his apprentice from the feast of St. Michael the Archangel next [29 Sept.] for seven years.

Lune xviij die mensis Septembris in presencia M. et custodum.

    This day the master paid to Robert Walthew and Thomas Robyns, almsmen of this fraternity, for the last 15 days 5*s.* 8*d.*

    This day Thomas Peryson presented here William Heron, son of Thomas Heron of Cargo in Cumberland, yeoman, from the feast of St. Michael the Archangel next [29 Sept.] for eight years.

    And the said Thomas Perison paid the Maister for the same apprentice x*s.*

Veneris xxij° die mensis Septembris in presencia M. et custodum.

    This day Thomas Dyker presented here Robert Stabuls, son of Richard Stabuls of Nottingham, yeoman, who bound himself as an apprentice of the said Thomas from the feast of Pentecost last [14 May] for seven years.

---

76   See above n. 53.

And the said Thomas Dicar promiseth to pay the Maister according to the ordinaunce xxs. at the sealyng of the indenturs. Rec[eyved].

Lune xxv die mensis Septembris in presencia M. et custodum.

This day Thomas Dicar, citizen and tailor of London, presented Robert Stables, son of Richard Stables of the town of Nottingham, as his apprentice from the feast of Pentecost next [3 June 1487] for seven years.
And the said Thomas Diker paid to the Maister according to the ordinaunce for the maisters part xs.
And the said Thomas Dakers browght a indenture of prentisod of Richard Pain the son of Robert Payn, parisshe clarke in the [county] of Cumbyrlon, the wiche prentize was set over from Richard Kelly unto the said Thomas Dyker the termes comyng of his apprentisod by the chamberleyn.[77]

This day the Maister resceyved of William Shotiswall for occupyeng of a foreyn xijd.

Lune secundo die mensis Octobris in presencia M. et custodum.

This day Edward Moleners presented here Robert Mason, son of John Mason of Cockermouth in Cumberland, as his apprentice from the feast of Easter 3 Ed. IV[78] for seven years.

This day Oliver Warner presented here Roger Radeclyff, son of William Radeclyff late of the town of Calais, as his apprentice from the feast of St. Michael the Archangel last [29 Sept.] for nine years.
And the said Olyver promiseth to pay to the Maister accordyng to the ordinaunce xxs.

This day the master paid to Robert Walthew and Thomas Robyns, almsmen of this fraternity, for the last 15 days 5s. 8d.

---

[77] In the event of the death of a master, or in certain other circumstances such as imprisonment or bankruptcy, the remainder of the term to be served by an apprentice could be 'set over' or transferred to another master by the city chamberlain. The language used emphasises the fact that apprentices themselves were not chattels and that it was their terms of apprenticeship which could be bought, sold or transferred with the permission of the city and the relevant guild.

[78] Probably an error for Easter 3 Hen. VII [6 Apr. 1488].

Veneris vj die mensis Octobris in presencia M. et custodum.

This day the Maister paid to John Savage the kynges Bargeman for the Barge to Westmynster for the felaship to bryng M[ayor and] shrevys to Westminster[79] xiijs. iiijd.
Item gevyn to the Bargemen to drynke xijd.

> This day Ralph Traford presented here Hugh Wilson, son of Adam Wilson of the Episcopate of Durham, yeoman, who bound himself as an apprentice of the said Ralph Traford from the feast of St. Michael the Archangel next [29 Sept.] for eight years.

And the said Rawfe Traford promiseth to pay the Maister accordyng to the ordinaunce xxs. resceyved in party of paiment vs. at Crystmas vs.

[f. 8] Cotton.

Lune xvj die mensis Octobris in presencia M. et custodum.

> This day Henry Hawkyns was admitted into the freedom of this fraternity, and paid for his redemption £3.

> This day the master paid to Robert Walthew and Thomas Robyns, almsmen of this fraternity, for the last 15 days 5s. 8d.

Dies quarterii tentus xvij die mensis Octobris videlicet in presencia M. et custodum et totius comunitatis istius fraternitatis, Tego, Stodard, Cays, West, Barlow, Materdale, Pemberton, Lee, Stalworth.

> This day the wills of John Stone, Thomas Reymond, Hugh Cavendish and John Churchman were read out.[80]

This day where was admitted for the oversight with the vewers[81] of this citee for the lyvelode on the grund of Bassettes Inne[82] thes persones folowyng[83]

---

79 This waterborne procession to Westminster took place following the annual election of the mayor on 13 Oct. This custom was said to have begun in the mayoralty of John Norman (1453–4): C. L. Kingsford (ed.), *The Chronicles of London* (Oxford, 1905), p. 164.

80 For these men see nn. 38, 50, 53 and 129.

81 For the history and work of London's viewers see J. S. Loengard (ed.), *London Viewers and their Certificates, 1508–1558*, London Record Society, 26 (1989), esp. pp. xi–lxv.

Maister Galle	William Bukke
Maister Keys	Stephyn Janyns
Maister Materdale	William Harte
Maister Pemberton	John Hardyng

This day it [was] graunted by the Maisters above wrytten that wher Richard Derby handes by graunted to hym a peire of Endenturs of lees the Tenement the wiche he now dwellith in for the termes of xx yeers undir this condicion he shuld not lett to ferme the same tenement withowt licens of the Maister and wardens. Where as now for the benevolens that he hath promysed to make a chimney and a seler in the same is graunt a new lese for xx yeers and of lycens to lette the same to what man he will excepte to a pewterer, fuller, sherman, blaksmyth or founder.

Veneris vicesimo die mensis Octobris in presencia M. et custodum.[84]

On Tuesday[85] 20 October the obits of John Halygate and Idonea his wife[86] were held in the church of St. Martin Outwich and Mass was held on the morrow. For bread 6*d.*, for ale 8*d.*, to the rector of the church 6*d.*, to six priests 22*d.*, to a child 2*d.*, to the clerk of the church 6*d.*, for offerings 2*d.*

---

[82] The company began receiving rent from Bassett's Inn in 1422-3: Accounts, I, f. 133.

[83] For the biographies of these court members see Appendix IV.

[84] It was relatively unusual for the court to meet three times in a week.

[85] Error for Friday.

[86] John Halygate was a London mercer who was apprenticed to Thomas Saccheford, had joined the livery of his craft by 1412 and was a merchant adventurer by 1421. In 1428 the wardens of the Skinners' Company charged him before the mayor with mixing seasoned and unseasoned furs together, these having been found in his house in the parish of St. Mary le Bow. He died in 1432 and his widow, Idonea, subsequently joined the Tailors' fraternity, becoming a sister at some point after 1445. In her will dated 12 Oct. 1451 she left lands in the parish of St. Margaret Pattens to the master and wardens of the Tailors for the celebration of an obit in the church of St. Martin Outwich. GL, MS 9171/3, f. 308; 5, f. 30v; Clode, *Early History*, I, p. 410; Accounts, II, f. 15v; *Cal. Letter Bk. L*, p. 89. I am grateful to Dr. Anne Sutton for information on Halygate's career taken from the biographical index cards compiled by Miss Jean Imray for the Mercers' Company.

Lune xxiiij[87] die mensis Octobris in presencia M. et custodum.

The obit of John Stone, late sheriff of this city, held the 24th day of October, with exequies and Mass held on the morrow. For bread 18*d.*, for ale 2*s.* 2*d.*, for spices 14*d.*, for cheese 12*d.*, to the rector of the church 12*d.*, to five chaplains 20*d.*, to a ?carter (*clarator*) 2*d.*, to a child 1*d.*, to the clerks of the church 12*d.*, for wax 12*d.*, to the master of the fraternity 3*s.* 4*d.*, to each of the wardens 20*d.*, to the clerk and the beadle 22*d.*, for offerings 4*d.*, for alms ..., for wine 18*d.*

Veneris xxvij die mensis Octobris in presencia M. et custodum.

The obits of William Jowderell and Alice his wife,[88] held in the church of St. Mary Abchurch the 26th day of October, according to his will 2*s.* 4*d.*

Lune xxx[to] die mensis Octobris

The master paid to Robert Walthew and Thomas Robyns, almsmen of this fraternity, for the past quindene 5*s.* 8*d.*

This day Richard Radclyf, junior, was admitted into the freedom of this mistery by redemption for £3, of which he will pay at Christmas next 10*s.*, at Easter next 10*s.*, on the feast of the Nativity of St. John the Baptist 10*s.*, on the feast of St. Peter's Chains 10*s.* and on the feast of St. John the Baptist following 20*s.*

[f. 8v] Cotton.

Lune vj° die mensis Novembris in presencia M. et custodum.

This day Ralph Baily, son of John Baily of Willingham in Lincolnshire, yeoman, bound himself as an apprentice to John Brownyng, citizen and tailor of London, from Christmas next for seven years. Received from the said John Brownyng by the master 6*s.* 8*d.*

---

[87] Error for 'xxiij'.

[88] William Jawdrell, master of the Tailors in 1415–16. He died in 1448 and was buried in St. Mary Abchurch. His will makes no mention of his obit which was probably established by his widow, Alice in 1463–4 when it is first recorded in the Tailors' accounts: PRO, PROB 11/1, f. 96; Accounts, II, f. 245v.

The same day the master received from Edmund Warfeld for employing foreigns 3s. 4d.

The same day the master paid to the Five of the Bachelors for their labour 20d.

Item the [Maister] resceyved of Huetsons man for openyng without licence xijd.

This day ther it is condiciend by the Maister and wardeins that where Richard Marchall, apprentice to Richard Borne, is dissmissed of his termes comyng of his apprentizod from the same Richard Born and for more record it is regestryd in this Boke by as moche as the said Richard [Born] promysed the Maister and wardeins to have browgh in the said indenturs of apprentizode and dothe not.

Lune xiij die mensis Novembris in presencia M. et custodum, Tego, Stodard, Gall, Barlow, Materdale, Pemberton, Hede, Adyf, Ffytte, Hardyng.[89]

This day the Maister receyved of Thomas Madisson for ocupieng of a fforen viijd.

This day it [was] condicendid by all the maistres above wrytten that there shall be taken out of the treser for Maister Percyvele shreve xl marke.
And also to be taken out of the tresure for the menstrelles and the new baners and hattes.[90]

This day Humfrey Stephynson the son of Reynold Stephyn of Machefed[91] in the counte of Chesshire, yeman, aprentice to Richard Gryston, citizeyn and Thailour of London, is set over by the chamberleyn unto Thomas Dyker, citezeyn and Tailowre of the same cite, the termes of apprentizode comyng.

---

[89]   John Hardy: see Appendix IV.
[90]   John Percyvale, master of the Tailors' Company for 1485–6, had been chosen as one of the sheriffs of the city on 21 Sept. 1486. These entries almost certainly relate to the company's participation in the procession of the new mayor and sheriffs which took place after the mayoral election on 13 Oct. For Percyvale's career see Appendix IV.
[91]   Almost certainly Macclesfield in Cheshire.

Item in lyke wyse this same day William Fyze jon the son of William Fytz john of Westmynster in Middlesex yeman is set over by the chamberleyn un to Thomas Dyker the termes of his apprentizod comyng.

This day the Maister paid to Robert Walthow and Thomas Robyns for a xv daies passed vs. viijd.

Veneris xviij die mensis Novembris in presencia M. et custodum.

This day the Maister resceyved of John Landysdale for ocupieng of a foren viijd.

This day Richard Page was admitted into the freedom by redemption for £3 of which he will pay at Christmas next 10s., at Easter [15 Apr. 1487] 10s., on the feast of St. John the Baptist [24 June] 10s., on the feast of St. Peter's Chains next [1 Aug.] 10s., and on the feast of the Nativity of St. John the Baptist following [24 June 1488] 20s.

This day Herman Walrafe[92] presented here William Gest, son of Hugh Gest of Crofton (*Croftwot*) in the county of Cumberland and the said William bound himself as an apprentice to the said Herman from the feast of All Saints last [1 Nov.] for seven years.

[f. 9] Cotton.

Lune xx° die mensis Novembris in presencia M. et custodum.

Veneris xxiiij° die mensis Novembris in presencia M. et custodum.

This day William Danyell, son of Robert Danyell late of Ribchester in Lancashire yeoman, bound himself as an apprentice to Robert Graple, citizen and and tailor of London, from the feast of St. Katherine the Virgin next [25 Nov.] for seven years.
And the said Robert Graple promiseth to pay for the maisters parte xs. Paid this same day to the Maister in parti of payment iijs. iiijd., at Ester [15 Apr. 1487] iijs. iiijd., and Witsontyde [3 June] iijs. iiijd.

---

92   Walrafe, a German, along with his wife, Alice, and two servants, was listed as a resident of Dowgate ward in the alien subsidy roll of 1483-4. He was assessed to pay 6s. 8d. while his wife and servants were assessed for 2s. each: Bolton (ed.), *Alien Communities*, p. 56.

Item the Maister resceyved of John Coppyn foren for ocupieng within the fraunches of this citee xd.

This day John Wotton senior, and Robert Stephynsson, tailors and citizens of London, submitted themselves to the arbitration of Hugh Pemberton and John Lee, tailors and citizens of London, an award to be made by the feast of the Epiphany [6 Jan. 1486/7].

Lune xxviij[93] die mensis Novembris in presencia M. et custodum.

<u>Edward Newton admissus operandum shopam in the old change</u>
This day Edward Newton was admitted as a shop-holder and paid in part payment 5s. at Easter 5s.

This day the master paid to Robert Walthew and Thomas Robyns, almsmen of this fraternity, for the past 15 days 5s. 8d.

This day Richard Radclyf, senior, was admitted into the freedom of this fraternity by redemption for £3, of which the master received from the said Richard in part payment 10s., and will pay at Easter next [15 Apr.] 10s., on the feast of the Nativity of St. John the Baptist next [24 June] 10s., at Easter next [6 Apr. 1488] 15s., and at Easter following [19 Apr. 1489] 15s.

This day John Simcokke, son of William Simcokke of the town of Westminster in the county of Middlesex, tailor, bound himself as an apprentice to John Hubanke from the feast of the Nativity of St. John the Baptist last past [24 June] for seven years.
And the said John Hubanke paid the Maister the same day in party of paiment iijs. iiijd. and promiseth to pay the Maister at Ester [15 Apr.] iijs. iiijd., and at Midsomer than nex folowyng [24 June] iijs. iiijd.

This day William Dodde was admitted [to the freedom] by redemption for £3. of which he will pay next Friday 10s., at Easter [15 Apr.] 10s., on the feast of the Nativity of St. John the Baptist [24 June] 10s., at Easter following [6 Apr. 1488] 15s., and at Easter next following [19 Apr. 1489] 15s.

---

[93] An error for 'xxvij'.

Veneris primo die mensis Decembris in presencia M. et custodum.

This day Thomas Hatton, son of John Hatton of Dunley in Worcestershire, yeoman, bound himself as an apprentice to Ralph Traford citizen and tailor of London, from Christmas next for seven years.

Item resceyved of a Bocher[94] for make of new werke xx*d*.
Item resceyved of a foren for werkyng within this ffraunches viij*d*.
Item resceyved of Harry Wodemose of ocupyeng within this fraunches xviij*d*.

This day Thomas Brocton presented here Thomas Cartlage, son of John Cartlage of Dronfield (*Drufeld*) in Derbyshire, yeoman, and the said Thomas bound himself as an apprentice to the said Thomas Brocton from the feast of All Saints last [1 Nov.] for nine years.
 And the same Thomas Brocton paid at the sealing of the denturs for the sam prentice xx*s*.

[f. 9v] Cotton.

Lune iiij die Decembris in presencia M. et custodum.

This day the master paid to Thomas Percy, prior of Holy Trinity Priory[95], London, a quit-rent arising from tenements in the parish of St. Martin Outwich, London, for a whole year to the morrow of St. John the Baptist last [24 June] 7*s*.

This day John Dawson, son of James Dawson of Hull in Yorkshire, bound himself as an apprentice to Randell Newell, citizen and tailor of London, from Christmas next for seven years.
And the said Randell promiseth to pay the Maister accordyng to the ordinaunce xx*s*. that is to sey at the sealyng of the indenturs v*s*., at Witsontyde [3 June] v*s*., and to the Bachelers felashippe x*s*.

---

94 A mender of old clothes. The Tailors were keen to regulate this sector of the industry which, for much of the fifteenth century, was dominated by aliens and other unenfranchised workers whose activities were not at that point seen as threatening the livelihoods of freemen tailors: see Davies, 'Artisans, Guilds and Government', pp. 146-7.
95 Holy Trinity priory (or Christ Church), situated within the city walls near Aldgate, was founded as a house of Augustinian canons by Queen Matilda 1108: Lobel (ed.), *Atlas*, p. 77.

This day John Parker was admitted to the freedom by redemption for £3, of which he paid 5s. in part payment and will pay on the feast of the Purification of Mary the Virgin next [2 Feb.] 5s., at Easter next [15 Apr.] 10s., on the feast of the Nativity of St. John the Baptist following [24 June] 10s,. at Easter following [6 Apr. 1488] 15s., and at Easter next following [19 Apr. 1489] 15s.

And for the suerte of the same paiments the said Johanni Parcar and John Mortyn tailowr promiseth to be bound in an obligacion.

This day John Stafford Boccher[96] made a fyne for oc ...
This day the Maister payd to the almesmen Thomas Robyns and Robert Walthowe vs. viijd.

Lune undecimo die mensis Decembris in presencia M. et custodum.

This day the master paid to Robert Walthew and Thomas Robyns, almsmen of this fraternity, for the past 15 days 5s. 8d.
This day John Mendall was admitted as a shop-holder and paid to the master in part-payment 5s., and is to pay on the feast of the Purification of the Blessed Virgin Mary next [2 Feb.] 5s.
This day John Scotton was admitted to the freedom by redemption for five marks, to be paid at Easter next [15 Apr.]

The obyte of Thomas Carlton[97] holden in Seint Johannis chapell in Powles the xij day of Decembre accordyng to the compocision xs.

Veneris xv die mensis Decembris in presencia M. et custodum.

This day the Maister resceyved of John Bell for ocupyeng of a foren viijd.
Item resceyved by the Maister of Edmond Warvyle for ocupyeng of a foren xijd.

---

96 See Glossary.
97 Thomas Carleton (d. 1389) was a wealthy embroiderer and alderman, and one of the earliest benefactors of the Tailors' fraternity. He left property in the parish of St. Alban Wood Street to the Master and wardens for the maintenance of an obit and a perpetual chantry in the chapel which the Tailors' fraternity had maintained in St. Paul's from at least the 1370s: CWCH, vol. 2, pp. 272–3; Davies, thesis, p. 57. See also H. Kleineke, 'Carleton's Book: William Fitzstephen's Description of London in a Late 14th-Century Common-place Book', Historical Research (forthcoming).

Item resceyved by the Maister of William Duncan for ocupyeng of a foren xij*d*.

This day the Maister paid to the chamberleyn of Westmynster for a quiterent goyng oute of a tenement in the parissh of Seint Mathei in Fryday strete for halfe a yere at Mighelmas last passed x*s*.

This day the Maister paid to the same chamberleyn for a quiterent goyng oute of a tenement in the parissh of oure Lady Colchirch for halfe a yere at Mighelmas last passed iij*s*. vj*d*.

Lune xviij die mensis Decembris in presencia M. et custodum Stodard, West, Barlow, Duplage, Pemberton, Lee, Bukke, Hoberd, Spencer, Hardyng, Ffytte, Jenyns.

This [day] it is condicendid and a greed by the Maisters above written and thoos persones of the xxiiij^ti in lyke wyse that no man of this worshipfull felashippe shall not go to no markettes nor feiers in to the contre with waris the forto sell.[98]

This day it is a greed by all the worshipfull personys above written that William Gray, browderer, shall have termys in the howse the wich he dwellyth in for the terme of x yerys begynnyng at Crystmas next comyng.

This day John Burgh presented here George Cartlage, son of John Cartlage of Willingham.[99]
This day John Burgh presented here George Sparke, son of Richard Sparke late of Newcastle, yeoman, who bound himself as an apprentice to the said John from the feast of All Saints last [1 Nov.] for seven years.
And the said John Bourgh paid to the Maister in parti of paiment x*s*

[f. 10][100]

[1487]

---

[98] For the controversy surrounding fairs and the rights of citizens to attend them, see above, pp. 39–40.
[99] Perhaps Derbyshire – see earlier entry for 1 Dec.
[100] There is a gap in the original foliation (ff. 235–44v), corresponding to missing entries for the 11 months from 18 December 1486 to 12 November 1487. These pages, like the first 227 folios of the volume, were probably lost in the early 17th century, before the surviving folios were bound together and renumbered. The text resumes in a different hand, that of William Duryvale who held the post of clerk from June 1487 (see below n. 118) and is now written almost entirely in Latin.

Lune xij° die Novembris[101] in presencia Magistri et custodum.

This day the master paid to Robert Walthew and Thomas Robyns, almsmen of this fraternity, for the quindene before the 7th day of January 5s. 8d.

Item the master granted Richard Sharp licence to open his shop. And the said Richard paid in part payment of his fine 5s. and has until the feast of Pentecost [25 May] to pay the residue of 5s.

Item Richard Quykrell, citizen and tailor of London, presented Matthew Long, son of John Long, citizen and brewer of London, and desired that the said Matthew should be admitted as an apprentice. The said Matthew then bound himself as an apprentice to the said Richard, to remain with him from the feast of St. Michael the Archangel, 3 Hen. VII [29 Sept. 1487] for seven years, and paid according to the ordinance 3s. 4d.

Item Thomas Bodley, citizen and tailor of London, presented John Harryson, son of William Harryson, deceased, late of Alnwick in Northumberland, shearman, and it was agreed that the said John should be admitted as an apprentice of the said Thomas, to remain with him from Christmas next for fourteen years. And since he has a large number of apprentices he paid 40d.

Veneris xvj° die Novembris in presencia Magistri et custodum.

This day Thomas Brounfeld and Thomas Petyt, citizens and tailors of London, on the one part, and Richard Geffrey, citizen and tailor, on the other part, submitted themselves to the arbitration of Thomas Randyll and ... Redeknap.

John Harryson citizen and tailor of London paid a fine for not enrolling his apprentice etc. 20d.

William Boyland made a fine for offending against the ordinances 4d.

Richard Sharp and John Swetyngham have submitted themselves, upon a penalty of 40s., to the arbitration of Thomas Skylman and William Norton, an award to be made by the feast of the Epiphany next [6 Jan.]

---

[101] 12 November 1487.

This day Thomas Bankes, citizen and tailor of London, presented Christopher Baldewyn, [son of] Richard Baldewyn of Lacton[102] in Yorkshire, weaver. And it was agreed that he should be admitted into apprenticeship, and the said Christopher bound himelf as an apprentice to the said Thomas Bankes from the feast of St. Michael the Archangel 3 Hen. VII [29 Sept. 1487] for eight years and paid 40d.

[f. 10v]

Lune xix° die Novembris in presencia Magistri et custodum.

This day John Bell and Robert Walthowe have submitted themselves, on a bond of 40s. each, to the arbitration of Richard Joskyn and Roger Mone, an award to be made between them before Christmas next.

Lune xxvj^to die Novembris in presencia Magistri et custodum.

This day the master paid to the master of the Hospital of St. Katherine by the Tower of London for a quitrent arising from tenements in the parish of St. Mary Abchurch, London, for the year ending on the feast of St. Michael the Archangel last [29 Sept.] 10s.

This day the master paid to Thomas Robyns and Robert Walthew, almsmen of this fraternity, for the last quindene 5s. 8d.

Item the master paid to Robert Savage for a barge to Greenwich to meet the Queen on the occasion of her coronation 20s.[103]
Item the master paid for boatmen and minstrels for the same boat and for a potation held among divers masters the same day and for accompanying the boat 3s. 10d.

---

[102] Probably Laxton in the E. Riding.

[103] The actual coronation took place on St. Katherine's day, Sunday 25 Nov. 1487. This entry refers to the river journey undertaken by Elizabeth of York from Greenwich to the Tower on the Friday before. Her barge was attended by barges of the mayor and aldermen of London as well as those of the guilds, adorned with their respective arms and devices. The following day saw a procession from the Tower through the streets of London to Westminster: Anglo, *Spectacle*, p. 49. For a description of these events see John Leland, *De Rebus Britannicis Collectanea*, ed. T. Hearne, 6 vols (London, 1770), vol. 4, pp. 216–33. On 7 November the Common Council had agreed a gift of 1,000 marks to the Queen: CLRO, Journals, 9, f. 161.

Memorandum that William Boston is indebted to Roger Maynell, tailor, executor of the will of John Comber[104] for the sum of 42s. 2d. by his signed bill etc. This day it is ruled by the master and wardens that the said William should pay to the said Roger 26s. 8d. of the aforesaid sum and that the residue should be remitted and that the said 26s. 8d. should be paid 40d. quarterly, the first term of payment to be at Christmas next.

This day William Bekeham, citizen and tailor of London, presented John del Stable, son of Roger del Stable, deceased, late of London, waterman. And it was agreed that he should be admitted as an apprentice etc. And the said John bound himself as an apprentice to the said William Bekeham from the feast of St. Michael the Archangel 3 Hen. VII [29 Sept. 1487] for nine years and paid acording to the new ordinance 40d.

Item the master received from Hamo Wichecot, who was the apprentice of Roger Doget[105] and who served a term of five years, for his admission into the freedom 26s. 8d.

Item paid for 12 quarters of coals for the almsmen in the parish of St. Martin Outwich, from the bequest of Hugh Cavendish 4s. 6d.

[f. 11]

Lune iiij[106] die Decembris in presencia Magistri et custodum.

This day Walter Webbe, citizen and tailor of London, presented Edward Gough, son of David Gough, deceased, late of Queenhope in Wales, tailor, and it was agreed that he should enter into an apprenticeship etc. and he was admitted for the term of seven years from the feast of St. Michael the Archangel 3 Hen. VII [29 Sept. 1487] and paid according to the new ordinance ...

---

104 Comber obtained the freedom by redemption 1466-7 and was admitted to the livery of the Tailors the same year. His will has not been located. Accounts, II, ff. 292v, 296v.

105 This is almost certainly a clerical error for John Doket (or Doget), who was a member of the Tailors' court and served as warden in 1488-9 and 1492-3 and was chosen as master of the company in 1500. His kinsman Roger was one of the chantry chaplains employed by the company. Hopkinson, *Ancient Records*, pp. 114-5.

106 An error for 'iij'.

This day William Hille and Thomas Chamberleyn submitted themselves, on a bond of 40s. each, to the rule of Alan Hoberd and Roger Doket[107], arbiters etc. an award to be made before the Epiphany of Our Lord [6 Jan.]

This day Richard Penne, citizen and tailor of London, presented Richard Penne, son of John Penne deceased, late of Penn in Buckinghamshire, gentleman,[108] and it was agreed that he should be admitted as an apprentice from Easter next [6 Apr.] for seven years and paid according to the ordinance ...

This day William Brownyng and Richard Thomasson, tailors, submitted themselves, on a bond of twenty marks each, to the arbitration of David Jenkyns and Richard Acres, tailors and arbiters etc. an award to be made between them before the feast of the Epiphany [6 Jan.]

Item the master paid to the warden of the house of St. Giles in the Fields[109] for a quit-rent arising from tenements in Candlewick Street for half a year to the feast of St. Michael last [29 Sept.] 13s.
Item paid to the same warden for a quit-rent arising from tenements in Garlickhithe for the year ending at the [said] feast 23s.

William a Bristowe, son of Thomas a Bristowe of Wirrall in Cheshire, shearman, was apprenticed to Robert Wylkynson from the feast of St. Bartholomew next [24 Aug.] for ten years.

[f. 11v]

Veneris vij° die Decembris in presencia Magistri et custodum.

This day the master paid for 14 quarters of coals to be distributed in alms among the poor of the parish of St. Mary Abchurch according to the last will of Elene Langwith 5s. 5d.[110]

Once again an error for John Doket, see above n. 105.
[108] The identity of the father is unclear, although he was perhaps the merchant of the staple who, in June 1478, acquired the title to lands and tenements in Calais from his brother, Philip, *CCR 1476–85*, p. 115. Part of the manor of Penn in Bucks. had been in the hands of the family since 1222: VCH, *Buckinghamshire*, III (1925), p. 237.
[109] See above n. 21.
[110] For John and Elene Langwith see above n. 63.

This day John Taillour, citizen and tailor of London, presented John Bury, son of Oliver Bury of the town of Derby, carpenter, and it was agreed that he should be admitted as an apprentice etc. and the said John bound himself as an apprentice of the said John Taillour from the feast of All Saints 3 Hen. VII [1 Nov. 1487] for nine years and paid 3s. 4d.

Lune xj° die Decembris in presencia Magistri et custodum.

This day the master received from the executors of the testament of William Felde,[111] brewer, from the bequest of the said William 3s. 4d.

Item the master paid to Robert Walthewe and Thomas Robyns, almsmen of this fraternity, for the past quindene 5s. 8d.

Item the master paid to the treasury of St. Peter's Westminster for a quit-rent arising from tenements in Abchurch formerly of Elene Langwith and from a tenement in Fridaystreet 13s. 6d.

Item the master paid for the obit of John[112] Carleton, held in St. John's chapel in St. Paul's 10s.

Veneris ...[113]

This day the master paid to the dean of the cathedral church of St. Paul, London, for a quit-rent arising from tenements in [the parish of Holy] Trinity the Less for the year ending at the feast of St. Michael next [29 Sept.] 5s.

[f. 12]

Lune xxiiij° die Decembris.

Item the master paid to Robert Walthewe and Thomas Robyns, almsmen of this fraternity, for the past quindene 5s. 8d.
Item paid to William Haccomplayn, almsman, for the quarter ending at Christmas 5s.

---

[111] Felde's will, containing this bequest, was proved on 5 Nov. 1487: PRO, PROB 11/8, ff. 37–37v.
[112] An error for 'Thomas'.
[113] Either 14 or 21 Dec.

Item paid to Christopher Kyrke, almsman, for the quarter ending at Christmas 10s.
Item paid to Thomas Hosyer, almsman, for the quarter ending at Christmas 10s.[114]

Item the master paid to the prioress of Clerkenwell[115] for a quit-rent arising from tenments in Colechurch for the year ending at the feast of St. Michael the Archangel 13s. 4d.

Item paid to Thomas Grysyle, beadle of this fraternity, for his wages for the quarter ending at Christmas 13s. 4d.
Item for the wages of the wardens of the craft for the same time 5s

Termino Natalis Domini anno regni regis Henrici vij tercio[116]

Veneris xj° die Decembris[117] in presencia M. et custodum.

This day Richard Trewe and John Harryson submitted themselves, on a bond of 40s. each, to the rule of William Alye and William Batyson, tailors and arbiters etc. to arbitrate upon all matters etc. before the day of the Purification of the Blessed Virgin Mary next [2 Feb.]

This day the master received into this fraternity by redemption Richard Bayle, tailor, and the said Richard promised to pay to the master 53s. 4d. of which he paid in person 26s. 8d., and the residue of 26s. 8d. is to be paid by the feast of the Holy Trinity next [1 June].
And finally the said Richard is licensed to open a shop etc. And the said Richard agreed to pay according to the custom at the aforsaid feast etc. At which day he paid 13s. 14d. and owes 13s. 4d. to be paid within a quindene after the Nativity of St. John [24 June].

Item the master paid to William Duryvall, clerk of this fraternity, for his wages for half a quarter ending at the feast of St. Michael the

---

114 Haccomplayn, Kyrke and Hosyer were paid their alms quarterly whereas Walthewe and Robyns received theirs every fortnight.
115 The priory of St. Mary Clerkenwell, a house of Augustinian canonesses founded c.1145. VCH, *Middlesex*, I (1969), pp. 170–3. For the administration of the rents and properties of the priory see Paxton, 'Nunneries of London', pp. 226–63.
116 Christmas term 3 Hen. VII (1487–8). The company's year was divided into four terms, each commencing on one of the four quarter-days of Christmas, the Annunciation (25 Mar.), the Nativity of St. John the Baptist (24 June, the company's annual feast day) and Michaelmas (29 Sept.).
117 An error for 'Januarii'.

Archangel last [29 Sept.] 12s., and for the quarter ending at Christmas the said year 25s. Total 37s.[118]

[f. 12v]

Item the master paid to Geoffrey atte Welle, almsman, for the term ending at Christmas last 6s. 8d.

Item the master paid to Robert Walthewe and Thomas Robyns, almsmen, for the quindene ending on the 7th day of January 5s. 8d.

Item the master paid to Sir[119] Robert Urton,[120] chaplain celebrating in St. Martin Outwich, for the quarter ending at Christmas 16s. 8d.

Item the master paid to Roger Doget[121] chaplain, for his salary for the quarter ending at Christmas 33s. 4d.

Item the master paid to Richard [Wheler][122] chaplain, for his salary for the quarter ending at Christmas 33s. 4d.

Item paid to Sir[123] John Radclyf for his salary 30s. 4d.

Item paid to Sir William Camell,[124] chaplain, for his salary for the quarter etc. 40s.

---

[118] Duryvale's tenure of the clerkship therefore began in about June 1487, although none of the minutes for which he was responsible survive until 12 November.

[119] See Glossary.

[120] Chaplain of the chantry of John and William de Oteswich: see Appendix III.

[121] Little is known of the background or education of Doket (or Doget), who was appointed in 1442–3 as one of the three stipendiary chaplains employed by the fraternity of St. John the Baptist. He continued to serve in this capacity for almost fifty years at a salary of £6 13s. 4d. and was active elsewhere in London as a feoffee. He died at some point between 22 March 1491, when his last quarterly wages are recorded in the minutes, and 13 June when his name was absent from the list of chaplains to be paid. In his will, proved on 12 July, he asked for burial in the chapel dedicated to St. John the Baptist in St. Paul's (where the Tailors' employed a chaplain) and left a bequest of 20d. to the altar of St. Martin Outwich 'next the Taylours hall'. He left the Tailors' fraternity a mazer with a cover, the yeomen tailors 10s. and further bequests to the master, wardens, clerk and beadle if they attended his funeral. One of his executors was Richard Wheler, one of his fellow chaplains, who was left a 'portewys' ('porteous' or portable breviary, OED). Accounts, I, f. 360; CLRO, HR 193/42, 200/8–9; GL, MS 9171/8, f. 22v.

[122] Wheler was appointed as one of the fraternity's three stipendiary chaplains in 1468–9. Although little is known of his education it is probable that he was from Preston in Herefordshire where he established an obit. He was an executor of the will of his fellow chaplain, Roger Doket (q.v.) in 1491 and continued to be employed until his death in 1495. In his will, proved on 12 April, he asked for burial in the church of St. Martin Outwich, close to Tailors' Hall. Accounts, II, f. 331v; GL, MS 9171/8, f. 124.

[123] See Glossary.

Item paid to John Palmer,[125] chaplain for his wages for the quarter ending at Christmas 30s. 4d.

Item this day William Avenell presented William Middleton, son of Henry Middleton, as his apprentice etc. and the said William Middleton bound himself as an apprentice to the said William Avenell from the feast of Christmas 3 Hen. VII [1487] for ten years and paid 40d.

Item the master received from Edmund Gerard for his redemption for Christmas 6s. 8d.

Item paid to Robert Boylet,[126] almsman 10s.

Item the master has licensed William Asshby, tailor, to open a shop etc. And he must pay before the feast of Easter next [6 Apr.] 10s. And afterwards he paid 5s. and so owes ...

[f. 13]

Lune xiiij° die Januarii in presencia Magistri et custodum.

This day Vincent Depres, son of Nicholas Despres of the town of Southampton, tawyer,[127] bound himself as an apprentice to William Stalworth, citizen and tailor of London, from the feast of the Purification of the Blessed Virgin Mary [2 Feb.] next for seven years, who paid nothing for him because ... late apprentice of the said William has withdrawn within a year and a day.

---

[124] Camell was chaplain of the chantry established Lady Beatrice de Roos (d. 1414). He appears to have replaced Henry Cheshire whose appointment was noted on 21 July 1486: see above p. 66.

[125] Appointed in Easter term 1480 as chaplain of the chantry of Peter Mason (d. 1412) in St. Peter Cornhill. Mason, a tailor, left the Tailors property in the parish of St. Mary Colechurch, near the Great Conduit: Davies, thesis, p. 60; GL, MS 9051/1, ff. 274–6; Accounts, I, f. 69; III, f. 128v.

[126] Probably the RB who was an officer of the Great Wardrobe from at least 1462–5 until the late 1480s. Several other Boylets were almsmen of the Tailors in this period, including John Boylet, another employee of the Great Wardrobe. For these men see *Coro. Richard III* ed. Hammond and Sutton, p. 316. A William Boylet was master of the Tailors' Company in 1458–9: Hopkinson, *Ancient Records*, p. 112.

[127] Nicholas Depres was fined the sum of 20d. by the authorities in his native town in August 1486 'for mysgovernaunce of his wiff of her body and for bawdrye', *The Book of Remembrance of Southampton, III: AD 1483- AD 1563*, ed. H. W. Gidden (Southampton Rec. Soc., 1930), p. 41.

This day William Hewelet and Thomas Cope submitted themselves, on a bond of ten marks each, to the rule of Richard Norton and John Stoyle, arbiters, an award to be made before Shrove Tuesday [18 Feb.]

Veneris xviij° die Januarii in presencia [Magistri et] custodum.

This day in the presence of the aforesaid, William Hamond, son of Richard Hamond of Byrsam[128] in Oxfordshire, yeoman, bound himself as an apprentice to John Bowman, citizen and tailor of London, from the feast of Christmas next for nine years, and in the presence of the aforesaid paid 40*d.*

Lune xxj° die Januarii in presencia Magistri et custodum.

Item the master paid to Robert Walthewe and Thomas Robyns, almsmen of this fraternity for the past quindene 5*s.* 8*d.*

This day Nicholas Bushbury, tailor, agreed to pay 20*s.* to William Gybson, tailor, that is to say at the feast of the Purification of the Blessed Virgin Mary next [2 Feb.] 6*s.* 8*d.* and the middle Sunday in Lent following [9 Mar.] 6*s.* 8*d.* and on the feast of Pentecost [25 May] 6*s.* 8*d.*, on a bond of 26*s.* 8*d.*

The obit of John Churchman[129] held on the 24th day of January. For bread, ale and cheese 2*s.*, to the rector of the church 6*d.*, to five other priests 20*d.*, to the parish clerk 8*d.*, for offerings 2*d.*, for candles 12*d.* [Total] 6*s.*

---

128   Probably Burford.

129   Churchman was a prominent member of the Grocers' Company in the late 14th century, serving as warden for 1383–4. An alderman 1381, and 1383–91 and mayor of the Calais staple 1389. In 1382 he rebuilt the customs house in London after purchasing the wool wharf in the parish of All Hallows Barking. Closely associated with the Tailors from the 1380s onwards, in 1405 he conveyed 4 messuages and 17 shops in the parish of St. Martin Outwich, as well as the advowson of the church itself, to the Tailors' fraternity of St. John the Baptist. He died in 1412 and in January 1412/13 the Tailors celebrated his obit for the first time. Churchman's perpetual chantry was also administered by the fraternity from that year onwards. The lands given by Churchman in 1405 included a plot next to the Hall on which the Tailors started to construct an almshouse soon after their benefactor's death. Nightingale, *Grocers*, pp. 238, 280, 293, 296–8, 315; Davies, thesis, pp. 55–6; idem, 'Charity', pp. 182–3.

[f. 13v]

Lune xxviij° die Januarii in presencia Magistri et custodum ac Stodard, Tego, West, Deplache, Galle.

This day William Grene and Thomas Stratton submitted themselves, on a bond of £10 each, to the arbitration of William Galle and Robert Duplech, arbiters concerning all matters etc. to make an award by the middle Sunday in Lent [9 Mar.]

This day John Bemond, son of Robert Bemond of Ambury[130] in Yorkshire, husbandman, bound himself as an apprentice to John Cok, citizen and tailor of London, from the feast of the Purification of the Blessed Virgin Mary [2 Feb.] next for eight years, and paid 3s. 4d.

Veneris primo die Februarii in presencia Magistri et custodum ac Tego, Stodard, Barlowe, Pemberton, Deplech, Jenyns et Randyll[131]

Isto die John Bernes dyer Thomas Taillour et John Dorkynghole testificaverunt quod Ricardus West non vocitavit Radulfum Bukberd modo et forma prout allegatum fuit etc. Sed solomodo quod idem Ricardus dixit eidem Radulfo hec verba sequencia etc. videlicet Goo oute of my hous Benche whistler.

[translation] This day John Bernes, dyer, Thomas Taillour and John Dorkinghole testified that Richard West did not call out to Ralph Bukberd in the manner and form that was alleged, but only that the said Richard said to the same Ralph these words following, namely 'Goo oute of my hous Benche whistler'.[132]

Lune iiij^to die Februarii in presencia Magistri et custodum.

This day the master received from John Combes for a fine for not enrolling his apprentice etc. 20d.
Item the master paid to Robert Walthewe and Thomas Robyns, almsmen of this fraternity, for the past quindene 5s. 8d.

---

130 Perhaps Almondbury, or Ambry Well in the W. Riding.
131 For West and Bukberd see Appendix IV.
132 'Bench-whistler': a term of reproach implying great idleness. The earliest usage of this term given by the OED is 1542.

This day William Kesteven, son of John Kesteven of Tickhill in Yorkshire, husbandman, bound himself as an apprentice to Thomas Bromefeld, citizen and tailor of London from the feast of the Purification 3 Hen. VII [2 Feb. 1487/8] for seven years and paid 3s. 4d.

This day Thomas Ethell was licensed to open shop etc. and paid 10s.
This day Richard Trewe was licensed to open shop etc. and paid 10s.

This day John Harryson and Richard Trewe submitted themselves, on a bond of 40s. each to the arbitration of William Batyson and William Alye, an award to be made by the feast of the Annunciation next [25 Mar.]

Isto die Johannes Sparman et Johannes Barowes arbitraverunt Johannem Combes solvere gardianis de lez yomen felasship xls. videlicet pro duobus apprenticiis suis xxs. et pro uno apprenticio Bygges xs. et pro uno apprenticio de Doves xs.
  [translation] This day John Sperman and John Barowes arbitrate that John Combes is to pay 40s. to the wardens of the yeomen fellowship, that is to say for two of his apprentices 20s., for one apprentice of Bygges 10s., and for one apprentice of Doves 10s.

[f. 14]

Jovis vij die Februarii in presencia Magistri et xxiiij magis fidedignorum videlicet Tego, Stodard, West, B ..., Deplage, Pemberton, Galle, Lee, Jenyns, Spencer, Povey, Randyll, Adyff, Ffittz, Bromefeld,[133] Howden,[134] Grene.[135]

Memorandum that John Watertoft which was chief cook with M. Horn[136] meyre, at the makyng of his feest the morne after the day of Symond and Jude [29 October 1487] in this place of Taylours halle[137] holden and kept ayenst all equytie and ryght brake and bare a wey a peyre of Rostyng Rakkes belongyng to this place, that tyme beyng in the kechen, and at such season as he was

---

[133] Thomas Bromeflete: see Appendix IV.
[134] Thomas Howdan: see Appendix IV.
[135] William Grene: see Appendix IV.
[136] William Horn, citizen and salter, was mayor for 1487-8: Beaven, *Aldermen*, II, p. 16.
[137] Sir John Shaa (mayor in 1501-2) was the first to hold his feast at Guildhall. Prior to his mayoralty this event was held elsewhere, including both the Tailors' and Grocers' halls: Caroline M. Barron, *The Medieval Guildhall of London* (London, 1974), p. 32; Stow, *Survey*, I, p. 273.

demaunded therof he gave croked and ungodley answere and langage affyrmyng his said symple dede and never would recompens the same. Therfor it is ordeyned that the said John Watertoft from hensforth in no wise shall not occupye with noo persone in this place beyng at noo feests nor dyners here to be made withoute a speciall licence be had upon payne that every master for the tyme beyng soo licensyng hym to pay at eche defaute xls. to the almes of this crafte.

Veneris viij° die Februarii coram Magistro et gardianis.

This day George Bolton presented John Asshpull his apprentice etc. from the feast of Easter next for nine years and paid 40*d.*

Isto die Willelmus Batyson concessit terminos Willelmi Smyth apprenticii sui Ricardo Gryffeth ab isto die usque ad finem trium annorum etc pro xxiijs. iiij*d.* per annum solvendis quarteriatim unde soluit in manibus pro primo anno xxiijs. iiij*d.*
[translation] This day William Batyson granted the terms of his apprentice, William Smyth, to Richard Griffith from this day until the end of three years etc. for 23*s.* 4*d.* a year, to be paid quarterly, of which he paid in hand for the first year 23*s.* 4*d.*

Item Robert Benet presented Thomas Vyncent as his apprentice from the feast of the Annunciation next [25 Mar.] for seven years and paid according to the new custom 40*d.*

[f. 14v]

Lune xj° die Februarii in presencia Magistri et custodum.

This day Richard Bernard, son of the late Edward Bernard, deceased, late of Uxbridge in Middlesex, yeoman,[138] bound himself as an apprentice to Thomas Sharparow, citizen and tailor of London, from the feast of the Purification 3 Hen. VII [2 Feb. 1487/8] for nine years and paid 40*d.*

This day Sir[139] Richard Jakes[140] began to celebrate in St. Martin's church and was admitted by the master and wardens etc.

---

138 For Bernard, a Middlesex lawyer, see *CCR 1476-85*, p. 294.
139 See Glossary.
140 One of the chantry chaplains in St. Martin Outwich. Not otherwise identified.

This day John a Cote, son of John a Cote, bound himself as an apprentice to John Dyconson from the feast of All Saints 3 Hen. VII [1 Nov. 1487] until the end of seven years and paid according to the new[141] custom 40d.

This day William Blyman, son of W[illiam?] Blyman of Bishop Aukland in the episcopate of Durham, bound himself as an apprentice to Robert Byllyngham from the feast of St. Matthew next for eight years, and paid according to the custom ...

William Peyrson, son of Matthew Peyrson deceased, late of Kirkby Kendall in Westmoreland, bound himself as an apprentice to Peter Halle, citizen and tailor of London, from the feast of the Purification of the Blessed Virgin Mary 3 Hen. VII [2 Feb. 1487/8] for seven years and paid according to the custom ...

James Thomson, son of the late John Thomson, deceased, late of Catterick Bridge in Yorkshire, tailor, bound himself as an apprentice to John Abbot,[142] citizen and tailor, from the feast of the Annunciation of the Blessed Virgin Mary next [2 Feb.] for nine years and paid according to the custom ...

John Bayncroft bound himself as an apprentice to John Stokwell from the feast of St. ... until the end of ...

Item received from Robert Benet for a fine for foreigns 6s. 8d.
Item from John Dyconson for not enrolling his apprentice 20d.
Item the master paid for coals according to the last will ... almsmen etc. that is to say for 12 quarters 5s.
Item for coals in the parish of St. Mary Abchurch according to the last will of [John] Creke[143] 5s. 5d.

---

[141] *'antiquam'* in the text has been altered to *'novam'*. This refers to the reduction of the enrolment fee for an apprentice from 10s. to 3s. 4d. for which see Introduction, pp. 31–2.

[142] Perhaps the John Abbot who worked for 2¾ days in the Great Wardrobe for the coronation of Richard III in 1483: *Coro. Richard III* ed. Sutton and Hammond, p. 303.

[143] See below n. 148.

[f. 15]

Quarter-day (*dies quarterii*)

Mercurii xiij°[144] die Februarii in presencia Magistri et custodum ac Percyvale, Tego, Stodard, West, Barlowe, Galle, Lee, Deplech, Pemberton, Materdale.

This day the last wills of John Churchman and Hugh Champernon were read.[145]

Veneris quintodecimo die Februarii in presencia Magistri et custodum.

This day William Popes and Thomas Ethell submitted themselves, on a bond of £20 each, to the arbitration of John Borowes and Richard Joskyn tailors. An award to be made by Palm Sunday next [30 Mar.]

This day Richard Cornhill presented William Dorkyng his apprentice etc. from the feast of Christmas 3 Hen. VII [1487] for eight years and paid 40*d*.

Item William Cok presented Richard Wolsale his apprentice from the feast of the Purification of the Blessed Virgin Mary 3 Hen. VII [2 Feb. 1487/8] for seven years.

[f. 15v]

Veneris xxij° die Februarii in presencia Magistri et custodum.

This day Robert Johnson presented Thomas a Borowe his apprentice etc. from the feast of Christmas 3 Hen. VII [1487] for eight years and paid 40*d*.

John Batyson presented John Worth, son of the late William Worth, late of Macclesfield in Cheshire, as his apprentice from the feast of the Annunciation of the Blessed Virgin Mary next [25 Mar.] for seven years and paid 40*d*.

This day the master paid to Robert Walthewe and Thomas Robyns, almsmen of this fraternity, for the quindene before the 18th day of February 5*s*. 8*d*.

---

[144] An error for 'xij'.
[145] See above nn. 40, 129.

Veneris xxvij°[146] die Februarii in presencia Magistri et custodum.

This day William a Lye and John Doket, arbiters between Richard Bothom and Thomas Wytney, make their award in this manner, that is to say that each is to make an acquittance to the other. And in consideration that the said Richard gravely insulted and rudely gestured[147] to the aforesaid Thomas it is declared that the said Thomas should be quit of his service etc. And that the said Richard should acknowledge the faithful service of the said Thomas to his master before the [city] chamber. And that the said Richard Bothom should return the gown, hose and shirt which the same Thomas left in the house of the said Richard.

This day William Gerves and John Lucas submitted themselves, on a bond of 40s. each, to the arbitration of John Povey and Robert Kelham etc. an award to be made before Palm Sunday next [30 Mar.]

The obit of John Creke[148] held in the parish of St. Mary Abchurch the first Sunday of Lent [23 Feb.], that is to say for bread and wine 2s. 8d., for figs and raisins 6d. ob., for candles 12d., for priests and clerks 2s., and for offerings 2d.
[Total] 6s. 8d.

[f. 16]

Lune iij° die Marcii in presencia Magistri et custodum.

This day the master received from John Bodyam for Edmund Poley his apprentice ...
Item the master paid to the almsmen of this fraternity for the past quindene 5s. 8d.

---

146 An error for 'xxix'.
147 Text reads *'graviter lesit et male' prebuit in digito'*.
148 John Creek (d. 1413) was almost certainly a former master of the Tailors. The celebration of the obit of Creek and his wife, Joan (d. 1414) was administered at first by William Turnell, his executor, who then entrusted the task to his widow, Cecily. On the latter's death in 1441 the tenement in Tower Street used to fund the obit was conveyed to the Tailors and in that year the accounts of the fraternity recorded the payment of 2s. 6d. for the obit and a further payment for 13 quarters of coals to be distributed to 13 poor men. See Davies, thesis, pp. 58–9; *CWCH*, vol.2, p. 417; GL, MS 9051/1, ff. 308v–309v, 324–325; Accounts, I, f. 350.

Item cum diverse contraversie sunt pendentes inter Willelmum Gerveys et certos alios de les commons nuper tent' etc. consideratum fuit per magistrum [et] gardianos quod Johannes Povey et Robertus Kelham audirent omnimodis variaciones etc. inter predictum Willelmum habiteo ex una parte ac predictos alios ex altera parte etc.

[translation] Item that divers controversies are pending between William Gerveys and certain others of the Commons[149] lately held etc. It was considered by the master [and] wardens that John Povey and Robert Kelham should hear all variances etc. between the said William on the one part, and the said others on the other part etc.

This day Robert Greves and Ralph Traford submitted themeslves, on a bond of £20 each, to the arbitration of Richard Adyff and Owen Boughton, an award to be made by Palm Sunday [30 Mar.]

This day Robert Barber and Robert Johnston submitted themselves, on a bond of 40s. each, to the arbitration of John Combes [and] Richard Semer,[150] an award to be made by Palm Sunday next [30 Mar.]

William Norton and Thomas Kynmond arbiters between ... Swetyngham and Richard Sharp rule that the said ... Swetyngham should pay 20s. that is to say 5s. today, 5s. at Easter [6 Apr.], 5s. at Pentecost [25 May], 5s. on the Sunday before the feast of the Nativity of St. John [22 June], on a bond of 40s. payable to the use of the alms and the chamber of the Guildhall.

[f. 16v]

Veneris vij die Marcii in presencia Magistri et custodum ac Percyvale, Stodard, Tego, Keys, Pemberton, Deplage, Galle, Jenyns, Adyf, Hardy.

Isto die ordinatum est quod Reginaldus Walker apprenticius Cristoferi Laurens serviret terminos apprenticiatis sue cum Roberto Lokkey pro eo quod idem Cristoferus recessit extra civitatem etc.

---

149 Probably referring to M.P.s who attended the Parliament held at Westminster from 9 Nov. to 18 Dec. 1487, during which the city's ban (1486) on citizens attending provincial fairs, was overturned. It may be significant that Hugh Pemberton, master of the tailors in 1482–3, was one of London's four representatives at this assembly: see Introduction, pp. 39–40 and Appendix IV for Pemberton's career.

150 Semer, a resident of Portsoken ward, was listed in the alien subsidy roll for 1483–3 as an employer of Gillam Taillour, whose nationality was not recorded: Bolton (ed.), *Alien Communities*, p. 84.

[translation] This day it is ordained that Reginald Walker, apprentice of Christopher Laurens, should serve out his apprenticeship with Robert Lokkey, because the said Christopher has left the City etc.

Item the master received from the said Robert Lokkey as a fine for not enrolling etc. 20*d*.
Item John Harryson paid for his disobedience to the master of this fraternity 26*s*. 7*d*.
Item the same John acknowledged that he owes to the master and wardens of this fraternity £10, since the same John shamefully insulted John Hede, the master.

Lune ix°¹⁵¹ die Marcii in presencia Magistri et custodum.

This day Richard Quykrell presented Richard Halle as his apprentice from the feast of Christmas last for eight years, and paid today 40*d*.

Item the master licensed John a Chambre to practise his craft etc. and is to pay 10*s*. at Holy Trinity [1 June].

Item the master receieved from John Spencer for John Brokholles his apprentice 40*d*.

Veneris xiiij die Marcii.

This day Thomas Porter and William Howlet submitted theselves, on a bond of £10 each, to the arbitration of Thomas Howe and William Morton, an award to be made before Maunday Thursday (*diem Jovis in cena Domini*) [3 Apr.]

[f. 17]

Lune xvij° die Marcii in presencia Magistri et custodum.

Item the master paid to the almsmen of this fraternity for the past quindene 5*s*. 8*d*.
Item the master licensed William Fayrford to occupy [his craft] etc. and paid this day 10*s*.

---

¹⁵¹ An error for 'x'.

Item the master received from William Shotteswold for not enrolling an apprentice 16*d*.

Veneris xxj° die Marcii in presencia Magistri et custodum.

This day received of Richard Lytell for the rent of his tenement for the past year 6*s*. 8*d*.

Lune xxiiij° die Marcii in presencia Magistri et custodum.

The obit of Richard Benton held in the church of Holy Trinity the Less. For bread 18*d*., for ale 2*s*., for spices 12*d*., for wine 16*d*., to the rector 8*d*., to a chaplain 4*d*., to a clerk 8*d*., for offerings 4*d*., for wax 12*d*., the master's fee 20*d*., and the residue in alms. Total 13*s*. 4*d*.

This day Richard Orme, son of Thomas Orme of Shepshed in Leicestershire, husbandman, was apprenticed to Walter Stalworth from the present day until the end of ten years and it is agreed by Sir Robert Orme[152] in person.

John a Kechyn presented William Holme as his apprentice from next Easter for seven years and paid ...

Robert Barker presented David Gough as his apprentice from the feast of the Aunnunciation next for seven years.

[f. 17v]

Veneris xxviij° die Marcii in presencia Magistri et custodum.

This day Thomas Hore and William Morten, arbiters between William Howlet and Thomas Porter, have adjudged that each should seal to the other a general acquittance and make peace etc. And that the said William should pay 10*s*. to the master to the use of the said Thomas.

Item the master received from John Lewes for John Wandelace his apprentice 40*d*.

---

[152] The Latin title 'dominus' is used here (see Glossary), suggesting that Orme was a priest or chaplain and not a knight. The entry suggests that he was Richard Orme's guardian and as such was required to agree to the apprenticeship.

Item the master licensed Edmund Caryngton[153] to occupy [the craft] and has a day of payment on Friday before the Nativity of St. John [20 June].

Lune xxxj° die Marcii in presencia Magistri et custodum.

Peter Forster presented William Robynson as his apprentice from the feast of Easter next [6 Apr.] for eight years and paid in person 40*d*.

Item paid to William Hacomplaynt, almsman, for Easter term 5*s*.

Item paid to Robert Boylet, almsman, for Easter term 10*s*.

Item paid to the prioress of Clerkenwell for a quit-rent arising from tenements in Colechurch 13*s*. 4*d*.

Item paid to William Duryvale the clerk, for his wages for the term of the Annunciation of the Blessed Virgin Mary[154] 25*s*.

Item paid to Thomas Gresyle for his wages for the same term 18*s*. 4*d*.

Item paid to Geoffrey atte Welle for his stipend 6*s*. 8*d*.

Item paid to John Radclyf clerk for his wages for the same term 23*s*. 4*d*.

Item paid to Roger Doket for his wages for the same term 33*s*. 4*d*.

Item paid to Sir[155] Richard [Wheler] for his wages for the same term 33*s*. 4*d*.

Item paid to John Palmer clerk for his wages 33*s*. 4*d*.

Item paid to Christopher Kyrke almsman for his stipend 10*s*.

Item [paid to] Richard Jakson clerk for his wages for the same term 26*s*. 8*d*.

Item paid to Thomas Hosyer almsman for the same term 10*s*.

This day William Ayleward granted the terms of his apprentice, Patrick Stafford, to William Maryot from the feast of Easter next [6 Apr.] for a quarter, and the same apprentice has, over and above this, agreed to serve for three quarters as compensation for his offences etc. And the same William Maryot owes to the said William Ayleward 20*s*., that is to say 5*s*. on the feast of the Nativity of St. John the Baptist [24 June] and 5*s*. quarterly thereafter etc. And if the apprentice dies then [the sum] to be paid on his death.

Item paid to Robert Walthowe and Thomas Robyns, almsmen of this fraternity, for the past quindene 5*s*. 8*d*.

---

153 Caryngton had been employed for 1½ days by the Great Wardrobe prior to Richard III's coronation in 1483 and was employed there for a further 11 days in 1492–4: *Coro. Richard III* ed. Sutton and Hammond, p. 319.

154 25 March to 24 June.

155 See Glossary.

Item Henry Grene presented George Thomas from the 10th day of April for seven years and ...

[f. 18]

Lune xiiij° die Aprilis in presencia Magistri et custodum ac Percyvale, Tego, Stodard, West, Galle, Duplech, Keys, Hardy, Martyn, Randall, W. Grene.

This day William Walker, the apprentice of Thomas Madisson, was committed to Master John Hede to serve him from the feast of Easter 3 [Hen. VII] [6 Apr. 1488] until the end of the terms of the indenture.

This day the master licensed John Copeland to open his shop etc. and has a day of payment three weeks after the Nativity of St. John [24 June].

Item the master received from Hugh Hebbys for occupying foreigns 14*d*.

Item David Michell presented John Orum as his apprentice from the feast of St. Michael the Archangel 3 Hen. VII [29 Sept. 1487] for nine years and paid in person 40*d*.

From the same as a fine for occupying foreigns 20*d*.

Item the master paid to the almsmen of this fraternity for the past quindene 5*s*. 8*d*.

Veneris xviij° die Aprilis in presencia Magistri et custodum.

This day the master paid to the prior of St. Mary Overey[156] for a quit-rent arising from tenements in the parish of St. Martin Outwich for a whole year 8*s*.

Isto die Ricardus Adyf et Owinus Boughton arbitratores inter Radulfum Traford ex una parte et Robertum Greves ex altera parte videlicet quod In primo in presencia Magistri uterque pars faceret alteri eorum amiciciam etc. Et quod dictus Radulfus solvat predict Roberto xj*li*. videlicet in manibus xl*s*. et quod dictus Robertus haberet vj virgas dimidiam de panno per ipsum sinditas de panno predicti Radulfi pro iij*li*. in partem solucionis dictarum xj*li*. et in festo Pentecostes xl*s*. et in festo Nativitatis Johannis xl*s*. et in festo Sancti Michaelis Archangeli xl*s*.

---

156   For the history of the Augustinian priory of St. Mary Overey ('over the river'), in Southwark see Carlin, *Southwark*, esp. pp. 67–75, 285–6.

[translation] This day Richard Adyf and Owen Boughton, arbiters between Ralph Traford on the one part and Robert Greves on the other part [make their award as follows], that is to say first, peace is to be made between the two parties in the presence of the master etc. And that the said Ralph is to pay to the said Robert £11, that is to say 40s. in advance, and that the said Robert should have 6 and a half yards of cloth, cut from cloth belonging to the said Ralph for £3 in part payment of the said £11, and 40s. on the feast of Pentecost [25 May] and 40s. on the feast of St. Michael the Archangel [29 Sept.]

Item that the remenaunt of cloth and the ruges shall remayne in the handes of me the said Richard Adyf for suretie and plegge of payment of the said money and that eyther of them shall have free course to the sale therof and that eyther of them shall quitunce etc. and that the said Rauf shall be bounde by obligacion et quod denarii solvantur in aula in vigilis festonum predictorum.

Item the master received of Edmund Gererd for his redemption 6s. 8d. This day Thomas Algore agreed to pay William Pryor 6s. 8d., that is to say 20d. at Pentecost [25 May], 20d. on the Nativity of St. John [24 June], 20d. on St. Peter's Chains [1 Aug.] and 20d. at Michaelmas [29 Sept.]

[f. 18v]

Lune xxj° die Aprilis in presencia Magistri et custodum ac xxiiij^or videlicet Tego, Keys, Barlowe, West, Buk, Galle, Randyll.

This day John Burnam, clerk, was admitted by the master and wardens to celebrate in the church of St. Martin Outwich according to the ordinance.

This day Roger Mone presented William Patryk as his apprentice from the feast of Easter 3 Hen. VII [6 Apr. 1488] for seven years and paid ...

Item John Combes presented John Danyell as his apprentice from the feast of the Annunciation next [25 Mar.] for seven years and paid 40d.

Lune xxviij° die Aprilis in presencia Magistri et custodum.

This day Ralph Traford presented William Fisshpoole as his apprentice from the feast of Pentecost [25 May] next for ten years.

This day John Colman was licensed to open shop and paid 5s. in person and is to pay 5s. before the Nativity of St. John [24 June].

Item the master paid to the almsmen of this fraternity for the past quindene 5s. 8d.

Martis xxix die Aprilis in presencia Magistri et custodum ac Swan, Percyvale, Materdale, Tego, Stodard, Barlowe, West, Gall, Duplage, Pemberton, Lee, Buk, Keys, Jenyns, Hardy, Stalworth, Martyn, Crosby, Hoberd.

Isto die concessa fuit quedam concessio sive dimissio de quadam parcella muri de lez Saresyns hede Rectori et custodibus Sancti Mathei in Frydaystrete prout latius patet per indenturas inde factas.
[translation] This day it was agreed that the grant or demise of that parcel of wall of the Saracen's Head[157] to the rector and wardens of St. Matthew's in Fridaystreet [to be made] according to the dimensions specified by the indentures made.

Item John Harryson was judged by the said masters as to the imposition of his fine of 40s. for his disobedience to the master, and he gave into the hands of the master the same day etc.

[f. 19]

Veneris ij° die Maii.

This day Robert Segge presented William Fuller as his apprentice from the feast of the apostles Philip and James 3 Hen. [VII] [1 May 1488] for seven years and paid in person 40d.
Item the master received from Thomas Howdan for William Langfeld 40d.
Item Richard Spicer presented Hugh Adam as his apprentice from the feast of Pentecost next [25 May] for seven years.

---

157   For this property see above n. 56 and pp. 18–19.

Item from Thomas Sharparowe for Edmund Margeretrod his apprentice 40*d*.
Item received from John Semer for an apprentice [not] enrolled 20*d*.
Item from the same for occupying foreigns 20*d*.
Item from John Skefe for William Cokbene his apprentice 40*d*.

Dies quarterii

Mercurii vij° die Maii in presencia Magistri ac Stodard, Tego, West, Barlowe, Materdale, Pemberton et Stalworth.

This day the master received from William Joynour for his apprentice 40*d*.
Item received from Robert Kellom for [Bartholomew] Maundevile 40*d*.

Item paid to William Camell for his wages for last Easter term 40*s*.

The obit of Ralph Basset held in the church of St. Martin on the 9th day of May. For bread 4*d*., for ale 5*d*., to the rector 6*d*., for 7 chaplains 2*s*. 4*d*., to the clerk 8*d*., for offerings 2*d*., for candles 12*d*., for alms 13*d*. Item for children 5*d*.
Total 7*s*.

[f. 19v]

Veneris xiiij°[158] die Maii.

This day Richard Hill, son of the late John Hille, deceased, late of Romford in Essex, yeoman, bound himself as an apprentice to Richard Dakers from the feast of Pentecost next for seven years and paid in person 40*d*.

Item James Fitte granted the terms of his apprentice Thomas Myles to William Hewetson, citizen and tailor of London, and in respect therof made letters of sale.
Item the master received from Thomas Felle for Robert Brendewode 40*d*.

---

[158] An error for 'xvj'.

Item John Sparman presented Richard Cokson, son of John Cokson of Derby, tailor, from the feast of St. George the Martyr 3 [Hen. VII] [23 Apr. 1488] for seven years.
Item the master received from John Sparman 20s.
Item from a foreign for making new work 8d.

Veneris xxiiij[159] die Maii.

This day the master paid to the almsmen of this fraternity for a month ending on Monday next 11s. 4d.
Item the master received from Thomas Speight,[160] a new brother 20s.
Item of John Harryson for his disobedience 13s. 4d.

Sabbati sequente in presencia Magistri et custodum ac Percyvale, Tego, Stodard, Pemberton, Galle, Lee, West, Keys, Materdale.

Isto die Johannes Hardy electus est in unum sex ad interessendum cum magistri ad convivium.
[translation] This day John Hardy was chosen as one of the six to be present with the master at the feast.

The obit of Hugh Talbot, held on Friday before the feast of the Holy Trinity. For bread 4d., for ale 5d., for offerings 2d., to the Rector 6d., for 6 chaplains 2s., to a clerk 8d., to the waxchandler 12d.
[Total] 5s. 11d.

Item concessa fuit quedam dimissio Rectorii et custodibus ecclesie Sancti Mathei in Frydaystrete ut patet minuta inde facta.
[translation] Item it was agreed that the demise to the rector and wardens of the church of St. Matthew Friday Street to be according to the minute made in respect thereof.

Item Richard Griston paid for Richard Rich his apprentice 40d.
Item Richard Colston paid for Mallone Broun his apprentice 40d.

---

159 An error for 'xxiij'.
160 Speight presented his first apprentice in 1476–7, was chosen as warden of the company for 1499–1500 and 1503–4, and went on to become master for 1509–10: Hopkinson, *Ancient Records*, p. 116.

[f. 20]

Lune ij° die Junii.

This day the master paid to the prioress of Kilburn[161] for a quit-rent arising out of tenements formerly of Master Langwith 8s. 6d.

Item the master received from Thomas Bankes for Edmund Clyfton from the feast of Pentecost 3 [Hen. VII] [25 May 1488] for eight years 40d.

Item received from William Batyson for an apprentice not enrolled 8d.

Veneris vj° die Junii.

This day the master received from George Bolton for John Bolton his apprentice 40d.

This day the master received from David Roche for Thomas Belle 40d.

Item from Robert Yngill for William Asshton 40d.

Item from William Buk for Richard Cartelage 40d.

Item from John Abbot for James Thomson 40d.

Lune viij°[162] die Junii in presencia Magistri ac Barlowe, Galle, Pemberton, Tego, Hardy, Martyne.

This day the master paid for the obit of Thomas Reymond in the church of St. Thomas the Apostle. To the Rector 6d., to the clerk 8d., for 3 chaplains 12d., for offerings 2d., and the residue in alms. Total 10s.

Item the master received from Roger Barlowe for William Dalton his apprentice, who is to serve him from the feast of the Nativity of St. John the Baptist 3 [Hen. VII] [24 June 1488] for nine years 40d.

Item the master paid to the almsmen of this fraternity for the past quindene 5s. 8d.

Item paid for a copy of the plea of Danyell's wife 8d.

This day Thomas Pole was sworn as a new brother and paid 20s.

---

[161] Kilburn priory, founded c.1130: see VCH, *Middlesex*, I (1969), pp. 178–82.
[162] An error for 'ix'.

Veneris sequente.

The obit of Hugh Cavendish held in the church of St. Martin the 12th day of June. For bread 6*d*., for ale 12*d*., for cheese 6*d*., to the parish chaplain 6*d*., for seven chaplains 2*s*. 4*d*., to the clerk 8*d*., for offerings 4*d*., for candles 12*d*., for alms 4*d*., to the master 3*s*. 4*d*., to the four wardens 6*s*. 8*d*., to the clerk and beadle 20*d*.
Total 18*s*. 10*d*.

Item the master received from Richard Smyth for John Tancok his apprentice 40*d*.
Item from John Tofte for a fine 40*d*.
Item received from Richard Quikrell for his admission 20*d*.
Item from Richard Bayly in part payment of his redemption 13*s*. 4*d*.

Item paid to the treasury of Westminster for a quitrent 13*s*. 6*d*.

[f. 20v]

Memorand' that these ordenaunces underwriten were made ordeigned and establisshed by Gilbert Keys, Maister, Richard Adyff, John ...[163]

Lune ...[164]

Thomas Petyt presented Edward Ame as his apprentice from the feast of Christmas 3 [Hen. VII] [1487] for nine years and paid in person 40*d*.
Item paid to the master of St. Giles for a quit-rent 14*s*.
Item [from] Reginald Trayford for John Trayford 40*d*.
Item from John Flemyng for Robert Barker 40*d*.
Item from Richard Flemmyng for William Rich 40*d*.
Item from Richard Radclyf senior for part payment of his redemption 12*s*.
Item from Thomas Gardener for his entrance 20*s*.
Item from the same for his [shop] opening 10*s*.

Item soluit pro expensis in eundo usque Fulham ad Episcopum London' videlicet pro cimba xiij*d*., in potacione vij*d*., in pane iij*d*., in speciebus ij*d*.,

---

[163] This heading is in a smaller, more formal, hand. Keyes was master of the company for 1473–4.
[164] 16 or 23 June.

in cervisia jd., in vino ijs. viijd., pro carubus[165] xd., pro dentruce[166] xiiijd. vijs. xd.

> [translation] Item paid for expenses in going to the bishop of London at Fulham,[167] namely for a boat 14d. for a potation 7d. for bread 3d. for spices 2d. for ale 1d. for wine 2s. 8d. for carts 10d. for pike 14d. [Total] 7s. 10d.

For the obit of Ralph Holand 13s. 4d.
From Robert Colson for Mallone Broun his apprentice 3s. 4d.
From John Shotbourn for Patrick O'Brother 3s. 4d.
From John Lewes for ... his apprentice 40d.

In vigilia Nativitatis Sancti Johannis Baptiste.

John Gayton, son of Master William Gayton, deceased, late citizen and barber of London, bound himself as an apprentice to William a Lye from the feast of the Nativity of St. John the Baptist 3 [Hen. VII] [1488] for 13 years and paid ...
From John Herst for his redemption 20s.
Item paid to William Hacomplayne almsman for the term of the Nativity of St. John 5s.
Item to Sir[168] John Palmer at St. Peter's[169] 33s. 4d.
Item to Christopher Kyrke almsman 10s.
Item to Thomas Hosyer almsman 10s.
Item to Sir Richard 33s. 4d.
Item paid to him for bread and wine 20d.
Item to Sir John Burnam clerk for his wages 16s. 8d.
Item to Sir Roger Doket 33s. 4d.
Item paid to the same for bread and wine 20d.
Item paid to Camerty serjeant at arms for his wages 6s. 8d.
Item to John Radclyf clerk 33s. 4d.
Item paid to the same for bread and wine for a year 20d.
Item for oil for the lamp in St. Martin's church 9s. 6d.
Item paid to the minstrels 6s. 8d.

---

165 'pro carubus', probably from 'carrus' (cart). This should be 2nd decl. but may have been treated as 4th decl. I am grateful to Dr. Stephen O'Connor for his suggestion on this point.
166 Possibly confused with 'dentrix' (dentrice) = pike.
167 The reason for this visit is not recorded.
168 See Glossary.
169 Chantry of Peter Mason (d. 1412), see above n. 125.

Item for putting hoops on barrels (*pro hopyng de le tobbys*)[170] 4s.
Item paid to the almsmen of this fraternity on the vigil of the Nativity of St. John [24 June] 10s. 8d.

[f. 21]

Item paid to Robert Boylet almsman for the term of the Nativity of St. John ~~vii~~
Item paid for the hood given to Master Vavasour[171] 10s. 3d.
Item paid for the hood given to Thomas Cambery[172] 8s. 6d.
Item William Spencer who was the apprentice of Richard Burton ...

---

[170] For this phrase see *Middle English Dictionary* (Ann Arbor, MI, 1956-), *G–H*, pp. 934-5. The expression may also refer to putting a rim on a wheel. In 1466 the Carpenters paid 6d. 'For howpyng of Towbys': *Records of the Worshipful Company of Carpenters*, ed. B. Marsh, J. Ainsworth and A. M. Millard, 7 vols (Oxford 1914-68), vol. 2, p. 12.

[171] John Vavasour (d. 1506), was a prominent lawyer who was educated at Lincoln's Inn, was created a serjeant-at-law in 1478 and served as a justice of assize for the Midland circuit from 1483-95. He was concerned in a number of important legal cases during his career, and was involved in a conspiracy to influence the course of the law in a dispute concerning the Plumptons. He was renowned for his disagreeable character and for his parsimony. His admission to the Tailors' fraternity suggests that he had provided them with legal advice, as he had the Mercers five years before. E. Ives, *The Common Lawyers of Pre-Reformation England* (Cambridge, 1983), esp. pp. 69, 415, 478-9; J. C. Wedgwood, *History of Parliament: biographies of the members of the commons house, 1439-1509* (London, 1936), p. 905; *Coro. Richard III* ed. Sutton and Hammond, p. 408; *Acts of Court*, pp. 150, 152.

[172] Probably the Thomas Cambray who was returned to Parliament for Wenlock in 1478: Wedgwood, *History of Parliament*, p. 151 Little is recorded of him, but the fact that he was granted a hood with Vavasour suggests that he too was a lawyer.

VOLUME II: 24 JUNE 1488—9 AUGUST 1493

[f. 1]¹⁷³

Jhesus. Maria

Memorandum quod xxv⁰ die mensis Junii videlicet die Martis in festo Nativitatis Sancti Johannis Baptiste anno domino milessimo CCCC^mo octogesimo octano, et anno regni regis Henrici Septimi tercio Willelmus Buk electus est in magistrum istius fraternitatis.
Item eidem festo et anno Oliverus Warner Jacobus Wilford Thomas Petyt et Johannes Doket electi sunt in custodes ejusdem fraternitatis.

> [translation] Memorandum that on the 25th¹⁷⁴ day of June that is to say Tuesday, the feast of the Nativity of St. John the Baptist in the year of Our Lord 1488 and the third year of the reign of King Henry VII, William Buk was elected as master of this fraternity.
> Item that on the same feast and year Oliver Warner, James Wilford, Thomas Petyt and John Doket were elected as wardens of the same fraternity.¹⁷⁵

Lune iiij⁰ die Julii anno predicto.

> Henry Hatherwyck was licensed to hold a shop and paid in person 10s. [mainprised] by Thomas Dyker, John Wareyn, William Person, and John Tayllour.
> Robert Noreys, son of William Noreys of Barnet in Middlesex, ferrour, bound himself as an apprentice to George Burdon, citizen and tailor of London, from the feast of St Peter's Chains [1 Aug.] for seven years and paid ...

---

¹⁷³ A heading at the top of the page in a 17th-century hand reads: 'D. Libri nota. Liber continens fo. 75 de rebus gubernacionem mistere tangentibus'.
¹⁷⁴ The clerk has the correct day of the week for the feast in 1488 but has wrongly dated it to 25 instead of 24 June.
¹⁷⁵ For brief biographies of Warner, Wilford, Petyt and Doget see Appendix IV.

Veneris xjº die Julii anno predicto.

Thomas Glover has a licence to hold a shop and paid in person 10s. [mainprised] by Robert Archer, Henry Brewster, John Waren and William Person, brethren.

Item Herman Neuce paid to the master for John Cok his apprentice 40d.

Item the master paid to the almsmen of this fraternity for the quindene before the 14th day of July 5s. 8d.

Lune xiijº[176] die mensis Julii anno predicto in presencia Magistri et custodum ac Stodard, Barlowe, West, Lee, Dupleche, Materdale, Galle, Hede, Spencer, Fittz, Hoberd, Randyll.

This day Richard Tolle presented Richard Trunbys, son of Richard Trunbys, as his apprentice from the feast of the Nativity of St. John 3 [Hen. VII] [24 June 1488] for seven years and paid in person 40d.

[f. 1v]

Mercurii xvjº die Julii in presencia Magistri et custodum ac Swan, Percyvale, Barlowe, Keys, West, Duplech, Materdale, Galle, Stodard, Lee, Hede, Jenyns, Spencer, Hoberd, Povy, Crosby.

res publica
Communicacio quedam habita fuit de quodam actu de non comparendo confratrem istius fraternitatis cum premuniti fuerint etc. et inde compilata fuit quedam billa ostensura ad diem quarterii proxime
[translation] public matters
A discussion took place in regard to an ordinance concerning the non-attendance of brothers of this fraternity warned to appear. And to this end a certain bill was drawn up, to be presented at the next quarter-day.

Item Johannes Smyth, Johannes Laurens, Robertus Peris, Willelmus Grey et Johannes Bernard appunctuati sunt ut duo eorum eligentur in supervisores reparacionum istius fraternitatis ad diem quarterii nominandos.
[translation] Item John Smyth, John Laurens,[177] Robert Peris, William Grey and John Bernard were required to choose two of their number as

---

[176] An error for 'xiiij'.

111

supervisors of repairs for this fraternity, and to name them at the quarter-day.

Veneris xviij die Julii.

No business (*nichil*).

Lune xxjᵒ die Julii.

Memorandum that the master paid for the obit of John Langwith held in the church of St. Mary Abchurch 10s.

Item that it should be granted to the master, wardens, clerk and beadle, for their labour, according to the last will of the said John Langwith 6s. 8d.

Item the master received from John Povy[178] for Ralph Robert his apprentice 40d.

Item the master received from Thomas Egerton for employing (*occupacione*) foreigns 40d.

Item from William Clerk for employing foreigns 8d.

Item paid to the almsmen of this fraternity 5s. 8d.

Lune xxviij die Julii.

Ranulph Nowell presented Richard Iryell as his apprentice and paid ...

John Copland presented Geoffrey Peerson as his apprentice and paid ...

Item John Sexi presented John Rysely as his apprentice and paid 40d.

Item Gilbert Keys presented William Gaucell as his apprentice and paid 40d.

[f. 2]

Dies quarterii tentus die Mercurii [xxx die Julii].[179]

[f. 2v]

---

[177] Perhaps the John Laurens, tailor, who was listed on the 1483–4 alien subsidy roll as the employer of two German servants: Bolton (ed.), *Alien Communities*, p. 84.

[178] For John Povey and his brother Walter see Appendix IV.

[179] The rest of this page is blank and there are no surviving proceedings for this quarter-day.

Veneris primo die Augusti.

Robert Halle presented John Reynold as his apprentice and paid 40*d*.

Lune iiij^to die Augusti.

Item the master received from a certain ... Galyman for occupying the craft of tailoring in the liberty of this city for the month up to ... last 2*s*.

Item Richard Swan presented Roger Sambroke as his apprentice and paid 40*d*.

Item paid to the almsmen of this fraternity 5*s*. 8*d*.

Veneris viij° die Augusti.

Item the master paid to the Abbot of Bermondsey for a quit-rent arising from tenements of this fraternity in Abchurch Lane for a whole year to the Nativity of St. John the Baptist last [24 June] 2*s*. 6*d*.

Lune xj die Augusti in presencia magistri et custodum ac xxiiij^pr magis fidedignorum videlicet M. Percyvale militis, Pemberton, Deplech, Materdale, Barlowe, Hede, Tego, Stodard, Lee, Galle, Spencer, Hardy, Boughton, Crosby, Fitz.

[f. 3]

Lune xviij° die Augusti

This day James Wilford presented master William Wilford as his apprentice and paid in person 40*d*.

Item John Grene presented Thomas Thorneton as his apprentice and paid 40*d*.

Item Thomas Trymmer agreed terms with the master and wardens for the sum of 53*s*. 4*d*. for his redemption, of which he paid in person 20*s*. and of the residue he is to pay 20*s*. at Christmas, and on the feast of the Annunciation of the Blessed Virgin Mary [25 Mar.] 13*s*. 4*d*.

Item paid to the almsmen of this fraternity for the past quindene 5*s*. 8*d*.

Jovis xxj° die Augusti in presencia Magistri et custodum ac Swan, Percyvale, Pemberton, Lee, Deplech, Stodard, Hede, Adyf, Boughton, West, Fittz, Materdale, Stalworth.

Item paid for the obit of Bernard Dax[180] according to the composition 6s. 8d.

Item Hugh Davy was licensed to hold a shop etc. and paid in person 5s. and is to pay the residue on ...

Item John Hede petitioned for a day on which to bring in the accounts of this mistery. This was agreed and he is to have until Wednesday 3 September.[181]

Lune primo die Septembris in presencia Magistri et custodum ac Percyvale, Swan, Stodard, Pemberton, West, Stalworth, Tego, ..., Hardy, Jenyns, Randyll, Fyttz, Martyn.

Item the master received from Benedict de Cenia galyman[182] for two months for himself and his family 4s.

Item it is agreed that the evidences gathered concerning the lands and tenements in Aldermanbury, formerly called B[assets Inn] ...

Item David Johnson presented Owen ap Meredith and paid ...

Item paid to the almsmen of this fraternity for the past quindene 5s. 8d.

[f. 3v]

Veneris v^to die Septembris.

This day Christopher Bankys presented John Brouwnes and paid 40d.

Item this day Richard Botham, Charles Caryngton, John Plomer and John Wright[183] were sworn as wardens of the Bachelors of this fraternity.

---

180 Bernard Dakers, see above n. 70.

181 Heed was master of the company for the previous year (1487–8) and like his predecessors was responsible for the compilation of the accounts for his year in office. For biographical details see Appendix IV.

182 See Glossary.

183 As a young man Wright may have worked at the Great Wardrobe for Richard III's coronation. It was almost certainly this warden of the Bachelors who went on to become a warden of the company as a whole in 1503, 1507 and 1511 before being chosen as master in 1515: Hopkinson, *Ancient Records*, pp. 115–6; *Coro. Richard III* ed. Sutton and Hammond, p. 414.

Veneris xij° die Septembris.

Matthew Reynold obtained the freedom of this mistery for £3 sterling of which he paid in person 6s. 8d. And he has days of payment of the residue of 53s. 4d., namely at Christmas 10s., at Easter [19 Apr.] 6s. 8d., at the Nativity of St. John [24 June 1489] 6s. 8d., at Michaelmas [29 Sept.] 6s. 8d., at Christmas 6s. 8d., at Easter [11 Apr. 1490] 6s. 8d., and at the Nativity of St. John [24 June] 6s. 8d. and he was sworn.
Item John Stoyle presented Richard Eldemer as his apprentice and paid 40d.
Item from Simon Lytell for occupying foreigns 12d.
Item William Ashby paid for William Pynder 40d.
Item John Wright paid for William Dorset his apprentice 40d.
Item the master paid to Richard Batte for a quit-rent as made clear by an acquittance 6s. 8d.

Lune xv° die Septembris in presencia Magistri et custodum ac xxiiij^(or) videlicet Percyvale, Tego, Stodard, Pemberton, Lee, Barlowe, Marchall,[184] Hoberd, Adyff, Povey, Boughton.

This day the master paid to the almsmen of this fraternity for the past quindene 5s. 8d.

Item[185] concordatum est quod lez yoman tayllours abhinc nuncupentur the company de lez Bachelers etc.
[translation] Item it is agreed that from henceforth the yeomen tailors are to be known as the Bachelors' company.[186]

Item William Pecok was presented as an apprentice by Thomas Sterne and ...

Item M. soluit pro duobus libris emptis pro necessariis istius loci vs. viijd.
[translation] Item the master paid for two empty books for the use of this place 5s. 8d.

[f. 4]

---

184 For William Marchall see Appendix IV.
185 The margin has a drawing of a hand pointing to this entry.
186 For the Bachelors' Company see Introduction pp. 23–5.

Veneris xix° die Septembris in presencia Magistri et custodum.

Item the master received from Peter de Catero, galyman[187] 2s.
Item from a servant of Benedict de Cena,[188] galyman 12d.
Item from Michael de Ragos, servant of the said Peter 2s.
Item paid for expenses incurred for St. Bartholomew's fair[189] 20d.
Item Robert Barker presented William Hynseley as his apprentice and paid ...
Item John Povy presented Roger Wenteworth his apprentice and paid 40d.
Item received from Robert Thomson for opening his shop on St. John's day 2s.

Lune xxij° die Septembris in presencia Magistri et custodum.

Item [from] Margery Gresacre[190] for Robert Smyth 40d.
Item William Kyrkeham presented Henry Venables and paid 40d.

Veneris xxvj^{to} die Septembris in presencia Magistri et custodum.

Nota. Isto die Magister dimist Willelmo Balard alias dicto March' Regi armorum quoddam tenementum istius fraternitatis in Ancre Lane in parochia Sancti Martini in Vinetria London'. Tenendum sibi a festo Sancti Michaelis Archangeli proximo per x annos reddendo inde annuatim per idem tempus xxiijs. iiijd. ad terminos consuetos etc. prout patet per indenturas etc.

[translation] Note. This day the master demised to William Balard *alias* March King of Arms,[191] the fraternity's tenement in Anchor Lane in the parish of St. Martin in the Vintry, London. To hold the same from the

---

187 For this term see Glossary.
188 De Cena was among those galleymen who were also active in Southampton, see *Book of Remembrance of Southampton, III*, ed. Gidden, p. 46.
189 See above n. 73.
190 Possibly the widow of the John Grisacre who worked for 3¼ days in the Great Wardrobe before Richard III's coronation in 1483: *Coro. Richard III* ed. Sutton and Hammond, p. 351.
191 Ballard was herald to Henry, duke of Exeter, by 1460 and, after becoming March King of arms (c.1480), compiled a roll of arms of the nobility and gentry (College of Arms MS M. 3) which included epitaphs on King Arthur and Richard, duke of York, as well as descriptions of royal ceremonial occasions such as the coronation of Elizabeth Woodville: A. R. Wagner, *Heralds and Heraldry in the Middle Ages* (Oxford, 1956), pp. 58-9, 107-9; *idem*, *A Catalogue of English Medieval Rolls of Arms* (London, 1950), pp. 111-12.

feast of St. Michael the Archangel next [29 Sept.] for 10 years, rendering yearly during the same time 23s. 4d. at the usual terms etc. specified by indentures etc.

Item John Cok presented William Williamson and paid 40d.

Veneris iij° Octobris in presencia Magistri et custodum ac xxiiij°ʳ videlicet Tego, Stodard, Pemberton, Deplech, Lee, Galle, Jenyns, Fittz.

This day the master granted licence for Henry Beauford to hold a shop and he paid in part payment of 10s. according to the custom 6s. 8d.

Item it is agreed that the aforsaid William Balard shall have the said tenement for 23s. 4d. a year for 10 years as set out above.

Item William Cok presented William Ogyll his apprentice.

Item Roger Harrys was licensed to hold a shop and paid 40d. in person and is to pay the residue by the Na[tivity of St. John] [24 June].

Item paid to Thomas Say for arresting Lodowic John 12d.

[f. 4v]

Lune vj°° die Octobris in presencia Magistri et custodum.

Item paid to Sir[192] John Radclyf, chaplain, for Michaelmas term 32s. 4d.

Item paid to Sir Roger Doket, chaplain, for Michaelmas term 32s. 4d.

Item paid to Sir William Camell, chaplain, for Michaelmas term £4.

Item paid to William Boylet, almsman, for Michaelmas term 10s.

Item paid to Christofer Kyrke, almsman, for Michaelmas term 10s.

Item paid to Robert Walthewe and Thomas Robyns, almsmen, for the quindene before the 30th day of September 5s. 8d.

Item paid to William Hacomplayn, almsman 5s.

Item paid to Sir John Burnam[193] for half his salary for this term 16s. 8d.

Item paid for a barge on the morrow of St. Michael's day 13s. 4d.

Item paid for drink for the boatmen 20d.

Item paid for coals distributed in the almshouse of this fraternity 4s. 8d.

Item paid to the prioress of Kilburn for a quit-rent arising from tenements formerly of Elene Langwith for half a year to the feast of St. Michael 8s. 6d.

---

192   For the use of the Latin title 'Dominus' (Sir) see Glossary.

193   Burnham replaced Robert Urton as chantry chaplain of John and William de Oteswich in St. Martin Outwich. The Tailors paid half his salary, the other half being paid by the churchwardens: see Appendix III.

Item paid to the same for a quit-rent arising from tenements in Bread Street 6s. 8d.

Item Henry Alexaunder presented William Brewton his apprentice and paid 40d.

Item Laurence Bardeney presented John Carter his apprentice and paid 40d.

Item paid to Thomas Hosyer, almsman, for Michaelmas term 10s.

Item paid to William Duryvale, clerk of this fraternity, for the same term 25s.

Item paid to Thomas Gresyle, beadle 18s. 8d.

Item paid to Sir John Palmer at St. Peter Cornhill 35s.

Item paid Sir Richard Wheler, chaplain 33s. 4d.

Item paid to Robert Walthewe for a gallon of oil to be used in the light in St. Martin's 11d.

Item paid to Geoffrey atte Welle, almsman of this fraternity 6s. 8d.

Dies quarterii tentus die Mercurii viij° die Octobris in presencia Magistri et custodum ac Magistri Swan, Percyvale, Stodard, Barlowe, Materdale, Pemberton, Keys, West, Deplech, Jenyns, Spencer ac totius comunitatis istius mistere.

This day the last will of Hugh Champernoun was read.

Item ordinatum est quod lez yomen company abhinc nuncupentur les company de lez Bachelers in hac mistera ut lacius patet in magno registro.
[translation] Item it is ordained that the yeomen company from henceforth shall be known as the Bachelors' Company[194] of this mistery, as is set out more fully in the great register.[195]

Item quod quilibet confrater auxilians erit ad sepeliendum confratres et sorores mortuos istius mistere ut patet per magnum registrum.
[translation] Item that every brother is to assist at the burial of deceased brothers and sisters of this mistery as specified in the great register.

Item ad hummilem supplicacionem Galfridi atte Welle confratris istius fraternitatis concessum est eidem Galfrido xxvjs. viijd. de elemosina istius fraternitatis percipiendos annuatim a festo Nativitatis Sancti Johannis Baptiste ultimo durante vita sua cum una domo pro mansione sua infra domum elemosinariam.

---

194 See Introduction, pp. 23–5.
195 This probably refers to a book of ordinances of which only four folios now survive as Guildhall Library, Merchant Taylors' Co., Ancient MS. Book A.2.

[translation] Item at the humble supplication of Geoffrey atte Welle, brother of this fraternity, the said Geoffrey is granted 26s. 8d. in alms of this fraternity to be received yearly from the feast of the Nativity of St. John the Baptist last [24 June] for the term of his life, together with a dwelling in the almshouse.[196]

[f. 5]

Veneris x° die Octobris in presencia Magistri et custodum.

This day the master licensed Robert Ferrour, dwelling in the parish of St. Ewen within Newgate, to hold a shop and he agreed to pay according to the ordinance 10s. that is to say at Christmas 40d., at Easter [19 Apr.] 40d., and on the feast of the Nativity of St. John [24 June] 40d.
Item James Shirwode presented William Halle and paid 40d.

Lune xiij° die Octobris.

Item paid to Robert Walthewe and Thomas Robyns, almsmen of this fraternity, for the past quindene 5s. 8d.

Veneris xvij die Octobris in presencia Magistri et custodum.

Item John Warner presented William White his apprentice and paid ...
Item Lodewic John presented John Heweson his apprentice and paid ...

This day William Crosby and Thomas Martyn, arbiters between Richard Quykrell and Henry Brewster, make their award in this manner, that is to say that the aforesaid parties are to make peace in the presence of the master.

Item the master received from John Skeef for employing a foreign 4d.

Item the master licensed George Wilson to hold a shop, paying 40d. today and 6s. 8d. at Christmas.

---

196   For the Tailors' almshouse see Davies, 'Charity', pp. 182–3.

Lune xx° die Octobris in presencia Magistri et custodum.

Item Gilbert Keys presented William Gauncell and paid 40*d*.
Item Thomas Porefyssh presented John Cook and paid 40*d*.
Item William Gerveys presented Roger Andover and paid 40*d*.

The obit of John Halygate and Idonea his wife[197] in the church of St. Martin Outwich. For bread 6*d*., for ale 8*d*., for cheese 8*d*., to the parish priest 6*d*., for five other priests 20*d*., to the clerk of the church 6*d*., for help for a poor man 2*d*., to various children 1*d*., for offerings 2*d*., for candles 2*d*.
Total 5*s*. 11*d*.

[f. 5v]

Veneris xxiiij^to die Octobris in presencia Magistri et custodum.

John Skefe presented John Gregory, his apprentice, and paid ...

Lune xxvij° die Octobris.

This day the master licensed Thomas Robertson, who was the apprentice of James Shirwode, to hold a shop and he is to pay 10*s*. in the manner following, that is to say at Christmas 5*s*. and on the feast of the Annuciation 5*s*.

Item the master paid for the obit of Master Stone held in the church of St. John the Evangelist, the 23rd day of October. For bread 13*d*., for ale 2*s*., for offerings 5*d*., to the rector of the church 12*d*., to the clerk of the church 12*d*., for three priests 12*d*., for assistance for two poor men 8*d*., for wine 3*s*., for confections[198] 20*d*., to the master of the craft 40*d*., to the four wardens 6*s*. 8*d*., to the clerk of the craft 12*d*., to the beadle 12*d*., for candles 12*d*., to two children 2*d*., for the alms of John Stone 8*d*., to Laweles 4*d*., to Balle's wife 4*d*., to Henry Armorer 4*d*.
Total 26*s*. 8*d*.

Item paid for the obit of John[199] Jawdrell in the church of St. Mary Abchurch, according to the composition 2*s*. 4*d*.

---

[197] For the Halygates see above n. 86.
[198] 'pro comfectis'.
[199] Error for William: see above n. 88.

Item the master licensed John Tanner, dwelling in the parish of St. Bride Fleet Street, to hold a shop, and he paid 6s. 6d. in person and is to pay the residue on the feast of St. Andrew [30 Nov.] next.

Item paid to the almsmen of this fraternity for the past quindene 5s. 8d.

Veneris xxxj° die Octobris in presencia Magistri et custodum.

Item Henry Percy paid for a fine because he attended the mayoral dinner[200] 2d.

Item from Thomas Tromy for the same 4d.

Item from John Swetyngham for the same 4d.

Item from Richard Trewe for the same 2d.

Item paid to John Heth bargeman for a barge for the presentation of the mayor 13s. 4d.

Item paid for the boatmen 12d.

Item received from the bequest of Robert Lyndesey, a brother 20d.

[f. 6]

Veneris vij° die Novembris in presencia Magistri et custodum.

Item received from Roger Mone for not attending the funeral of Robert Hille[201] 4d.

Item John Skeef presented Reginald Donne his apprentice and paid 40d.

Item from Alan Hille for occupying a foreign 4d.

Item from the same for his breakfast at the mayoral feast 4d.

Item John Clerk presented John Parkynson ...

Item William Werton made an agreement with the master and wardens for his redemption which was granted to the said William for 26s. 8d. of which he paid in person 13s. 4d. and James Wilford was surety for the residue.

Item William Brownyng presented John Locoke and paid 40d.

---

[200] *'quia sedebat in prandio maioris'*. Perhaps fines imposed on individuals who attended the mayor's feast at Tailors' Hall without permission: see Introduction, p. 41.

[201] Robert Hill 'gentleman otherwise called Robert Hill citizen and tailor' drew up his will on 17 Oct. 1488 and asked for burial in his parish church of Holy Trinity the Less. He owned property in Essex and in Cornwall. He must have died in late Oct. or early Nov. although the will was not proved until 17 Dec. PRO, PROB 11/8/13.

Lune x° die Novembris.

Item received from Richard Dove for dining at the mayoral feast 4d.
Item Hamo Wichecote presented John Rodeley and paid 40d.
Item from Hugh Gybson for his dinner 4d.
Item [from] Thomas Shirbourne for his dinner 2d.
Item from Robert Dawes in full [payment] of his redemption 20s.
Item from Thomas Dawes in full payment of his redemption 20s.
Item paid to the almsmen of this fraternity for the past quindene 5s. 8d.
Item from William Maryot for his dinner at the mayoral feast 4d.
Item paid for expenses in inspecting the rents at the Three Kings[202] 4d.
Item received from Edmund Gerard in full payment 6s. 8d.

Lune xvij die Novembris in presencia Magistri et custodum ac Percyvale, Stodard, Barlowe, Pemberton, Materdale, Deplech.

Item John Brigge presented Roger Glossop and paid 40d.
Item from Benedict de Cena in full payment for 4 months 2s.
Item William Witworth, [dwelling] near the Cross Keys in Gracechurch Street, was licensed to open a shop etc. and paid in person 5s. 6d. and is to pay the residue of 6s. 8d. at Christmas.
Item John Bayon compounded with the master for his freedom of this mistery, which he has for 40s. which he paid.

[f. 6v]

Veneris xxj° die Novembris.

Item Robert Archer presented Thomas Godfrey as his apprentice and paid 40d.
Item paid to the chamber at Westminster for a quit-rent specified by an acquittance 10s.
Item to the same by way of another acquittance 3s. 6d.
Item paid for a gift for the mayor[203] 40s.

---

[202] This property, opposite Houndsditch in the parish of St. Botolph Aldgate, was one of those left to the Tailors by Ralph Holland (master 1419–20) in his will of 3 May 1452: Clode, *Early History*, vol. 1, p. 411; *CWCH*, vol. 2, p. 526.

[203] Robert Tate, mercer and merchant of the staple, was mayor 1488–9: Beaven, *Aldermen*, II, p. 16.

Lune xxiiij^{to} die Novembris.

Item soluit Cristofero Haryngton de cancellaria domini regis pro consilio suo ad querelam uxoris Danyell habendo xxd.

> [translation] Item paid to Christopher Haryngton[204] of the royal Chancery for his counsel concerning the suit of Danyell's wife 20d.

> Item Richard Semer presented Peter Thomasson and paid 40d.
> Item paid to the prior of St. Mary Overey for a quit-rent 10s.
> Item to the master of St. Katherine's Hospital for a quit-rent 8s.
> Item paid to the almsmen of this fraternity for the past quindene 5s. 8d.

Lune primo die Decembris.

> No business (*nichil*).

Veneris quinto die Decembris.

> Item Thomas Mathyson presented John Carre and paid ...
> Item received from Philip Davy in part payment of his redemption 6s. 8d.
> Item from Henry Beauford for Richard Hawkyns his apprentice 40d.
> Item from Edward Smyth for Nicholas Robynson 40d.
> Item from Richard Sharp in full payment of his redemption 5s.
> Item from Richard Alenson for Gilbert Dowell ...

> Item paid to the master of St. Giles Hospital 23s.
> Item paid to the same as it appears by an acquittance 13s.

[f. 7]

Veneris xij^o die Decembris.

> No business (nichil).

---

204 Haryngton's name first occurs on writs issued by the royal Chancery in 1461, although his main period of service was from 1472 to 1490. His will, drawn up in 1486, was proved on 19 July 1490. As well as having strong links with Hampshire he was a parishioner of St. Dunstan in the West in London and asked to be buried at White Friars. His executors were left detailed instructions concerning his business affairs, notably sums of money he had lent to various individuals. PRO, Card Index of Chancery Clerks, 'Haryngton'; PROB 11/8, ff. 201v–203.

Lune xvj°[205] Decembris in presencia Magistri et custodum.

The master paid to the dean of St. Paul's for a quit-rent arising from tenements in Holy Trinity the Less for this year 5s.
Item paid to the almsmen for the quindene before the 7th day of December 5s. 8d.
Item received from Hugh Davy in full payment of his shop-opening 5s.
Item from Thomas Perte for John Bykeryng 40d.
Item paid for the obit of John[206] Carleton held in the church of St. Paul 10s.
Item paid for 12 quarters of coals distributed among the almsmen 5s. 6d.

Veneris xx°[207] die Decembris.

Item received from John Bigge for not enrolling his apprentice 8d.

Lune xxiij°[208] die Decembris.

Item the master paid to the almsmen of this fraternity for the past quindene 5s. 8d.
Item paid to William Boylet, almsman, for Christmas term 10s.
Item paid to Thomas Hosyer for the same term 10s.
Item paid to William Hacomplayne for the same term 5s.
Item paid to Christopher Kyrke for the same term 10s.
Item paid to Thomas Gresyll for his wages for the same term 18s. 8d.
Item paid to William Duryvale, the clerk, for his wages 25s.
Item received from John Harryson for Robert Jakson 40d.

[f. 7v]

Lune v°to die Januarii in presencia Magistri et custodes ac Tego, Stodard, Keys, Materdale, Deplech, Pemberton, Galle, Hede, Hert,[209] Hardy, Adyff, Povy, Fitz.

Item William Olyver presented Thomas Smyth and paid 40d.

---

205 An error for 'xv'.
206 An error for Thomas: see above, n. 97.
207 An error for 'xix'.
208 An error for 'xxij'.
209 William Hert: see Appendix IV.

Item John Clerk presented Hugh Egerton and paid 40*d*.
Item William Olyver presented Robert Jakson 40*d*.
Item the master paid to the almsmen of this fraternity 5*s*. 8*d*.

Veneris xv[210] die Januarii.

Item John Lye made an agreement with the master and wardens for his redemption for £3 of which he paid in hand 13*s*. 4*d*. And for the residue of 46*s*. 8*d*. he has days of payment as follows: at Easter [19 Apr.] 10*s*., on the feast of Pentecost [7 June] 6*s*. 8*d*., at Christmas 10*s*., on the feast of the Nativity of St. John the Baptist next [24 June 1490] 10*s*. and at Christmas next following 10*s*.

This is thawarde of us Walter Povy and Thomas Martyn arbitours bitwene Margaret Carden and John Swanton that is to sey we awarde that the said John before Monday next comyng shall bryng in before the M. in this place a wollen cloth of the colour of blak conteinyng xxx yerds by the said Margaret to the same John late delyvered if the same cloth may be brought forth And the same cloth if it be hole there to be kyt and the said Margaret to have therof xx yerdes and the said John x yerdes for dyverse consideracions us movyng in recompence of all maner thyngs which the said John claymeth of the said Margaret or of Nicholas late apprentice of the said John. And if the said cloth can not be brought forth than we awarde the said John to pay to the said Margaret for the said xx yerds v*li*. sterlinges videlicet in hande l*s*. and l*s*. at our lady day anunciacion [25 Mar.] next comyng. And also that either of them at the gevyng out of this awarde shall geve to the other a generall acquytaunce. Also that the same John on his owne costes shall withdrawe all maner actions taken by hym ayenst the same Margaret in spirituell lawe or at temporell lawe and also that the said John shall delyver to the said Nicholas his endentures with with acquytance generall or unto the said Margaret for hym.

Item we William Crosby and Thomas Howden arbitrours bitwene William Marchall thelder and William Marchall the yonger make awarde in this wise that is to sey that eyther of the said partyes shall geve unto the other of them a generall acquytaunce And that doon we awarde the said William the yonger to pay to the said William thelder x*li*. sterlinges in full payment of all dueties and summes of money by the same William the yonger to the same William thelder due. And that also the same William thelder shall be quit of all maner dueties that the said William the yonger claymeth of hym And also that the

---

[210]   An error for 'xvj'.

said William the yonger before Candelmes next comyng shall bryng in before the M. sufficient suretie after the M. discression to be bounden to the seid William thelder in the said x*li.* to be payde x*ls.* by yere till it be payde the first payment of x*ls.* to be payde at our lady day annunciacion anno lxxxx° and if the said William the yonger can fynde no such suretie than he to bryng in plegge to the value of x*li.* to remayne still in the Halle tyll the some be paid and the same plege to be delyvered rately as the money as the money shall be paid. And we remytte to the Maisters jugement whether the said x*li.* shall be paid x*s.* quarterly or x*ls.* yerely.

John a Waltone presented John Hokeham and paid 40*d.*

[f. 8]

Veneris xxiij die Januarii in presencia magistri et custodum.

This day the master licensed Robert Wampole in Fleet Street to open a shop and he agreed to pay 10*s.* of which he paid in hand 5*s.* and is to pay the residue at Easter [19 Apr.]

Item paid for the obit of John Churchman held in the church of St. Martin the 24th day of January the same year. For bread 6*d.*, for ale 10*d.*, for cheese 6*d.*, to the rector 6*d.*, for eight chaplains 2*s.* 8*d.*, for offerings 5*d.*, to the clerk of the church 8*d.*, for candles 12*d.* [Total] 7*s.* 1*d.*

Veneris xxx die Januarii.

Item John Yon presented Thomas Neleson and paid 40*d.*
Item Richard Grove was licensed to hold a shop and paid in part 5*s.*

Item Walter Povy presented Robert Sexton and paid ...
Item paid to the almsmen of this fraternity for the quindene before the day of the Purification [2 Feb.] 5*s.* 8*d.*

Lune [ii die Februarii]

Robert Fitz Water was licensed to hold a shop etc. and agreed to pay the sum of 10*s.* as follows that is to say at Easter [19 Apr.] 5*s.* and at Pentecost [7 June] 5*s.*

Item James van Sand presented Matthew Kyve his apprentice and paid
...
Item Alan Hoberd presented Richard Stanes his apprentice and paid ...

Lune ix° die Februarii in presencia Magistri et custodum ac Percyvale, Barlowe, Keys, Pemberton, West, Materdale, Lee, Hede, Jenyns, Hoberd, Spencer, Boughton, Fitz, Martyne.

Item paid to the almsmen of this fraternity for the past quindene 5s. 8d.
Item David Michell presented John Bisshop and paid in hand 40d.

[f. 8v]

Lune xxiij° die Februarii in presencia Magistri et custodum ac Magistrorum Percyvale, Stodard, Galle, West, Barlowe, Lee, Hoberd, Spencer, Hardy, Adyf, Ffitz, Martyn.

Item received from John Williamson,[211] bocher,[212] for making new work
20d.
Item of John Baynard for John Turlesley his apprentice 40d.

Dies quarterii tentus xxvj° die Februarii anno regni regis Henrici vij iiij^to in presencia Magistri et custodum ac Percyvale, Stodard, Galle, West, Barlowe, Pemberton, Lee, Heed, Hoberd, Spencer, Hardy, Adyf, Boughton, Fitz, Martyn, ac tocius comunitatis hujus mistere.

This day the last wills of John Churchman and Hugh Champernon were read.

Item Galfridus atte Welle qui habet ex elemosina istius fraternitatis xxvjs. viijd. humilime supplicavit Magistro et comunitati istius fraternitatis de habendo elemosinam sanam istius fraternitatis. Cui concessum est in augmentacione elemosine xiijs. iiijd. Ita quod habeat per annum in futurum ab isto die xls. primo termino solucionis inde incipiente in festo Annunciacionis proximo et quod habeat tunc xs. et sic quarteriatim etc.

---

[211] Possibly the man of this name, a German tailor, who was listed among the alien residents of Castle Baynard ward in the subsidy roll of 1483–4: Bolton (ed.), *Alien Communities*, p. 99.
[212] See Glossary.

[translation] Item Geoffrey atte Welle, who receives 26s. 8d. from the alms of this fraternity, humbly beseeched the master and the commonalty of this fraternity that he might have sufficient alms of this fraternity. To whom is granted 13s. 4d. in augmentation of alms. Thus he is to have in future from this day 40s. yearly, the first term of payment to be the feast of the Annunciation [25 Mar.] next, and that he is then to have 10s. quarterly etc.

Item in hac congregacione Johannes Hardy, Walterus Povy, Thomas Martyn et Henricus Clough assignati fuerunt per totam comitivam ad prosequendum recognirionem omnium illorum alicujus alterius artis qui occupant nostram misteram contra tenorem et formam recognitionis sue etc.
[translation] Item at this assembly John Hardy, Walter Povy, Thomas Martyn and Henry Clough were asssigned by the whole company to prosecute the recognizances of all those of other crafts who practice our craft against the spirit and letter of their recognizances.

Item ad hunc diem stabilite fuerunt iij seperales ordinaciones pro bono regimine istius fraternitatis habendo ut lacius patet magno registro istius fraternitatis.
[translation] Item on this day 3 several ordinances for the good governance of this fraternity were ratified, as set out in the great register of this fraternity.[213]

Veneris xxviij°[214] die Februarii in presencia Magistri et custodum ac ..., West, Keys, Pemberton, ..., Hoberd, Spencer, Hardy, Adyf, Bowton, Fitz.

Veneris vj[to] die Marcii in presencia Magistri et custodum ac Pemberton, Barlowe, Lee, Hede, Spencer, Hardy, Adyf, Martyn.

This day William Peerson presented Cuthbert Belle and paid 40d.
Item it is agreed that Thomas Croucheman is to have the brewery called the Three Kings[215] for the term of 20 years from the feast of Christmas last.
Item paid for faggots for the Hall 2d.
Item John Lye paid in part payment to the mayor for his redemption 6s. 8d.

---

[213] See above n. 195.
[214] An error for 'xxvij'.
[215] See above n. 202.

Item paid to the almsmen of this fraternity for the quindene before the second day of March 5s. 8d.

[f. 9]

Lune ix° die Marcii in presencia Magistri et custodum.

This day John a Worteley, who was the apprentice of John Cawdry, brought in his copy of his freedom dated 20 February 4 Hen. VII [1488/9] and petitioned for a licence to hold a shop, which was granted to him for 10s., of which he is to pay 5s. at Easter [19 Apr.] and 5s. at Pentecost [7 June].

Item paid for 12 quarters of coals distributed among the almsmen 5s.
Item paid for the obit of John Creke held in the church of St. Mary Abchurch the first Sunday in Lent [1 Mar.] For bread and wine 17d., for figs and raisins 6d., to the rector of the church 6d., for five chaplains 20d., to the clerk of the church 8d., to the sub-clerk 4d., for offerings 3d., for candles 12d., for alms 4d.
[Total] 6s. 8d.

Veneris xiij° die Marcii.

This day John Shymell, dwelling in the parish of St. Nicholas Wolhous, who was the apprentice of Richard Wyly, brought in a copy of his freedom dated 11 March 4 Hen. VII [1488/9], and petitioned for a licence to hold a shop etc. and it was granted to him for 10s. to be paid by the middle Sunday in Lent [29 Mar.], of which he paid 5s.
From the same John Shymell for Hugh Crampton his apprentice ...

Item paid to the prioress of Clerkenwell for a quit-rent 26s. 8d.

Lune sequente.

Item the master paid to the almsmen of this fraternity for the past quindene 5s. 8d.
Item received from Wiliam Swanston for Nicholas ... his apprentice 40d.
Item received from the same for not enrolling his apprentice 30d.

Veneris xx° die Marcii.

John Yong presented John Sympson and paid ...

Lune xxiij° die Marcii.

Item the master paid for the obit of Richard Benton held in the church of Holy Trinity the Less. For bread 18*d.*, for ale 2*s.* 2*d.*, for wine 2*s.*, for offerings 4*d.*, for candles 12*d.*, for confections 7*d.*, to the rector 8*d.*, for 2 other priests 8*d.*, to the clerk of the church 8*d.*, for the master's fee 20*d.*, for alms 20*d. ob.*
[Total] 13*s.* 4*d.*

Item received from William Hulot for disobedience 12*d.*
Item paid for the arrest of William Gerveys and John Warder for disobedience 2*s.*
Item William Norton presented Thomas Goodson ...

[f. 9v]

Veneris xxvij° die Marcii.

Item John Hardy presented John Benet and paid ...
Item Robert Grapeles presented Richard Young and paid 40*d.*
Item received from the Pinners for the cleaning of a latrine 16*s.* 8*d.* (*de le Pynners pro purgacione unius latrine*)[216]

Item of Richard Lytell for the farm of his tenement for this year 6*s.* 8*d.*

Item received from Janot Frensshman foreyn for shaping[217] of new work (*pro aptacione novi operis*) 4*s.*

Lune xxx die Marcii.

Item received from John Warner for a fine for disobedience 2*s.*
Item paid to the almsmen of this fraternity for the past quindene 5*s.* 8*d.*

---

[216] The Pinners were renting their Hall from the Tailors: see above pp. 19–20.
[217] See Glossary.

Veneris ij°[218] die Aprilis in presencia Magistri et custodum.

Item the master paid to William Hacomplayne, almsman, for the term of the Annunciation of the Blessed Virgin Mary 5s.
Item paid to Geoffrey atte Welle almsman for the same term 10s.
Item paid to Thomas Hosyer for the same term 10s.

Mercurii viij° die Aprilis in presencia magistri et custodum ac Swan, Percyvale, Tego, Lee, Duplech, Hede, Jenyns.

Ricardus West promisit media fide pro se et familia sua quod ipsi et eorum quilibet bene et honeste se gerent et habebunt erga Radulfum Bukberd et familiam suam tam in verbis quam in factis.
Item Stephanus Jenyns concesit media fide forma predicta pro se et familia sua.
Item Thomas Randyll concessit media fide forma predicta pro se et familia sua.

> [translation] Richard West promised under oath, on behalf of himself and his household, that he and they will behave and conduct themselves rightly and honourably towards Ralph Bukberd and his household, in words as well as in deeds.
> Item Stephen Jenyns conceded under oath in the same manner for himself and his household.
> Item Thomas Randyll conceded under oath in the same manner for himself and his household.[219]

From Walter Hay for Henry Hawkyns 40d.

Lune xiij° die Aprilis in presencia Magistri et custodum ac Swan, Tego, Stodard, West, Lee.

Item James Grene presented Thomas Tomlynson and paid 40d.
Item paid to John Boylet, almsman of this fraternity, for the same term 10s.
Item paid to the almsmen of this fraternity for the past quindene 5s. 8d.
Item paid to Sir[220] Roger Doket for the same term 33s. 4d.
Item paid to Sir Richard Wheler for the same term 33s. 4d.

---

218 An error for 'iij'.
219 All of these men were senior members of the court: see Appendix IV. The dispute between West and Bukberd was particularly bitter: see above p. 91.
220 For the use of the Latin title 'Dominus' (Sir) for a priest see Glossary.

Item paid to Sir William Camell for the same term 40s.
Item paid to Thomas Gresyll, beadle, for the same term 18s. 4d.
Item paid to Sir John Radclyf for the same term 33s. 4d.
Item paid to Sir John Palmer for the same term 35s.
Item to Sir John Burnam 16s. 8d.

[f. 10]

Lune iiij^{to} die Maii.

Item received from John Harryson for a payment for his redemption for last Easter 10s.
Item Master Stalworth presented Richard Brown and paid 40d.
Item the same presented Thomas Edy and paid 40d.

Item Willelmus Marchall junior pro disobediencia committitur prisone ad manucapcionem Magistri per Johannem Halle sergeant ad instanciam M. Warner et M. Wilford.
[translation] Item William Marchall the younger, at the instance of Master Warner and Master Wilford, shall be committed to prison for disobedience on the mainprise of the master, by John Halle, sergeant.

Item received from John Lye for a payment for his redemption for last Easter 5s.
Item received from the same for a fine for shaping work in another's shop 4d.

Dies quarterii tentus vij° die Maii in presencia magistri et custodum ac Percyvale, Tego, Stodard, Keys, West, Materdale, Pemberton, Depleche, Lee, Hede, Hoberd, Jenyns, Crosby, Povy, Martyn et tocius communitatis istius mistere.

This day Nicholas Foderey was chosen as sergeant-at-mace of this mistery and is granted the customary fees of the said office.

Item habentur certe communicaciones quo ad certas ordinaciones lez bachelers concernentes pro dismissione cene sue post Epiphaniam Domini et aliorum prandiorum etc.
[translation] Item certain discussions were held about various ordinances of the Bachelors concerning the grant of their feast after Epiphany [6 Jan.] and other dinners.

Item habentur communicaciones quedam pro die festi nostri mutandi et super hoc assignantur xij persone sequentes ad simul loquendum de predicto festo nostro videlicet

> [translation] Item certain discussions were held concerning our feast day ... and above this were assigned the 12 persons following to discuss together our aforesaid feast, namely
>
> Master Tego
> Master Pemberton
> Master Lee
> Master Materdale
> Roger Mone
> Ralph Bukberd
> John Festam
> Robert Kelham
> Henry Kellowe
> Richard Dyngley
> William Batyson
> John Cok

Paid for the obits of Hugh Shirley, Ralph Basset etc. For bread 6*d*., for ale 8*d*., for cheese 6*d*., for offerings 4*d*., for candles 12*d*., to the rector 6*d*., for 8 chaplains 2*s*. 6*d*., for alms 13*d*. Total 7*s*.

From Henry Kellowe for John Sampy his apprentice 40*d*.

[f. 10v]

Lune xviij° die Maii in presencia Magistri et custodum ac Swan, Percyvale, Tego, Stodard, Deplech, Pemberton, Lee, Hede, Hoberd, Jenyns, Spencer, Herte, Hardy, Povy, Adyf, Martyn, Fitz.

Publicate fuerunt quadam rumores ostensi Magistro et custodibus in Guihald per Maiorem et aldermannos per literas missas a domino Rege Maiori et aldermannis directas.

> [translation] There were published certain rumours, shown to the master and wardens in the Guildhall by the mayor and aldermen, contained in letters sent by the lord the King, directed to the mayor and aldermen.[221]

Item from John Batyson for John Wynter 40*d*.
Item from Geoffrey Mone for ... 40*d*.

---

[221] The nature of these 'rumours' is not revealed by the city records.

[f. 11]

Veneris v^{to} die Junii.

Isto die dominus Robertus Cudworth admissus est in cantiariam perpetuam pro anima ... fundatam in ecclesia Sancti Petri in Cornhill et presentatur per rectorem et custodes ejusdem ecclesie.

> [translation] This day Sir Robert Cudworth was admitted into the perpetual chantry founded for the soul of ... in the church of St. Peter Cornhill, and was presented by the rector and wardens of the same church.[222]

Item Hugh Acton and William Charfull submitted themselves, on a bond of £40 each, to the arbitration of John Spencer and Robert Kelham. An award to be made by the feast of St. Peter's Chains [1 Aug.]

Item paid for the obit of Hugh Talbot for bread 4*d*., for ale 6*d*., for offerings 4*d*., to the rector of the church 6*d*., to other chaplains 2*s*. 4*d*., to the clerk of the church 8*d*., for candles 12*d*. [Total] 5*s*. 8*d*.

Item paid to the almsmen of this fraternity for the quindene before the 8th day of June 5*s*. 8*d*.

Item received from William Harryson in part payment for his redemption for the term of the Nativity of St. John the Baptist 10*s*.

Sabbati[223] in presencia Magistri etc. ac Swan, Percyvale, Galle, Keys, Barlowe, Deplech, Tego, Pemberton, Lee, Hede, Jenyns, Spencer, Hert, Hardy, Povy, Adyf, Fitz.

This day the master granted the terms of Christopher Armstrong, formerly the apprentice of Richard Vertycas, to David Michell, to serve the same until the completion of the terms specified in his indenture, and he has paid nothing etc.

The obit of Hugh Cavendish. For bread and ale 6*d*., for offerings 4*d*., for candles 12*d*., to the rector 6*d*., for seven other chaplains 2*s*. 4*d*., to the clerk of the church 6*d*. Total 5*s*. 2*d*.

---

[222] Cudworth replaced John Palmer. This was the chantry of Peter Mason (d. 1412), for whom see above, n. 125.

[223] The date of this meeting is not given but must be either 6, 13 or 20 June.

Item paid to the master, wardens, clerk and beadle according to the composition 11s. 8d.
Item paid for the obit of Thomas Reymond according to the precedents 10s.

[f. 11v]

Die Martis xxiiij^{to} die Junii videlicet in vigilia Nativitate Sancti Johannis Baptiste anno regni regis Henrici septimi quarto in presencia Magistrorum subsequencium Stephanus Jenyns electus est in magistri istius fraternitatis per magistros Swan, Percyvale, Tego, Stodard, Keys, Galle, Barlowe, West, Pemberton, Materdale, Deplech, Lee, Hede.

Item eodem die electi sunt in custodes ejusdem fraternitatis persone subscripte videlicet
Willelmus Grene
Johannes Bernard jur'
Thomas Bodley jur'
Petrus Forster jur'
  [translation] Tuesday 24 June, that is to say on the vigil of the Nativity of St. John the Baptist 4 Henry VII in the presence of the following masters Stephen Jenyns was chosen as master of this fraternity by Masters Swan, Percyvale, Tego, Stodard, Keys, Galle, Barlowe, West, Pemberton, Materdale, Deplach, Lee, Hede.
  Item the same day the following persons were chosen as wardens of the same fraternity[224]
William Grene
John Bernard sworn
Thomas Bodley sworn
Peter Forster sworn

Lune vj^{to} die Julii.

Henry Brewster presented John Brewster, his apprentice, and paid 40d.
William Grene presented John Bonde, his apprentice, and paid 40d.
Item paid to the almsmen of this fraternity for the past quindene 5s. 8d.
Item paid for going by water to Westminster with the mayor 6d.

---

[224] For biographies of these men see Appendix IV.

Veneris x° die Julii.

Item John Wright paid for George Meryk 40*d*.

Lune xiij° die Julii.

Item the master licensed Thomas Cheyne to occupy and hold a shop, and he paid in hand 10*s*.

[f. 12]

Veneris xvij° die Julii.

Item the master received from William Werton for William Werton his apprentice 40*d*.
Item received from the same for John William 40*d*.

Lune xx° die Julii.

Item the master received from Thomas Perte for Thomas Herde his apprentice 40*d*.
Item the master paid to the almsmen of this fraternity for the past quindene 5*s*. 8*d*.
Item Richard Bothom paid for Simon Wede his apprentice 40*d*.

Veneris xxiiij° die Julii.

Item paid for the obit of Elene Langwith 16*s*.
Item the master granted the terms of John Harvy, formerly the apprentice of Robert Bate, to William Alye, tailor, for 40*d*. paid to the master.

Lune xxvij° die Julii.

From Robert Dobson for William Miller his apprentice 40*d*.
Item paid to the almsmen of this fraternity for the quindene before the 3rd day of August 5*s*. 8*d*.
Item from Richard Stodard for a licence to open a shop 10*s*.

Veneris vij die Augusti.

This is thawarde of us Thomas Hore and Geffrey Here arbitrours electe and chosen by the Right worshipfull the master and wardeyns of the craft of Tayllours betwene Cristofre Banks and ... tayllours, by us made in fourme folowyng that is to sey that eyther of the said parties shall first and formest before our master and wardyens aforeseid seale delyver to the other of them a generall acquitauns etc. and that doon we awarde that the seid ... shall seale and delyver for his dede to the said Cristofre an obligacion of hym bounde to the same Christofre in xs. payable xxd. quarterly till it be payde the first payment to begynne at Halowmesse next comyng. And also that eyther of the said parties shall be bounde by recognisauns to our said master and wardeyns in xxs. with condicion that if eyther of them have or speke herafter eny ungodely or inconvenyent langage by the other of them and therof a due proof be made that than he soo spekyng to forfeyt xxs. to the behoof of the almesse of the said ffelasship.

[f. 12v]

Veneris xiiij° die Augusti.

> John Dykke, son of Thomas Dykke, who was the apprentice of William Barough, brought in the copy of his freedom dated 15 February 4 Hen. VII [1488/9] and petitioned for a licence to open shop, which he has on payment of 10s.
> Item John Cruse[225] paid for William Maye 40d.
> Item paid to the almsmen of this fraternity for the quindene before the 17th day of August 5s. 8d.

Veneris ... die Augusti.[226]

> Thomas Blokley presented Robert Kyng and paid 40d.

Item Willelmus Brownyng electus est et juratus in unum xvj personarum ad gubernacionem de les Bachelers company assignatarum.
> [translation] Item William Brownyng was chosen and sworn as one of the 16 men appointed to govern the Bachelors' company.

---

[225] Cruse had been employed by the Great Wardrobe for 6¾ days prior to Richard III's coronation: *Coro. Richard III* ed. Sutton and Hammond, p. 330.
[226] Either the 21st or 28th.

Veneris iijº²²⁷ die Septembris.

William Shotteswold paid for John Dokeson 40*d*.
Item John Bigge, Robert Ingle, Lancelot Holme, and Richard Kyrkeby were sworn as wardens of the Bachelors of this mistery.
From Thomas Egerton for occupying foreigns 8*d*.
From Thomas Speight for Robert Wytter 40*d*.

[f. 13]

Veneris xº²²⁸ die Septembris.

Item William Swanston granted the terms of his apprentice, William Hugh, to William Hewlot, tailor, to remain with him until the end of the term and year specified in the indenture and the said William paid to the master in hand for the same 6*s*. 8*d*.
Item received from William Hewlot for ...
Item paid for the almsmen of this fraternity for the quindene before the feast of the Exaltation of the Holy Cross [14 Sept.] 5*s*. 8*d*.

Dies quarterii tentus sextodecimo die Septembris in presencia Magistri et custodum ac tocius communitatis hujus mistere.

This day the last will of John Churchman was read.

Item consideratum fuit per magistros et xxiiijᵒʳ quod Robertus Jacson qui fuit apprenticius Johannis Harryson dimitteretur a servicio suo pro eo probatum fuit quod idem apprenticius coloratus fuit²²⁹ etc. in scandalum evitandum etc.
[translation] Item it was considered by the masters and the 24 that Robert Jackson, who was the apprentice of John Harryson, should be dismissed from his service for it was proved that the same apprentice had concealed etc. to avoid scandal etc.

Item that Robert Greves is to pay a fine for his contemptuous behaviour towards James Grene and John Povy, brothers.²³⁰

---

²²⁷ An error for 'iiij'.
²²⁸ An error for 'xj'.
²²⁹ '*Colorare*', meaning to pass, cover up, gloss over or conceal, a fault etc.
²³⁰ 'Brothers' in the sense of 'brothers of the fraternity of St. John the Baptist', i.e. liverymen.

Item quod Alanus Hoberd et Walterus Povy pro secucionem facerent in billa versus forinsecos attempta.

[translation] Item that Alan Hoberd and Walter Povy might prosecute the attempted bill against foreigns.

Item it is ordained that the master for the time being should not spend more than £20 on repairs without licence to do so.

[f. 13v]

Item Robert Shakelton for his licence to open shop 10s.

Item John Lucas presented John Cork and paid 40d.

Item Richard Dakers presented John Fasset and paid 40d.

Item Hugh Hebbys through his servant presented John Gerard and paid 40d.

Item the master received from William Swanston for Thomas Robynson 40d.

Item from the same for a fine for concealing [the errors of?] an apprentice (pro coloracione apprenticii)[231] 10s.

Item paid to the almsmen for the quindene before the 28th day of September 5s. 8d.

Item paid to Geoffrey atte Welle, almsman, for Michaelmas term 10s.

Item paid for coals at the feast of St. Peter's Chains [1 Aug.] 5s.

Item received from Humfrey Trotte in part payment of his redemption 6s. 8d.

Item received from William Fletcher, who was the apprentice of Robert Faryngton, tailor, and who brought in the copy of his freedom dated 29 April 4 Hen. VII [1489] and petitioned for a licence to hold a shop, which was granted to him for 10s. paid in hand.

Item of William Barley for a fine for foreigns 4d.

Veneris ijº die Octobris.

Thomas Cheyney presented John a Bynkes and paid 40d.

Item William Mey settled with the master for his redemption for £3, of which he paid in hand 15s. and is to pay the residue on days specified by an obligation.

Item William a Barre was licensed to hold a shop and paid in hand 10s.

---

[231] See above, n. 229.

Item John Clerk and Thomas Dawes submitted themselves to the arbitration of William Howlet and Nicholas John, an award to be made by All Saints' day [1 Nov.] next.

[f. 14]

Lune v^to die Octobris.

Item paid to Sir[232] William[233] Cudworth for his salary for last Michaelmas term 35s.

Item paid to Sir Richard Wheler for his wages for the same term 33s. 4d.

Item paid to Sir John Burnam for his wages for the same term 16s. 8d.

Item to Sir Roger Doket for his wages for the same term 33s. 4d.

Item paid to William Hacomplayne, almsman, for the same term 5s.

Item paid to Thomas Hosyer, almsman, for the same term 10s.

Item paid to Sir Robert Cardemaker[234] for his wages for the half-year ending on the feast of St. Michael last £4.

Item paid to Christopher Kyrke for the same term 10s.

Item John Hynde presented Robert Atkynson and paid 40d.

Item paid to Robert ... almsman of this fraternity for the same term 10s.

Item cum diverse discordie arte existunt inter Johannem Nayler et Johannem Fayreford pro uno anulo per ipsum Fayreford de dicto Nayler empto adjudicatum fuit per M. Percyvale tunc locumtenentem magistri quod idem Johannes Nayler haberet xviijs. et solutum est et sic eque.

[translation] Item that divers trade disputes are pending between John Nayler and John Fayreford concerning a ring which the said Fayreford bought from the said Nayler. It was ruled by Master Percyvale, at that time master of this place, that the same John Nayler should have 18s. which was paid and thus he is quit.

Item paid to Thomas Grysyll beadle for his wages for his office and for the wardens of the craft 18s. 4d.

---

232 For this title see Glossary.
233 Error for Robert (see above p. 134).
234 Cardemaker replaced William Camell as chantry chaplain of Beatrice de Roos in St. Paul's. He served until Michaelmas term 1491, when he was replaced by Thomas Roos, and on 31 Aug. 1492 was appointed as rector of St. Mary Bothaw in London. G. Hennessey, *Novum Repertorium Ecclesiasticum Parochiale Londinense* (London, 1898), p. 390.

Veneris x°²³⁵ die Octobris.

Item John Alye paid in part payment of his redemption for Michaelmas term 5s.
From Thomas Richardson for William Lee 40d.
From William Tayweys for occupying foreigns 12d.
From Robert Serle for John Badger 40d.

[f. 14v]

Lune xij° die Octobris in presencia Magistri et custodum ac Swan, Percyvale, Pemberton, West, Lee, Buk, Stodard, Galle, Hoberd, Povy, Bowghton, Fitz, Randyll, Martyn, Wilford.²³⁶

Item paid to the prioress of Kilburn for a quit-rent arising from tenements in Abchurch Lane, formerly belonging to Elene Langwith,²³⁷ for half a year to the feast of Michaelmas 8s. 6d.
Item paid to the same for a quit-rent arising from tenements in Bread Street 6s. 8d.
Item received from certain foreigns 8d.
Item paid to Sir John Radclyf for his wages 33s. 4d.
Item paid to the almsmen of this fraternity for the past quindene 5s. 8d.
Item that Robert Grevys is to pay for disobedience towards James Grene and John Povy 10s.

Veneris xvj° die Octobris.

Jacobus Grene et Robertus Johnson arbitratores inter Willelmum a Lye et Johannem Iryssh arbitraverunt quod dictus Willelmus deliberabit dicto Johannis omnes pecias panni lanei per ipsum Johannem nuper cissas in aptacione unius toge muliebris etc. Et quod dictus Johannis solvet eidem Willelmo in recompensacione dampni sui etc. vs. iijd. Et eo facto quod uterque eorum acquietabit etc. alium eorum de omnibus accionibus.

[translation] James Grene and Robert Johnson, arbiters between William a Lye and John Iryssh have awarded that the said William shall deliver to the said John all those pieces of woollen cloth that the said John lately cut for shaping a woman's gown etc. And that the said John

---

²³⁵ An error for 'ix'.
²³⁶ James Wilford's first appearance on the court after his service as warden: see Appendix IV.
²³⁷ See above n. 63.

should pay to the said William in recompense of his losses 5s. 3d. And that each should make an acquittance to the other of all actions etc.

Item Christopher Bankes presented William Morton and paid 40d.
Item paid for a barge for the presentation of the sheriffs at Westminster on the morrow of Michaelmas 13s. 4d.
Item paid for drink for the boatmen 20d.
Item received from Christofer Bankes for William Morton 40d.

[f. 15]

Lune xix° die Octobris.

Item Master Materdale presented John Kelly and paid 40d.
Item the same presented Robert Marche and paid 40d.
Item paid to the 'masters de lez lokes'[238] for a quit-rent 13s. 4d.
Item paid to the mayor for a gift as on previous occasions 40s.

Item Thomas Martyn et Thomas Howdan arbitratores inter Willelmum Shotteswold et Willelmum Asshwell de et super omnibus etc. arbitraverunt in hac forma videlicet first we awarde that eyther of the said parties shall seale and delyver to the other of them in the presence of our m[aister] and wardeyns a generall acquitaunce of all maters etc. and that doon we awarde that that the said William Shotteswold shall delyver to the said William Asshwell a gowne that the said W.S. gave to the said W.A. Item we awarde that the said William Asshwell nowe forthwith shall entre into the service of the said William Shotteswold and so shall contynue from this day unto Mighelmas next comyng and that by all the said tyme the same W.A. shall diligently serve to his said m[aister] W.S. all rankours stryves bytwene them to be leyde apart. And that the said William Shotteswold shall pay to the said William Asshwell for his wages by all the same tyme xls. to be payde quarterly at iiij the next pryncipall termes of the yere. And that the said William Asshwell in the presence of our said master and wardeyns shall beseche the said William Shotteswold to be his good master and to submytte hym self as a servaunt owth for to doo and to aske forgevenes all false ungodely langage as he hath ayenst the said W.S.

---

[238] The Lock hospital in Southwark, one of 4 leper hospitals outside the capital, was situated on the stream between St. George's parish and Newington: VCH, *Surrey*, II (1905), pp. 124–5, IV (1967), p. 162; Honeybourne, 'Leper Hospitals', pp. 44–54.

Veneris xxiij° die Octobris.

Item paid for the obit of John Halygate and Idonea his wife, held in the church of St. Martin Outwich, London 6s. 8d.
Item received from Thomas Brokton for Thomas Lynton 40d.
Item received from John Broughton for Thomas Clerk 40d.
Item received from John Nicholas for Robert Holme 40d.
Item received from Robert Ferrour in full payment of his opening 2s. 6d.
Item [from] Richard Hylle for disobedience 5s.
Item received from Henry Alisaunder for Alan Lambe 40d.
Item received from the same for William Metcalf 40d.
Item Richard Frecok, son of John Frecok formerly of this mistery, for his admission 4s. 8d.
Item from Philip Davy for arrears of his redemption 10s.
Item John Combes presented William Donatson and paid 40d.

[f. 15v]

Lune xxv°[239] die Octobris.

Item the master paid to the almsmen of this fraternity for the past quindene 5s. 8d.
Item paid to the wardens of the chapel of St. Mary in St. Paul's Cathedral[240] for a quit-rent 5s.
Item the master received from John Newenton for his licence to open a shop 10s.
Item paid for the obit of Master Stone[241] in the church of St. John the Evangelist 26s. 8d.

Veneris xxx° die Octobris.

Item John Flemmyng presented Roger Kyrton and paid 40d.

---

239 An error for 'xxvj'.
240 Probably the Lady Chapel in the cathedral: Dugdale, *St. Paul's*, pp. 13–14. This quit-rent is elsewhere listed as having been paid to the dean or just to 'St. Paul's'.
241 John Stone: see above, n. 38.

Veneris vij²⁴² die Novembris.

Nicholas John presented Nicholas Dawsyng and paid 40d.
Thomas Greves was admitted as a shop-holder and is to pay 5s. at
Christmas and 5s. at the feast of the Annunciation [25 Mar.]

Lune ix° die Novembris in presencia Magistri et custodum ac Percyvale, Stodard, West, Keys, Galle, Hoberd, Spencer, Povy, Boughton, Adyf, Fitz.

Item it is granted that the master may repair the lands and tenements of
this fraternity to the sum of £10 above the sum of £20 specified in the
ordinance concerning repairs.²⁴³

Item that our tenement called the Saracen's Head²⁴⁴ is in a great state of
ruin, and that since Richard Dyngley intends to hold the same house, he
should pay a rent of 10 marks a year, and the sum of 40 marks in
advance for repairs to the said tenement.

Item paid to the almsmen of this fraternity for the past quindene 5s. 8d.
Item paid for coals distributed to the almsmen 6s.

[f. 16] Genyns

Veneris xiij° die Novembris.

Item the master paid to the master of the house of St. Giles for a
quit-rent issuing from tenements in the parish of St. Mary Abchurch,
formerly belonging to Elene Langwith, for the year ending at the feast
of St. Michael last 14s.
Item paid to the same for a quit-rent issuing from tenements in
Garlickhithe for the same term 23s.
Item the master received from Stephen Eburton for his excessive words
towards Robert Shakelton 20d.
Item received from the said Robert Shakelton for his excessive words
towards the said Stephen 20d.
Item the master licensed Christopher Braunton, late the apprentice of
Roger Warynges, to hold a shop and he paid in hand 10s.

---

²⁴² An error for 'vj'.
²⁴³ See above, p. 139.
²⁴⁴ See above, pp. 18–19.

Item William Swanston presented George Spotte his apprentice and paid
Item paid for a barge to attend upon the mayor 13s. 4d.
Item paid for drink for the boatmen 16d.

Lune xvj° die Novembris.

Item received from Thomas Rubton for working in his chamber contrary to the ordinance 2s.[245]

Veneris xx° die Novembris.

Nicholas John and William Howlet arbiters between John Clerk and John and Thomas Dawes award that the said John Clerk, in full payment of all moneys owed by him should pay 13s. 4d. in the following manner, namely at Christmas 4s., at Easter 4s., and at Pentecost 5s. 4d. and that the said John should be bound etc.

Item paid to the master of St. Katherine's Hospital for a quit-rent 10s.
Item John Broughton presented Richard Wilford and paid 40d.
Item John Davy, late the apprentice of Thomas Tromy, brought in the copy of his freedom dated 1 April 7 Hen. VII [1492][246] and petitioned for a licence to open shop for which he paid in hand 5s. and is to pay the residue at Christmas. The copy of his freedom was given as a pledge.
Item John Davy presented James Kyngsey and paid in hand 40d.

[f. 16v]

Lune xxiij° die Novembris.

Item paid to the almsmen of this fraternity for the past quindene 5s. 8d.
Item Robert Bolton presented James Archer and paid 40d.

Item for makyng a newe gowne taken of a foren iiijd.

---

[245] This may refer to an ordinance of 1450 which sought to prevent freemen from working in attic rooms or chambers, away from the scrutiny of the wardens of the craft. Such men were known as 'chambur holders': GL, Merchant Taylors' Co., Misc. Docs. A.2., f. 10.
[246] Error, possibly for 4 Hen. VII [1490].

Item the M. and wardeyns have ordeyned and adjuged that thawarde before made bytwene William Shotteswold and Will Ashwell shall be sette aparte and that the said William Asshwell shall serve the said William S. unto the feest of Cristemas next comyng and to take for his wages ij*s*. et hoc factum est cum assensu dicti W.S.[247]

Veneris iiij^{to} die Decembris.

Item the master paid to the prior of St. Mary Overey for a quit-rent arising from tenements in the parish of St. Martin Outwich 8*s*.

Item paid to the chamber of St. Peter's Westminster for a quit-rent arising from tenements in Friday Street 10*s*.

Item paid of a tenement in the parish of St. Mary Colechurch for a quit-rent 4*s*. 6*d*.

Item the master received from Edmund Gerard for his licence to open shop 10*s*.

Item Thomas Hore presented Richard Tayllour and paid 40*d*.

Item received from Thomas Person for 'settyng over'[248] John Langryk his apprentice 6*s*. 8*d*.[249]

Item received from the same for William Shawdeford his apprentice 40*d*.

Item from John Barbour who did not enroll his apprentice within a year etc. 20*d*.

Item William Swanston presented George Spotte and paid 40*d*.

Item paid to William Duryvale for his wages for Christmas term 25*s*.

Item paid to Thomas Gresyll for his wages for the same term 18*s*. 4*d*.

[f. 17]

Lune vij die Decembris.

Item Ranulph Newell presented Robert ... his apprentice and paid 40*d*.

Item paid to the almsmen of this fraternity for the past quindene 5*s*. 8*d*.

Item paid to Hassok, bargeman, for his barge for the encounter with the Prince (*ad obviandum Principem*)[250] 13*s*. 4*d*.

---

[247] See above, p. 142.

[248] See Glossary.

[249] The high level of the fine suggests that this was not a temporary suspension of the apprenticeship but a 'settyng over', or transfer, to another master.

[250] The event referred to is almost certainly the ceremonial surrounding the creation

Item paid for a kilderkin of ale 2s.
Item paid for bread, rushes and the hiring of boats 8d.

Item paid to Sir[251] Richard Wheler for Christmas term 33s. 4d.
Item paid to Sir Richard Burnam for his wages 16s. 8d.

Veneris xij[252] die Decembris.

Item paid to Sir Roger Doget for his wages for the aforesaid term 33s. 4d.
Item paid to Sir John Radclyf for the aforesaid term 33s. 4d.

Lune xiiij° die Decembris.

Item paid for the obit of Thomas Carleton in the chapel of St. John the Evangelist[253] the 12th day of December 10s.

Item Willelmus Bryan qui fuit apprenticius Rogeri Shavelok qui quidem Rogerus obiit intestatus peciit intrari in papirum istius fraternitatis pro eo quod non presentabatur ante hec tempora per dictum Rogerum in vita et ei conceditur etc. Et ulterius peciit licenciam serviendi cum aliquo alio libero istius fraternitatis usque ad finem termini sui iam venturi et in ei concessa etc.
[translation] Item William Bryan, late the apprentice of Roger Shavelok, petitioned that, for as much as the said Roger died intestate, and because he was not presented before this time by the said Roger while alive, he should be entered in the book of this fraternity. And this should be granted to him etc. And finally he petitioned for a licence to serve with another freeman of this fraternity until the end of his term still remaining, and this is granted to him etc.[254]

---

of Prince Arthur (b. 1486) as Prince of Wales. On 29 November 1489 the young Prince travelled by barge from Sheen to Chelsea where he was met by the mayor, aldermen and guilds of London and on to Lambeth where the ambassadors of Spain greeted him: Anglo, *Spectacle*, p. 52.

251 For this title see Glossary.
252 An error for 'xj'.
253 The Tailors' chapel in St. Paul's Cathedral was in fact dedicated to St. John the Baptist: see Davies, thesis, esp. pp. 18–20.
254 According to the author of the Great Chronicle, Shavelok 'kut his awne throte', leaving a draper's shop containing cloth and other goods worth more than 1,000 marks. His career to that point had been a successful one: he was apprenticed to Thomas Gresill in 1455–6 and had completed his training and established a business of his own within ten years. He was admitted as a liveryman in 1469–70:

147

Veneris xviij die Decembris.

Item John Doget presented Richard Case and paid 40*d*.
Item paid to Christopher Kyrke almsman for this term 10*s*.
Item Thomas Patynson presented George ad Wren 40*d*.
Item from the same for ocupying foreigns 4*d*.
Item from Hugh Bercher foreign 8*d*.
Item Robert Catelyn was licensed to open shop and paid 10*s*.
Item paid for a key 4*d*.
Item [from] John Belle for Robert Gylberd his apprentice 40*d*.
Item John Warner for William White not enrolled 4*d*.
Item paid to the prioress of Clerkenwell for a quit-rent arising from tenements in Colechurch for half a year ending at Michaelmas 3*s*. 4*d*.
Item paid to Geoffrey atte Welle almsman of this fraternity for the same term 11*s*. 8*d*.
Item paid to William Hacomplaynt almsman for the same term 5*s*.
Item paid to the almsmen of this fraternity for the quindene before St. Thomas's day next 5*s*. 8*d*.
Item from William Tate foreign 8*d*.
Item [from] John Tayllour for working in his chamber[255] 4*d*.

Item paid to Robert Cudworth for his salary 35*s*.
Item paid to Thomas Hosyer for the same term 11*s*. 8*d*.
Item paid as a reward to John Smyth, viewer 40*s*.

[f. 18]
Termino Natalis Domini

Veneris xiiij°[256] die Januarii[257]

Hugh Gybson presented William Orfor his apprentice 40*d*.
Item James Harryson presented Nicholas Snell and paid 40*d*.
Item paid for 13 quarters of coals distributed for the soul of John Creke 5*s*. 11½*d*.
Item paid for 13 quarters of coals for the soul of Elene Langwith 5*s*. 11½*d*.[258]

Great Chronicle, eds Thomas and. Thornley, pp. 243-4; Accounts, I, f. 3v, II, ff. 62, 274v.

[255] See above, n. 245.
[256] An error for 'xv'.
[257] 1489/90.
[258] For Creek and Langwith see above, nn. 63, 148.

Item Thomas Walker came to this place and petitioned to have the freedom of this fraternity which was granted to him, and he paid to have the said freedom £3

Item Roger Butrode, son of Hugh Butrode of Yorkshire, deceased, who was the apprentice of John Pyers, brought in a copy of his freedom dated 15 January 22 Ed. IV [1482/3], in the time of Edmund Shaa mayor, and paid for his licence in part payment 4s. 8d. and 5s. 4d. [Total] 10s.

John Reynold was sworn as the clerk of the fraternity of the Bachelors' company.

Lune xviij die Januarii.

From Herman Wylde bocher[259] for making new work 4d.
From Richard Crofte for Ranulph Palmer 40d.
From William Hewelot for Robert Strother 40d.
Item paid to the almsmen of this fraternity for the quindene before the 4th day of January 5s. 8d.
Item paid to the same for the quindene before the 18th day of January 5s. 8d.

Veneris xxij° die Januarii.

William Ager of the parish of St. Andrew by the Wardrobe was admitted into the freedom of this mistery by redemption for £4 [of which he paid] in hand 15s. and [is to pay] on the Nativity of St. John [the Baptist] [24 June] 15s. and at each half year thereafter 6s. 8d.

Item Rowland a Maugham brought in a copy of his freedom dated ... January 5 Hen. VII [1489/90] and petitioned for a licence to hold a shop, which was granted to him, and he paid in hand 10s.

Item Richard Grove and Thomas Skydmore submitted themselves, on a bond of 40s., to the rule of John Stoyle and Richard Bothom, arbiters, an award to be made by the first Sunday in Lent.

Item Edmund Floure agreed to pay 30s. in hand for his redemption.

---

259 A repairer of old clothes. During the fifteenth century the Tailors allowed immigrants, including aliens such as Wylde, to practice as tailors as long as they confined their activities to the second-hand market: see Glossary.

[f. 18v]

Dies quarterii tentus die Veneris[260] xxv° die Januarii in presencia Magistri et custodum ac Swan, Percyvale, Tego, Galle, West, Materdale, Keys, Deplech, Lee, Hede, Buk, Hoberd, Spencer, Povy ac omnium aliorum istius cometive etc.

This day the last wills of John Churchman and Hugh Champernoun were read according to the precedents.[261]

Veneris xxix° die Januarii.

From Richard Hille for John Dey 40*d*.

Mercurii iij° die Februarii in presencia Magistri et custodum ac Stodard, Galle, Keys, West, Pemberton, Deplech, Lee, Hoberd, Adyf, Randyll, Wilford.

Item forasmoch a grete cryme and defamacion renneth upon this fraternytie by cause that sum persones of this felaship excede in ther behavour and demeanyng amonges men of worship and other honest persones and namely at Blakwellhall amonges which Robert Greves ys one. And therfore this day the said Robert beyng called to this place and examyned of the premisses hath knoweched hym self to be bounde to this place in xl*li*. that he shall from hensforth shall be of honest demeanyng in bying and sellyng aswell in the said place or elleswhere.
Item in lyke wise Roger Mone beyng examyned and called to this place for lyke maner thyng hath graunted in lyke wise to be bounden to this place to be of good and honest demeaner in bying and sellyng etc. ut supra under the peyne of xl*li*. for every defaulte.

[f. 19]

Veneris v^to die Februarii.

---

[260] This may be an error for '*Lune xxv Januarii*', although quarter-days were normally held on Wednesdays.
[261] See above, nn. 40, 129.

Item William Patenson came here this day and petitioned for a licence to open shop and it was granted to him and he paid in hand 10s.
Item Henry Dakyns came here the same day and petitioned for a licence etc. and paid in hand 5s.

Lune viij° die Februarii.

Robert Barker presented Thomas Benet and paid 40d.
Item from the same for not presenting the aforesaid apprentice 12d.
Item George Harryson came here and petitioned for a licence to hold a shop and paid in hand 10s.

Veneris xij die Februarii.

From John Hynde for James Blande 40d.
From Richard Smyth for Henry Levered 40d.
From John Gatford for Silvester Crakenthorpe 40d.
From the same for not presenting him 4d.

Item Thomas Ethell and John Copelond submitted themselves to the arbitration of Robert Kelham on all causes which took place or were pending between them before Monday, provided this occurs before Septuagesima Sunday (*diem dominicam in Carniprevio*) [14 Feb.] next, on pain for each of 40s.

From William Cok for Alexander Turnebull 40d.
From Edmund Brittowe for William Kyrkhous 40d.
Item George Salle petitioned for a licence to hold a shop and paid 10s.
Item John Willyngham was licensed and paid 6s. 8d. in hand and afterwards paid 40d. and thus paid in total 10s.

Lune xv° die Februarii.

Item Thomas Warde made an agreement with the master concerning his shop opening and paid in hand 10s.
Item the master paid to the almsmen of this fraternity for the quindene before the 15th day of February 5s. 8d.

[f. 19v]

Veneris xix° die Februarii

> From John Reynold for Richard Lynet 40*d*.
> From William Polgrave for employing foreigns 20*d*.

Item Robertus Kellam arbitravit inter Thomam Ethell et Johannem Copelond in hac forma videlicet first I awarde that eyther of the said parties shall take the other of them by the hande and to desyre that good love may be had bytwene them from hensforth. Item I awarde that the said John Copelond in full payment of all and singuler dueties and soms of money as the said Thomas Ethell claymeth of the said John Copelond.

> Item Edmund Floure presented John Harrop and paid in hand 40*d*.
> From Robert Hertyshern for Ambrosius Bredeman 40*d*.

Veneris xxvj die Februarii.

> Item William Tetworth presented John Smyth and paid 40*d*.

Item we Richard Bothom and John Stoyle arbitrours electe bytwene Richard Grove and Thomas Ferne otherwise called Skydmore make our awarde bytwene them in the fourme folowyng that is to sey first we awarde that eyther of the said partes shall seale to the other of them a generall acquytaunce of all maner maters. And that doon we awarde that the said Thomas shall pay to the said Richard v*s*. in this wise that is to sey ij*s*. vj*d*. at Ester and ij*s*. vj*d*. at Penticost
Item [we] awarde that eyther of the said parties shall take the other by the hande in the presence of the master and wardens and that if eyther of them eny tyme herafter revile, rebuke and shlaunder the other of them that than he of them so doying shall pay vj*s*. viij*d*. to our crafte for a fyne.
And afterward it was adjuged by John Spencer, m[aister] and his wardens that for the more ease of the said Thomas the same Thomas shall pay the said v*s*. wekely iiij*d*. tyll it be payde this beyng adjuged the xxviij day of Juyn.

> Item from William Norton for Henry Broun 40*d*.
> Item from a foreign 6*d*.

[f. 20]

152

Lune primo die Marcii.[262]

Item paid for the obit of John Creke held in the church of St. Mary Abchurch the first Sunday of Lent [28 Feb.] For bread and wine 17d., for offerings 2d., to the rector 6d., for three chaplains 12d., for two clerks 8d., for candles 12d. Total 4s. 9d.

Item paid to the almsmen of this fraternity for the past quindene 5s. 8d.

Item paid for coals distributed to the almsmen 5s.

Veneris v^to die Marcii.

Item paid to the prioress of Clerkenwell for a quit-rent arising from tenements in the parish of St. Mary Colechurch for the year ending at Christmas 13s. 4d.

Item Robert Asshton, foreign, paid for a fine 6d.

Item Roger Clay presented Thomas Wylkynson and paid 40d.

Lune viij° die Marcii.

Edward Robson granted the terms of Andrew Chesham his apprentice to John Morton, citizen and tailor of London, to remain with him from the present day until the end of the term specified in the indenture. And the aforesaid John has agreed to pay for the same apprentice 40s., of which 13s. 4d. is to go to the alms [of the fraternity] and 26s. 8d. to the aforesaid Edward. And 20s. of the said sum of 40s. is to be paid at Easter [11 Apr.] and 20s. at Pentecost [30 May]. And he is to be bound by obligation to the master. And at the end of the term the said Edward is to acknowledge the service of the said apprentice before the City Chamber.

Item Willelmus Asshwell peciit libertatem tenendi shopam et soluit xs. et monstravit copiam etc. libertatis sue per quam apparet quod dictus Willelmus xxij die Junii anno regni regis Henrici vij quarto tempore Roberti Tate maioris et Willelmi Purches camerarii civitatis London et [sic] intratur in libro cum litera J. de empcione libertatis.

[translation] Item William Asshwell petitioned for a licence to hold a shop and paid 10s. and he showed the copy of his freedom by which it appears that on the 22nd day of June 4 Hen. VII [1489], in the time of Robert Tate, mayor, and William Purchas, chamblerlain of the city of

---

[262] 'Februarii' is crossed out in the text.

London, the said William was entered into book J of freedom purchases.[263]

[f. 20v]

Veneris xij die Marcii.

Alanus Bolton qui preantea fuit in occupacione de lez foysters venit hic et peciit ut M. et gardiani dignarentur accipere illum in libertatem istius mistere et quod translaretur a dicta occupacione de Foystres in hanc misteram et ei concessum est et dictus Alanus concessit solvere pro hac mutacione xxs. videlicet ad Nativitatis Johannis xs. et ad Natalem Domini proxim' xs.

> [translation] Alan Bolton who formerly occupied the craft of fusters[264] came here and petitioned that the master and wardens should condescend to accept him into the freedom of this mistery and that he should translate from the said art of Fusters into this mistery, and it is granted to him and the said Alan agreed to pay 20s. for this translation, namely 10s. at the Nativity of St. John [24 June] and 10s at Christmas next.

From David Johnson for Maurice Meredeth 40d.

Lune xv° die Marcii.

Item paid to the almsmen of this fraternity for the quindene before the present day 5s. 8d.
Item John Batyson presented John Broun as his apprentice 40d.
Item Richard Seymer presented Robert Moreys and paid 40d.
Item William Domesday who was the apprentice of Richard Seymer brought in the copy of his freedom dated the 9th day of October 5 Hen. VII [1489] and petitioned for the right to hold a shop, which was granted to him and he paid in hand 10s.

---

[263] In other words Ashwell obtained his Freedom by redemption (by paying an entry fee) rather than through apprenticeship. The medieval records of the chamberlains of London were destroyed in a fire in the Chamber of the Guildhall in 1786: see *Chamber Accounts of the Sixteenth Century*, ed. B. R. Masters, London Record Society, 20 (1984), p. ix.

[264] Fusters were makers of wooden saddle-trees, and in London members of this craft were frequently in dispute with the Saddlers themselves: e.g. *Cal. Letter Bk. K*, p. 37.

Veneris xix° die Marcii.

Item paid to Sir[265] Richard Wheler for the term of the Annunciation 33s. 4d.
Item paid to Thomas Hosyer, almsman, for the same term 11s. 8d.
Item paid to Sir John Burnam for the same term 16s. 8d.
Item paid to Geoffrey atte Welle for the same term 11s. 8d.
Item paid to Thomas Gresyll for the same term 18s. 4d.
Item paid to William Duryvale, clerk, for the same term 25s.
Item paid to Christopher Kyrke, almsman, for the same term 10s.

Lune xxij die Marcii.

Item paid to Sir John Radclyf for the same term 33s. 4d.
Item paid to William Hacomplaynt, almsman of this fraternity, for the same term 5s.
Item paid to Sir Roger Doket for the same term 33s. 4d.

[f. 21]

**Mercurii xxiiij^to die Marcii in presencia Magistri et custodum ac Swan, ...,
Tego, Stodard, Galle, Deplech, Pemberton, Keys, West, Lee, Buk,
Hoberd, Spencer, Randyll, Adyf, Fitz, Warner,[266] Brounflete[267] et Wilford.**

This day Master Galle, Master Pemberton and John Spencer were chosen to arbitrate upon all matters between Master West, Thomas Randyll, William Grene and Ralph Bukberd.

Item it is ordained that the master should determine for the repair and building of the inn called 'Le Saresyns [Hede]' etc.
And William Galle, John Lee, John Bernard and Thomas Martyn were appointed as supervisors of the rebuilding of the same inn.[268]

---

[265] For this title see Glossary.
[266] For Oliver Warner see Appendix IV.
[267] Thomas Bromeflete (or Bromefeld): see Appendix IV.
[268] Further details of the rebuilding of this property are contained in the company's treasury accounts which cover the period 1489–1503 and are printed in Clode, *Memorials*, pp. 69–92.

Veneris xxvj^{to} die Marcii.

Item Oliver Warner presented John Stubbes and paid 40*d*.
Item John Harper for ... 40*d*.
Item Ralph Traford presented Gilbert Owen 40*d*.

Lune [x]xix die Marcii in presencia Magistri et custodum ac M. Swan, Percyvale, Tego, Barlowe, Pemberton, Deplech, Hede, Hoberd, Spencer, Povy, Adyf, Randyll, Fytz, Martyn, Wilford.

Item it is ordained that the aforesaid Master Galle, Master Pemberton, John Spencer and Walter Povy are to arbitrate upon all matters between the said Master West, Thomas Randyll, William Grene and Ralph Bukberd with the assent and supervision of Master Swan, Master Percyvale and Master Jenyns.

Item paid to the almsmen of this fraternity for the past quindene 5*s*. 8*d*.
Item paid to Robert Boylet almsman of this fraternity for the said term 10*s*.

Veneris ij^{do} die Aprilis.

Item Geoffrey Mone presented Thomas a Lee his apprentice and paid 40*d*.
Item Robert Debenham presented Thomas Yenson and paid 40*d*.
Item Thomas Randyll presented William Traps and paid 40*d*.
Item the same Thomas presented Jeremy Edlyn and paid 40*d*.
Item Nicholas Glossop was licensed to hold a shop and paid 10*s*.

[f. 21v]

Mercurii vij^o die Aprilis in presencia Magistri et custodum ac Swan, Percyvale, Pemberton, Galle, Spencer et Povy.

Ralph Grene came here and petitioned for the freedom of this mistery and it was granted to him for the sum of £3 to be paid in this manner, namely 30*s*. before the feast of the Nativity of St. John the Baptist next [24 June] and 30*s*. at the feast of the Nativity of St John the Baptist 1491.

Item this day a finall ende and accorde was made by the said masters bitwene Thomas Randyll and Rauf Bukberd of and upon all maner maters and causes dependyng bytwene them in eny wise before this day and therupon it is specially awarded that all thyngs bytwene them dependyng to be sette aparte.

Lune xix die Aprilis.

Item paid to the almsmen of this fraternity for the quindene before the 12th day of April 5s. 8d.
Item Nicholas John presented John Martyn and paid 40d.
Item from Charles Caryngton for an apprentice not presented 6d.
Item Richard Bothom presented John Judson and paid 40d.

Lune xxvj die Aprilis.

Item received from William Harryson in full payment of his redemption 20s.
Item paid to the prioress of Kilburn 8s. 6d.
Item from Richard Tofte for Nicholas Forde 40d.
Item paid to the almsmen of this fraternity for the past quindene 5s. 8d.

[f. 22]

Mercurii v^to die Maii Dies quarterii tentus in presencia M. Percyvale, Galle, Pemberton, Keys, Deplech, Materdale, Hede, Buk, Hoberd, Spencer, Povy, Randyll, Fitz, Bromflete ac tocius communitatis hujus mistere.

Ordained on this day:
First that Robert Rede, serjeant-at-law,[269] was admitted as a brother of this fraternity without payment.
Item Reynold Bray, knight,[270] should be admitted as a brother of this fraternity without charge.

---

[269] Robert Rede (d. 1519) of Kent and London was a prominent lawyer who was admitted to Lincoln's Inn in 1467 and became a serjeant-at-law in 1486. For details of his legal career see Ives, *Common Lawyers*, pp. 474–5.

[270] For the career of Sir Reynold Bray (d. 1503), steward to Lady Margaret Beaufort, knight of the body to Henry VII, and chancellor of the duchy of Lancaster see Wedgwood, *History of Parliament*, 104–5; M. M. Condon, 'From Caitiff and Villain to Pater Patrice: Reynold Bray and the Profits of Office', in *Profit, Piety*

Item Philip Lewes, esquire, [271] was admitted as a brother of this fraternity.

Item where as in tyme past it hath ben used and accustumed that the brethern of this ffraternitie yerely the morne after mydsomer day shuld pay ther duetie for ther mete and almes in the cloystre wherby sum persones goyng there forth have spoken and sayde sum wordes soundyng rather to dishonour than to worship wherfore it is ordeyned that brethern of this felasship from hensforth shall pay their dueties aforesayd the morne after Mydsomer day [24 June] in this place and not in the said cloystre as it hath be used before.

Also where as in tyme past it hath ben used and accustumed in this place that at the quarterday comonly holden next before the fest of the Nativitie of Saynt John Baptist [24 June] that such brethern as shuld be admitted in to this fraternytie shuld be admitted at the same quarterday and where also at the same day sum persones have bene admitted in to the fraternytie have bene in substaunce of goodes as it hath bene supposed wherby they have lytely fallen into the almes of this fraternytie to the grete charge of the same fraternytie. Wherefore it is ordeyned that from hensforth there shall be noo persone admitted into this fraternytie but at such tyme as the hole lyvere shall be geven in this fraternytie. Except that if eny persone of this fraternytie be marryed to eny maistres or wardeyns wif in this craft or that he be promoted by maryage of eny other woman oute of the felasship or otherwise which persone so promoted by maryage or otherwise shall than be admitted into the clothyng by the discression of the master, wardens and xxiiij men of this crafte or the more part of them.

Item eodem die persone subscripte admissi sunt in confratres istius fraternitatis non obstante quod liberata non datur hoc anno juxta ordinacionem predictam qui ambo iidem fratres nupcerunt uxores qui preantea fuerunt uxores gardianorum juxta ordinacionem predictam

    Willelmus Fitzwilliam jur'

    Edmundus Floure jur'

---

and the Professions in Later Medieval England ed. M. A. Hicks (Gloucester, 1990), pp. 137-68; D. J. Guth, 'Climbing the Civil-Service Pole during Civil War: Sir Reynold Bray (c.1440-1503)', in *Estrangement, Enterprise and Education in Fifteenth-Century England*, eds. S. D. Michalove and A. Compton Reeves (Stroud, 1998), pp. 47-61. The admission of Bray was in keeping with the Tailors' long-standing policy of admitting prominent figures in government and the church to their fraternity: see Davies, 'Charity', pp. 166-7 and *idem*, thesis, pp. 27-47.

[271] Almost certainly Philip Lewis, lieutenant of the Cinque Ports 1476-92, for whose career see Wedgwood, *History of Parliament*, p. 539.

[translation] Item the same day the following persons were admitted as brethren of this fraternity, notwithstanding that the livery is not being granted this year according to the aforesaid ordinance, as both brethren were married to wives who were formerly the wives of wardens according to the aforesaid ordinance.

William Fitzwilliam[272] sworn

Edmund Floure[273] sworn

[f. 22v]

Veneris vij° die Maii.

William Rubton, son of William Rubton of Cockermouth in Cumberland, yeoman, came here and petitioned for a licence to hold a

---

[272] Following his admission to the livery Fitzwilliam was chosen warden of the company in 1494 and 1498 and was master for 1499–1500. He became a merchant of the Calais staple and was alderman for Broad Street from 1503–11. His candidacy for the shrievalty in 1506 was rejected, probably as a consequence of his role in securing the company's controversial charter of January 1502/3; he secured the post only through the intervention of Henry VII. In 1510 the mayor and aldermen required him to serve for a second term as a demonstration of their unhappiness with the earlier election. He refused and was deprived of the freedom and fined 1,000 marks. These punishments were overturned by the Star Chamber July 1511 but Fitzwilliam chose to leave the city and enter the service of his patron, Cardinal Wolsey, becoming the latter's treasurer and high chamberlain. Lived first at his estates at Chigwell, Essex (sheriff of the county 1513, 1515) and then at Milton, Northants. Knighted 1515. Sheriff Northants. 1523–4, 1528–9. Settled 1200 marks upon the Merchant Taylors' Company May 1533 which was used to fund services in Crowland Abbey and four almshouses at Marholm, Northants. Died in the summer of 1534 and was buried in Marholm church. The first of his three wives was Anne, daughter of John Hawes, mercer and alderman, and it is presumably her status as a widow of a master or warden that enabled Fitzwilliam to enter the livery on this occasion. For his biography see the *Dictionary of National Biography* (and esp. the revised article in the forthcoming *New DNB*); Clode, *Early History*, vol. 2, pp. 39–53;

[273] Floure became warden of the company in 1495 and 1499 and was chosen as master for 1503–4. Exported cloth through the port of London with Stephen Jenyns (see Appendix IV) Jan. 1506. Will dated 11 July and proved 13 Aug. 1521. Buried in Cuckfield church, Sussex where 'at certeine yeris past' he had founded a grammar school. The endowment of the school was purchased later that year and increased in 1528. His wife had predeceased him and her identity and that of her first husband are not recorded. Hopkinson, *Ancient Records*, pp. 114, 116; PRO, PROB 11/20, ff. 56v–58; VCH *Sussex*, II (1905), pp. 416–21.

shop, and showed his copy dated 21 April 5 Hen. VII [1490], which was granted to him and he paid in hand 10s.

Item William Wotton who remains with William Fletcher made an agreement with the master for his redemption for £3, of which he paid in hand 13s. 4d. and is to pay 6s. 8d. in the week after Pentecost [30 May], 20s. at Christmas, 20s. at the feast of the Nativity of St. John the Baptist [24 June]. Item he paid for his payment at Pentecost 6s. 8d. Item for Christmas term 20s.

Lune x° die Maii in presencia M. et custodum ac M. Percyvale, Galle, Barlowe, Pemberton, Hede, Deplech, Keys, Lee, Buk, Hoberd, Povy, Randyll, Bromeflete.

Item paid for the obit of Ralph Basset, Gerard Braybroke and Hugh Shelley knights,[274] held in the church of St. Martin. For bread 6d., for ale 8d., for cheese 7d., for an offering 4d., to the rector 6d., for 4 other chaplains 16d., to the clerk of the church 8d., for candles 12d., for alms 13d. Total [6s. 8d.]

Item it [is] accorded bytwene the M. and the crafte and Simond Byrlyngham and John Benkes carpenters that the same carpenters shall bylde newe the Saresyns Hede[275] accordyng to a patron[276] therof to be made by endentours and the said carpenters shall have for ther labour and all maner stuff of tymber and bourde cc*li*. in this wise that is to sey ...

Item paid to Sir[277] Robert Cardemaker for Easter term, that is to say for half a year £4.
Item paid to the almsmen of this fraternity for the past quindene 5s. 8d.

Lune xviij[278] die Maii.

John Bode presented Thomas Dyson and paid 40d.
The same John Bode presented William Shepperd and paid 40d.
Item Thomas Robertson paid in part payment for his opening 6s. 8d.

---

274 See above, n. 32.
275 See above, pp. 18–19.
276 An architect's design or plan: *OED*.
277 For this title see Glossary.
278 An error for 'xvij'.

[f. 23]

Lune xxiiij^{to} die Maii.

Item paid to the almsmen of this fraternity for the past quindene 5s. 8d.

Veneris xxviij° die Maii.

Item Richard Seymer presented Edward Belle and paid 40d.
Item [received] from Peter Barbour for a fine for disobedience 6d.
Edmund Floure and William Bryan submitted themselves to the arbitration of Richard Gryffyth and Peter Forster, an award to be made before the Sunday after Trinity.
Item from Henry Dakyn in full ...

Veneris iiij^{to} die Junii in presencia Magistri et custodum ac Percyvale, ..., Galle, Tego, Barlowe, West, Materdale, Depleche, Hede, ..., Hert, Povy, Haydyf, Bromeflete.

From Thomas Bodeley for John Hareys 40d.
From John Parker in part payment of his redemption 6s. 8d.

Memorandum that where there is wreten in the iiijth leef of the grete boke²⁷⁹ of ordenaunces of this crafte an ordenaunce concernyng the warnyng of vj men of the said crafte to be warned ayenst the feest day to be at the dyner in the hall the same day under a certayn peyne as by the same ordenaunce therof made more playnly appereth. For certeyn consideracions now moevyng and had the said master and maisters and other persones beforewreten have ordeyned and enacted that the same olde ordenaunce from hensforth shall not be occupied nor used but that the maister that shall be newe chosen from hensforth shall be named and chosen by them that have ben maisters in the parlour on midsomer even before dyner as it hath ben used before tyme. And also it is ordeyned that the wardeyns for the tyme beyng shall have preeminence to goo next unto the masters and before all other of the crafte in processions, rydyngs, diriges and all other assembles.

[f. 23v]

---

²⁷⁹ See above, n. 195.

Lune vij° die Junii.

Item paid for the obit of Hugh Talbot 5s. 2d.
Item paid to the almsmen of this fraternity for the past quindene 5s. 8d.
Item from William Joynour for occupying foreigns 12d.
Item Rowland Hyneson was licensed to hold a shop and paid 10s.
Item from Richard Swynderby for William Edmondson 40d.

Veneris xj die Junii.

Item received of Thomas Trymmer in arrears 6s. 8d.
Item paid to the chamber of Westminster for the tenements in Friday Street 10s.
Item paid to the same for the tenements in Colechurch 4s. 6d.

Lune xiiij die Junii.

Item paid for the obit of Hugh Cavendish. For bread 6d., for ale 8d., for cheese 7d., to the rector 6d., for 3 chaplains 12d., for offerings 4d., to the clerk of the church 6d. [Total] 4s. 7d.
Item [paid to the] master, wardens, clerk and beadle 11s. 8d.
Item for the obit of Thomas Reymond 10s.
Item from John a Toure 5s.
Item received from John a Lye 10s.
Item from John Harryson for ... his apprentice 3s. 4d.
Item paid to Sir[280] Richard Wheler 35s.
Item paid to Sir John Burnham 16s.
Item paid to Sir Roger Doket 35s.

[f. 24]

Veneris xviij° die Junii in presencia Magistri et custodum ac Tego, Galle, Deplech, Pemberton, Lee, Buk, Hede, Hoberd, Povy et tocius comitive fraternitatis hujus mistere

Isto die pronunciata fuit per magistrum quedam billa pro solucione clxxxxiij*li*. vjs. viijd. parcelle mm*li*. ex mutus concessarum domino regi. Et super hoc ordinati sunt assessores persone sequente

---

[280] For this title see Glossary.

[translation] This day a certain bill was announced by the master for the payment of £193 6s. 8d., part of a loan of £2000 granted to the King.[281] And for this the following persons were chosen as assessors

Assessors
Master Lee
Master Deplech
Master Buk
Thomas Bromflete
~~Thomas Howdan~~
Henry Clough
Thomas Werton
William Free
John Feston
James Grene

Collectors
Thomas Petyt
Thomas Howdan
Roger Mone
Ralph Bukberd

Item this day Richard Gristen, a brother of this mistery, was appointed as collector of the rents of the lands and tenements of this mistery, receiving the same tallies and wages as Simon Lorymer[282] had before this time, holding the office from the feast of the Annunciation of the Blessed Virgin Mary last.

Item from William Asshwell for his disobedience 12d.

[f. 24v]

Lune xxj° die Junii.

We Thomas Martyn and James Shirwode arbitrours electe and chosen by the Maister and wardeyns to arbitre and juge all maters and causes dependyng bytwene William Swanston on that one part and Sir Edmond Verty clerk[283]

---

281 This loan had been agreed by the Common Council on 11 June: CLRO, Journals, 9, f. 251v.
282 Lorymer, Gristen's predecessor as rent collector, had been admitted to the Scriveners' fraternity on 9 July 1474: *Scriveners' Common Paper* ed. Steer, p. 23.
283 Unidentified, although Verty may well have been the apprentice's guardian. For a

and George Spotte apprentice of the said William on that other part make our awarde bytwene them in fourme folowyng that is to sey First we awarde that the said William Swanston whansoever he shall be commaunded by the master and wardens shall bryng yn and delyver to ther handes thendenture of apprenticehode of the said George and also an obligacion of xx*li*. wheryn the said Edward stondeth bounde to the said Swanston for the said apprentice. The same endenture and obligacion there to be cancelled. And that doon we awarde that the said Sir Edmond in full contentacion and satisfaccion of all such demandes as the said William claymeth of the said Sir Edmond and for all maner recompence of the service of the said George and for all costes by the said William had and susteyned in this behalf the said Sir Edmond shall pay to the said William xxs. in fourme folowyng that is to sey at Mighelmas next comyng xs. and at Cristemas next folowyng xs. and that the said Sir Edmond for surete of payment of the said xxs. shall bynde hymself to the said William by lawfull bondes and wrytynges therof to be made.

[f. 25] Johannes Spencer.

Die Mercurii xxiiij die Junii videlicet in vigilia Nativitatis Sancti Johannis Baptiste anno domini millesimo ccccxxxxx Et anno regni regis Henrici vij quinto, Johannes Spencer electus est in Magistrum istius fraternitatis per Magistrum et custodes ac Percyvale, Swan, Tego, Galle, Keys, West, Barlowe, Materdale, Deplech, Pemberton, Lee, Hede, Buk.

Item eodem die electi sunt in custodes istius fraternitatis persone quorum nomina sequuntur
    Thomas Bromeflete jur'
    Thomas Howdan jur'
    Rogerus Mone jur'
    Ricardus Hille jur'

[translation] Wednesday 24 June, that is to say on the vigil of the Nativity of St. John the Baptist 5 Henry VII, John Spencer was chosen as master of this fraternity by the master and wardens and Percyvale, Swan, Tego, Galle, Keys, West, Barlowe, Materdale, Deplech, Pemberton, Lee, Hede, Buk.

Item the same day the persons whose names follow were chosen as wardens of this fraternity:[284]

comparable case see the biography of Richard West, Appendix IV.
284   For biographies of these men see Appendix IV.

Thomas Bromeflete sworn
Thomas Howdan sworn
Roger Mone sworn
Richard Hille sworn

Lune xxviij die Junii.

Item Richard Russell was licensed to hold a shop and paid 10s.

Lune v^{to} Julii.

Thomas Wytney and Rowland Walker submitted themselves, on a bond of £10 each, to the arbitration of John Stoyle and John Byg, an award to be made before St. Peter's Chains [1 Aug.]

[f. 25v]

Veneris xvj° die Julii in presencia Magistri et custodum ac Percyvale, Pemberton, Keys, Lee, Deplech, Jenyns, Povy, Grene, Martyn, Wylford.

A communicacion was had bytwene the maisters aforesaid for a newe Thresory hous to be made for the Thresory of this fraternytie.

Veneris xxiij° die Julii.

Item paid to Richard Batte for a quit-rent issuing from tenements in in Bread Street for the year ending on the morrow of St. John [the Baptist] [24 June] 6s. 8d.

Veneris xxxj[285] die Julii.

Item John Baynard presented Thomas Raven 40d.
Item from William Hewetson for Hugh Stodeley 40d.

---

[285] An error for 'xxx'.

Lune ij^do die Augusti.

Item paid to the almsmen of this fraternity for the past quindene 5s. 8d.

Veneris v^to286 die Augusti.

From Alan Hoberd for Roger Leke his apprentice ...

Veneris xiij° die Augusti.

Item paid to the Abbot of Bermondsey for a quit-rent arising from the tenements formerly of Elene Langwith 2s. 6d.
Item John Hewe presented Thomas Halton and paid 40d.

[f. 26]

Lune xvj° die Augusti.

Item Johannes Morten promisit solvere xls. de denariis per ipsum debitis comitive de lez bachelers de tempore quo fuit gardianus ejusdem fraternitatis et quod pignus suum iacebit in cista et custodia gardianorum pro secura solucione de. Rec'
   [translation] Item John Morten promised to pay 40s. of monies owed by him to the Bachelors' company for the time he was warden of the same fraternity and that his pledge lies in the chest and in the custody of the wardens to secure payment. Received.

Item paid to the almsmen of this fraternity for the past quindene 5s. 8d.

Mercurii xviij° die Augusti in compoto Stephani Jenyns magistri istius fraternitatis in presencia magistri et custodum ac M. Swan, M. Percyvale, Keys, West, Barlowe, Pemberton, Deplech, Lee, Buk, ac gardianorum ac tocius communitatis istius mistere.
   [translation] Wednesday the 18th day of August in the account [year] of Stephen Jenyns, master of this fraternity, in the presence of the master and wardens and Master Swan, Master Percyvale, Keys, West, Barlowe, Pemberton, Deplech, Lee, Buk, and the wardens and the whole

---

286 An error for 'vj'.

community of this mistery.[287]

Memorandum that where as by the olde ordenaunces had and used in this place It hath ben used that the master yerely at his accompt shulde have allowaunce of certen parcelles hereafter followyng toward his charges at the feest of Midsomer [24 June] that is to sey of xiijs. iiijd. for the gaderyng yn of the prentys money. Item of iiijli. for a tonne wyne. Item for the dyner at the vewyng of the lyvelode xxvjs. viijd.

Item for the Garlondes at the feest vjd. Item for the clothyng of the master, wardeyns, clerk and bedell vjli. xs. and at his rekenyng sum tyme the master hath ben rewarded sumtyme xx markes, sumtyme xijli., sum tyme xli., sumtyme x markes and sum tyme lesse and sum tyme more which is to the grete charge and hinderaunce of the same crafte. Therfore these premisses considered it is ordeyned and enacted that from hensforth the master for the tyme beyng shall never have alowaunce of eny parcelles aforesaid. And to that entent Stephen Jenyns late master of the said crafte hath geven yn at his accompt the some of xijli. which was to hym alowed at his accompt for a rewarde xijli. Item xls. payde to John Smyth vewer for his fee in the tyme of M. Buk. Item xjs. which he hath payde for a quyte rente due by M. Cotton and M. Hede.

[f. 26v]

Item asmoch lath as amounted to the some of iiijli. iiijs. iiijd. Item liijs. iiijd. spent in the lawe ayenst the parsone and wardeyns of Saynt Mathewes in Frydaystrete for the byeldyng of the stepyll.[288] Item xs. for makyng of the cupbourde in the Erber in the gardyne. Wherof sum totall is xxjli. xixs. The which premisses John Spencer nowe beyng master of the said crafte and Thomas Bromeflete, Thomas Howdan, Roger Mone and Richard Hille wardeyns for ther tyme have graunted to holde ferme and stable. This foresaid acte beyng made and establisshed by the auctorytie of the masters and wardeyns whos names bene before wreten and by the auctorytie and wille of the hole body of the said crafte in this halle assembled. And what persone that

---

[287] Although held on a Wednesday this was not a quarter-day meeting of the court and seems to have been a special meeting called to discuss issues connected with the annual feast, notably the inconsistent nature of the rewards granted to the outgoing master.

[288] The Tailors' main property in Friday Street, the Saracen's Head (the site of the present nos. 5, 6 and 7) abutted on St. Matthew's church and the decision to rebuild this property (see Introduction, pp. 18-19) probably contributed to this litigation with the parson and churchwardens. For the settlement of this dispute in favour of the Tailors by the mayor and sheriffs see below, pp. 185-6 (meeting held on 31 Aug. 1491).

hereafter shall attempt to breke this ordenaunce shall forfeit xl*li*. that is to sey xx*li*. to the almesse and xx*li*. to the chambre of the gilde halle and that the masters from hensforth to be chosen at the tyme of ther admission shall make bodely othe upon a boke to observe the premisses.

Veneris xx° die Augusti.

Item Robert Griston who was the apprentice of Richard Griston, was licensed to hold a shop and paid in hand 10*s*.
And he brought in the copy of his freedom dated the 13th day of August 5 Hen. VII [1490].

Veneris xxvij° die Augusti.

Item John Davy was licensed to hold a shop and paid in hand 6*s*. 7*d*. and the residue to be paid before the feast of the Annunciation [25 Mar.] next on the mainprise of Thomas Bromeflete.
Item Robert Saunderson settled with the master and wardens for his freedom for £3 to be paid in the following manner, that is to say 10*s*. in hand, 10*s*. on the feast of St. John [24 June]. Item 15*s*. at Easter [22 Apr.] 1492, and 15*s*. at Easter [7 Apr.] 1493.
Item the same [Robert] was licensed to hold a shop and to hold two apprentices for 10*s*. to be paid by next Christmas.

[f. 27] Spencer

Lune xxx° die Augusti in presencia Magistri et custodum ac Swan, Percyvale, Galle, Pemberton, Lee, Jenyns.

Item paid to the almsmen of this fraternity for the past quindene 5*s*. 8*d*.
From Alan Hille for Christopher Pursell 40*d*.
From the same for a fine for not presenting him 20*d*.
From the same for disobedience 16*d*.
From Thomas Speight for John a Craven 40*d*.

Veneris iij° die Septembris.

From George Bolton for John Suggenor his apprentice 40*d*.
From Thomas Pyerson for Robert Eryngton 40*d*.

Item Richard Seynier, John Broughton, Thomas Shirbourn and William Polgrave were elected and sworn as wardens of the Bachelors' Company on the feast of the Decollation of St. John the Baptist [29 Aug.] last.[289]

Lune xiij° die Septembris in presencia magistri et custodum.

Item paid to the almsmen of this fraternity for the past quindene 5s. 8d.
Item received from Lionell Baker for not presenting his apprentice 4d.

Veneris xvj°[290] die Septembris.

Item Andrew Robynson was licensed to hold a shop and paid in hand 10s.
Item Thomas Richardson for Swythin a Craven 40d.
From William Gerveys for John Pecche 40d.
From Hugh Lannoy for Thomas Harryson 40d.

Veneris xxiiij die Septembris.

From Roger Clay for Richard Clerk 40d.

[f. 27v] Spencer

Lune xxviij°[291] die Septembris.

Item the master received from John Dyconson for Laurence Apostelet 3s. 4d.
Item paid for coals distributed among the almsmen according to the last will of Elene Langwith 4s. 10d.
Item paid to the almsmen of this fraternity for the past quindene 5s. 8d.
Item paid to William Hacomplaynt for Michaelmas term 5s.
Item [paid to] Thomas Hosyer for the same term 11s. 8d.
Item paid to Geoffrey at Well 11s.
Item paid to Christopher Kyrke 10s.

---

[289] The Bachelors held their feast on the Decollation (29 August) rather than the Nativity (24 June) of St. John the Baptist which was the livery's annual feast day.
[290] An error for 'xvij'.
[291] An error for 'xxvij'.

Item to Sir[292] Roger Doket 33s. 4d.
Item to Sir Richard Wheler 33s. 4d.
Item to Sir John Burnam 16s. 8d.
Item to Sir William[293] Cudworth 35s.
Item to William Duryvale, clerk 35s.
Item to Thomas Gresyll, beadle 18s. 4d.

Veneris viij die Octobris.

Robert Deplech and George Bolton submitted themselves, on a bond of
20 marks each, to the arbitration of William Buk and Stephen Jenyns,
an award to be made by the feast of All Saints next [1 Nov.]
Item received in rent from Robert Saunderson 10s.
From Richard Toll for occupying foreigns 40d.
From John de Boe, galleyman 3s.
From John Festam for Robert Thurlond 40d.
From Robert ... with Master Buk 10s.
[f. 28]
The obit of John Halygate and Edith[294] his wife held in the church of St.
Martin Outwich. For bread, ale, cheese, priests and alms 6s. 8d.

Lune xxv^to die Octobris.

The obit of John Stone, late sheriff of London, held the 24th day of
October. For bread 18d., ale 2s. 4d., for wine 21d., for offerings 5d.,
for a confection 14d., to the 4 wardens 6s. 8d., to the master 40d., to
the clerk and beadle 2s., to the rector 12d., for 2 priests 8d., for candles
2d., to the clerk of the church 12d., in alms 2s. 8d. [Total] 26s. 8d.
Item paid to the almsmen of this fraternity for the past quindene 5s. 8d.

Veneris v° die Octobris[295]

Item William Palgrave presented Dionisius Pully and paid 40d.

---

[292] For this title see Glossary.
[293] Error for Robert.
[294] Idonea or Ydonia, see above, n. 86.
[295] An error for 'Novembris'.

Lune viij° die Novembris.

Item paid to the almsmen of this fraternity for the past quindene 5s. 8d.

Item William Batyson mainprised John Batyson, his brother, that the said John will obey the judgement of Richard Adyf and John Doget, arbiters, on all disputes between the said John and William Smith and Henry Clough on the other part. And the said Henry mainprised for the said William Smyth that the same will likewise obey, on a bond of £10 payable by each to the master. An award to be made by the feast of St. Thomas the Apostle [21 Dec.] next.

Item the said William Batyson submitted himself, on a bond of £10, to the rule of Robert Kelham and John Povy and a settlement to be made of all matters between him and William Crisby, with an end to be made by the 16th day of November next.

Item David Roche, a brother, and Stephen Baker, a foreign (*extraneus*) submitted themselves to the arbitration of Master Galle and Thomas Bromeflete, an end to be made by next Friday coming.

Item John Marchall, late the apprentice of John Campynet, brought in the copy of his freedom dated the 6th day of November 6 Hen. VII [1490] and petitioned for a licence to hold shop, which was granted to him for 10s. paid in hand.

[f. 28v]

Veneris xiij[296] die Novembris.

Item paid to the prior of St. Mary Overey for a quit-rent 8s.

Lune xv die Novembris.

From William Burton for John Herde 40d.
From William Popes for Richard Palmer 40d.

Item William Avenell brought in certain indentures in which John Vaux is bound to Richard Gryffyn from the 12th day of March 5 Hen. VII [1489/90] for 7 years, and the same William petitioned that, because the said Richard has refused (*recusavit*) the service of his apprentice, he

---

[296] An error for 'xij'.

should be bound to him. And it was granted to him and he [i.e. John] was bound to the said William, to serve until the end of his term, and the said William paid according to the custom of this mistery   40*d*. because he was not presented by the said Richard Gryffyn.

Veneris xix die Novembris.

Item John Robynson was licensed to hold a shop and paid in hand   40*d*. and is to pay the residue by the feast of Easter. And Thomas Howdan stood surety for him.
From Henry Beaufeld for ...   40*d*.
From Robert Ingle for William Cowley   40*d*.
Item paid to the prioress of Clerkenwell for a quit-rent   13*s*. 4*d*.

Lune xxij° die Novembris in presencia M. et custodum ac Swan, Percyvale alderman, Galle, Lee, Buk, West, Pemberton, Barlowe, Keys, Povy, Adyf, Martyn, Wilford, Grene.

Richard Seymer submitted himself to the arbitration of John Festam and Richard Quykrell, arbiters between him and ... Symson brothers, an award to be made by the Feast of the Conception [8 Dec.] next.

Item where as Symond Lorymer late renter etc. hath put yn his supplicacion to the master, wardens and hole company of this crafte for recompence of dyvers losses by hym susteyned in the said office as by the said supplicacion appereth and where as the same Symond dysyreth by the said supplication to have in reccompense for terme of his life fre a tenement which he holdeth in Trynete parissh the lytell of the yerely value of xxvj*s*. viij*d*. It is graunted that he shall have the same tenement with reparacions [for] terme of his lyf for xiij*s*. iiij*d*. by yere orelles the place in the Vyntre for terme of his lyf with reparacions for xx*s*. by yere. And he has answered to have the tenement in Trenetie parish as it is more playnly endorsed upon the said supplicacion.

Item where as Richard Bothome hath mys behaved hym ayenst the ordenaunce to John Doget. Yf the said Richard woll submyt hym to the said John than he shal pay but v*s*. and if he woll not than he shall pay xx*s*.

Item paid to the almsmen of this fraternity 5*s*. 8*d*.

[f. 29] Spencer.

Nicholas Nynes presented Thomas Chybold as his apprentice and paid 40*d*.

The same Nicholas presented Simon Nynes as his apprentice and paid 40*d*.

Thomas Dobson brought in the copy of his freedom and petitioned for a licence to hold a shop and paid in hand 6*s*. 8*d*.

Item Master Galle and Master Jenyns, together with Henry Clough and John Doget were assigned for the supervision of the repairs and rebuilding of the Saracen's Head.

Item Master Pemberton and all the aforesaid masters, together with Walter Povy and James Wilford were assigned for the supervision and reckoning of the Treasury etc.

Lune xxix° Novembris in presencia [M.] et custodum ac Swan, Percyvale, West, Lee, Buk, Galle, Pemberton, ..., Povy, Adyf, Wilford, Fittz.

William Brownyng was ordered to pay 13*s*. 4*d*. for his behaviour towards Richard Thomasson.

Item Richard Thomassson was ordered to pay 10*s*.

Veneris iiij^{to297} die Decembris.

Richard Popley presented Henry Tederowe and paid in hand 40*d*.

From the same for not presenting him 4*d*.

From John Tanner for John Johnson his apprentice 40*d*.

Martis viij°298 die Decembris.

Robert Adelyn who was the apprentice of William Wytney brought in his copy, dated the 14th day of August and petitioned for a licence to hold a shop, which was granted to him. And he is to pay 5*s*. at Easter and 5*s*. at Pentecost.

Item paid to the prioress of Kilburn for tenements in Abchurch 17*s*.

Item paid to the same for tenements in Bread Street 6*s*. 8*d*.

---

297 An error for 'iij'.
298 An error for 'vij'.

Richard Quykrell submitted himself to the arbitration of William Batyson and ..., who are to arbitrate upon all matters between himself and Lady Frowyk,[299] an award to be made before the feast of Christmas and if agreement is not reached then he is to bound in £10 to abide by the judgement of the master and wardens.

From William Batyson for disobedience 12d.

[f. 29v]

Item Robert Wilkynson who was the apprentice of William Hulot brought in the copy of his freedom dated 4th day of August 5 Hen. VII [1490] and petitioned for a licence to hold a shop. And it was granted to him, for a payment to be made by the feast of the Annunciation next. William Hulot was surety for him.

Item the said Robert Wilkynson presented Henry Adam and paid 40d.

Veneris xvj°[300] die Decembris.

Item paid for the obit of Thomas Carleton 10s.
Item paid for a quitrent to St. Paul's church 5s.
Item paid to the abbot of Westminster by 2 acquitances 13s. 6d.
Item Richard Grey junior, formerly the apprentice of Richard Alenson, was licensed to hold a shop and paid in part payment 8s. [Total to be paid] 10s.

Lune xx° die Decembris.

Item paid for coals at Christmas according to the will of Creke[301] 5s. 10d.
Item paid to the almsmen of this fraternity for the past quindene 5s. 8d.

---

[299] Joan, daughter of Richard Sturgeon and widow of Sir Thomas Frowyk (d. 1485): see A. F. Sutton and L. Visser-Fuchs, 'The Making of a Minor Chronicle in the Household of Sir Thomas Frowyk (died 1485)', *The Ricardian*, 10 no.126, pp. 86–103; Wedgwood, *History of Parliament*, pp. 357–8; Thrupp, *Merchant Class*, p. 343. The precise cause of the dispute is not recorded in the minutes: the judgement entered in the minutes for 22 Feb. 1491 required Quykerell to pay her 18s. but authorised him to recover cloth he had probably supplied to her household.

[300] An error for 'xvij'.

[301] John Creek: see above, n. 148.

Veneris in vigilia Natalis domini.

Item paid to John Radclyff, chaplain, for his wages for the same term 33s. 4d.
Item paid to the almsmen for the quindene before the ... day of January next 5s. 8d.
Item paid to Geoffrey atte Well almsman for the same term 11s. 8d.
Item Christopher Kyrke for the same term 10s.
Item Thomas Hosyer for the same term 11s. 8d.
Item paid to Sir[302] Richard Wheler for the same term 33s. 4d.
Item paid to William Duryvale, clerk, for his wages 25s.
Item paid to Sir Roger Doget for the aforesaid term 33s. 4d.
Item paid to Thomas Gresyll for the same term 18s. 4d.
Item paid to Sir Robert Cudworth 35s.
Item paid to William Hacomplaynt almsman 5s.

From ... for occupying foreigns 3s. 4d.
From Robert Debenham for ... apprentice 40d.
From William Wotton, redemptioner 20s.

[f. 30]

Veneris xvj⁰[303] die Januarii.[304]

From John Kechyn for ... 40d.
From Robert Bacon for Christopher Boys[305] his apprentice 40d. And if he withdraws before the feast of the Nativity of St. John [24 June] he may take on another in his place.
From William Werton for William Robynson 40d.
From William Olyver for William Walton 40d.

Lune ...[306]

From John Shemell for John Broun 40d.
From John a Toure for Edward Wakefield 40d.

---

302   For this title see Glossary.
303   An error for 'xiv'.
304   1490/1.
305   Perhaps a son of Josse de Boys, a German tailor, and his wife Elizabeth, who were resident in Aldgate ward in 1483: Bolton (ed.), *Alien Communities*, p. 76.
306   Should be 'xvij Januarii'.

Lune xxiiij° die Januarii.

Item paid to the almsmen of this fraternity [for the quindene before the] 17th day of January 5s. 8d.
Item paid to the almsmen for coals according to the last will of Elene Langwith at the feast of the Purification [2 Feb.] 6s.
From William Olyver for not enrolling ... his apprentice 8d.
From Stephen Everton for George Cok 40d.
From the same for Richard Tatem 40d.
Robert Robson brought in the copy of his freedom dated the 15th day of May 5 Hen. VII [1490] and petitioned for a licence to hold a shop, which was granted to him and he paid in hand 6s. 8d. and is to pay the residue by the feast of Easter [3 Apr.] [Total paid] 6s. 8d.
From Robert Stephenson for ... 40d.

Item Robert Parker and John Shemell submitted themselves, on pain of 100s. to the arbitration of John Sperman and John Borowes, an award to be made before the first Sunday of Lent [20 Feb.]
Item [from] William Joynour for Rowland Fenwyk 40d.

Hugo Stokes recusavit servicium Willelmi Devenyssh apprenticii sui in presencia M et custodum et dictus apprenticius peciit admitti uno alio magistro istius mistere et isto die admissus est cuidam Johanni Shemell cissori ad serviendum usque finem termini in dicta indentura specificati.
[translation] Hugh Stokes has refused the service of William Devenish his apprentice in the presence of the master and wardens, and the said apprentice petitioned to be bound to another master of this mistery, and this day he was bound to John Shemell, tailor, to serve until the end of the term specified in the said indenture.

[f. 30v]

Lune ultimo die Januarii.

Item paid to the almsmen of this fraternity for the past quindene 5s. 8d.
Item paid for the obit of John Churchman 6s. 8d.

Veneris iiij^to die Februarii.

Item Thomas Nutman and William a Barre submitted themselves, on a bond of 100s. each, to the arbitration of Thomas Egerton and Dionisius

Burton, an award to be made before the middle Sunday in Lent [13 Mar.]

And if agreement is not reached they are to abide by the rule of John Spencer the master.

From John Wright for Thomas Fykkes 40*d*.

From Thomas Bankes for Walter North 40*d*.

John Clerk and Elizabeth Bulfynche submitted themselves on a bond of £10 to the arbitration of Thomas Martyn and Henry Clough, an award to be made before Palm Sunday [27 Mar.]

Lune vij° die Februarii.

Hugh Lannoy and Nicholas ... submitted themselves to the arbitration of William Olyver and Henry Grene, an award to be made before Shrove Tuesday [15 Feb.]

And Henry Caminy in Tower Street was licensed to hold a shop, and he brought in his copy dated the 28th day of August 6 Hen. VII [1490]. He paid in hand 5*s*. and is to pay to residue of 5*s*. by the first day of May.

The last day of January anno regni regis Henrici vij vj^{to} [1490/1] we John Lee and William Buk arbitrours electe and chosen bytwene Walter Povy tayllour on that one part and John Stokes draper on that other part make our awarde bytwene them in fourme folowyng that is to sey where as we fynde by thexaminacion of bothe said parties that the variaunce and controversye bytwene the said partes beganne and felle by reason of multyplyng of certen langage bytwene the said partes and therupon the said Walter vyolent handes shuld smyte the said John Stokes upon the face and other wise entrete hym than well and by reason therof the same John Stokes hath lost ij of his thet[307] as he hath deposed. We awarde that the said Walter shall bryng yn to our halle xiijs. iiijd. byfore the master and wardeyns of the which xiijs. iiijd. we awarde that the master shall delyver to the sayd John xs. and reserve to the said Walter iijs. iiijd. And that eyther of the said parties from hensforth shall be of good aberyng that one to the other of them in words and dedes.

[f. 31]

---

[307] 'Teeth': *Middle English Dictionary*, *T (8)*, p. 906.

Veneris xviij° die Februarii.

This day Thomas Mors made an agreement with the master and wardens for his redemption which was granted to him for £3 etc.

Item paid to the almsmen of this fraternity for the quindene before Monday after Quinquagesima, that is to say the 14th day of February 5s. 8d.

This day Thomas Bedford submitted himself to the arbitration of Richard Adyf and James Grene on a bond of 20 marks, an award to be made before the Annunciation of the Blessed Virgin Mary [25 Mar.]

And if agreement is not reached then he is to abide by the judgement of the master and Master Barlowe to be made before Low Sunday (*diem dominicam in Albis*) [10 Apr.] next following.

Item William Olyver and Henry Grene render judgement that Hugh Lannoy should pay 40d. to ... Makerell his servant in full payment of all monies etc.

Lune xxj° die Februarii.

Item paid for the obit of John Creke held in the church of St. Mary Abchurch the first Sunday of Lent [20 Feb.] 3s. 3d.

Martis xxij° die Februarii in presencia Magistri et custodum ac Keys, Barlowe, Galle, Pemberton, Deplech, Hede, Povy, Russh,[308] Martyn, Hoberd, Boughton, Randyll.

John Benet, son of Thomas Benet, came here and petitioned to have the freedom of this mistery which was granted to him, and he paid for the same redemption 16s. 4d.

Item Thomas Mors was admitted by the the master and the others above named into the freedom of this mistery, granted to him for 53s. 4d.

Item it is ruled that Richard Quykrell is to pay to Lady Frowyk 18s. and is to recover his cloth etc.[309]

Item the demise of a corner tenement in Wodestrete was made to John Bulle, tiler, according to indentures made therefore.

From Hugh Lannoy for William Stele 40d.

---

[308] Only meeting of the court attended by John Russh: see Appendix IV.
[309] See above, n. 299.

[f. 31v]

Lune vij° die Marcii in presencia Magistri et custodum ac Swan, Percyvale, Keys, Barlowe, Hede, Jenyns, Deplech, Buk, Hoberd, Povy, Russh, Adyf, Fittz.

Edmund Caryngton agreed to pay to William Becan all those monies that he owes by tally before the Month of Easter (*mensem Pasche*) next coming.

Veneris xj die Marcii.

Thomas Egerton and Dionisius Burton have arbitrated that William a Barre is to pay to Thomas Nutman 3s. 4d. in full payment of his debts etc.
From Thomas Egerton for Robert Nyghtyngale ...
From Robert Colson for John Goldthwayte 40d.
Item paid to the prioress of Clerkenwell for a quit-rent 13s. 4d.

Lune xiiij° die Marcii.

Item paid to the almsmen of this fraternity for the past quindene 5s. 8d.
From William a Barre for a fine for occupying foreigns 8d.

Lune xxij°³¹⁰ die Marcii.

From Richard Lyttyll for the farm of his tenement in which he dwells 6s. 8d.

[f. 32]

Martis xxij° die Marcii.

This day the master paid to Sir³¹¹ John Radclyf for his wages for the term of the Annunciation this year 33s. 4d.
Item paid to Sir Richard Wheler for the same term 33s. 4d.

---

³¹⁰ An error for 'xxj'.
³¹¹ For this title see Glossary.

Item paid to Sir Richard Burnam for the same term 16s. 8d.

Item paid to Sir Robert Cudworth for the same term 35s.

Item paid to Thomas Hosyer, almsman, for the same term 11s. 8d.

Item paid to Geoffrey at Well for the same term 11s. 8d.

Item paid to William Hacomplaynt for alms of 20s. a year, from the feast of Christmas until Shrove Tuesday [15 Feb.] 2s.

Item paid to Robert Boylet for the same term 10s.

Item paid to Christopher Kyrke for the same term 10s.

Item paid to William Duryvale, clerk of this fraternity 25s.

Item paid to Thomas Gresyll, beadle 18s. 4d.

Item paid to Sir Roger Doget for the same term 33s. 4d.

Lune xxviij° die Marcii.

Item paid to the almsmen of this fraternity for the past quindene 5s. 8d.

Aldrichegate.

William Thomas, formerly the apprentice of Edward Robson, brought in the copy of his freedom dated the 22nd day of September 4 Hen. VII [1488] and petitioned for a licence to hold a shop which was granted to him on payment of 3s. 8d. in hand and he is to pay the residue at Pentecost [22 May].

From Robert Gysbourn for Richard Frisden 40d.

Thomas Gresyll and Robert Godere submitted themselves to the arbitration of John Kyrkeby and Robert Halle, an award to be made before the last day of April.

From John Lynton for Robert Staunford 40d.

Item paid for the obit of Richard Benton 15s.

[From] Simon Ady 'opner'[312] ...

[f. 32v]

Lune xj° die Aprilis.

From Henry Kellowe for John Halle his apprentice 40d.

From John Sutton for Henry Newson 40d.

From William Stockbridge for Richard Dawson 40d.

From Robert Palmer for Ranulph Palmer 40d.

From Robert Adeleyn 'opener'[313] for his Easter payment 5s.

---

[312] See Glossary.

From William Dryffeld for William Atwode 40*d*.
Item paid to the almsmen 5*s*. 8*d*.
Ralph Wodeward and Richard Fowler submitted themselves, on a bond of £10 each, to the arbitration of Thomas Broughton, John Cok, John Kechyn [and] Thomas Galle, with an award to be made before the feast of Pentecost [22 May] next.

Veneris ...[314] die Aprilis

John Roundethwayte, who was the apprentice of Thomas Felle, brought in the copy of his freedom dated the 18th day of March 5 Hen. VII [1489/90] and petitioned for a licence to hold a shop and paid in hand 10*s*.
John Smyth, who was the apprentice of James Grene, brought in the copy of his freedom dated the 17th day of November 4 Hen. VII [1488] and petitioned for a licence to hold a shop which was granted to him and he paid in hand 10*s*.

Lune xxv die Aprilis.

Item paid to the almsmen 5*s*. 8*d*.
From Patrick Patenson for John Browell 40*d*.

Lune ij° die Maii.

And Benedict de Cena, galleyman,[315] was licensed for himself and his household to hold shops, and he agreed to pay 6*d*. a week, that is to say 3*d*. for each.
From Walter Povy for Ralph Middelton ...

[ff. 33-33v blank[316]]

[f. 34]

---

[313] See Glossary.
[314] Either 'xv' or 'xxij'.
[315] See Glossary.
[316] The blank folios correspond with the gap in the minutes for the period 3 May – 3 June, possibly indicating that notes taken at meetings held in these weeks were mislaid.

Veneris iij° die Junii.

From John Lucas for Michael Daldy 40*d*.

Lune xiij° die Junii.

From Joan Geffrey, administrator (*collectrice*) of the goods of Richard Geffrey[317] who died intestate, for Richard Bonde who was not presented 40*d*.
From John Broughton for William Wayte 6*s*. 8*d*.
From Edmund Bretowe for Geoffrey White 40*d*.
From William Worthy for a fine for not enrolling his apprentice 4*d*.

Delyvered to John Doget a box with the warde and endentures of the stepyll of Seint Mathies.[318]

From Thomas Egerton for ... his apprentice 40*d*.
Item paid for the obit of Ralph Holand held in the church of St. Mary Aldermary 13*s*. 4*d*.
Item paid to Sir[319] Robert Cudworth for the term of the Nativity of St. John [24 June] 35*s*.
Item paid to the chamber of Westminster for a quit-rent for tenements in Colechurch 4*s*. 6*d*.
Item paid to the same chamber for a quit-rent for tenements in Friday Street 10*s*.
Item paid to Sir John Radclyf 33*s*. 4*d*.
Item paid to the same for bread and wine 20*d*.
Item paid to Sir Richard Wheler 33*s*. 4*d*.
Item paid to the same 20*d*.
Item paid to Sir John Burnam chaplain 16*s*. 8*d*.
Item paid to Geoffrey at Welle 11*s*. 8*d*.
Item paid to Christopher Kyrke 10*s*.
Item paid to Thomas Hosyer 10*s*.
Item paid to William Duryvale 25*s*.
Item paid for paper and parchment 3*s*. 4*d*.
Item paid to Thomas Gresyll 18*s*. 4*d*.
Item paid to Nicholas Foderey serjeant 13*s*. 4*d*.

---

[317] Little recorded of Geffrey apart from his appearance before the chamberlain in Oct. 1486 as surety for the patrimony of the children of John Benet, a draper: *Cal. Letter Bk. L*, p. 236.
[318] St. Matthew's Friday Street: see above, p. 167.
[319] For this title see Glossary.

[f. 34v] W. Hert.

Die Jovis xxiiij° die Junii in vigilia Nativitatis Sancti Johannis Baptiste anno domini millesimo cccclxxxxj Et anno regni regis Henrici Septimi sexto in congregacione Magistri et custodum ac Swan Percyvale Pemberton aldermannorum Galle Keys Barlowe West Deplech Materdale et Jenyns William Hert electus est [in] magistrum istius fraternitatis ac eodem die Henricus Clough Nicholaus Nynes Henricus Kellowe et Radulphus Bukberd electi sunt in custodes ejusdem fraternitatis.

[translation] Thursday the 24th day of June on the vigil of the Nativity of St. John the Baptist AD 1491 and in the sixth year of the reign of King Henry VII at the assembly of the master and wardens and Swan, Percyvale, Pemberton aldermen, Galle, Keys, Barlowe, West, Depleche, Materdale and Jenyns, William Hert was elected as master of this fraternity and the same day Henry Clough, Nicholas Nynes, Henry Kellowe and Ralph Bukberd were elected as wardens of the same fraternity.[320]

Die Veneris primo die Julii in presencia Magistri et custodum.

Nichil

Die Lune iiij^to die Julii in presencia Magistri et custodum.

Thomas Dyker presented Philip Wenslond his apprentice and paid 40d. Nicholas Sawer, who was the apprentice of Robert Tewesdale, citizen and tailor of London, brought in the copy of his freedom dated the 2nd day of June 4 Hen. VII [1489] in the time of Robert Tate, mayor, and the same Nicholas petitioned for a licence to hold a shop which was granted to him and he paid in hand 10s.

Robert Catelyn presented Henry Smyth his apprentice and paid 40d.

Item paid to the almsmen of this fraternity for the quindene to the 8th day of July 5s. 8d.

---

[320] For the biographies of Hert, Clough, Kellow, Nynes and Bukberd see Appendix IV.

Die Lune xj° die Julii in presencia magistri et custodum.

Thomas Pole presented John Pryngle and paid 40*d*.

Item paid for the obit of John and Elene Langwith in the church of St. Mary Abchurch 16*s*.

[f. 35] Hart

Die Lune xviij° die Julii in presencia Magistri et custodum ac Swan, Percyvale, West, Deplech, Galle, Lee, Buk, Jenyns, ..., Fittes, Randyll, Martyn, Bromeflete.

Item concordatum est die predicto quod Thomas Davy excellentissime principis et domine Domine Elizabethe Regine Anglie ad humilem supplicacionem predicte Regine per litteram missivam Magistro et custodibus missam et deliberatam haberet libertatem istius fraternitatis et ad solvendum ad sui placitum pro hujusmodi.

[translation] Item it is agreed on the aforesaid day that Thomas Davy[321] [?servant of] the most excellent Princess and Lady, Elizabeth the Queen of England, at the humble supplication of the said Queen by letters missive sent to the master and wardens, should have the freedom of this fraternity and is to pay the usual fee.

Die Lune primo die Augusti in presencia Magistri et custodum.

Item paid to the almsmen of this fraternity for the past quindene 5*s*. 8*d*.

[f. 35v]

---

[321] A Thomas Davy was master of the company in 1436–7 and was a long serving warden of London Bridge. It may be this man's son who is referred to here, another tailor who was apprenticed in 1458–9 to Henry Matthew but whose career is less well-documented. This entry suggests, however, that his absence from the records of the company and the city may have resulted from employment as a tailor to Elizabeth of York. Hopkinson, *Ancient Records*, p. 111; *Cal. Letter Bk. K*, pp. 287, 329, 395; *L*, p. 299; Accounts, II, f. 151.

Lune xxij° die Augusti anno vij Henrici vij

John Baynard and Laurence Bardeney and Alan Scarlet submitted themselves, on a bond of 100s. each, to the arbitration of Richard Seymer and John Broughton, an award to be made before the day of the Nativity of the Blessed Virgin Mary [8 Sept.]

From Laurence Bardney 12d.

Mercurii ultimo die Augusti. Dies quarterii tentus fuit in presencia Magistri et custodum ac Swan, B ..., Barlowe, Buk, Hede, Jenyns, Galle, ..., Povy, Adyf, Fitz.

In the tyme of John Mathewe,[322] mayre of London, Hugh Pemberton and Henry Cote shyryffes[323] of the same cite, a contraversie and discorde was had and moeved bytwene the master, wardens and commaltie of this crafte of tayllours and the parson, chirchewardens and parisheners of Saynt Mathie in Frydaystrete London for a stone wall stondyng at the west ende on the Northsyde of the tenement called the Saresyns Hede in Frydaystrete of London. The vewers[324] of the said citie by the said Mayre were commaunded to vewe the said stone walle which have vewed the same stone walle and have therof geven their verdyt in fourme folowyng which verdet was presented at the said quarterday.

To the right full honourable lord and right wise soverayns the Mayre and Aldremen of the citie of London. Shewen unto your grete wisdomes William Ray, Thomas Kid, Thomas Wode and John Burton the iiij masters of masons and carpenters sworne to the said citie that where as late they were charged by your honourable commaundement to oversee a noyaunce in the parissh of Saint Mathewe in Frydaystrete of London bytwene the master wardens and commaltie of the crafte of tayllours of London, playntyfs on that one partye, and the parson, chirche wardens and parissheners of the parissh of Saint Mathewe, defendauntes on that other partye. The which noyaunce the said iiij[or] masters have serched, seen and rypely examined by their aller discresions. And therupon they sey that they fynde a stone walle ther the which stretcheth in lengthe from the south est corner of a principall post that belongeth to a tenement in Chepeside called the Saresyns Hede at height of the nether egge of the plate of the said principall post in the West [f. 36]

---

[322] Mathew, a mercer, was mayor 1490–1: Beaven, II, p. 16.

[323] Pemberton was chosen as sheriff after the death in office of Robert Revell: *Great Chronicle*, p. 244; Thrupp, *Merchant Class*, p. 363.

[324] See above, n. 81.

estward unto the northwest breche of the said stonewalle nowe begunne xliij fete of assise. They sey also that by their aller discressions the said walle and grounde from the south est corner of the said principall post unto the said northwest corner of the said breche upn the south side therof lyneright and plomright belongen to the said playntyffes [i.e. the Tailors] of lesse than the said defendauntes can shew eny evidence or specialty unto the contrary.

> Item the last wills of John Churchman and Hugh Champernoun[325] were read.
> Item on this day Robert Stephenson was admitted as a brother of this fraternity and paid in hand 20s.

Item Nicholaus Salman qui [fuit] apprenticius Edwardi Lytelhand admissus fuit pro uno fre sower isitus fraternitatis pro eo quod non potest admitti in libertatem istius civitatis non obtstante quod deservivit terminum apprenticialitis sue quia non irrotulatur in camera Guihald

> [translation] Item Nicholas Salman, who was the apprentice of Edward Lytelhand, was admitted as a free sewer[326] of this fraternity because he cannot be admitted into the freedom of this city, notwithstanding that he served out the terms of his apprenticeship, which was not enrolled in the chamber of the Guildhall.

Robert Stephenson was admitted into the freedom of this fraternity and paid 20s.

Veneris ij° die Septembris.

Richard Swan presented Richard Feyrecok and paid in hand 40d.

That William Cok, tailor, remains indebted to John Lynton, tailor, in the sum of 17s. 8d. The said William promised faithfully to pay back the

---

325 See above, nn. 40, 129.
326 Most 'free sewers' were newly qualified apprentices, most of whom, unlike Salman, had obtained the freedom but were not yet ready to open a shop. The Tailors, like other guilds, tried to regulate their activities and in 1449 they required all 'free sowers' to live together 'in the comons among other servauntes sawers' so that other freemen with their own shops could employ them 'for competent wages by the day or by the garment'. This case shows that this category of worker could also include men such as Salman who, although fully trained, was unable to obtain the freedom because of the failure to enrol his apprenticeship at Guildhall. GL, Merchant Taylors' Co., Misc. Docs. A.2, f. 10.

said 17s. 8d. in this manner namely 20d. at Michaelmas [29 Sept.], 4s. at Christmas and 4s. quarterly thereafter.

We Thomas Bromeflete and Thomas Howdan and Richard Hille, arbitrours electe and chosen bytwene Roger Mone and Geffrey Mone of and upon all maters and causes bytwene them, make and geve our awarde bytwene them in the premisses in this wise, that is to sey we awarde that the said Geffrey shall bryng yn xx marc' and therof the said Roger shall have xij*li*. and the said Geffrey to have the xxxiijs. iiijd. residue and that doon we awarde that eyther parte shall seale to the other of them a generall acquitauns.

[f. 36v]

Lune xiij³²⁷ die Septembris.

Robert Fitzwater and John Goos submitted themselves, on a bond of 100s. each, to the arbitration of Dionisius Burton and William Casson, an award to be made before the feast of Michaelmas [29 Sept.].

That Geoffrey Mone, by a certain writings dated the 10th day of September, was bound in an obligation to pay Roger Mone £12, to be paid by the 12th day of September. Nevertheless the said Roger has agreed that the said Geoffrey is to pay the said £12 in the form following, that is to say 6s. 8d. on the said 12th day of September and then 6s. 8d. each week on Mondays until the aforesaid £12 is fully paid.

Item paid to the almsmen of this fraternity, that is to say Geoffrey at Welle 11s. 8d., Christopher Kyrke 10s., Thomas Hosyer 11s. 8d. and Robert Boylet 10s.

Item paid to the chaplains of this fraternity that is to say to John Radclyf 33s. 4d., Sir³²⁸ Richard Wheler 33s. 4d., Sir Robert Cudworth 35s., Sir John Burnam 16s. 8d. and to Sir Thomas Roos³²⁹ £4.

---

327 An error for 'xij'.
328 For this title see Glossary.
329 Thomas Roos replaced Robert Cardemaker as chantry chaplain of Lady Beatrice de Roos in St. Paul's. The Tailors paid the priest's salary but the appointment was made by her family: Thomas Roos was almost certainly a relative of some kind. He is to be identified as the Thomas Rose who was previously rector of St. Mary Bothaw in London, but who resigned in 1492. His successor as rector was Cardemaker, whose appointment was noted on 31 Aug. 1492. Hennessey, *Novum Repertorium*, p. 390.

Lune iij° die Octobris in presencia Magistri et custodum ac Swan, Percyvale, Pemberton, Depleche, Hede, Buk, Galle, Spencer, Jenyns, ..., Povy, Hoberd.

In presencia predicta consideratum est quod Robertus Stephenson confrater istius fraternitatis pro diversis contumaciis et inobedienciis suis contra magistrum et custodes ac alios magistros istius fraternitatis perpetratis exoneraretur de vestura sua de liberata istius fraternitatis et oneratur bidellum fraternitatis predicte. Et ulterius ordinatum est quod idem Robertus pro dictus contumaciis suis subiret penam prisonamenti.

> [translation] In the presence of the aforesaid it is considered that Robert Stephenson, brother of this fraternity,[330] for his various contumacies and disobediences against the master and wardens and other masters of this fraternity, should be discharged from his clothing of the livery of this fraternity and should be charged by the beadle of the aforesaid fraternity. And finally it is ordained that the same Robert for his said contumacies should undergo the penalty of imprisonment.

Item where as by ordenaunce made in the tyme of Stephen Jenyns, master,[331] made at his accompt it was ordeyned that the clerk and bedyll of this fraternytie shall not from thensforth have no money for ther lyvery clothyng as they were wont to have. Neverthelesse the said maisters and felasship callyng to their remembraunces that the clerk and bedyll may not so well forbere their advauntages and dueties as the master [and] wardeyns may have ordeyned that the clerk and bedyll in augmentacion of their wages shall have that is to sey the clerk xiij*s.* iiij*d.* in money which was wont in the old ordenaunce to be geven to him for his gowne that yere that no lyvery was geven and in lyke wise the bedyll to have x*s.* in augmentacion of his wages x*s.* which was wont to be allowed to hym for his lyvere clothyng that yere that no lyvere was geven. And whan lyvere is geven to have the lyvere as they were wont [to] have.

[f. 37] Hart.

Lune x° die Octobris in presencia Magistri et custodum.

Thomas Shirbourne and Christopher Bank have acknowledged that they are bound to William Hert, master, and the wardens of this

---

330 Stephenson had been admitted to the livery on 31 Aug. less than five weeks previously: see above, p. 186 and below, p. 195.
331 Jenyns was master for 1489-90.

fraternity in £10, that is to say for each of them 100s., on condition that each is to be of good behaviour towards the other in words as well as deeds.

Thomas Chawny, son of William Chawny of Boston in Lincolnshire, baker, who was the apprentice of William Newport, tailor, brought in the copy of his freedom dated the 13th day of December 6 Hen. VII [1490] and petitioned for a licence to hold a shop, which was granted to him and he paid in hand 10s.

Richard Hansell, son of Robert Hansell, late of Marton in Lincolnshire, husbandman, who was the apprentice of Robert Dobson, brought in the copy of his freedom dated the 17th day of September 6 Hen. VII [1490] and petitioned for a licence to hold a shop, which was granted to him and he paid in hand 10s.

Nicholas Gressop and Andrew Robertson submitted themselves, on pain of 40s., to the arbitration of Thomas Shirbourne and Thomas Cape etc. an award to be made before the feast of St. Martin [11 Nov.]

Veneris xiiij die Octobris.

Rowland Hymeson and John Langryk submitted themselves, on a pledge of 100s., to the arbitration of Richard Adyf and John Doget etc. an award to be made by the feast of SS. Simon and Jude the apostles [28 Oct.]

Thomas Belly and John Nicholson submitted themselves to the arbitration of John Combes and Richard Seymer,[332] tailors, an award to be made before the feast of All Saints [1 Nov.] next.

Thomas Ethel and Peter Barbour submitted themselves, on a bond of 40s. each, to the arbitration of James Grene and John Sperman etc. an award to be made before the feast of All Saints [1 Nov.]

[f. 37v]

---

[332] The names of the original arbiters, John Festam and William Burton, are scored out.

Lune xxxj° die Octobris.

We Richard Adyf and John Doket, arbitrours electe and chosen bytwene Rowland Hymeson and John Langryk, make and geve oute our award bytwene them in maner and fourme folowyng that is to sey first that the said Rowland shall delyver unto the said John all his weryng gere and stuf beyng in the hous of the same Rowland. And also that the said John shall delyver unto the same Rouland a peyre sheres which the same John toke from the stall of the said Rowland. Also where as the said John stondeth bound by covenaunt [to] the said Rouland for a yere and where as the same John hath withdrawen hymself from the service of the said Rouland, therupon we awarde that the same John forthwith at the gevyng out of this awarde shall delyver and pay to the said Rouland for a recompence of such withdrawyng and for a full dismission oute of the said covenaunt xs. Also we awarde that than the said parties shall seale eyther of them to the other a generall acquituns. Also we awarde that the said John shall be bounde by recognisaunce in xiijs. iiijd. to be of good aberyng in wordes and dedes ayenst the said Rouland to be levable one half to the chambre and other half to the almes of the crafte. Also we awarde that the said Rouland at his owne costes shall withdrawe all such accions as he hath taken ayenst the said John. Also we awarde that the cost of wrytyng and makyng of this our awarde shall be equally borne bytwene the said parties.

> John Langryk of London, tailor, has acknowledged that he is bound to William Hert, the master, and to Henry Clough, Nicholas Nynes, Henry Kellowe and Ralph Bukberd the wardens of this fraternity, in 13s. 4d. to be paid at the feast of Christmas, on condition that the said John from henceforth is to behave well towards Rowland Hymeson as well in words as in deeds etc. the said 13s. 4d. once levied is then to be paid to the chamber of the city of London and to the alms of this fraternity.

Martis viij° die Novembris.

> Henry Fylberd presented Walter Tancok and paid ...

Lune xxj° die Novembris.

> Robert Atkynson, who was the apprentice of Ralph Osbolston, brought in the copy of his freedom dated the 16th day of November and petitioned for a licence to hold a shop and paid in hand 5s., and is to

pay the residue, on the surety of William Grene, by the feast of Christmas.

[f. 38]

Eodem die.

We James Grene and John Spereman arbitrours bytwene Thomas Ethell and Pyers Barbour make and yeve oute our awarde bytwene them in the premisses in maner and fourme folowyng, that is to sey Where as the said parties have acompanyed and conspereted them self by appoyntment bytweene them made to occupie an hous joyntly, and where as the said partyes nowe no longer can contynue togider in the said covenaunt, Therupon for dyvers consideracions us moevyng we awarde that the said Pyers shall departe from the said hous and company of the said Thomas Ethel bytwene the day aforesaid and Cristmas next comyng if the said Pyers so woll doo. And also that the said Thomas shall sufer the said Pyers to take and have with hym all such goodes and stuf as to the same Pyers is belongyng and beyng [in] the said hous. And also we awarde that the said Pyers shall be charged and chargeable with the half of the rent due for the said tenement and the halvendele of all such charges as concerne the same tenement as offeryng and clerkes wages bedyll and raker from the feest of Saint Mighell last past until Cristemas next nowe comyng.

Mercurii xiij° die Decembris in presencia Magistri et custodum ac Swan, Pemberton, West, Deplech, Lee, Buk, Jenyns, Grene, Bromeflete.

In the presence abovesaid Rauf Bukberd, one of the wardeyns of this fraternytie, for dyvers inordinate and inconvenyent dealyngs and demeanours by hym had and doon unto Master John Swan, aldreman, hath made submyssion unto the said Master Swan and the said Rauf hath umbeley besought the said Master Swan of forgevenes. And the said M. Swan hath forgeven unto the said Rauf all such offences as the said Rauf hath doon unto hym.

Memorandum that the xix day of Decembre a communicacion and mocion was had bytwene the Maisters and wardeyns and other of the xxiiij for to knowe and understond howe and in what wise a certeyn some of money shuld be reysed of the body of the crafte to content and pay werkmen and laborers at the Saresyns Hede[333] and bycause of shortnesse of tyme that a

---

[333] For the re-building of the Saracen's Head in Friday Street see Introduction, pp. 18–19.

sessyng coude not be had and made in the crafte before the feest of Cristemas next comyng Therfore the right worshipfull Sir John Percyvale, Hugh Pemberton aldremen and M. Roger Barlowe have graunted to lone of ther goods to thuse of the fraternytie amotes [sic: among] them the some of xl*li*. that is to sey M. Percyvale xx*li*., M. Pemberton x*li*. and M. Barlowe x*li*. tyll the said assessyng shall be made and gadered and therof they to be repayed.

And therupon Henry Clough and John Doget, supervisours of the said werkes, have receyved of the said M. Percyvale the some of xx*li*.

Item they have receyved of the said M. Pemberton x*li*.

> Thomas Cape, tailor, acknowledged that he has received 20*s*. from William Werton, which the said William agreed to pay to the said Thomas. The same William was mainprised by John Bradwode, barbour, for the said 20*s*. in the presence of Henry Clough and Walter Povy.

[f. 38v]

Lune ix° die Januarii.[334]

> Richard Symer and John Deplech submitted themselves, on pain of 100*s*., to the arbitration of Robert Kelham and Thomas [S]peight etc. and award to be made before the feast of St. Paul [10 Jan.] If no award is made then they are to be ruled by the judgement of John Spencer before the feast of the Purification next [2 Feb.]

> William Gerveys submitted himself to the arbitration of Henry Brewster and John Broughton, arbiters chosen between him and Thomas Mytton etc., an award to be made before the feast of the Purification next [2 Feb.]

Where as certeyn varyaunces and controversyes were late moeved and dependyng bytwene the Maister, wardeyns and commaltye of this felaship of Tayllours on that one part and Richard Dyngley, broder of the said felaship on that other part, of and for the lees and terme of yeres of all that inne called the Saresyns Hede[335] in Frydaystrete of London which the said Richard hath and holdeth of the graunte of the said felasship. Which varyaunces the said Maister, wardeyns and commonaltye for ther part and also the said Richard for his part have put in the awarde and jugement of us John Swan, John

---

[334] 1491/2.
[335] For the rebuilding of the Saracen's Head see Introduction, pp. 18–19.

Percyvale, knyght, and Hugh Pemberton, aldreman, and therupon the said Maister, wardeyns and commonaltye and also the said Richard hath promysed to us the said John, John and Hugh to fulfylle all such decree and jugement as we shuld make bytwene them of and in the premisses. Wherupon we the said arbitrours with good advice and deliberacion make and yeve oute our awarde and decree bytwene them in this wise, that is to sey First we the said arbitrours callyng to our remembraunces the grete and manyfold costes and charges which the said Maister, wardeyns and commaltye have had and borne in and aboute the newe byldyng of the said inne, and also callyng to our remembraunce the good and fryndely brotherhode of the sayd Richard in dyvers wise before tyme had and doon to this said felasship and for a contynuans of the same we willyng the said Maister and wardeyns and commaltye sumwhat to be relieved and eased of ther said grete costes and willyng also the said Richard for his good and lovyng brotherhode before tyme had and in tyme comyng to be contynued in the said felasship awarde ordeyne and deme that the said Richard shall surrendre to the said Maister, wardeyns and commaltye the lees which the said Richard hath nowe in the same inne. And that doon we awarde that the said master, wardeyns and commaltye under ther commen seall make a newe graunt and lees of the said inne to the said Richard and his wif for lyke yeres as be conteyned in the olde lees. The same Richard paying yerely for the same for the terme of iiij the first yeres of the said terme to the said Maister, wardeyns and commaltie on Midsomer day a Rede rose if it be asked. And of the which terme of iiij the first yeres twoo yeres bene passed at Cristemas last past and yerely after the said iiij yeres complete xiij*li*. vj*s*. viij*d*. sterlinges at iiij termes of the yere usuell etc. by even percions. Of the which yerely rente of xiij*li*. vj*s*. viij*d*. we awarde that the said Richard of the some of xxvj*li*. xiij*s*. iiij*d*. by hym leyde downe aforehand towarde the byldyng of the said inne in two the first next after the said terme of iiij the first yeres. Beyng present at the makyng of this awarde the master and wardeyns, M. Swan, M. Percyvale, M. Pemberton, Keys, Barlowe, Deplech, Buk, Bowghton, Fittz, Randyll, Grene, Bromeflete and the said Richard Dyngley.

[f. 39 blank][336]

[f. 39v]

Richard Alenson, tailor, and William Crochewell submitted themselves to the arbitration of Thomas Petyt and Richard Hille, an award to be made before the feast of the Annunciation next [25 Mar.]

---

[336] The blank page corresponds to a gap in the minutes from 9 Jan. to 9 Mar. 1491/2.

Veneris ix° die Marcii.

Nicholas Assh and Paul Berkby submitted themselves, on a bond of 40s., to the arbitration of Alexander Carvanell and John Carvell, tailors, an award to be made before the feast of the Annunciation of the Blessed Virgin Mary next.

Ralph Osbolston and Robert Atkynson submitted themselves, on a bond of 40s., to the arbitration of Stephen Jenyns and Walter Povy, an award to be made before the first day of April next.

Robert Walssh, son of William Walssh of Trymme in the county of Meath (*Medie*) in the land of Ireland, husbandman, formerly the apprentice of Richard Cornhill, tailor, and admitted into the freedom, brought in the copy of his freedom dated the last day of January 7 Hen. VII [1491/2] and petitioned for a licence to hold a shop and paid in hand 10s.

William Molle, linendraper ...[337]

[f. 40] Hart

Lune xix° die Marcii.

Item Richard Lytell brought in 6s. 8d. for the farm of his tenement.
Item paid to the almsmen of this fraternity for the quindene before last Monday 5s. 8d.
From William Gybson for a fine for chastising his apprentice in the workshop 6d.

Lune xxvjto die Marcii.

John Breton, tailor, and Robert Cook, dyer, submitted themselves to the arbitration of John Lee and William Buk, an award to be made before the feast of Easter [22 Apr.] And if an agreement is not reached then they are to abide by the judgement of the master and wardens.

---

[337] Entry incomplete.

Veneris xiij° die Aprilis in presencia Magistri et custodum ac Percyvale, Galle, Keys, Barlowe, Lee, Jenyns, ..., Povy, Randyll, Bromeflete.

Geoffrey Mone and John Chapman submitted themselves to the arbitration of William Batyson and ... Lubsede, goldsmith.

Lune xvj° die Aprilis.

William Flecher and John Rogerson submitted themselves, on a bond of 40s., to the arbitration of Henry Alisaunder and William Gybson, an award to be made before Low Sunday [29 Apr.] next.

Richard Robynson who was the apprentice of Edward Smyth was committed to Peter Halle to serve until the end of his term.

Laurence Holme and John Shemell submitted themselves, on a bond of 40s., to the arbitration of John Baynard and Robert Stauncer etc. an award to be made before the quindene of Easter.

[f. 40v]

Veneris x°³³⁸ die Maii in presencia Magistri et custodum ac Percyvale, Pemberton, Keys, Barlowe, Galle, Jenyns, Spencer, Russh, Fittes, Bromeflete.

Robert Stephenson, brother of this fraternity, has acknowledged that he is bound to William Hert and the wardens of this fraternity in £10, on condition that the same Robert is of good behaviour and governance towards the aforesaid master and wardens and all and singular of this mistery as well in words as in deeds, and is to obey all the ordinances and statutes of this mistery, in order to preserve the good name of this mistery.

Item a meeting (*communicacio*) was held here concerning disputes between Master Spencer and Robert Grevys. And it is commanded that the same Robert should bring in the sum of 100s. on the next Monday and is to abide by the rule of the master, wardens and the 24.

---

338 An error for 'xj'.

The dispute between Richard Quykrell and William Alweder was submitted to the arbitration of James Fitz and John Povy, an award to be made before St. John's day [24 June].

Dies quarterii tentus xiij die Maii[339] in presencia Magistri et custodum ac Percyvale, Pemberton, Galle, Keys, Materdale, Lee, Deplech, Buk, Jenyns, Spencer, Russh, Hoberd, Adyf, Bromeflete, Wilford.

The aforenamed Robert Grevys, according to the aforesaid commandment, brought in the said 100s. It is ruled that he is to pay to the alms of this fraternity, acording to the ordinance made therefore, for his many contumacies towards the said Master Spencer, then master of this fraternity, 26s. 8d. which he paid and received the residue of the said 100s.

And it is determined this year that, for certain considerations moving this commonalty, no livery should be had.
And it is determined that this year there should be no livery and no new brethren.[340]

Sabbati xxvij[341] die Maii in presencia Magistri et custodum.

Thomas Petyt and Richard Hille, arbitrators between William Crochon and Richard Alenson have announced their award etc. And the said William agreed to abide by his part of the award, and the said Richard has refused.

[f. 41] Hart.

Lune iiij[to] die Junii

Launcelot Holme and Robert Stauncer, arbitrours electe and chosen bytwene William Gerveys and Thomas Mytton, have reported that they were aggreed bytwene the said parties before the day to them assigned. And they have awarded that where as the said Thomas by meanes of the said William was arrested at the sute of ij sundry persones, that is to wete a bruer and a pulter,

---

339   13 May 1492 was a Sunday which suggests that the meeting was in fact held on Monday the 14th.

340   This may relate to the restrictions placed upon admission to the livery introduced at the meeting held on 5 May 1490 (see above, p. 158).

341   An error for 'xxvj'.

and also at the sute of the same William That the same William shall cause all the same accions to be withdrawen at his owne costes and also that the same William shall discharge the said Thomas ayenst the same persones of all maner dettes and claymes which the nowe have ayenst hym. Also we award that the said Thomas in full payment and contentacion of all maner dettes and summes of money due by the said Thomas to the said William and also to the said bruer and pulter shall pay to the said William before the M. and wardeyns in Tayllours Halle viijs. and also we awarde that the said Thomas shall bryng and delyver to the said William a coyne of beyonde the see called the Sleper[342] and that than the said William shall delyver to the said Thomas a ryng of sylver wrought iij rynges all in one. And then eyther of them to geve other a generall acquitaunce.

Item we John Baynard and Robert Stauncer, arbitrours electe and chosen bitwene Launcelot Holme and John Shefeld, have awarded that the said John shall pay to the said Launcelot at Pentecost next comyng viijs. for recompence of all such trespasses and damages as the said John hath doon to the said Launcelot etc. Item that eyther of the said parties shall geve other a generall acquitaunce.

John Hede and John Spencer have submitted themselves to the arbitration of Henry Kellowe and Ralph Bukberd, arbiters impartially chosen by Master Percyvale, Master Pemberton, William Galle, Gilbert Keys, Roger Barlowe, John Lee, William Buk, Master Hert and the wardens, to rule upon all disputes concerning the sum of £5 which the said John Hede demands from the said John Spencer. And the aforesaid parties have agreed to obey the judgement of the arbiters, an end to be rendered by the said master and those who have been master.[343]

[f. 41v]

Concerning Archer and his apprentice. (*In Archer et apprenticium suum.*)

Memorandum that in the tyme of us William Hert, master,[344] Henry Clough, Nicholas Nynes, Henry Kellowe and Rauf Bukberd, wardeyns, Thomas Godfrey apprentice of Robert Archer,[345] Tayllour, for dyverse enormyous and ungodelely demeanynges doon by the said Robert to his said apprentice as principally in noon fyndyng hym competent and convenyent mete and drynk

---

[342] Unidentified.
[343] A number of phrases relating to a payment of 20s. were crossed out by the clerk.
[344] 1491–2.
[345] Godfrey had been apprenticed to Archer on 21 Nov. 1488: see above, p. 122.

and clothyng and also in unreasonable and undue chastesyng as the said apprentice seyde and also for noun fyndyng the same apprentice to scole contrary to thendentures and covenauntes bytwene the said Archer and his apprentice. Wherupon the same Archer at the commaundement of the said master and wardeyns executed by Thomas Gresyll, bedyll of the crafte, was warned to come to this place to answere to the premisses which Archer so came. And than the said master and wardeyns, examynyng this mater and heryng the excuses and seyinges of the said Archer, gave credence unto the same Archer and therupon commaunded the said apprentice to doo service [to] the said Archer as he was bound to doo. And so they departed and eftesones withyn short tyme after the said apprentice cam ayen and complayned hym in fourme abovesaid. And the said master and wardeyns not gevyng credence unto the same apprentice commaunded hym ayen to doo his master service as he was bound to doo. And so he departed and withyn a short while after the said apprentice camme ayen unto the said master and wardeyns pyteously compleynyng unto them of the unresonable and undue chastesyng and also of unclene kepyng, shewyng for the undue chastesyng howe that his master with a mete yerd[346] had sore bette hym aboute the hede as it than appered and also upon the naked body of the said apprentice as well in betyng as in unclene kepyng as foule shirtyd above his midyll and full of vermyn etc. Which seyng the said master and wardeyns sent for the said Archer and shewed unto hym all the premisses. And for his ungodeley dealyng in this behalf they having respecte to the tendre age of the said apprentice, beyng faderles and moderles, and also of the undue and unreasonable kepyng of the same apprentice commaunded the said Archer to bryng yn his endenture etc. and therby to sette over the same apprentice. Which to do the said Archer by long processe of tyme denyed to delyver. Wherupon by the advice of the said master and wardeyns the said apprentys asmoch as in them was was dismissed from the said Archer. And the said Archer for disobedyence was to committed to warde and so the cause and premisses were brought the Meyre and Chaumberleyn where and by whom it was remytted ayen to this place.

[f. 42] Walterus Povey.

Die Sabbati xxiiij° die Junii in vigilia Nativitatis Sancti Johannis Baptiste anno domini millesimo cccclxxxxij et anno regni regis Henrici septimi septimo In congregacione Magistri et custodum ac Percyvale, Pemberton,

---

346 A yardstick used by tailors and drapers to measure cloth. The company had its own official cloth-yard and in 1455-6 the sum of 4d. was paid 'pro tynnyng of the standard metyerd': Accounts, II, f. 75. A silver cloth-yard dating from the reign of Henry VII is still in the possession of the company: F. M. Fry and R. S. Tewson, *An Illustrated Catalogue of the Silver Plate of the Worshipful Company of Merchant Taylors* (London, 1929), pp. 5-9.

Galle, Keys, Depleche, Lee, Hede, Buk et Spencer, Walterus Povy electus est in magistrum istius fraternitatis ac eodem die Johannes Doget, Thomas Petyt, Ricardus Dyngley et Johannes Povy electi sunt in custodes ejusdem fraternitatis.

[translation] On Saturday the 24th day of June on the vigil of the Nativity of St. John the Baptist AD 1492, and in the seventh year of the reign of King Henry VII, at an assembly of the master and wardens and Percyvale, Pemberton, Galle, Keys, Depleche, Lee, Hede, Buk and Spencer, Walter Povy was chosen as master of this fraternity and the same day John Doget, Thomas Petyt, Richard Dyngley and John Povy were chosen as wardens of the same fraternity.

Walter Povy   master[347]

John Doget
Thomas Petyt
Richard Dyngley
John Povy   wardens[348]

Veneris vj^{to} die Julii in presencia Magistri et custodum.

John Hede presented Percyvale Otwell his apprentice.

The same day the following four good men of this fraternity were chosen as wardens of the keys to the common chest.[349]

Walter Povy, master
John Percyvale, alderman
Hugh Pemberton, alderman
Roger Barlowe

[f. 42v] Povey

Lune xvj° die Julii.

Charles Caryngton promised to pay 11s. to William Rubton, which he is to do within fifteen days.

---

[347] For Walter Povy see Appendix IV.
[348] For Doget, Petyt, Dyngley and John Povy see Appendix IV.
[349] The margin has a small sketch of a key by this entry. Wardens of the keys were first noted in the Tailors' records in 1410–11: they normally included the current master as well as three former masters of the craft: Accounts, I, f. 54v.

Henry Belle came here before the master and wardens and made a settlement for his freedom. It was granted to him for 32s. 4d. of which 6s. 8d. was paid in hand. And 6s. 8d. is to be paid at the feast of St. Michael the Archangel [29 Sept.] next, 6s. 8d. at Christmas, 6s. 8d. at Easter next [7 Apr. 1493] and 6s. 8d. at the feast of the Nativity of St. John the Baptist [24 June] then following.

And furthermore it was granted to the same Henry that he should pay nothing for his shop opening.

Martis xvij° die Julii in presencia Magistri et custodum ac Percyvale, Hert, Depleche, Lee, Buk, Jenyns, Adyf, Wilford, Boughton, Fittz, Grene, Bromeflete, Nynes.[350]

Master Buk, Master Deplech, Master Jenyns and Master Lee were assigned to prosecute the bill against foreigns (*forinsecos*).[351]

Item ordinatum est quod si aliquis confrater istius mistere in aliquo modo inhonesto garilat cum aliquo conquerenti versus aliquem istius fraternitatis in presencia magistri et custodum hic in aula seu alio loco solvat ad elemosinam xls.

[translation] Item it is ruled that if any brother of this mistery in any shameful way chatters with any plaintiff who is suing a member of this fraternity in the presence of the master and wardens, here in the Hall or in another place, he is to pay to the alms 40s.

Mercurii xvij[352] **die Julii dies quarterii in presencia Magistri et custodum ac Percyvale, Pemberton, Keys, Galle, Barlowe, Deplech, Lee, Buk, Hert ac tocius comitive istius fraternitatis.**

This day the last will of Hugh Champernon was read.
This day the last will of [John] Churchman was read.

Item this day, at the humble supplication of Geoffrey atte Welle, almsman who formerly received 46s. 8d. a year from this fraternity, it is granted to him, in augmentation of his said alms, 6s. 8d. Thus he now receives 53s. 4d. a year

Item the same is granted to Thomas Hosyer, almsman.

---

[350] Nicholas Nynes: see Appendix IV.
[351] Both the Tailors and Skinners were active in trying to persuade the city government to introduce more stringent controls on the activities of 'foreign' workers in London: see Introduction, pp. 40–1.
[352] An error for 'xviij'.

[f. 43] **Povey.**

Veneris iij° die Augusti in presencia Magistri et custodum.

Richard Halle, who was an apprentice of John Bode, brought in the copy of his freedom and petitioned for a licence to hold a shop, which was granted to him and he paid in hand 6s. 8d. and, mainprised by John Copelond, he agreed to pay 40d. at the feast of the Assumption next [15 Aug.]

Lune vj^to die Augusti.

Walter Povy, Maister of this felasship, as arbitrour electe and chosen bytwene Lyonell Baker and ... his wyf on that one party, and John Stokkall on that other partye, hath arbitred and awarded that for a perpetuell peas and amytie to be had bytwene the said parties from hensforth the said John shall pay to the said Lyonell xls. in this wise that is to sey before Sonday next comyng xxs. and in the feest of All Halowen [1 Nov.] next comyng xxs. And for the suretie of payment of the same xxs. to be paide at Halowemes the said John shall be bound to the said Lyonell with such suretie as the master shall admytte to pay the said xxs. at Halowemes. Item that doon the said parties that is to sey the said Lyonell and his wyf and the said John and his wif hall make eche to other a generall acquytans. Item I award that eyther of the said Lyonell and John for them and their wifes shall be bound to the master of the crafte for the tyme beyng in xli. to be of good aberyng eyther of them to other bothe in words and dedes and all other demeanynges and what partye that offendeth to forfeyt the same xli. that is to sey vli. therof to the chambre of the Gylde Halle of London and ls. therof to the almes of this craft and ls. resydue therof to the party of them that is so revyled or spoken by upon due proef therof had and made.

Item the same fifth[353] day John Baker compounded with the master and wardens to have the freedom of this mistery, which was granted to him for 40s. which he paid in hand etc.

[f. 43v] **Povey**

---

[353] 'quinto' clearly an error for 'sexto'.

Iovis xv^{o354} die Augusti in presencia Magistri et custodum ac Pemberton, West, Deplech, Hede, Galle, Buk, Jenyn, Hert, Hoberd, Fitz, Grene, Nynes.

Memorandum that this day a communicacion was had for the mater bytwene this crafte and Thomas Payne, carpenter, for the lece of the house in Adlane and it is dicted to the master and wardens to take an ende with the said Payne and therof to yeve relacion to the xxiiij.[355]

Item it [is] ordeyned and aggreed that the master and the wardeyns shall have full power and auctoritie to lete the newe tenement by the Saresyns Hede in Frydaystrete so alwey that they lete it for v*li.* or above.

Item the dispute between Master Hede and William Bunt was submitted to the arbitration of William Grene and Nicholas Nynes. Master Jenyns was chosen as umpire.

William Chawny, who was the apprentice of William Newport, brought in the copy of his freedom dated the 13th day of August 7 Hen. VII [1492] and petitioned for a licence to hold a shop, for which he agreed to pay at Michaelmas.

Vicesimo secundo die Augusti.

James a Penbury compounded with the master and wardens for the freedom in this mistery and he agreed to pay 53s. 4d. of which he paid in hand 10s. Of the residue he is to pay 6s. 8d. at Michaelmas [29 Sept.], 6s. 8d. at Christmas, 6s. 8d, at Easter [7 Apr. 1493], 6s. 8d. at the Nativity of St. John [24 June], 6s. 8d. at Michaelmas and 10s. at Christmas.
The said James acknowledged himself bound to serve with the said John Copeland from the feast of St Bartholomew [24 Aug.] next until the end of one year for 46s. 8d. with his food, and linen and woollen clothing (*victu et pannorum suorum lineorum lot*').

---

[354] An error for 'xvj'.

[355] Adlane = Adelstrete, in the parish of St. Alban Wood Street: Lobel (ed.), *Atlas*, p. 63. The Tailors' tenements in this parish were given to them by Thomas Carleton (d. 1389), whose chantry the Tailors administered in their chapel in St. Paul's: see above, n. 97. This particular property was in fact sublet by Payne to the Pinners' guild from 1480: see Introduction pp. 19–20.

Thomas Cressy brought in the copy of his freedom dated the 2nd day of May and petitioned for a licence to hold a shop and paid in hand 10s.

Veneris xxx[356]° die Augusti.

Thomas Bredmere compounded with the master and wardens for Thomas Smyth the apprentice of William Olyver for 23s. of which 10s. is to be paid in hand and 7s. at the feast of All Saints [1 Nov.] and 7s. at the feast of the Purification [2 Feb.]

And it is agreed that Thomas Payn will surrender the lease of Pinners' Hall (*indenturam de Pynners halle*)[357], and that the same Thomas is to have in recompense a tenement in Lymestrete to the value of 10s. a year.

[f. 44]

Lune tercio die Septembris.

The dispute between William Greves and Agnes Waleys was submitted to the arbitration of Edward Fenkell and William Baker etc. an award to be made before St. Michael's day [29 Sept.]

Lune x° die Septembris in presencia Magistri et custodum ac Percyvale, West, Deplech, Buk, Lee, Boughton, Fyttes, Randyll, Grene, Wilford et Clough.

Thomas Gresyll reported that he had summoned Master Heed to come here on this day, and he did not come. Therefore it is determined that he should be fined.

Item this day a communicacion was had by the said Maister and wardeyns and other worshipfull persones aforesaid of the eleccion namyng and chosyng of the xxiiij men to be assigned to stond and be of the councell of this crafte. And it was ordeyned and condescended that the persones whos names ensue shall stond before the xxiiij of the councell of the said crafte. And also for as moch as the councelles and secretes of the said crafte by som persones

---

[356] An error for 'xxxj'..
[357] See Introduction, pp. 19–20.

beforetyme have ben disclosed and discovered oute of the said crafte wherby grete incovenyences have ensued therfore it is ordeyned that the said xxiiij and all the [persones] herafter shall be chosen and named to be of the xxiiij shall be sworne accordyng to othe therof made and wreten in the boke of othes of the said crafte.[358]

M. Walterus Povy jur'	Alanus Hoberd jur'
M. Johannes Percyvale aldermannus jur'	Owinus Boughton jur'
M. Hugo Pemberton aldermannus jur'	Johannes Rissh
M. Galle jur'	Jacobus Fites jur'
M. Keys jur'	Thomas Randyll jur'
M. Barlowe jur'	Willelmus Grene jur'
M. Materdale	Jacobus Wilford jur'
M. Duplech jur'	Ricardus Adyf jur'
M. Lee jur'	Thomas Bromflete jur'
M. Hede jur'	Nicholus Nynes jur'
M. Buk jur'	Johannes Doget jur'
M. Jenyns jur'	
M. Spencer jur'	
M. Hert jur'	

Item eodem x[mo] die
Robertus Spryngfelde jur'
Thomas Sharparowe jur'
Robertus Benet'
Willelmus Caston'
electi sunt in custodes societate Baculariorum fraternitatis Sancti Johannis in die decollacionis ejusdem Sancti Johannis ultimo iam preterito.

> [translation] Item the same 10th day Robert Spryngfelde, Thomas Sharparowe, Robert Benet, and William Caston were chosen and sworn as wardens of the society of the Bachelors of the fraternity of St. John the Baptist from the feast of the Decollation of the same St. John [29 Aug.] last past.

[f. 44v] Povey[359]

358   Anc. MS. Bk. 1 in the company's archive, now in Guildhall Library.

359   At least two separate hands were responsible for the entries on this page, which seems to herald the end of William Duryvale's career as clerk. He was paid his salary for Michaelmas term on 12 October 1492 (see below, p. 207), but was not replaced for at least two months, no clerk being among the officers paid their salaries for the quarter before Christmas (below, p. 218). Henry Mayour was paid for the first time on 3 March 1493 when his salary was for the quarter up to the feast of the Assumption (25 March). Given that the hand in fact changes

Lune xvij° die Septembris in presencia Magistri et custodum ac Percyvale, Pemberton, Keys, West, Barlowe, Deplech, Lee, Buk, Jenyns, Spencer, Hoberd, Boughton, Fittes, Adyf, Grene, Randyll.

The wife of John Bode was granted authority by the master and wardens to act as master of Thomas Dyson, her apprentice, according to the ordinance.[360]

The dispute between Master Lee and John Barton[361] was examined by the 24 above named, and it was commanded that John Kyrkeby should testify and the same John was examined and testified that the said Barton used insulting language (*male gessit seipsum in aliquibus verbis*).

Item concordatum est quod cum M. Johannes Hede qui preantea pluries summonitus fuit ad veniendum ad aulam et non venit sed contempsit quod idem Johannes distringatur et quod materia ostendatur maiori. Et ...

[translation] Item it is agreed that as Master John Heed, who was previously summoned on many occasions to appear at the Hall, did not come but was in contempt, that the same John should be distrained and that the matter should be shown to the mayor. And ...

Item concessum est Willelmo Purches aldermanno qui modo electus est in vicecomitem habebit occupacionem aule hujus ad festum.

[translation] It is concluded that William Purches, alderman,[362] who is now chosen as sheriff, is to have the use of this Hall at the feast.

Mercurii iij° die Octobris in presencia Magistri et custodum ac Percyvale, Pemberton, Barlowe, West, Deplech, Lee, Buk, Jenyns, Boughton, Fittz, Grene et Bromeflete.

Johannes Hede qui preantea pro multipliciis contumaciis et disobedienciis suis incarceratus fuit submisit et compromisit se obedire ordinacionibus.

---

permanently on 10 October, it seems probable that, rather than rely upon temporary staff to enter the minutes of meetings during this interregnum, the court left a backlog of entries for Mayour to deal with on taking office in January.

[360] Dyson had been enrolled as an apprentice by John Bode on 18 May 1490 (see above, p. 160). This formal transfer of the apprenticeship to his wife in September 1492 suggests that he had recently died. The ordinance referred to here does not survive.

[361] Probably William Barton: see below, pp. 217–18.

[362] A mercer who was city chamberlain Sept. 1484–92, sheriff 1492–3, and alderman 1492–1502: Beaven, *Aldermen*, vol. 2, p. 18.

[translation] John Hede, who was previously imprisoned for his many contumacies and disobediences, submitted and promised to obey the ordinances.

Mercurii x° die Octobris in presencia Magistri et custodum ac M. Percyvale, M. Pemberton, Keise, Barlow, West, Deplege, Hede, Buk, Fittes, Boughton, Randell.[363]

Robert Deane the same xth day in the presence of the worshipful persones aforenamed hath compounded with the Maister and wardeyns for his libertee and fraunchesie in this crafte to be had and the same with thassent of the samer persones is graunted unto hym for xl*s*. sterlinges to be paid in fourme folowyng that is to sey the same xth daye in hand xiij*s*. iiij*d*. which he so paid and at the feste of Purificacion of Seint Mary Virgyn [2 Feb.] than next ensuying xxvj*s*. viij*d*. as by a bill obligatory therof made more playnly is conteyned.

Thomas Barbour, corsour,[364] for divers causes by hym the same day shewed and at thinstaunce of divers worshipfull persones to the maister and wardeyns in this present place made was aggreed to translate his copy of the felaship of corsours aforsaid to be a broder of this company which was graunted unto hym for viij*s*. iiij*d*. which he furthwith paid etc. And therupon he was admitted and sworen.

[f. 45]

Veneris xij^{mo} die Octobris

prestes wages
First paid to Sir[365] John Ratclyf for his salary for Mighelmasse terme xxxiij*s*. iiij*d*.
Item paid to Sir Richard Wheler for his salary the same terme xxxiij*s*. iiij*d*.
Item paid to Sir John Burnam for his salary the same terme xvj*s*. viij*d*.
Item paid to Sir Robert Cudworth for his stipend the same terme xxxv*s*.

---

363 The hand changes permanently here to that of Henry Mayour (see above, n. 359, and Introduction, pp. 8–11).
364 The corsours of London were horse-dealers. By 1520 they had been 'taken over' by the Innholders' Company: W. C. Hazlitt, *The Livery Companies of the City of London* (London, 1892), pp. 155, 537–42; W. H Harris, *The History of the Worshipful Company of Innholders of the City of London* (London, 1922), p. 12.
365 For this title see Glossary.

Item paid to Sir Thomas Roos for his salary for half a yere ended at feste of Seint Mighell last passed the daye aforsaid iiij*li*.

Item paid to Sir George Bromehill[366] for his wages the same terme xxxiij*s*. iiij*d*.

wages of officers

Item paid to William Duryvale, clerke of the feliship, for his salary and wages the same terme of Mighelmasse xxv*s*.

Item paid to Thomas Gresill, bidell of the said feliship, for his salary and for the kepyng of the gardyn the same terme xviij*s*. iiij*d*.

Be it remembered that a complaynt was made unto the Maister and wardeyns by John Darby ayenst M. Heed for and in the cause of William Bunt late apprentice with the same M. Heed. Which variaunce and cause by the said Maister and wardeyns in this present place was discretely and sadly examyned and in the tyme of such examynacion the said M. Heed in the presence of the said Maister and wardeyns and also other worshipfull persones than beyng togiders assembelled in ungoodly wise reviled, rebuked and spake unto the said Derby unmanerly upon an answere by the same Derby made unto a question leyed by the same M. Heed. The same M. Heed answered and seide unto the said Derby with an unmeeke spirit, a rude voice, unsad demeanure and irreverent maner:

Thou liest falsely lyke a false harlot as thou arte.

Wherunto the said Derby answered soberly with a well advised mynde and sad demeanure and seide:

Sir I note and remembre in what place and whose presence that I am in. And if I were in an other place and from hensse and worshipfull company I wold speke as playne Englissh unto you as ye have don unto me.

All this not withstandyng upon a request made to the said M. Heed by the foresaid Maister and wardeyns the same M. Heed had aggreed to stand unto thaward of Aleyn Hubert and Richard Hyll, arbitratours there and than indifferently named and chosen, wherupon ij obligacions of arbitrament were made and sealed bitwene the said parties. And although the said M. Heed was bound as is aforsaid yet he delayed the tyme to the arbitratours lymyted and wold never sen[d] unto theym nor shewe unto theym his cause and matiers. Wherupon William Duryvale, clerke of the crafte by the commaundement of the Maister went unto [f. 45v Povey] the said M. Heed willyng desiryng and exortyng hym in the maisters name to be at Seint Thomas of Acres upon Monday next than comyng bitwene the houres of viij and ix the same day

---

[366] Bromehill replaced Roger Doket who died in 1491 (see above, n. 122) as one of the three stipendiary chaplains employed by the Tailors' fraternity: see also Appendix III.

there before noon than to purpose and shewe all such thinges of complaynte as he couth allege ayenst William Bunt late his apprentice before the ij arbitratours that were elect in that behalf for as moche as the daye of arbitrament lymyted unto theym approched and drue nere. And also the frendes of the said William Bunt dwellyng in the countrey purposely were comen to have an end in the matier that it wold please the said M. Heed to excite and stere the said arbitratours to make an end in the said matier wherunto the same M. Heed answered seiyng this wyse that he never complayned hym in the Hall ayenst the said Bunt, and as for the arbitratours shuld not be desired nor prayed by hym, wherfore he wold not com to Seint Thomas of Acres to labour theym theirin. Also he seyd that the Maister toke the seiyngs and complayntes of the said Bunt and he herd such witnesses as the same Bunt brought in his owne hous where he shuld have don it at the Hall. And furthermore he seynd that he wold that the Maister wold speke as well in his matier for the *vli.* that he delivered unto M. Spencer, later Maister etc. as he dyd in this matier for which seiynggs the said M. Heed was sent fore by the bydell for to com unto Taillours Hall there tanswere and shewe whye and for what cause he denyed and refused to com and do as he was instaunced etc.

Wherupon the same M. Heed in the presence of the Maister and wardeyns and of the right worshipfull persones Maister Pemberton aldreman, M. West, M. Gall, M. Duplach, M. Buk, M. Jenyns, M. Hert, Aleyn Hubert, James Fitte, William Grene and Nicholas Nynes beyng at Taillours Hall, upon a long communicacion had there in this matier it was agreed to make and seale new obligacions for asmoche as the olde obligacions were expired. And than and there by the said maister and worshipfull company William Grene and Nicholas Nynes were of new electe and named to here and determyn this matier. And if they couth not aggree be Halowmasse [1 Nov.] next than ensuyng M. Stephen Jenyns than to be umpiere to make an ende in the matier before Martynmasse [11 Nov.] next than comyng and therto as well the said M. Heed as the frendes of the said William Bunt aggreed. And accordyng to that aggreament the said frendes of the said William Bunt sealed their obligacion and afterward for asmoch as the said M. Heed had not sealed his obligacion, Thomas Petyt one of the wardeyns and William Duryvale, clerk, by the commaundement of the Maister went to the same M. Heed willyng hym to seale his obligacion as the other partie had don wherunto he answered precisely that he wolde seale none obligacion for none horemonger as he was. And therupon he was commaunded by the said wardeyn to com to the hall the Monday next than ensuyng to shew the matier and the cause whye he refused so to do. At which daye lymyted the said M. Heed came to the Taillours Hall and at his comyng thidre the Maister demaunded hym why he delayed to seale his obligacion accordyng to his promyse. Wherunto the said M. Heed answered precisely that he wolde noone seale all be it though

that he had promysed before to seale it he wold than revoke it for his
counceill advised hym so to do and that Stephen **[f. 46]** Jenyns shuld not be
his jugge nor the Maister neither for Stephen Jenyns had caused hym to lose
xxxviij*li*. And therupon the Maister answered:

> Sir, I most be your juge this yere.

Than the said M. Heed seyed:

> Sir, ye take to moche upon you for I have sitten in the Rome[367] as well
> as ye now do and was as able therto for I may expende xxx*li*. by yere as
> long as I lyve and ye take upon you more than ye nede and so wole xx
> moo sey aswell as I.

And thus the said M. Heed made grete comparisons with the Maister as in
beyng charge in the crafte and other thinges without regardyng or
reverencyng his office or the place. Wherunto the said Maister seyed:

> Sir, ye usyng no better condicions nor demeanure than ye now do it is
> pitee that ever ye bare the Rome or worship in this felaship as ye have
> don.

The said M. Heed answered ayen uncharitably seiyng this wyse:

> It is more pitee that ye sit ye sit in the Rome that ye sitte in and so moo
> sey as well as I.

Wherupon the said maister for the ungoodly dealyng of the said M. Heed at
that tyme and also affore that tyme caused certeyn ordynaunces and statutes
which bene made for the good rules and governaunces of the men of the said
crafte to be redd in which the said M. Heed had offended contrary to his othe
demaundyng hym whether he wold abide by the said ordynaunces or not.
The said M. Heed answered seiyng:

> Sir, I know thise ordynaunces as well as ye do but I wole not abide nor
> fulfill theym.

For asmoche as the said M. Heed renounced and denyed to be ruled and
governed by the old auncyent ordynaunces and laudable constitucions of this
present place but wold folow his own sensualitee and froward appetyte,
therfore his ungoodly demeanure and wilfull maner was shewed unto my lord
the mayre[368] of this noble citee which instaunced excited and moved the said
M. Heed to confourme hym self to the Maister and wardeyns and to the rules
and ordynaunces of his crafte which to do he precisely denyed. The Meyre
seyng his obstynate wilfull presumpcion and continuell disobedience and
wold not refourme hym self commytted the said M. Heed unto warde and
there he remayned v dayes in which tyme he sobred and mollified his
impetuouse agony and ire. Wherupon he was dismyssed oute of duresse and
came to this present place and humbly submytted hym self to the Maister and
wardeyns hertily desiryng theym to be good Maister and frendes unto hym

---

[367] 'Room', meaning in this case the office or position of Master of the craft: *OED*.
Heed held the post in 1483–4.

[368] Hugh Clopton, mercer, was mayor for 1491–2.

for he knewe well that he had mysse used hym self in brekyng of the ordynaunces wherfore he was penitent. The Maister and his wardeyns consideryng his lowly submyssion and reconsiliacion and how he confourmed hym self to the good ordynaunces and rules of this place admytted reputed and toke hym in every degree condicion and maner as he was afore for the fyne of xxs. which he paid.

All which premisses afore declared and specified not withstondyng the said M. Heed sealed thobligacion in which Nicholas Nynes and William Grene were named and indifferently electe arbitratours bitwene the said M. Heed on that one partye and William Bunt, late his apprentice on that other [f. 46v Povey] partye, by force and virtue of ij obligacions with condicions of arbitrament in the which the same parties bene bounden to stand unto thearbitrament ordynaunce and jugement of the said Nicholas Nynes and William Grene. First they awarde ordeigne and deme that the said William shall com and appere in his own persone before the Maister and wardeyns of the feliship of taillours in Taillours Halle and before the said M. Heed his maister and there shall knele down upon his knee and shall in lowly wise aske forgyfnese of the said M. Heed for all trespasses and hertily beseche thesaid M. Heed to be his good maister.

Also they awarde that the said William Bunt shall deliver unto the Maister and wardeyns of the forseid feliship immediately at the pronouncyng of their awarde iij*li*. vj*s*. viij*d*. unto thuse of the said M. Heed.

Also they awarde that the same M. Heed atte costes of the said William shall present the same William in the Chambre of Guyldhall of London before the chambreleyn or his deputee there and shall cause the same William to be admytted into the fraunchise of London and to be freman of the crafte of taillours.

And also they awarde that assone as the said William is made freman the said M. Heed shall have the foresaid iij*li*. vj*s*. viij*d*. and that than either of the forseid parties shall enseale and deliver unto other a generall acquietaunce of almaner accions personels from the begynyng of the world unto the day aforsaid.

Lune quintodecimo die mensis Octobris

Quiete rentes

Also paid to the Priour of Cristes Chirch[369] in London for a quiete rent of vij*s*. goyng oute yerely of certeyn landes and tenementes in the parisshe of Seint Martyn Oteswich for the yeres of M. Jenyns, M. Spencer and M. Hert xxj*s*.

---

[369] Holy Trinty priory near Aldgate.

and for this present yere vij*s*. Sum total xxviij*s*. as by acquietaunce therof made for iiij yeres more playnly shall appere xxviij*s*.

Also paid to Richard Haynes and to Richard Broude, wardeyns of the house of lepres of Kyngeslond and the Loke,[370] as by acquietaunce therof made more clerely is shall appere xiij*s*. iiij*d*.

Also paid to George Sutton, Maister of Burton Seint Lazar' Jerusalem in Englond and keper of thospitall of Seint Giles without London[371], for a quiet rent of xxvj*s*. yerely goyng oute of the tenementes that late were of John Langwith for half a yere ended at Mighelmasse as by acquietaunce therof made more playnly it shall appere xiij*s*.
Also paid to the said George for half a yere ended at the fest of Thannunciacion of Seint Mary Virgyn [25 Mar.] next folwyng the day aforsaid xiij*s*.

[f. 47]

Quiete rentes

Also paid to the said George Sutton for a quiete rent of xxiij*s*. yerely goyng oute of certeyn landes and tenementes in Garlekhyth parisshe for an hole yere ended at Mighelmasse last passed [29 Sept.] as by acquietaunce therof made more openly it shall appere.

Also paid to the Prioresse of Clerkenwell[372] for a quiet rent of xxvj*s*. viij*d*. by yere goyng out of a tenement somtyme of John Winchecombe in the parisshe of Oure Lady of Colchirch for an hole yere ended at Mighelmase last passed as by acquietaunce therof made more playnly is conteyned xxvj*s*. viij*d*.

Also paid to the Prioresse of Kylbourn[373] for a quiet rent of xvij*s*. goyng oute of certeyn tenementes in the parisshe of Our Lady of Abchirch for one hole yere ended at Mighelmasse last passed as by acquietaunce therof made more openly it shall appere xvij*s*.

---

[370] Kingsland Hospital in Hackney was founded by the City *c*.1280 and was administered by two wardens who, as this entry confirms, also supervised the Lock hospital in Southwark: Honeybourne, 'Leper Hospitals', pp. 31-8, 44-54; VCH, *Middlesex*, I (1969), p. 210 and see above, n. 238.
[371] For the connection between St. Giles and the house of Burton Lazars see above, n. 21. Sutton occurs as Master from 1484 to 1493 when he was succeeded by Thomas Harringwold: Honeybourne, 'Leper Hospitals', p. 28.
[372] See above, n. 115.
[373] See above, n. 161.

Also paid to the said Prioresse of Kylbourn for a quiet rent of vjs. viijd. yerely goyng out of a tenement set in Bredestrete for an hole yere ended at the same Mighelmasse as by acquietaunce therof made more playnly appereth vjs. viijd.

Also paid to the Priour of Seint Mary Overey in Suthwerk[374] for a quiet rent of viijs. yerely goyng oute of certeyn landes and tenementes in the parisshe of Seint Martyn Oteswich for an hole yere ended at Mighelmasse last passed as by acquietaunce therof made more playnly it apereth viijs.

Also paid to the Chamberleyn of the Monastery of Seint Petre of Westminster for a quiete rent of xxs. by yere goyng oute of certeyn tenementes in Frydaye strete for half a yere ended at Mighelmasse last passed as by acquietaunce therof made more playnly is conteyned xs.

Also paid to the said Chamberleyn for a quiet rent of ixs. by yere goyng oute of certeyn tenementes in the parissh of Our Lady of Colchirch for half a yere ended at the said feste of Mighelmasse as by acquietaunce therof made more playnly is declared iiijs.vjd.

Also paid to the maister of Seint Kateryns[375] for a quiet rent of xs. by yere goyng out of certeyn tenementes in the parisshe of Our Lady of Abchirch for an hol yere ended atte feste of Seint Mighell last passed as by acquietaunce therof made more playnly is specified xs.

[f. 47v] Povey

Veneris decimo nono die Octobris.

Randolph Nowell promytted the same daye before the Maister and his iiij wardeyns to present John[376] Greye late his apprentice before the chambreleyn of the citee of London for that tyme beyng for his fraunchise to be had there. And the same John the said daye and tyme before the forsaid maister and wardeyns promytted and graunted to pay to the said Randolph xiijs. iiijd. sterlinges for divers trespasses and offenses by hym don to the same Randolph the dayes of payment of which xiijs. iiijd. appere suyngly that is to sey in hand iijs. iiijd., in the feste of Cristemas than next suyng iijs. iiijd., in the feste of Candilmasse [2 Feb.] next than folowyng iijs. iiijd., and at Our Lady Daye in Lent [25 Mar.] iijs. iiijd. All which paymentes be perfourmed.

---

374 See above, n. 156.
375 St. Katherine Cree: see above, n. 16.
376 'Thomas' in margin.

Adhuc die Veneris predicto nono die Octobris.

Thward made by Alayne Hubert, Henry Clough, Thomas Bromefeld and John Bernard arbitratours indifferently named and electe bitwene Edmond Flour citezein and taillour of London on that one partie and John Saxy of London taillour on that other partie as by ij obligacions of arbitrament therof made more playnly is conteyned theffecte of which awarde herafter foloweth.

First we awarde ordeigne and deme that the said John Saxy furthwith at the yildyng up of this oure present awarde shall desire and besche the forsaid Edmond to be good maister to the same John at all tymes whan he shalbe therto resonably and manerly required.

Also we award and deme that eyther of the said Edmond and John shall ley doun into our handes in redy money vjs. viijd. which shalbe for the writyng makyng and engrocyng of this our said award and such other wrytynges as shall perteigne to the same.

Also we awarde and juge the said John Saxsy to pay to the forsaid Edmond xiij*li*. vjs. viijd. sterlinges in maner and fourme folowyng that is to sey in the feste of Nativitee of our Lord God next folowyng the daye aforsaid iij*li*. vjs. viijd., in the feste of thannunciacion of Seint Mary Virgyn [25 Mar.] next than suyng iij*li*. vjs. viijd., in the feste of Nativitee of Seint John Baptist [24 June] than next folowyng iij*li*. vjs. viijd. and in the feste of Seint Mighell tharchaungell [29 Sept.] next than folowyng iij*li*. vjs. viijd. as in iiij severall sengle obligacions therof made more playnly it shall appere.

[f. 48] Also we awarde ordeigne and deme that where the said John Saxsy claymeth a bargayne of cloth of the forsaid Edmond to the sume of an c*li*. as in certeyn parcelles specified in a bill of his own hand more at large it shall appere we decree and juge that if the said John Saxsy before the fest of Seint Andrew thappostell [30 Nov.] next suyng the daye aforsaid bryng such suertees that the said Edward wole holde hym contented with for the payment of the said c*li*. and the same suertees to be bounden with the said John that the same John shall enjoye and have the said bargayne and if he do the contrary and default in bryngyng in the suertees in the said feste of Seint Andrewe than the said bargayne to be utterly voide and of none effecte ne force.

And also we award that the said Edmond shall deliver to the forsaid John thise parcelles folowyng that is to sey

first a tawny conteignyng xxij yerds and di.
also a blak lynyng conteignyng xxiij yerds and quarter
also a remenaunt of blak lynyng of xj yerds iij quarters
also iij fleces of white wolle
also an olde blake goun and a buk skynne
also a walkyng bill[377]
also a pair of old crymsyn hosyn and ij olde botes.

Lune vicesimo octavo[378] **die Octobris.**

The same day John Bodyam and Roger Boterode before the Maister and his wardeyns are fully aggreed and accorded of and for almaner matiers, contraversies, variaunces, discordes and debates than moved or dependyng bitwene theym and so eyther of theym hath clerely before the said Maister and wardeyns relessed and pardoned to other of theym almaner offenses, trespasses and demaundes don affore the same daye. And over that the said Roger than graunted and promytted to departe from the house that he than dwelled in at the feste of thannunciacion of Seint Mary Virgyn [25 Mar.] next folowyng the daye aforsaid.

[f. 48v] Povey

Die Iovis ultimo[379] **die mensis Octobris**

le bargeman
First paid to Robert Hassok, bargeman, for the conveiyng and havyng up of the Maister and felaship to Westminster and ayen with and for the shrefes and mayre of London at ij severall tymes acordyng to the olde custome hertofore in this crafte of old tyme used and accustumed xxvj*s*. viij*d*.

Also paid the same tyme to his bargemen for a potacion in wey of rewarde and gentilnesse as of old tyme it hath be accustumed xx*d*.

Die Lune quarto die mensis Novembris.

The same daye John Geynes of London, steynour,[380] toke to ferme of the Maister and iiij wardeyns the tenement and gardyn and with all other appurtenaunces to the same apperteignyng set beside the tenement that the Pynners[381] holde to ferme of the crafte in the parisshe of Seint Albane of London for certeyn yeres at which tyme it was than aggreed that the said John atte his propre costes and charges shuld make a new chymney in the kechyn. Except that the Maister of the crafte hath promyssed to gyf and paye

---

377 A bill was a long-handled weapon, typically carried by watchmen, although a *walking* bill was probably just a staff of some kind.

378 An error for '*vicesimo novo*'.

379 An error for '*tricesimo*'.

380 Stainers of wood, paper, cloth etc. Joined with the Painters to form the Painter-stainers' Company in 1501–2: Unwin, *Gilds and Companies*, p. 384.

381 See above, pp. 19–20.

to the same John toward his said charges in brieke m¹ and in redy money vs. which ij thinges the maister hath perfourmed.

Die Lune undecimo³⁸² die dicti mensis Novembris.

The same Mondaye Randolph Nowell promytted before the Maister and his wardeyns to present John Grey late his apprentice before the chambreleyn of London for the tyme beyng for the injoynyng of the frauncheyse and libertee of this citee accordyng to his derservynges by reason of apprentishode fully served. Which John Grey the same daye before the said Maister and wardeyns promytted to paye unto the said Randolph for certayn offences and trespasses by hym commytted and don in tymes passed unto hys said maister xiij*s*. iiij*d*. in fourme folowyng that is to sey than in handes iij*s*. iiij*d*., atte feste of Cristmasse than next suyng iij*s*. iiij*d*., atte feste of Candilmasse [2 Feb.] next than folowyng iij*s*. iiij*d*. and atte feste of thannunciacion of Seint Mary Virgyn [25 Mar.] next than ensuyng iij*s*. iiij*d*. which dayes of payment were truly kept and the said John Grey is decessed.

[f. 49]

Adhuc die Lune undecimo die ejusdem mensis Novembris.

The same daye John Bodyam and Roger Boterode in the presence of the Maister and his wardeyns were fully accorded and aggreed of and for almaner matiers and causes at that daye bitwene they dependyng. Which Roger the same daye in the forsaid presence promytted and graunted to departe from the tenement and hous that he than dwelled in atte daye of thannunciacion of Seint Mary Virgyn [25 Mar.] next folowyng the daye aforsaid.

Die Veneris quintodecimo³⁸³ die predicti mensis Novembris.

The same daye M. Hert and Robert Tomson late his apprentice compromytted them self in the presence of the Maister and his wardeyns to stand and obey unto tharbitrament ordynaunce and juggement of M. William Galle and Nicholas Nynes arbitratours indifferently electe and named bitwene theym of and upon almaner matiers causes etc. as in ij obligacions of arbitrament therof made more playnly is conteyned.

---

³⁸² An error for 'duodecimo'.
³⁸³ An error for 'sextodecimo'.

Die Lune decimonovo die dicti mensis Novembris.

The same daye Thomas Wylmot, which than was apprentice of Richard Smyth, in the presence of the Maister and his wardeyns of his own aggreament and with the consent of the said Richard was commytted unto Roger Mone to serve hym as his apprentice unto the full end and accomplisshement of his termes specified in his indenture of apprentishode without any thing paiyng or gyffyng unto the forsaid Richard or to thuse of the crafte than for divers causes and consideracions by the forsaid Maister and wardeyns considered.

[f. 49v] Povey.

Die Veneris vicesimo tercio die mensis Novembris.

The same daye John Wendelesse, than apprentice of John Lewes, in the presence of the M. and his wardeyns of his own consent and free will with thaggreament of the said John Lewes his maister was commytted unto Richard Semar to serve unto hym as his apprentice unto the full end of the termes of his apprentishode recited and specified in his said indenture than for to com. For whose termes the said Richard Semar than graunted to pay xxxiijs. iiijd. in fourme folowyng that is to sey unto the M. to thuse and behofe of the crafte xiijs. iiijd. and to the said John Lewes xxs. for the which the said Richard sealed a bill obigatory payable at a certeyn day bitwene theym aggreed xiijs. iiijd.

Die Lune vicesimo sexto die mensis Novembris.

No business on account of the feast (*Nichil quia festivalis*).[384]

Die Iovis quarto[385] die mensis Decembris.

<u>Le quarter daye</u>
The same day was the quarter daye holden in the presence of the Maister, his iiij wardeyns, M. Percyvale, M. Pemberton, aldremen, Keys, Barlowe, West,

---

[384] The event referred to here is not recorded. It was probably a civic occasion such as the election dinner of the mayor which was commonly held in the Tailors' hall in the late 15th century: see above, p. 41.
[385] An error for '*sexto*'.

Duplach, Hede, Buk, Jenyns, Fittez, Boughton, Grene, Bromefeld and Randall and the hole body of the feliship than assembled.

It was than condescended and aggreed by the xxiiijti that William Styllyng of the towne of Westminster which instauntly desired to be of the fraternitee of Seint John Baptist founded in this crafte was admytted than to be free of the said crafte he paiyng to thuse of the same crafte xls. sterlinges in fourme folowyng that is to sey in handes xiijs. iiijd., atte feste of thannunciacion of Seint Mary Virgyn xiijs. iiijd. and at Pentecoste than next suyng xiijs. iiijd. as by an obligacion therof made more playnly is conteyned. And over that it was graunted to the said Stillyng to paye nothing for his openyng for dyvers causes than considered xls.

The same daye was the last will of Hugh Champernon redd.
Also the last wyll of John Chircheman redd.[386]

[f. 50]

Die Veneris duodecimo[387] die dicti mensis Decembris.

The same day in the presence of the Maister, his iiij wardeyns M. Pemberton, Gall, West, Barlow, Lee, Hede, Jenyns, Aleyn Hubert, Richard Haydyf and James Fittez, M. Lee shewed that William Barton had used hym self ungoodly toward the same M. Lee[388] and his wyf in unmanerly speche and unlefull language for which causes the said Barton was commoned with by the M. in the presence of the persones aforenamed. And he then of obstinacye and presumpcion not regardyng this place ne havyng reverence unto such persones as have ben governours and rulers of this worshipfull crafte accordyng to thordynaunces therof made, the M. of his pollicye seyng the firy heet and brennyng rancour of the said Barton intendyng to abate and mollifie his grete ire caused certeyn ordinaunces to be redd, the same William Barton heryng thextremitees and penalties set upon such transgressours and brekers of thordynaunces sobred hym self and humbly submytted hym to the good rules of this crafte and wolde be confourmable to the M. commaundement. The M. seyng his lowly submission enjoyned hym to paye to thalmes of the crafte for his myssebehavyng vjs. viijd. which furthwith he dyd. And over that to aske remyssion and pardon of the said M. Lee afore the forsaid persones for such offenses and trespasses that he had used, which he fulfilled. And than after that to goo unto the dwellyng place of the said M. Lee and

---

[386] For Churchman and Champernoun see above, nn. 40, 129.
[387] An error for '*quartodecimo*'.
[388] John Lee (master 1483–4). See Appendix IV.

there to aske forgyfnesse of Maistres Lee[389] for such unfittyng wordes that he afore tyme had seyde ayenst the same Maistres Lee. Whose injunction the same Barton performed in the presence of John Doget and John Povey than beyng wardeyns. vjs. viijd.

Die Lune quintodecimo[390] die ejusdem mensis Decembris ac in tota septimana sequente.

No business on account of the search (*Nichil quia scrutinium*).[391]

[f. 50v] Povey

Die Lune vicesimo secundo[392] die predicti mensis Decembris.

prestes wages
First paid to Sir[393] John Ratclyf for his salarye for a quarter of a yere endyng at Cristmasse than next xxxiijs. iiijd.
Item paid to Sir George Bromehill for his salary the same quarter xxxiijs. iiijd.
Item paid to Sir Robert Cudworth for his salary the same quarter xxxvs.
Item paid to Sir Richard Wheler for his salary the same quarter xxxiijs. iiijd.
Item paid to Sir John Burnam for his salary the same quarter xxvjs. viijd.

officers wages[394]
Item paid to Thomas Gresill bedill of the feliship for his wages the same terme and for kepyng of the Gardyn xviijs. iiijd.

almesmen
Item paid to Gefferey atte Welle almesman for the same quarter xiijs. iiijd.
Item paid to Robert Boylet almesman for the same terme xs.

---

389   The wife of a former master was able to use the title 'Mistress'.
390   An error for '*septimodecimo*'.
391   The wardens of London's crafts exercised rights of 'search' over their freemen on behalf of the mayor of the city. Searches were designed to uncover deceitful practices and sub-standard workmanship and to punish breaches of ordinances promulgated by the city and by the guilds themselves. In practice it is clear that guild officials often targeted areas of particular concern, such as the activities of 'foreigns', rather than attempting to enforce the whole canon of guild legislation: see Davies, 'Artisans, Guilds and Government', pp. 148-9.
392   Once again the clerk is two days out, the correct date being 24 December.
393   For this title see Glossary.
394   There is no salary listed for the clerk, the position then being vacant: see above, n. 359.

Item paid to Thomas Hosyer almesman in full payment of his quarter almes iijs. iiijd.

[f. 51]

Here after ensue all such obites which the Maister and his iiij wardeyns are boundeyn yerely to kepe at such seasons as it happen theym to fall.

First thobite of Elene Langwith[395] holden at Seint Mary Abchirch the xviij daye of July and there spent for prestes, clerkes, brede, wyne, chese and almes accordyng to the last will of the same Elene xvjs. viijd.

Item thobite of John Halyat and Eden his wyf[396] holden at Seint Martyns Oteswych the xxto daye of Octobre and there spent after the last will of the said John for a potacion and prestes, clerkes and offeryng vjs. viijd.

Item thobite of M. John Stone and his wyf[397] holden at Seint John Evaungelist the xxiiij daye of Octobre and there spent for the M. of the crafte, his iiij wardeyns, the clerk, the bedell, the person of the chirch, prestes, parisshe clerk, potacion and almes accordyng to the last will of the said M. Stone xxvjs. viijd.

Item thobite of William Jawdrell and Alice his wyf[398] holden at Seint Mary Abchirch the xxvj daye of Octobre and there spent for prestes, clerkes and offeryng accordyng to the last will of the said William ijs. iiijd.

Item thobite of Thomas Carleton[399] holden in the Chirch of Paules the xij daye of Decembre and ther spent aboute the charges of the same vs. vd.

Item thobite of John Chirchman[400] holden at Seint Martyns Oteswych the xxiiijto daye of January and than spent for a potacion and other charges vs. xd.

Item thobite of John Creke[401] holden at Seint Mary Abchirch the first Sondaye of Lent and than spent aboute the charges of the same accordyng to the last will of the said John iiijs. vjd.

---

[395] See above, n. 63.
[396] See above, n. 86.
[397] See above, n. 38.
[398] See above, n. 88.
[399] See above, n. 97.
[400] See above, n. 129.
[401] See above, n. 148.

Item thobite of Richard Benton[402] holden at Trinitee Chirch the Lytell the xxij daye of Marche and than spent in brede, ale, wyne, confectes, prestes, parisshe clerk, wexchaundeler, offeryng and almes acordyng to the last will of the said Richard xiij*s*. iiij*d*.

[f. 51v] Povey.

Item thobite of Rauf Basset Gerard Braybroke and Hugh Shyrley[403] holden at Seint Martyns Oteswich the x daye of Maye and than spent in brede, ale, wyne, chese, person, prestes, clerk, offeryng, almes, chaundeler, accordyng to their last wyll vij*s*. j*d*.

Item thobite of Hugh Talbote[404] holden at Seint Martyns Oteswich the last daye of Maye and than spent in brede, ale, wyne, prestes, clerk, chaundeler and offeryng accordyng to his last wyll v*s*.

Item thobite of Thomas Reymond[405] holden at Seint Thomas Apostelles the viijth daye of Juyn and than spent in potacion, prestes, clerkes, to viij pore men, vij pore women, chaundeler and offeryng accordyng to the last will of the said Thomas Reymond x*s*.

Item thobite of Hugh Caundishe[406] holden at Seint Martyns Oteswych the xij daye of Juyn and than spent in potacion, prestes, clerke, to the maister of the company, iiij wardeyns, the clerk, the bedell, chaundeler and offeryng and for xxxvj quarters of coles distributed to thalmesmen accordyng to the last will of the said Hugh xviij*s*. vj*d*. *ob*.

Item thobite of Rauf Holand[407] holden at the chirch of oure Lady at Aldermary the xviij daye of Juyn and than delivered the wardeyns of the same chirch accordyng to his last wyll xiij*s*. iiij*d*.

Sum total of thobites this yere cometh to [vj*li*. xv*s*. iiij*d*. *ob*.]

[f. 52]

---

402   See above, n. 39.
403   See above, n. 32.
404   See above, n. 36.
405   See above, n. 50.
406   See above, n. 53.
407   See above, n. 55.

In the moneth of November last passed the Mayre of this citee directed lettres unto the Maister and wardeyns of this mistere and crafte in thie wordes herafter folowyng that is to sey:

A direction
> To the Maister and wardeyns of Taillours

By the mayre

A commission
> Purveyeth xxx persones on horssebak in gownes of violet accordyng to thensample herunto annexed to meete with the kyng our soveraigne lord at his next comyng to London from the parties of beyond the see.[408]

A determynacion
> After which commyssion so directed it was fully aggreed and concluded by the common assent of the hole body of the felaship than assembled that thise persones undernamed shuld ryde and every maister to have toward his charges xiijs. iiijd. and everych other broder xs. and the same to be levied in the crafte and assessed by vj persones therto electe named and assigned.

Ryders

M. Povey, Maister
M. Gall
M. Bukk   iij*li*. vjs. viijd.
M. Jenyns
M. Spencer *per M. sol'*

horssemen
John Doget xs. sol'
John Povey wardens
Richard Haydyff ±[409]
William Grene xs. *sol'*   iiij*li*.
Nicholas Nynes xs. *sol'*
Rauf Bukberd
Richard Gryffeth xs.

---

[408] This refers to the arrangements made for the reception of the King in London following his return from France after the conclusion of the Treaty of Etaples on 3 Nov. For these events see Introduction, pp. 42–3.

[409] The meaning of this marginal annotation is unclear in these lists as 'sol[uit]' appears to have been used to refer to those whose payments had been received.

James Grene

Robert Kelham
Richard Smyth
William Batyson
George Bolton _sol'_
John Kyrkeby _sol'_
Hugh Acton _per M. sol'_   v_li_.
John Nayler
William FitzWilliam _per M. sol'_
Edmond Floure _per M. sol'_
James Assand _per M. sol'_

                  Sum total [xij_li_. vj_s_. viij_d_.]

[f. 52v]

M. West
M. Hede
James Fittez
Thomas Bromefelde   sessors named by the company
John a Kechyn
Richard Joskyn

M. Gylbert Keys vs.	Alisaunder Bassyngthwayte iij_s_. iiij_d_. ±
M. Richard West vs.	Thomas Broughton iiij_s_.
M. Roger Barlow vij_s_. ±	Richard Toll iij_s_. iiij_d_.
M. John Materdale vj_s_. viij_d_.	Thomas Werton iij_s_.
M. Robert Duplache vj_s_.	John a Kechyn ij_s_. vj_d_.
M. John Lee vj_s_.	Thomas Bond iij_s_.
M. John Heede vs. ±	Robert Parys iij_s_.
M. William Hert vj_s_. viij_d_. ±	

fotemen payers and assessed to pay

Thomas Petyt iiij_s_.	William Frene
Richard Dyngley iiij_s_. <u>wardens</u>	Thomas Burgate iij_s_. iiij_d_.
William Crosby ij_s_. vj_d_.	William Burton ij_s_.
James Fittez iij_s_. iiij_d_.	John Festam iij_s_. iiij_d_.
John Bernard iiij_s_.	Thomas Bodford iij_s_. iiij_d_.
Aleyn Hubert vj_s_.	John Bowman iij_s_. iiij_d_.

Owen Boughton vjs.
Thomas Randell vjs.
Thomas Martyn ijs.
Thomas Bromefeld iiijd.
Henry Clough iiijs.
Thomas Howden iiijs.
James Shirewood ijs.
Henry Iryell ijs. ±
John Rysshe iiijs.
Thomas Bodley iiijs.
Richard Hill vjs.
Roger Mone vjs.
Henry Kellow iiijs. ±
James Wylford vjs. viijd. _sol'_

Thomas Segge ijs. vjd.
William Orwell iiijs.
Robert Greves iiijs. ±
Richard Cornhill ijs. iiijd.
William Werton iijs.
Nicholas Asshe iijs. iiijd. ±
~~John Niche~~ ijs.
Richard Frere ijs.
Paten Patenson iijs.
Robert Hertishorne ijs.
Alexander Cavarell ijs. vjd.
Henry Payne ijs. viijd.
John Lyndon iijs. iiijd.
Richard Leman iiijs. _sol'_
William Bekeham ijs. iiijd.

[f. 53]

Richard Lynche iijs. iiijd.
Richard Joskyn iijs.
John Smyth ijs. Povey
William Snowdon iijs.
Thomas Pole iijs. iiijd.
William a lye ijs. vjd. ±
Richard Failer xijd.
David Roche ijs.
Thomas Gall xxd.
William Avenell viijd.
William Fox xijd.
John Laurence ijs. vjd.
William Erle xijd. ±
Robert Johnson ijs.
John Baskerfelde xvjd. ±
Richard Gyrston xvjd. _Povey sol'_
Roger Claye xxd.
John Cokke ijs.
John Spereman xxd.
Henry Dod xvjd.
William Gray ijs. viijd. ±
Richard Quykrell xijd.
John Chicheley iijs. iiijd. _Povey sol'_
Richard Thomasson iijs. iiijd.
Robert Stephenson iijs. iiijd. ±

John Dorking
Thomas Speight

John Hyrst iij*s*.
John Nicholas
Thomas Painson
William Gryndell

collectours
John Lynton
Richard Lynche

> summa in money of thise persones that have paid is ...

> summa in money of theym that have not paid is ...

[f. 53v] Povey.

Openers[410] licenced by the M.

First of Thomas Cressy accordyng to thordynaunce therfore made x*s*.
Also of George Spark for lyke cause x*s*.
Also of Aleyn Scarlet for lyke condicion x*s*.
Also of Humfrey Ryggeley late apprentice with M. Hert for lyke maner x*s*.
Also of John Todde for lyke condicion x*s*.
Also of Richard Hall in full payment for his openyng vj*s*. viij*d*.
Also of Edward Dudley x*s*.
Also of Richard Todde in full payment for his openyng vj*s*. viij*d*.
Also of John Shirley in partie of payment for his openyng vj*s*. viij*d*.
Also of Richard Brygge x*s*.
Also of Henry Tetworth x*s*.
Also of John Hodgeson in partie of payment of his openyng viij*s*. iiij*d*.
Also of John Tomson x*s*.
Also of John Johnson x*s*.
Also of William Greves in partie of payment for his openyng v*s*.
Also of John Bruer in partie of payment iij*s*. iiij*d*.

Biquestes

First of John Wotton by the handes of William Dormer for Maister Stone accordyng to his last will vj*li*. xiij*s*. iiij*d*.

---

[410] Freemen licensed to open a shop on payment of a fine of 10*s*.

Also of John[411] Kyrkton by thands of William Botiller of his benivolence to be registred in the bed roll[412] and remembred among other names at every quarter daye xiij*s*. iiij*d*.

[f. 54]

Sale and settyng over[413] apprentices to the advantage of this present place

First of Richard Semar for the settyng over of John Wendles late apprentice of John Lewes to the same Richard to serve unto hym in maner of his apprentice the residue of his termes for to com as it appereth in thendenture xiij*s*. iiij*d*.

Also of Rauf Bukberd for the settyng over of Richard Stanes late apprentice with Aleyn Huberd to the said Rauf to serve with hym in maner of his apprentice the residue of his termens that he hath to serve with the said Aleyn as it shall appere in his indenture vj*s*. viij*d*.

Also of the said Aleyn Huberd for the said Richard Stanys of his good will and benivolence toward thadvauntage of this crafte vj*s*. ij*d*.

Also of William Gerveys for the termes of Thomas Daniell late apprentice with John Combes which he hath to serve with the said John Combes as it shall more largely appere in his indentures of apprentishode vj*s*. viij*d*.

Also for the termes of John Brygge late apprentice with Thomas Bond now commytted unto Piers Barbour with the consent of the said Thomas to serve unto hym in maner of his apprentice the residue of his termes now for to com as it shall appere by his indenture.

---

411   The margin is annotated 'T. Kyrkton late clerk', suggesting a mistake on the part of the current clerk, Henry Mayour, in referring to one of his predecessors. Kirton's will, containing this bequest, had been proved in October 1490: PRO, PROB 11/9, f. 63. For his career and authorship of the minutes see Introduction, pp. 8–9.

412   A bede roll, or list of benefactors, was commonly kept by institutions such as parishes, lay fraternities and religious houses, as well as by craft organisations such as the London livery companies, many of whom were bequeathed lands and goods in exchange for prayers and masses for the souls of the deceased. Unfortunately, the Tailors' roll has been lost although the company's accounts, which are extant for the period 1398–1484, note bequests received from more than 230 individuals, many of whom were members of the fraternity recruited from outside the craft: Accounts, I–II and see Davies, 'Charity', pp. 166–71.

413   For this term see Glossary.

Also of John Cok late apprentice with John Stowtes of his owne aggreament and auctoritee of this place is commytted unto Henry Alisaunder to serve oute the residue of his termes now for to com as it shall appere more openly in his indenture of apprentishode.

Receiptes of rent

Of Richard Lytell for the ferme of his house that he now dwelleth in for an hole yere ended at feste of thannunciacion of Seint Mary Virgyn [25 Mar.] last passed accordyng to a graunte made unto hym for terme of his lyf by the company vjs. viijd.

[f. 54v] Povey.

Fines levied of those persones that sette foreyns[414] awerke contrary to thordynaunces made therfore.

First of Piers Barbour for thoccupiyng a foreyn vs.
Of William Joynour for the kepyng of a foreyn xxd.
Of Hugh Huchyns for thoccupiyng of a foreyn iijs. viijd.
Of Robert Hyde for thoccupiyng of a foreyn at ij sundry tymes iijs.
Of William Kyrkeham for thoccupiyng of a foreyn vs.
Of John Warner for thoccupiyng of a foreyn iiijd.
Of Robert Walter for thoccupiyng of a foreyn xijd.
Of John Harper for thoccupiyng of a foreyn xxd.
Of George Sparke for thoccupiyng of a foreyn xxd.
Of George Foster for thoccupiyng of a foreyn xxd.
Of John a Lye for thoccupiyng of a foreyn at ij severall tymes iiijs.
Of Richard Peynter for thoccupiyng of a foreyn xxd.
Of John Brown a pore foreyn iiijd.
Of Robert Colson for thoccupiyng of a foreyn xxd.
Of Petre a foreyn for shapyng [415]of a dublet viijd.

Chambre holders

Of Thomas Kyng for kepyng of a chambre contrary to the ordynaunces of this crafte made therfore[416] xijd.

---

414   See Glossary.
415   See Glossary.
416   This probably refers to an ordinance of 1450 in which concern was expressed about 'chambur holders', newly qualified tailors who produced garments hidden away in rented attic rooms, away from the scrutiny of the wardens of the craft. Instead, new freemen were ordered to covenant themselves as servants to

[f. 55]

Fynes and amerciamentes levied and percyved of such persones that appere not whan they be duly sommoned.

First of Robert Fitzwater for nonne apperaunce iiij*d*.
Of Roger Mone for his nonne apperaunce iiij*d*.
Of William Oliver for his nonne apperaunce iiij*d*.
Of Richard Crofte for his nonne apperaunce iiij*d*.
Of dyvers persones of the xxiiij[417] for their noune apperaunce at one tyme ij*s*.
Of John Baskerfeld for his nonne apperaunce iiij*d*.
Of Richard Toll for his nonne apperaunce iiij*d*.
Of Thomas Bedford for his nonne apperaunce iiij*d*.
Of Robert Greves for his nonne apperaunce viij*d*.
Of Thomas Wytteney for his nonne apperaunce iiij*d*.
Of Aleyn Hill for his nonne apperaunce iiij*d*.
Of Richard Semar for his nonne apperaunce iiij*d*.
Of William Polgrave for his nonne apperaunce iiij*d*.
Of Thomas Randell for his nonne apperaunce iiij*d*.
Of Rauf Bukberd for his nonne apperaunce iiij*d*.
Of William Grene for his nonne apperaunce iiij*d*.
Of Richard Hill for his nonne apperaunce iiij*d*.
Of Robert Kellow for his nonne apperaunce iiij*d*.
Of Thomas Bond for his nonne apperaunce iiij*d*.
Of dyvers brethern for their nonne apperaunce at a quarter daye ij*s*. vj*d*.
Of Ewen Boughton for his nonne apperaunce at ij tymes viij*d*.
Of Robert Johnson for his nonne apperaunce iiij*d*.

[f. 55v] Povey

Transgressours and Brekers of Ordynaunces of this crafte.

For as moch as it is enacted in this present place among other laudable and reasonable constitucions and ordynaunces of olde tyme made that no broder shuld myssebehave hym to any other broder of this crafte prively ne openly upon a certeyn peyne therfore lymyted, Richard Tolle but late in the open market at Blakwell Hall[418] in the presence of all comers and passers by to and fro in the same market unmanerly and indiscretely used hym self ayenst Thomas Bedford at one tyme in ungoodly language and unsad demeanur to

---

established freemen until they had built up the necessary resources to open a shop: Davies, 'Artisans, Guilds and Government', p. 148.
[417] Members of the court of assistants.
[418] For Blackwell Hall see above, n. 14, and Introduction, p. 16.

the grete infamy and sclaunder of the hole company. The M. of the feliship comyng to the market to bey as other persones dyd, heryng and seyng their both unmanerly doynges and seiynges commaunded theym to have silence and not to contynue ther jangelyng in open place and market at their perill and to be at the Taillours Hall at the next court day there to be holden and there either of theym to shew what matier or cause he cowde allege ayenst other of theym. Whose commaundement they both observed and there either of theym shewed his greefe and complaynt. The Maister heryng their causes and matiers of complaynte caused thordynaunce to be red and declared unto theym to thentent that they shuld be the more ware of theym self to eschewe and avoide the penalties ordeigned for such Transgressours and for their better remembraunces the said Maister with thadvice and counseill of his wardeyns adjuged the said Richard Toll to paye unto thuse of this feliship vjs. viijd.

Also the said Maister with thadvis and counseill of his said wardeyns adjuged the said Thomas Bedford for myssebehavyng hym ayenst the said Richard Toll atte same Blakwell Hall the same tyme vs.

Also the said Richard Toll at an other season myssebehaved hym self in the market openly holden at Blakwell Hall ayenst John Getteford in ungoodly speche and uncovenable wordes which was to the reproch and obloquie of the feliship. Wherfore he paid to the almes of this crafte vjs. viijd.

John Bolton enrolled not his apprentice within the furst yeres of his termes that he had served. Wherfore he made a fyne of xvjd.

[f. 56]

Adhuc transgressours

Where as ... apprentice with John Bowman complayned and showed unto the Maister and his wardeyns that the saide John Bowman gave unto his said apprentice unlefull and without reason chastisyng as well with wepyns defensyve as with lak of mete, drynke, vitailles and apparaill. For which causes the said Bowman was commoned with sadly, sobrely and discretely by the M. and his wardeyns which intended the honestee of the same Bowman and the reformacion of such defaultez that were than alleged and purposed ayenst hym. The same Bowman brennyng in grete malice ayenst his said apprentice and wold not be advertised by the M. and wardeyns sodenly in a grete agony and ire departed from theym and seide he wolde be maister over his own apprentice, the M. and his wardeyns seyng his firy heet and hastynesse, and wold not confourme hym self to reason. Than the M. desired John Doget than Upper wardeyn[419] to take home with hym the said apprentice for a season till his maisters malice was abated. The said Bowman havyng knowlege that his said apprentice was within [the] dwellyng hous of the said John Doget furthwith went to the Cownter[420] in Bredestrete and there attained an accion ayenst hys said apprentice and brought a sergeant with hym and of verry pure malice despite obstynacie and froward presumpcion arested the said apprentice within the hous of the said wardeyn which was to the obbrobry of the said wardeyn. That not withstandyng he and his broder wardeyn Richard Dyngley mayneprised the said apprentice and afterward shewed the demeanure of the said Bowman to the M. Wherfore he was adjuged by the M. and wardeyns to pay to thalmes of this crafte xs.

Also Richard Thomasson used and multiplied moch ungoodly spech and language ayenst Waltier Beaufeld in the presence of the Deane of Tharches[421] which was to the reprofe ofthe Company. Wherfore he made a fyne of iijs. xd.
Also the said Waltier in said presence had lyke demeanure ayenst the said Richard. Wherfore he mad a fyne of ijs. vjd.

[f. 56v] Povey.

Adhuc transgressours

Where as Thomas Grysell, Bedell of the crafte, was comaunded by the M. to goo into Fletestrete unto the dwellyng hous of William Tetford and there to take a distresse bicause the said William than occupied a foreyn, the said Bedell intendyng to execute his office and the Maisters comaundement wold have had by feyre meanes a distresse and that the said Tetford wold in no wyse suffre but rebuked the said Bedell and called hym carle[422] and manassed hym seiyng that he wold sette his heres on the poste at his shop dore, with many other unfittyng wordes, if the said Bedell toke any distresse there. Whose demeanure and ungoodly behaving the same Bedell shewed unto the M. and the M. the same unto my lord the Mayre.[423] The Mayre consideryng

[419] By this date two of the four wardens were known as 'upper wardens', indicating that they had served a previous term in that office. Their two more junior colleagues, the 'lower wardens', were serving for the first time. To be eligible for the mastership an individual normally had to serve as both a lower and an upper warden.

[420] There were sheriffs' prisons, or Compters, in The Poultry and in Bread Street: Lobel, *Atlas*, p. 70; H. Harben, *A Dictionary of London* (London, 1918), pp. 109–10.

[421] The Dean of the Arches was the lay judge of the Court of the Arches, having jurisdiction over 13 London parishes, exempt from the authority of the Bishop of London.

[422] A 'churl': *OED*.

[423] The mayor at that time was William Martin, a skinner: Beaven, *Aldermen*, II, p.

the grete presumpcion obstynacye and inobedience of the said Tetteford and his uncurteys dealyng with the common officer of this place sent for hym by Nicholas Foderey, sergeaunt, and commytted hym to prison and there contynued unto such tyme that he knew and sobred hym self better and submytted hymself unto the M. and wardeyns and to the good rules of the crafte. And for the deliveraunce of the said Tetford oute of pryson Richard Lytton, gentilman, and Robert Kymme, haberdassher, made grete instaunce and request as well to my said Lord Mayre as to the M. whose instaunce and request the Maire with the M. advise fulfilled and the said Tetford came to this place and shewed his submyssion and obedience affore the M. and his wardeyns and the said Robert Kyme and for his humble submyssion and obedience was pardoned of his fyne savyng onely the Sergeaunts fees.

[f. 57]

Die veneris quarto die Januarii.[424]

In the presence of the Maister, M. Pemberton aldreman, Gall, Duplach, Barlowe, West, Lee, Heed, Buk, Spenser, Hert, iiij wardeyns, Hubert, Haydyf, Boughton, Willeford and Nynes.

[f. 57v] Povey.

Die Veneris xviij die Januarii.

W. Cokke a blynde erroure taken by hym as ignoraunt of the lawes of this land
William Cokke beyng destitute of apprentice, not perfectly knowyng the lawes of this lande and good auncient Rules of this noble citee, contrary to both toke to his apprentice Richard Locan the son of Thomas Locan born in Berwyke upon Twede that tyme beyng Scottysshe and under thobeysaunce of the Kyng of Scottes for vij yeres as in ij indentures of apprentishode therof made more playnly it was conteyned. The Maister by wey of informacion herof heryng caused the said Cokke at a certeyn day to hym lymyted to appere personally before hym and his wardeyns at this place. Whose commaundement the same Cokke fulfilled wherupon he and his said prentised apprentice were of the covenaunt made bitwene theym examyned. And than the M. and his iiij wardeyns by long communicacion, rype

---

17.
[424] 1492/3.

deliberacion and sad advisement in eschewyng and avoydyng the incoveniencies that myght ensue and come and growe unto the infamye of the body of the hole fraternitee by the reason of the unsad dealyng and behavyng of the said Cok discharged the said apprentice from his said maister bicause he was not borne under the Kynges liegeaunce not withstandyng the contracte and covenaunt made affore by indenture bitwene theym and so thendentures of apprentishode were delivered and cancelled furthwith in the presence of the M. and his iiij wardeyns.

The same daye David Michell and Richard Todd compromytted they self in the presence of the M. his iiij wardeyns and the wardeyns of the Bachelers company to stand and obey unto tharbitrament of William Howlat and John Baynard arbitratours indifferently electe bitwene theym of and upon all and almaner matiers etc. bitwene theym etc. so that the end and determynacion be made bytwene theym by mydlent Sonday [17 Mar.] than next suyng etc. Which determynacion and juggement herafter foloweth and is this. It is awarded by the forsaid arbitratours that eyther of the said parties shall acquiete and discharge other of theym by wrytyng and also the said David shall deliver to the M. in this present place xiijs. iiijd. wherof the forsaid Richard shall have ayene vjs. viijd. and of that other vjs. viijd. the same David shall discharge the said Richard ayenst the M. for the openyng of his shop accordyng to thordynaunce therof made.

[f. 58]

Die Mercurii xxiij^{to} die Januarii.

In the presence of the Maister, M. Pemberton alderman, Duplach, Buk, Jenyns, the iiij wardeyns, Fittes, Bromefeld, the same Maister with thadvice of the worshipfull persones afore named and the consent of his wardeyns graunted and leate to ferme to M. Richard Laurence the new tenement with thappurtenaunces set in Fridaystrete next unto the Saresyns Hede[425] there on the parties of west and north. To have unto the said M. Richard from the feste of thanunciacion of Seint Mary Virgyn [25 Mar.] than next to com as long as it shall please either of the lessour or lessee with lawfull warnyng he paiyng yerely to the crafte vli. sterlinges at iiij termes of the yere in the citee of London usuell by even porcions and the lordes of the soile to kepe the reparacions necessaries of the forsaid tenement.

---

[425] This new tenement was constructed as part of the rebuilding of the Saracen's Head itself, for which see Introduction, pp. 18–19.

The same day it was commoned by the mouthes of the forsaid persones that the clothyng for gownes shuld be of feyir murrey in greyne and the lyverey in hodys shuld be partie of fyne murrey and scarlet.

And afterward at a quarterdaye holden the xvj[426] daye of February by the comon assent of all the feliship that the clothyng and colour of cloth for gownes and lyverey in hodes shuld be accorded to the commonycacion afore rehersed and so it was than fully aggreed concluded and clerely determyned.

The same daye the M. and his wardeyns with the consent of the wardeyns of the Bachelers company graunted and dispensed with Thomas Hubert that he shuld pay no more money by yere unto the Bachelers company but onely viij*d.* unto such tyme that he kepe household hymself.

The same daye John Johnson which was apprentice of Robert Dod, citezein and Tayllour of London, brought in a copy of his admyssion into the libertees and frauncheise of this crafte beryng date in the chambre of the Yeld hall the v day of February the fyrst yere of kyng Richard the iij[de] [1483/4].

[f. 58v] Povey.

Veneris primo die Februarii.

The same daye Robert Pawtrell[427] dwellyng without Bisshopesgate graunted and promytted in the presence of the Maister and his wardeyns to paye unto William Ayleward *vs.* sterlinges in fourme folowyng that is to sey the xv daye of this present moneth xx*d.*, the last daye of the same moneth xx*d.* and the xv daye of March than next ensuyng xx*d.*

Lune iiij[to] die Februarii.

The same daye Symond Motte, fleccher, which hath wedded the wyf late of Robert Faryngdon taillour confessed that John Rogerson served the said Robert in maner of his apprentice v yeres well and truly.

The same day Robert Fitzwater graunted and promytted upon his feith and trouth in the presence of M. Lee, M. Spencer, the iiij wardeyns, Roger Mone and Henry Mayour to pay unto the M. of the company at the fest of Pentecost now next comyng viij*s.*

---

[426]   Error for 'xv', see below, pp. 234–5.

[427]   Probably the Robert Pawtrell who was employed for ½ a day by the Great Wardrobe for the coronation of Richard III in 1483: *Coro. Richard III* ed. Sutton and Hammond, p. 381.

The said daye the forsaid John Rogerson covenaunted to serve Richard Crofte for xiiijd. a weke unto the feste of Pentecost than next ensuyng of which xiiijd. the said Richard shall receyve wekeley vijd. in his own handes till he be contented and fully satisfied of vjs. spent in the lawe for the cause of the said John and so the sewertees of the said John to be discharged clerely ayenst the said Richard Crofte.

The same daye M. Spencer in the presence of the forsaid M. Lee the iiij wardeyns Roger Mone and Henry [Mayour] promytted and graunted to paye unto the M. of the feliship for the dette of Robert Fitzwater ijs. over and above the forsaid viijs. whan it shalbe desired ijs.

The same day the said Fittzwater promytted to paye to Robert Archer vs. viijd. in fourme folowyng that is to sey the Fryday next comyng xxd., the xxiiij day of March than next suyng xxd. and at Easter next folowyng [7 Apr.] ijs. iiijd. Summe vs. viijd.

[f. 59]

Lune undecimo die Februarii.

The same day in the presence of the M. and his iiij wardeyns, William Marchall and Thomas Marchall compromytted theym to stand and obey tharbitrament of Richard Haydyff and Roger Mone arbitratours indifferently named and electe by the Maister bitwene theym as in ij obligacions of xlli. a pece with condicion upon theym indorsed more openly appereth.

The said daye John Sheffeld hath for xs. to hym paid and to be paid by William Devenyssh late his apprentice clerely relessed and discharged the same William of his termes of apprentishode specified in a payre of indentures therof made bitwene theym which he had to serve and the same John delivered his indenture unto the said William upon which delyveree the same William in partie of payment of the said xs. paid iijs. iiijd. and graunted to paye at Easter than next suyng vjs. viijs. for which vjs. viijs. M. Lee hath undertaken for the payment therof in the presence of the M. and John Goldsmyth of Canterbury, inholder.

The same daye John Wollaston graunted an promytted before the M. and his wardeyns that he and John Hill, joynour, and Thomas Bowre, hewrer, suertees for the same John Wollaston shuld seale and as their dede deliver unto John Copelond taillour an obligacion with condicion to pay wekely iiijd. till xs. be fully payd.

The same daye the M. with thadvis of his wardeyns at a request and prayer made by M. Pemberton gafe full power and auctoritee to the same M. Pemberton to lette and graunte the Sterre unto such an honest persone as he wole answere and pay the yerely rent fore. Orelles the same honest persone shall fynde other sufficient suertees by writyng to the M. of the feliship truly to pay the rent of the said Sterre[428] a long as he shall occupie it at iiij termes of the yere in the citee of London usuell by even porcions.

The same daye the M. and his wardeyns graunted to Robert Busshell a tenement within the aley in Cornehull[429] for xxxvjs. viijd. paiyng by yere his terme begynnyng atte feste of thannunciacion of Seint Mary Virgyn [25 Mar.] next and so he became tenaunt by jd. delivered to the M.

[f. 59v] **Povey.**

Veneris xv^{mo} **die Februarii.**

The same daye was the quarter holden in the presence of the Maister, M. Pemberton aldreman, West, Barlowe, Duplach, Lee, Hede, Buk, the iiij wardeyns and the feliship for divers causes than assembled.

Divers testamentes and last willes openly redde.[430]
First the testament and last wille of Thomas[431] redd.
Also the testament and last [will] of John Creke redd.
Also the testament and last will of John Chirchman redd.
Also the testament and last will of Thomas Reymond redd.

The same day by the consent of the feliship than assembled atte humble supplicacion of Christopher Kyrke than shewed and declared openly was graunted unto the said Christopher thalmes of xls. by yere the first payment

---

[428] 'Le Sterre', a brewery on the west side of Bishopsgate Street, was one of the four messuages acquired, along with 17 shops, from John Churchman, grocer and alderman, in July 1405 (see above, n. 129). By 1455 the property was rented out for £5 6s. 8d. p.a. Accounts, II, f. 58v.

[429] This was one of several properties, acquired by the Tailors in the mid-14th century, which lay to the north of Cornhill and which abutted on the south side of their hall. The alley referred to is probably the lane which ran north from Cornhill into White Lyon Court, the location of a southern entrance to Tailors' hall. See H. L. Hopkinson, *The History of Merchant Taylors' Hall* (London, 1931), pp. 5–16.

[430] For these men see above, nn. 50, 97, 129, 148.

[431] Probably Thomas Carleton.

begynnyng atte feste of Mighelmas next comyng [29 Sept.] and his entree into his [hous] at the almes hous at Midsomer [24 June].

For as moch as M. Hede and his wardeyns by their dede indented and sealed with their v seales beryng date the xx daye of March in the iij^de yere of the reigne of Kyng Henry the vij^th [1487/8] graunted and lette to ferme unto William Cok sadiller ij tenementes next adjoynyng unto the Saresyns Hede in Frydaystrete for xx yeres payng by yere liij*s*. iiij*d*. as in the said dede indented more playnly is conteyned. It was and is so that the said ij tenementes were taken down not withstandyng the lees made affore to thentent that the Sarsyns Hede and the same tenements shuld be new bielded.[432] For which cause the said William Cok toke the Swan[433] benethe in Fryday strete and there dwelled till the said ij tenementes were new bielded, set up, garnysshed and made tenauntable. The same William seyng the said tenementes tenauntable and in goodly maner as it is now many tymes and often as well in his own persone as with Maister Broke alderman[434], as other divers worshipfull persones desired and required the M. that now is that the same William myght occupie and enjoye the said new tenementes accordyng to his graunte made to hym for the rent and yeres specified in the said dede indented. [f. 60] The said Maister consideryng the grete costes and charges that the crafte had borne and susteyned in and aboute the new makyng of the said bieldynges there willyng as moch as in hym is the common encreace and advauntage of this present place havyng also perfyt knowlege that he myght lette the said ij tenements of new bielded ferre above the said rent of liij*s*. iiij*d*. by yere if he had the said dede indented in his hands purposyng in his mynde well sewerly and sadly to redeme the same dede indented if it myght be at easy price oute of the handes of the said Cok. Wherupon he sent for the same Cok to the taverne where he had long communicacion with hym for the redemyng of the right and title that the said Cok had of and in the said tenementes by vertue of his lees Than beyng present with the said M., John Doget his Upper wardeyn, Nicholas Nynes and Henry Mayour, clerk of the felaiship. The same Cok perceyvyng right well the M. mynde by reason of the communicacion that was than bitwene theym was verey hard herted to wyn and seide precisely that he myght have had many tymes and often for his interesse and title of and in the said tenementes vj*li*. xiij*s*. iiij*d*. All this not withstondyng atte last by the wyse and discrete meanes of the said M. and of his counceill there and than assembled compowned with the forsaid Cok for the surrendryng up of the said dede indented and for his said interesse and title for xx*s*. which was furthwith paid and also for brede and wyne there

---

432   See Introduction, pp. 18–19.
433   This property was not one of those acquired by the Tailors in Friday Street.
434   John Broke (d. 1511), grocer and alderman 1488–1502: Beaven, *Aldermen*, II, p. 18.

spend viijd. And so by and by the said Cok delivered to the M. the said dede indented which he this same present daye shewed openly before the company than assembled in the hall and caused the same dede indented to be cancelled before theym all in avoidyng such inconveniencies that myght folow if it were kept hole and unbroken. xxs. viijd.

The same daye William Moll, translatour of his copy from the crafte of lynen drapers[435] unto this crafte, brought in his copy of fredom and admyssion into this same crafte beryng date in the chambre of the Guyldhall of London the xiij daye of the moneth of March in the vij[th] yere of the reigne of Kyng H. the vij[th] [1491/2]

The said daye John Hodgeson which was thapprentice of Thomas Huetson brought in the copy of his fredom beryng date the xiij daye of Novembre in the viij[th] yere of the reigne of Kyng H. the vij[th] [1492].

[f. 60v] Povey.

Die Veneris vicesimo ij[do] die Februarii.

The same daye William Assheby shewed and complayned that John Hebelthwayte whom he had taken to his apprentice by colour and contrary to laudable custumes of this famous citee and the good rules of this place wold not be ruled by hym. Wherfore the Maister had both the said parties before hym and theym examyned sundrely of and upon the cause of variaunce bitwene theym. The said Assheby seid that his said apprentice used the company of a woman which was to his grete losse and hynderyng for asmoch as he was so affectionate and resorted dailly unto hyr. The M. heryng herof called the said apprentice before hym and alleged the seiyngs of the said Assheby ayenst hym. The said apprentice heryng the M. well denyed not all thinges that were alleged ayenst hym how be it he said that his resortyng to the said woman was not the breche bitwene theym but the cause of variaunce is this, the said Assheby had made with his said apprentice a private contracte by fraudelent meanes and under colour to gyfe unto the said apprentice yerely duryng the tyme of his apprenticehode xxxijs. and that to be paid quarterly by even porcions which is contrary to the old aunciett custumes of this said citee and the good ordynaunces of this present place[436] accordyng to which

---

435 The linen-drapers were recognised as a small, but distinct craft by the city government although a number of them were also members of the Drapers' Company. They specialised in the retailing of linen goods, many of which had probably been imported.

436 It was an established custom that apprentices should not receive wages.

covenaunt the said apprentice offered to bryng in ij honest men to witnesse
with hym the same at the nexte courte daye, orelles he wold be punysshed for
his demerytees as the M. wold adjugge hym. And bicause he asked his money
accordyng to his covenaunt therfore the said Assheby was at variaunce with
hym. The M. than lyke a man usyng pollicye heryng their bothe complaynts
wold not be to hasty to gyf sentence and juggement in this matier but respited
it till the next courte daye at which daye he enjoyned the said Assheby to be
here and to bryng with hym thendenture that his prentised apprentice is
bound and enrolled by and commaunded the said prentised apprentice to
bryng with hym the same daye the said ij wittenesses which dyd so. And than
the M. toke into his handes the said indenture and afterward examyned John
Greves, sherman, and William Barow, bowyer, witnesses in this matier and
what they knew of the covenaunt made bitwene theym and either of theym
after other severally shewed as he was a true Cristen man that the said
Assheby graunted and promytted before theym to gyf and pay unto the said
apprentice every quarter duryng the terme of his apprentishode viijs. and
upon holy dayes to go at his large and pleasure where he wold. The M.
consideryng this matier verrey heynous and ayenst all the good rules of this
said citee by a good deliberacion and sad advisement of his iiij wardeyns [f. 61]
commoned reasoned and argued the said matier and the grete infamy that of
lyklyhode myght have growen in tyme to com to the hoole body of the
feliship by reason of the symple dealyng and seducious demeanure of the said
Assheby if the said matier shuld be publisshed and com to lyght affore the
Chambreleyn of this citee and ferther peradventure affore the mair and
aldremen of the same citee and therupon openly shamed with a paper over his
hede as untrue citezein and perjured man. Wherfore and in avoidyng the
inconveniencies that myght ensue excited, moved and stered bothe the said
parties to abide his juggement and determinacion in this matier which aggreed
therto. And the M. with thadvis of his iiij wardeyns and consent of the said
Assheby dismyssed clerly the said apprentice from hym and either of theym
in this present place affore the M. and wardeyns sealed and as his dede
delivered to other of theym a generall acquietaunce and relesse of almaner
accions personelles and so either of theym was well contented and pleased.

Die Veneris primo die Marcii.

The same daye John Hewlyn hath taken of the Maister and wardeyns the
corner tenement in Wodestrete which John Bull dwell in for x yeres his terme
begynnyng at the feste of thannunciacion of Seint Mary Virgyn than next
ensuyng paiyng therfore yerely xls. sterlinges at iiij termes of the yere in the
citee of London usuell by even porcions. And therupon he became tenaunt by

j*d*. and the M. and his successours to kepe almaner reparacions and bere almaner changes goyng oute of the same.

More over the said John Hewlyn had of the M. in wey of loone the said daye xl*s*. sterling in redy money to releef and help hym with all at his begynnyng for suertee and contentacion ayen of the said xl*s*. David Berman, bruer, and Henry Sevenoke, sherman, bene bounden by ij severall obligacions the condicion wherof resteth in a paper specifiyng the daye of payment of the said xl*s*.

[f. 61v] Povey

Adhuc die Veneris primo die Marcii.

The same daye Thomas Halywell and Hugh Davy compromytted theym self before the M. and his wardeyns to stand and obey unto tharbitrament of Christopher Middleton and Thomas Imbroke procuratours of Tharches[437] arbitratours indifferently named bitwene theym etc. So that the said arbitratours ended the matiers of contraversy than hangyng undiscussed before the feste of Thannunciacion of Seint Mary Virgyn [25 Mar.] than next suyng. And if they ij arbitratours cowd not aggree by that feste than they to name an umpere and he to ende the contraversy by Palme Sonday [31 Mar.] than next as in ij obligacions of arbitrament therof made more playnly is conteyned.

Die Veneris octavo die Marcii.

The same daye Thomas Myles which was apprentice of James Fittez brought in the copy of his libertee of the citee of London beryng date in the chambre of the Guyldhall of London the vj daye of February the viij^th yere of the reigne of Kyng H. the vij^th [1492/3].

Die Lune undecimo die Marcii.

The same daye John Hebelthwayte compowned with the M. and iiij wardeyns for his redempcion to be admitted into the libertee of this feliship and to paye for his redempcion and admyssion unto thuse of the same feliship xlvj*s*. viij*d*. in fourme folowyng that is to sey in hand xiij*s*. iiij*d*., atte feste of the Holy Trinitee [2 June] than next suyng xiij*s*. iiij*d*., atte feste of All Seintes [1 Nov.]

---

437   Officials of the Court of the Arches, subordinate to the dean.

than next folowyng xs. and atte feste of Purificacion of Seint Mary Virgyn than next ensuyng [2 Feb. 1494] xs.

The same daye James Fittez and Thomas Miles compromytted theym to stand to tharbitrament of Richard Haydyff and Henry Iryell arbitratours indifferently chosen bitwene them of and upon all causes etc. So that thend be made by the last daye of this present moneth as in ij obligacions therof made more playnly it appereth.

[f. 62]

Die Veneris quintodecimo die Marcii.

The same daye the M. sent Thomas Gresyll unto William Barton commaundyng hym to be at this present place and to here such matiers as shuld be than alleged and proposed ayenst hym. The same Barton oberved the M. commaundement at whose comymg the M. shewed unto hym that he had broken thordynaunces of this place for as moch as he enrolled not Robert Robynson his apprentice within the first yere of his termes wherfore he shuld bere a fyne accordyng to the custume of this crafte. He made answere ayen and seyd that his said apprentice was long from hym wherfore he had litell joy to enroll hym and he rekked not whether he had or lost hym. The M. seyng his grete hastynesse willed hym to sobre and pacifie hym self. He that refused and said with grete violence and a fiery agony that he had never right in this present place and also he seyde that M. Jenyns served hym lyke a falsse Judas whan he was M. of the feliship.[438] Whose seiynges is a grete infamy and sclaunder to this worshipful place and company.

The said daye Edmond Brytour dettour unto M. Stodard graunted in the presence of the M. and Henry Mayour notary and clerk of this worshipful company to pay unto the said M. Stodard viijs. sterlinges in fourme folowyng that is to sey atte feste of Easter [7 Apr.] now next for to com iiijs. and at the first daye of May next than ensuyng iiijs. Summe viijs.

Die Lune xviij° die Marcii.

The same daye John Thomson shewed the copy of fredom of the crafte of Taillours under the autentyke seale of the Chambreleyn of London for the tyme beyng beryng date in the chambre of the Guyldhall of London the ix[th]

---

438 Stephen Jenyns, master of the company 1489-90: see Appendix IV.

daye of Novembre in the vijth yere of the reigne of Kyng Henry the vijth [1491].

[f. 62v] Povey.

Adhuc die Lune xviij° die Marcii

The same daye John Thomson had licence to open shop accordyng unto thordynaunces therfore made and hath paid in hand in partye of payment for his openyng vs. and John Edmyn pastiller dwellyng in the Vyntry hath undertaken as suretee that the other vs. shalbe paid by the first daye of Maye now next comyng.

The same daye John Seltman was pardoned and relesed by the M. and his wardeyns of a fyne that he shuld have paid bicause he bought cloth of a draper in Candelwyke strete contrary unto the ordynaunces of this place to the contrary therof made for asmoche as the same John Seltman is verrey indigent and in grete povertee and myserie.[439]

Die Veneris xxij^{do} die Marcii.

The same daye the M. as an arbitratour instaunced and specially desired by John Saxy and Thomas Symondes to here a matier hangyng in travers bitwene theym undecised and to take such direction in that behalf as the parties myght be breveley set in good accorde and amytee. The M. heryng the allegiaunces and seiynges of both the parties wisely in his mynd considered what shuld have folowed if either of theym shuld implete or sue other of theym in any courte spirituell or temporell wherfor he gave sentence and juggement with the consent of the parties and the wardeyns advice That the said Thomas shall pay unto the said John xxs. sterlinges in maner and fourme folowyng that is to sey in hand xs. which he dyd and xs. assone after as the same Thomas cowd or myght receyve it of John Wetnall, gentilman. And therupon the said Saxy delivered to the said Thomas an obligacion of xls. wherin the said John Wetnall is bounden to the said Saxy and Simondes.

Rauf Mauncell the same daye in the presence of the M. and his wardeyns graunted to paye unto the wardeyns of the Bachelers company for his

---

[439] This ordinance no longer survives. It is possible that the Tailors were trying to encourage their freemen to buy cloth at a market such as Blackwell Hall, where they could buy from one of an increasing number of fellow tailors who were involved in the cloth trade.

incomyng among theym vjs. viijd. in fourme folowyng that is to sey in hand
iijs. iiijd. and at Midsomer next than comyng iijs. iiijd. Summe vjs. viijd.

[f. 63]

Die Sabbati vicesimo tercio die Marcii.

Prestes wages
The same daye the M. paid to Sir[440] John Ratclyf for his stipend and salary for
a quarter of a yere endyng at feste of Thannunciacion of Seint Mary Virgyn
[25 Mar.] than next for to com xxxiijs. iiijd.
Also to Sir George Bromehill for his salary the same quarter xxxiijs. iiijd.
Also to Sir Richard Wheler for his salary the same quarter xxxiijs. iiijd.
Also to Sir Robert Cudworth for his salary the same quarter xxxvs.
Also to Sir John Burneham for his salary the same quarter xvjs. viijd.
Also to Sir Thomas Roos for his salary for half a yere ended at feste of
Thannunciacion of Seint Mary Virgyn [25 Mar.] aforsaid as it appereth by
acquietaunces therof made iiijli.

Officers wages
Also paid to Henry Mayour clerk of the feliship for his fee the same quarter
xxvs.
Also paid to Thomas Grysell bedell for his wages and kepyng of the Gardyn
for the said quarter xviijs. iiijd.

Almesmen
Also paid to Robert Boylet almesman for his almes the said quarter xs.
Also paid to Geoffrey atte Well for his almes the same quarter xiijs. iiijd.

A confession.
Also the same daye Rauf Bukberd confessed and knowleged afore the M. and
iiij wardeyns that William Skydmore his apprentice had fully served his
termes of apprentishode which by the procuryng of Richard Walker, weyer,[441]
went to the Guyldhall and there was made a freman of the crafte of Mercers
by reason of his faders copy. Which Skydmore was never presented here by
his maister accordyng to thordynaunces wherfore the said Rauf is in a

---

440 For this title see Glossary.
441 As the name suggests, a 'weyer' was an official responsible for weighing
merchandise, either appointed by municipal authorities or, as this entry suggests,
by guilds such as the Mercers or Grocers who regularly checked the accuracy of
the balances used by their freemen.

contempt to this place.[442]

[f. 63v] Povey

Die Lune primo die Aprilis.

The same daye the M. and his wardeyns gretely intaunced and hertily prayed by Aleyn Hubert and Richard Stanys his apprentice to here thallegiaunces complayntes and greves than dependyng in travers bitwene theym indecised and in especiall of and for iij yeres of termes of apprentishode which the same Richard hath to serve with the said Aleyn. The M. and his wardeyns well advisedly and by good deliberacion and sobrenesse intendyng to expell and put away all rancour, malice and ill will willyng that love, peace and charitee shuld reigne and contynue among theym wherfore the M. with thadvice of his said wardeyns toke upon hym the charge of an arbitratour and gyffeth sentence bitwene the said parties as herafter it shall ensue.

First the M. awardeth that the said Aleyn shall this present daye deliver or do to be delivered unto the said M. to and for thuse and behofe of the said Richard thendenture of apprentishode wherin the same Richard is bounde to the said Aleyn which the said Aleyn than perfourned.

Also he awardeth that the said Richard shall the same present day pay or do to be paid unto the said Aleyn or to his assignees xxvjs. viijd. sterling and after that don than the said Aleyn shall deliver unto the said Richard all such weryng gere and stuf a cheste with evidences and a pece of white cotton of vj yerds or there aboute as the said Richard hath within the hous of the said Aleyn.

And also he awardeth that the said Aleyn shall have a luyte which the said Richard affore tyme had bought.

---

442   Skydmore's father, also named William, had been apprenticed as a mercer in 1435–6 and served as warden of that company in 1467. The younger William was therefore entitled to become a freeman of the mercers by patrimony, but for some reason chose to serve an apprenticeship as a tailor with Bukberd as his master. This entry suggests that Walker had persuaded William to take up the freedom as a mercer after all, despite having completed his apprenticeship. His freedom was duly recorded in the Mercers' Company records for the year 1492. All information regarding the Skidmores kindly supplied by Ms Ursula Carlyle, Archivist and Curator, Mercers' Hall, London.

Die Lune xxij[do] die Aprilis.

The same daye a servant of M. Barlow delivered one of the iiij keyes of the grete cheste in the Tresour house unto the M. in the presence of the iiij wardeyns and of the clerk.[443]

[f. 64]

Die Veneris xxvij[444] die Aprilis.

<u>Assemblee of the xxiiij[ii]</u>
The same daye assemblee holden of the xxiiij in the presence of the M., M. Percyvale knight, M. Pemberton aldreman, West, Duplache, Buk, Jenyns, the iiij wardeyns, Boughton, Fittz, Grene, Bromfeld and Nynes.
Concluded and aggreed than that the M., M. Buk, M. Jenyns and N. Nynes in the name of the hole feliship and atte costes of the crafte shall pursue the bill and peticion put up unto my lord the Mair and to my maistres his brethern thaldremen for the reformacion of all foreyns that they herafter werke with no freman and citezein of this citee under a peyn therfore to be ordeigned by my said lord Mair and his brethern.[445]
Concluded and fully determynd the same daye that Richard Leman the baker[446] shalbe ruled and governed by thordynaunces of this place.

<u>A reporte of a sermoner at Seint Thomas of Acres</u>
Aggreed and concluded the same daye that the M., M. Jenyns, N Nynes and ij of the wardeyns shall the same daye at costes of the crafte go unto

---

[443] Roger Barlowe (Master 1478-9), one of the four holders of keys to the company's treasury chest, had died a few days previously. His will, dated 17 March 1492, was proved in the Prerogative Court of Canterbury on 24 April, two days after his servant brought in his key. Among his bequests was £10 towards 'an hangyng of fyne vedur' which the Tailors had commissioned for the Hall: PRO, PROB 11/9, f. 192.

[444] An error for 'xxvj'.

[445] The Tailors were particularly prominent among those crafts which lobbied the city government for tighter controls on the employment of immigrant workers: see Introduction, p. 40 and Davies, 'Artisans, Guilds and Government', pp. 145-8.

[446] Although a baker, Leman appears to have been granted a status within the craft identical to that of the freemen tailors. The previous November he had even contributed to the levy raised to pay for the Tailors' contingent at Henry VII's entry into London (see above, p. 223). The reason for this is unclear: it is possible that he was being rewarded for long service as the company's own baker, or else that he had married the widow of a tailor and had taken over responsibility for an apprentice tailor.

Grenewich[447] to speke with the sermoner that preched at Seint Thomas of Acres in Lent for asmoch as the same sermoner shewed openly affore a grete audience that many and divers taillours of this citee occupiyng shapyng and makyng of garmentes bene worsse extorcioners than they that lye in a wayte by a high wey side in robbyng and spoillyng the kynges liege people that passen furth by. For the said taillours taken brybes and grete rewardes of theym that they bey the cloth fore which is to the grete hurt and disceipte of the kynges liege people and also a grete infamy and open sclaunder to the hole feliship and body of the crafte of Taillours.

Concluded the same daye that M. Gall shall have the iiij[th] key of the chest in the Tresoury that M. Barlow had and afterwardes it was delivered unto hym.

[f. 64v] Povey.

Die Veneris iij[cio] die Maii.

The same daye Richard Fyllour of his free will and mere mocion graunted and promytted to gyfe unto thuse of this place to thentent that the M. wardeyns or ij of theym wold present hym afore the Chamberleyn of this citee to have the fraunchise and libertee of the same and be free of this crafte for asmoche as he had truly served therfore as apprentice with a man of this crafte. iijs. iiijd.

Die Martis vij[mo] die Maii.

Le quarter daye
The same day was holden the quarter day in the presence of the M., M. Percyvale, knight, M. Pemberton, aldreman, Keys, West, Duplache, Lee, Jenyns, Spenser, the iiij wardeyns and the hole feliship than to giders assembled.

Admyssion of new brethern
Concluded and fully aggreed by the comon assent of all the feliship than assembled that thise persones whose names herafter folowen shuld be admytted into hole brethern and clothyng of this worshipfull fraternitee and company.

---

[447] The first house of Friars Observants (Grey Friars) had been founded at Greenwich by Edward IV in 1482: Knowles and Hadcock, *Medieval Religious Houses*, pp. 230-1.

<u>New brethern</u>
John Bodyam
John Lucas
Thomas Newman
Andrew Botiller
Robert Colson
Henry Alisaunder
James Moncastre
Thomas Davy
George Bodeherst
Edward Dravyk
John Wright
admitted and sworen

Richard Smyth of Redyng admytted

Graunted the same day unto the M. accordyng to his desire to kepe a dyner the morow after Midsomer daye.

[f. 65]

For as moch as in old tyme passed it was enacted and made that noman of the crafte which hath borne thoffice and rome of a wardeyn shuld in the daye of the Nativitee of Seint John the Baptist be absent from his dyner in this present place but to be there to kepe his ordre and rome after his degree for the replenysshyng and garnesshyng of the wardeyns table withoute he were diseased orells had a lawfull and reasonable excuse undre a certeyn peyne theupon lymyted as in the said ordynaunces therof made more openly is conteyned. It is so now a dayes that many and divers persones of this same crafte which have borne thoffice and rome of a wardeyn have not in their myndes the grete othe and promys that they have taken and made unto God and Seint John their patron nether the penaltee that is assessed upon theym that breken thordynaunces nor, they fere not as it semeth, the grete and orrible peynes that God hath ordeigned for theym that wilfully be purjured, but folow their owne sensualitees and sinistre weyes intendyng by colour and fraudulent excuses to deceyve God and Seint John their foundour and the company also bicause they wold not bere the charges and rome of a maister. But God knoweth every hidd thyng and thought of mannes hert in avoidyng and eschewyng the manyfold inconveniencies that myght ensue by reason of pejuryie. Therfore it is now of new enacted, stablisshed and ordeygned by the discrete wysedomes of the worshipfull persones affore named with the consent and aggreament of the hole body than to gyders assembled that the wardeyns table from hensforth shalbe garnysshed and replenysshed at dyner

245

in the daye of Nativitee of Seint John Baptist with such persones as have bene wardeyns and with none other enlesse som straunge gentilman or other worshipfull persone be appoynted by the M. for the tyme beyng to sitte there. And if it so fortune in tyme to com any persone or persones of this crafte which hath or have born thoffice of wardeynhode be absent at dyner in the daye of the Nativitee of Seint John Baptist and hath or hath not a reasonable and lawfull excuse or excuses he or they so beyng absent and everich of theym shall pay at every tyme for his or their defaultes in that behalf unto thuse and behofe of the fraternitee of Seint John Baptiste xxs. sterlinges without any remission or pardon and that as often and whan as any such caas shall happen herafter.

[f. 65v] Povey

Adhuc le quarter daye

<u>A graunte of almes of xvij*d*. wekely unto G. atte Well and T. Hosyer</u>.
The same daye atte humble supplicacion of Geoffrey atte Welle and Thomas Hosyer, pore and indigent almesmen, was graunted by hole feliship than assembled to the said Gefferey and Thomas the full almes of xvij*d*. by the weke and their almes houses that they now dwell in to have to theym and either of theym the said almes of xvij*d*. by the weke from the feste of Nativitee of Seint John Baptist now next comyng duryng all the naturell lyfes of the said Gefferey and Thomas and of either of theym lenger lyvyng to be paid by thandes of the M. for the tyme beyng at their almeshouse or elles by thands of his assignees.

Die Veneris decimo die Maii.

The same daye the M. with thadvice of his wardeyns toke a direccion in a matier of accompte dependyng undiscussed bitwene Nicholas Asshe on that one partie and Richard Oldom late his servaunt on that other partie. Which Richard than knowleged to owe unto the said Nicholas iiij*li*. viij*s*. and the same iiij*li*. viij*s*. he and sufficient suertee with hym graunteth to be bound by obligacion to pay in maner and fourme folowyng that is to sey the xvij daye of this present moneth xxs., atte feste of Seint Mighel Tharchaungell [29 Sept.] than next xxij*s*., atte feste of Nativitee of our Lord God than next xxij*s*., and atte feste of Pasche than next [30 Mar. 1494] xxiiij*s*. Provided alwey that if it be proved and knowleged by the wyf of the forsaid Nicholas that he oweth unto the said Richard v*s*. than the same Richard and his suertees shall pay no more money but only iiij*li*. iij*s*. Not withtandyng the graunte of payment made afore to the contrary. iiij*li*. viij*s*.

The same daye William Kyrkeham in the presence of the M. his iiij wardeyns Fittez Bromefeld and Mayour promytted and graunted upon his faith and trouthe to pay unto Richard Smyth xiijs iiijd. in fourme folowyng that is to sey at Pentecost [26 May] iijs. iiijd., at Midsomer [24 June] than next iijs. iiijd., at Bartilmew tyde [24 Aug.] than next iijs. iiijd. and atte fest of All Seintes [1 Nov.] than next ensuyng iijs. iiijd. [Total] xiijs. iiijd.

John Cok the son of Henry Cok by indenture beryng date in the feste of Nativitee of Seint John Baptist anno viij° H. vij [24 June 1493] put himself apprentice to Harman Nuce for viij yeres.

[f. 66]

Die Veneris ultimo die Maii.

xxiiij^{or} assistentes
Assemblee holden than in presence of the M., M. Percyvale knight, M. Pemberton aldreman, Keys, West, Duplach, Lee, Hede, Jenyns, the iiij wardeyns, Hubert, Boughton, Randyll, Haydyff, Fittes, Grene, Nynes.

The same day it was aggreed and fully concluded by the comon assent of the worshipfull persones afore named that the nominacion and eleccion of the new Maister and iiij wardeyns that shalbe for the yere to com shalbe named and electe the Sonday affore none in the eve of Nativitee of Seint John Baptist [24 June] now next comyng accordyng to the old auncient ordynaunces and laudable custumes in this place hertofore made used and ordeigned.
Concluded and determyned than by and with thassent of the said persones that the M. for the tyme beyng iij iiij or mo of the xxiiij whiche as the M. wole call unto hym with his iiij wardeyns shall at the M. pleasure call all such persones before theym which have not paid the summes of money graunted by theym of their benivolence toward the new bieldynges in Frydaystrete[448] and to have communicacion of their grauntes and paymentes and if any man deny or refuse to make payment of his said graunte than he that so refuseth to make payment to be ordered and ruled by the good oredynaunces and constitucions of this place orelles sharply to be punysshed accordyng to his deservynges.

Concluded the same daye with thassent of the said persones that the M. and ij other persones which have bene M. such as the M. wole assigne and ij of his wardeyns shall goo unto M. Hert in Flete strete willyng hym in goodly maner

---

448   See Introduction, pp. 18–19.

bicause he is a sekeman to make perfite his accompts which is not yet engroced to thentent that the company may know wether they be advauntaged or no by reason of his office and to thentent also that the M. that now is may suerly and perfectly make and yeld up his accomptes accordyng to the good rules of this place.[449]

[f. 66v] Povey.

Die Lune tercio die Junii.

The same day Richard Semar and Broughton made reporte unto the Maister and his wardeyns on this wyse folowyng that where they as wardeyns late of the Bachelers company accordyng to their othe and office wente aboute the citee and subarbes of the same to aske levy, perceyve and gadre all such duties as every broder of this crafte by ordynaunces is bound to paye. Among which they came unto one Bukston a broder among theym dwellyng in Cornehull desiryng hym to make payment unto theym of his dette and dutie that he than owed he that to to utterly denyed and refused seiyng precisely that he wold none pay for noman. The said late wardeyns heryng and seyng his ungoodly answere and demeanure shewed unto hym that the M. of the feliship shuld send unto hym for a distresse:

> Let ne cause not the M. to distreyne me nor no man elles in his name for and if he doo he shalbe put in jeopardye of his lyf and endited of felony.

And over all this the said Bukston seyd that he cowde scathe and disadvauntage the hall of more money than an c. persones of the best perteignyng to the crafte were worth and also he knew and knowes where divers writynges be that perteignen to the crafte that the crafte wold gyf xl*li*. to have the same wrytyngs in their possession and handes.

The same day Andrew Robynson graunteth to paye unto Thomas Cape xij*s*. j*d*. ob. in fourme folowyng that is to sey upon Sonday than next ij*s*. j*d*. ob. and at Mighelmasse than next suyng by suretee and hym self bound x*s*. And [if] he can fynde no suertee than the same Thomas to be at his libertee and to take thadvauntage by the lawe.

The same day the old wardeyns of the bachelers company that is to sey David Michel and his felowes in the name of all their feliship have gyffen of their free will and benivolence towardes the reparacion and new makyng of the rayles in the gardyn x*s*.

---

[449]   Hert made his will in September 1493: see Appendix IV.

Die Veneris vij^{mo} die Junii.

The same daye William Barton and John Breton in the presence of the M. and the iiij wardeyns compromytted theym to stand unto the arbitrament of George Bolton and Richard Cornhill arbitratours bytwene theyn as in ij obligacions therof made playnly it appereth.

[f. 67]

Die Lune decimo die Junii.

The same day William Symson fuller and John Lynton have compromytted theym to stand unto thearbitrament of Nicholas Nynes arbitratour of almaner matiers of discorde dependyng than bitwene theym so that thend were made bitwene theym at such tyme as they wole require it.

The same daye Ambrose Bradman the son of Thomas Bradman of the town of Calice,[450] souldiour, with the consent of Robert Hertishorne his m[aister] in the presence of the M. and wardeyns is commytted unto Thomas Bradman his broder to serve oute the residue of his termes now for to com accordyng to theffecte of his indenture beryng date the vth daye anno v^{to} Henrici vij^{mi} [1490] his terme begynnyng at Midsomer [24 June] the same yere.[451]

Die Veneris xiiij^{mo} die Junii.

The same day John Bruer the son of William Bruer which was apprentice of Thomas Blokley brought in the copy of his fredom beryng date in the chambre of the Guyldhall the ix daye of Decembre in the vth yere of the reigne of Kyng Henry the vijth [1489].
The same daye the M. licenced the said John Bruer to open shop and he to pay accordyng to the ordynaunce *xs.* in fourme folowyng that is to sey the xxiiij daye of July next comyng *vs.* and the xxiiij daye of Marche than next ensuyng *vs.* and Thomas Blokley hath undertaken payment for the same *xs.*

Redempcionar' tempore M. Cotton.
The same daye John Scotton redempcionar graunted in the presence of the Chamberleyn of London to pay unto thuse of this place *xs.* sterlinges whan and assone as it shall happen hym to open occupie and hold shop of his own

---

450   Calais.
451   No month is given for the date of the indenture, but as his term was said to have started on Midsummer's day, the year is almost certainly 1490 rather than 1489.

and therupon he assured his feith and trouth before the said Chamberleyn into thands of the M. and his wardeyns and so he is licenced to open whan he wole makyng the said payment orelles not ... xs.

[f. 67v] Povey.

Adhuc die Veneris xiiij° die Junii.

The same day Thomas Chicheley in the presence of the M. Lee, Buk, wardeyns and Nynes upon his feith graunted to paye to Henry Brewster and William Polgrave vijs. ijd. in fourme folowyng that is to sey at Midsomer [24 June] now next iijs. vijd. and at Mighelmesse [29 Sept.] than next iijs. vijd.

The takyng doun of the chymney in the kyngs chambre[452]
The same day Richard Gyrston rentgaderer shewed unto the M. and to his wardeyns that the chymney in the Kynges chambre atte west end of the hall is so ruynouse and feble that it may in no wyse long stand and every daye is in all lyklyhode to fall down to the grete perill and jeopardye to the good man of the Cok[453] his gestes, servauntes and bestes. The M. heryng of this caas sawe the same chymneye and grete perill therof and the wekenesse and feblenes of the same wherfore he with thadvice of his wardeyns willed the said rentgaderer to cause the said chymney to be taken down from the upperest parte down unto the corbelles wherupon the same stode and for the upper part is lefte a pece of lede upon the said chambres side and the corbelles yet stand still in token and remembraunce that the same chymney was there set without any contradiction or impedyment of any man. And the same chymney to be bielded ayen as shall please the company therto to be advised.

---

[452] This upper room was originally part of the 'vielle hostel' which stood to the west of the hall itself and was acquired by the Tailors in the late 14th century. Previously referred to simply as the 'great chamber', the change of name may have followed a visit by Henry VII to Tailors' Hall, perhaps on the occasion of a mayoral dinner. In 1512 the chamber contained a long table with trestles, a bedstead and 'a staf for the Resurrexion the crosse thereof gilt'. The 'olde howse' was taken down in 1573 and a new building put up which incorporated a new 'King's Chamber' where James I dined in 1607. Following the Great Fire the west end of the hall site was remodelled around a grand staircase. Hopkinson, *Merchant Taylors' Hall*, pp. 20–1; Clode, *Memorials*, 40, 86, 150.

[453] Presumably an inn abutting the west end of the Hall.

Die Lune decimo septimo die Junii.

Assemblee holden the same day in the presence of the M., M. Percyvale, knight, M. Pemberton, aldreman, Keys, West, Lee, Buk, Jenyns, iiij wardeyns, Randall, Haydyf, Boughton, Fittez, Wylford and Nynes.

Concluded and aggreed than that Fader Payne,[454] carpenter, shall have the house in Lymestrete that he now dwelleth in for terme of his lyf paiyng therfore yerely xs. sterlinges at iiij termes of the yere in the citee of London usuell by even porcions and kepyng almaner reparacions of the same tenement well and sufficiently duryng all his naturell lyf tyme.

[f. 68]

Adhuc die Lune xvij^{mo} die Junii.

Concluded and aggreed the same day that Symond Lorymer, scryvaner, late rentgaderer shall have the termes of the tenement and house in Trinitee parissh the lytell accordyng to theffecte of thendenture of lees made and graunted unto hym and unto his wyf in the tyme of Maister Deplache than beyng M. for xl yeres as in the said indenture of ferme more openly is conteyned.

Reversyng of a graunte made to Fader Lytell
For asmoche as the same daye Richard Lytell an old fader of the company willed and desired to have his lyveree clothyng, hode and lynyng accordyng to a graunte made unto hym the vijth day of Marche in the xx^{ti} yere of the reigne of Kyng Edward the iiijth [1479/80] M. Barlow than beyng M. of the company as in the same graunte with the proviso therin expressed and therof made more playnly is conteyned and also where the same day the said Richard shewed unto the company a bill recytyng a graunte of the tenement that he now dwelleth in made in the tyme of M. Duplach than M. of the company To have to hym from the vijth day of Decembre in the xxj yere of the reigne of Kyng Edward the iiijth [1481] for terme of his lyf paiyng by yere therfore to the M. of the company for the tyme beyng vjs. viijd. and the said tenauntre to be repaired atte costes of the crafte as in the same graunte therof made more playnly it appereth. The ryght worshipfull persones before named caused the said ij grauntes to be redd divers tymes to thentent that they wold know well and advisedly what money and clothyng he had receyved more of the feliship than he gafe and so they found that the said Fader Lytell had receyved of the

---

454   Thomas Payne had formerly rented a property in Adlane (which he sub-let to the Pinners' Company) but then gave up the lease in exchange for this house in Lymestrete: see Introduction, p. 19.

company asmoch money as he delivered unto theym and vj*li*. above which is not in his power to recompence the feliship ayen. They remembryng his grete age, faderly maners, sad condicions, honest behavyng, vertuous disposicion and verrey true lover after his degree that he alwey bare to God, Seint John his patron and to the feliship wold not in nowyse that he shuld be as an abjecte from theym but that he shuld [have] som token of love and remembraunce. Wherefore they all with one assent and will aggreed and graunted the said Fader Lytell the said tenement that he now dwelleth in for terme of his lyf accordyng to his old graunte and to be repayred atte craftes cost.

[f. 68v] Povey.

Adhuc die Lune xvij° die Junii.

The same daye George Bolton and Richard Cornhill as arbitratours indifferently electe and named bitwene William Barton and John Breton of almaner matiers of travers bitwene theym dependyng undecised wherfore they awarde as it shall appere herafter folowyng that is to sey. First the said arbitratours awarde and deme in the presence of the M., ij of his wardeyns and the clerk, that either of the said William and John shall seale and as his dede deliver to other of theym a generall acquietaunce and relesse of almaner accions personell from the begynnyng of the world unto this present daye. And after [that] don the said William Barton shall seale and as his dede deliver unto the forsaid John a lawfull obligacion with condicion upon the same endorsed of xlvj*s*. viij*d*. wherin the same William shalbe bound unto the said John payable in the feste of Seint Mighell tharchaungell [29 Sept.] now next comyng than vj*s*. viij*d*. and every quarter after vj*s*. viij*d*. till the said xlvj*s*. viij*d*. be so fully paid as in an obligacion therof made more playnly it appereth etc.

Die Sabbati xxij^{do} die Junii.

Prestes wages
The same day the M. paid to Sir[455] John Ratclyf his stipend and salary for a quarter of a yere endyng at Midsomer now next to com xxxv*s*.
Also paid to Sir George Bromehill for his salary the same quarter xxxv*s*.
Also paid to Sir Robert Cudworth for his salary the same terme xxxv*s*.
Also paid to Sir Richard Wheler for his salary the same terme xxxv*s*.
Also paid to Sir John Burneham for his salary the same terme xvj*s*. viij*d*.

---

[455]   For this title see Glossary.

Wages of officers
Also paid to Henry Mayour, clerk of the company, for his fee the same terme xxvs.
Also paid to Thomas Gresyll, bedell, for his wages and kepyng of the gardyn the same terme xviijs. iiijd.

[f. 69]

Adhuc die Sabbati xxij^{do} die Junii.

Almesmen
Also paid to Thomas Hosier in full payment of his yeres almes ended at Midsomer now next comyng [24 June] iijs. iiijd.
Also paid to Robert Boylet for his quarter almes in full payment of this yere xs.
Also paid to Gefferey atte Well for his quarter almes in full payment of this yere xiijs. iiijd.
Also paid to Thalmesmen for their quarter almes ended at this Midsomer day [24 June] fully viijs. vjd.

[f. 69v blank]⁴⁵⁶

[f. 70]

Pateat universis quod die Dominica litera dominicali F in Vigilia Sancti Johannis Baptiste patroni nobilis mistere Scissorum et linee armature armurariorum hujus alme civitatis London anno incarnarcionis dominice Millesimo quadringentesimo nonagesimo tercio et anno regni metuendissimi nostri regis Henrici septimi octavo [1493]. In congregacione ac presencia honorabilium virorum Walteri Povey adhunc magistri mistere predicte, Johannis Percyvale militis, Hugonis Pemberton aldermannorum, Gall, Keys, West, Duplach, Lee, Heed, Bukk et Jenyns, venerabilis et discretis vir Thomas Randell nominatus et electus est in magistrum hujus famose fraternitatis et eodem die ex assensu honorabilium virorum predictorum Ricardus Hill, Johannes Kyrkeby, Thomas Bedford et Ricardus Smyth nominati et electi existunt in custodes ejusdem fraternitatis.

> [translation] Let it be known to all that on Sunday, dominical letter F,⁴⁵⁷ on the vigil of St. John the Baptist, patron of the noble mistery of tailors and linen-armourers of this beneficent city of London, in the

---

⁴⁵⁶ Five blank pages follow f. 69 and precede f. 70 (new numbering), coinciding with a change of hand to that of an unknown individual.

⁴⁵⁷ For the use of dominical letters see C. R. Cheney, *Handbook of Dates for Students of English History* (Bury St. Edmunds, 1991), pp. 8, 116–7.

year of the incarnation of Our Lord 1493 and in the eighth year of the reign of our most dread king, Henry VII. At an assembly and in the presence of the honourable men Walter Povey, late master of the aforesaid mistery, John Percyvale knight, and Hugh Pemberton, aldermen, Gall, Keys, West, Duplach, Lee, Heed, Bukk and Jenyns, that venerable and discreet man Thomas Randell was nominated and chosen as master of this renowned fraternity, and on the same day, with the assent of the aforenamed worshipful men, Richard Hill, John Kyrkeby, Thomas Bedford and Richard Smyth were nominated and chosen as wardens of the same fraternity.

Thomas Randell   master

Richard Hill
John Kyrkeby
Thomas Bedford
Richard Smyth   wardens

[f. 70v] Randyll

Veneris v^{to} die Julii.

The same daye the forenamed Maister and the iiij wardeyns sworen in the daye of Nativitee of Seint John Baptist last passed and his next predecessour Maister Povey and the iiij wardeyns late with the same M. Povey within the chapell perteignyng to this present place herd their Masse of tholy goste and after Masse don and seyde the new M. and the iiij wardeyns to hym electe came into this parlour and were sette in their romes and places by their said next predecessours accordyng to the auncient custume and rules heretofore in this present place used and accustumed.[458]

The same day the M. with the consent of the iiij wardeyns enjoyned Robert Hall to bryng in to this place the next Frydaye xx*d.* for nonne enrollyng of Thomas Fox his apprentice within the first yere accordyng to thordynaunce.

---

[458]   This is the earliest surviving description of the ritual surrounding the annual election of the master and wardens of the Tailors.

Lune 8ᵛᵒ die Julii.

<u>24</u>ᵒʳ. Assemblee than holden in the presence of the M., the iiij wardeyns, M. Percyvall Knyght, Keys, West, Lee, Buk, Jenyns, late M. Hubert, Fittes, Gre[ne], Bromefeld, Nynes, and Dogete.

The same day it was concluded and fully determyned with the consent of the persones afforenamed that Richard Smyth, than named the yongest wardeyn, shalbe charged with the leviyng, perceyvyng and gaderyng of all thissues, revenues and profettes comyng and growyng of all the lands and tenementes with their appurtenaunces perteignyng to this crafte and to do the reparacions of the same landes where nede shalbe accordyng to thordynaunces. And atte thend of the same yere to make therof a true accompte in writyng to the said M. of all his charges and discharges. [f. 71] And John Syth to gyf his best advis and mynde in counceillyng the said Richard for the profet of the said crafte where reparacions shalbe nedeful and they to have for their labours and busynes a rewarde orelles thank accordyng to their deservynges.

Concluded the same day that the M., the iiij wardeyns to hym electe, thold M. and wardeyns to hym asigned, M. Gall, M. Lee, M. Jenyns and Nicholas Nynes, Richard Gyrston, late rentgaderer, Henry Mayour, comon clerk of the company and William Erle, bedell of the same, shalbe redy upon Wednesdaye next at vj of the clok in the mornyng atte Seint Peters in Chepe[459] for the viewyng of all the landes perteignyng to this crafte.

Concluded also the said daye that M. Povey and the wardeyns to hym electe, M. Gall, M. Lee, M. Buk and M. Jenyns shuld go unto thous of M. Hert[460] and therto here his accomptes and rekenynges bilongyng to thuse of the crafte by reason of his office of maistership.

Determyned also that from hensforth the yongest wardeyn that shalbe for the tyme shalbe lyke wyse charged with the gaderyng of all the rentes and doyng reparacions as the said Richard Smyth now wardeyn is charged.

Ferthermore it was concluded and determyned the same daye that theste end of thall shalbe taken down unto the upper parte of the wyndow there and lower afterwardes if nede shall require and also thought convenient by workemen. And therupon provision to be had for the makyng of a scafold there shortily for the takyng down of the stone worke of the said Easte parte.

---

[459] St. Peter Westcheap.
[460] See above, pp. 247–8 and Appendix IV.

[f. 71v] Randyll

Veneris 12ᵐᵒ die Julii.

The same daye the Maister with the consent of the wardeyns enjoyned and comaunded William Gerveys to withdrawe thaccion that he had attained ayenst Thomas West taillour or elles at his perill and his demeanure to be shewed unto the counceill of the crafte. Which William [than] and there seide precisely that the seid accion shuld not be withdrawen for no man lyvyng but if the said West shuld put in suertee in the courte tanswere unto the said accion.

The said daye the said William Gerveys reported and seide in this present place before the said M. and wardeyns, M. Povey and John Doget, that the same M. Povey dyd unto hym whan he was ruler of this worshipfull fraternitee open wrong and intreated hym lyke no good M. And over this the said Gerveys seyde that the sad M. Povey was the covetouse man that ever was in his dayes gouvernour of the said company. And he had lever⁴⁶¹ forswere Englond for vij yeres rather than the said M. Povey shuld be ruler of the said company ayeyn.
The said Gerveys the said daye graunted and promytted in the presence of the said M. and wardeyns to paye unto the said M. Povey or to his assignees the xix day of the said moneth of July atte ferrest vjs. viijd.

Lune 15ᵐᵒ die Julii

The same daye John Bettes⁴⁶² alias Jenyn Bettes an aliaunt borne and made denizein by the Kynges lettres patentez hath compowned with the M. and wardeyns for his redempcion and is admytted into the crafte without any ferther charges to the crafte thofficers fees allowed for iijli. sterlinges to be paid in fourme folowyng that is to sey in hand xxs. which was paid attefeste of All Seintes [1 Nov.] than next suyng xiijs. iiijd. [f. 72] atte feste of Purificacion of Seint Mary Virgyn [2 Feb. 1494] than next folowyng xiijs. iiijd. and atte feste of Pentecoste [18 May] next than ensuyng xiijs. iiijd.
Memorandum quod dicto quintodecimo die Thomas Petyt civis et scissor London' manucepit pro predicto Johannis Bettes pro solucione quadraginta

---

⁴⁶¹ 'rather'.
⁴⁶² Bettes, a German, was recorded in the alien subsidy roll of 1483–4 as one of three servants employed by a German tailor, Peter Selonder, in Aldgate ward. Bolton (ed.) *Alien Communities*, p. 76. For his letters of denization see *CPR 1485–94*, p. 430.

solidorum residui de dictis lx^to solidis si predictus Johannes superstes fuerit in ultimo festo solucionis preallegato.

[translation] Memorandum that the said fifteenth day Thomas Petyt, citizen and tailor of London, mainprised the said John Bettes for the payment of 40s., the residue of the said 60s., if the aforesaid John meets the last repayment day specified before.

Veneris 19vo die Julii.

The same daye M. Nynes, in the name of M.[463] Rose Swan[464], shewed unto the M. and wardeyns there beyng present, M. Povey, John Doget and Richard Dyngley that the same M. Rose for the true zele good will and love that she bereth and oweth unto almyghty God and that holy martyr and patrone of the fraternitee of the crafte of Taillours of London wole deliver unto the M. and wardeyns of the same crafte for the tyme beyng liij^xxxv marc for thentent herafter folowyng that is to sey iij*li*. vjs. viij*d*. sterlinges therof yerely duryng the terme of xix yeres to a preste of the Convent of the Freres Carmelites in Flete strete of London, and x marcs yerely during the term of x yeres to a seculer preste singyng at Seint Dunstanes in the West for the soule of M. John Swan, late aldreman, and all cristen soules, and xxs. yerely duryng the terme of xix yeres for the kepyng of thobite of the said Maister Swan, and x*li*. to the M. and iiij wardeyns of this crafte for the tyme beyng to be devided among theym after the maner and fourme here ensuyng that is to wete to the maister of the crafte for the tyme beyng, beyng present at the said obite to have for his labour iijs. iiij*d*. as long as the said obite shall endure and to everich of the iiij wardeyns beyng present atte same obite xx*d*. as in the composicion therof made more playnly is conteyned.

[f. 72v] Randyll.

Adhuc Veneris.

The same daye William Gerveys reported that there were some persones which have sitten here that were gretter maynteners of foreyns other wyse than ever he dyd.

Lune 21^mo465 die Julii.

---

[463] Abbreviation of 'Mistress' in this instance.
[464] For John and Rose Swan see Appendix IV.
[465] An error for '22do'.

The same day Thomas West, late covenaunt servaunt with the said William Gerveys, graunted and promytted upon his feith and trouth assured in thandes of the M. that he the 6ᵗʰ daye of August next for to com wolde funde sufficient suertee to the said Gerveys for the contentacion and payment of xxxvs. xjd. to be paid at such dayes as shuld be stalled and aggreed bitwene theym the said 6ᵗʰ day of August.

The same daye John Danyell late apprentice of John ... with his own consent in the presence of the M. and wardeyns by thauctoritee of this place is commytted unto the said William Gerveys to serve unto hym in maner and fourme of apprentice the reste of his termes that he had than to serve with the said John as in thendentures of apprentishode therof made more playnly is conteyned.

Mercurii 23[466] die Julii.

The same daye Germane Gryffyth of Suth[amp]t[on] merchaunt hath compowned with M. Povey as deputee[467] to the Maister, Richard Hill, John Kyrkeby and Thomas Bedford than wardeyns to be admytted freman of this crafte for xls. sterlinges wherof the said Germane paid than in hand xxs.

[f. 73]

Veneris 25[to468] die Julii.

The same daye the Bachelers company with licence of the M. and wardeyns aforehad and graunted kepte their quarter daye in the presence of Richard Hill, John Kyrkeby and Thomas Bedford than wardeyns and divers ordynaunces were redd unto the said company by Henry Mayour, clerk of the M. clothyng.[469]

---

[466]   An error for '24'.

[467]   An unusual instance of a former master (Povey) acting in place of his successor (Thomas Randall). It is unclear why Randall was not present at this meeting.

[468]   An error for '26ᵗᵒ'.

[469]   Mayour was clerk of the fraternity of St. John the Baptist, the organisation for liveried members of the craft, rather than the Bachelors' Company which was made up of the freemen who were outside the livery. This entry illustrates the extent to which the fraternity of St. John the Baptist and its officers kept a careful eye upon the activities of the Bachelors, most obviously by requiring them to hold this particular quarter-day in the presence of the wardens of the senior fraternity.

Lune 29ᵐᵒ die Julii.

The same daye assemblee of thissistents and counceillours of the crafte was holden and kept in the presence of the M., the forsaid iij wardeyns, M. Pemberton aldreman, Gall, West, Jenyns, Povey, late M. Hubert, Grene, Bromefeld, Nynes and Doget.

It was concluded the same daye tht the iij actes conteyned in the Bachelers bill shalbe confermed and ratified atte next quarter daye.

Also it was concluded and determyned with the consent of the persones afforenamed that thoffer that Maistres Swane desired and offered by the mouthe of M. Nynes shalbe admytted and taken.

Also it was aggreed and concluded that John Bettes late made denizein shalbe made freman of this crafte for iij*li*. sterlinges.[470]

Also it was determyned that the money beyng behinde unpaid by John Wotton the yonger of the biquest of M. Stone[471] shuld be receyved of William Dormer which had bought the landes of the said M. Stone before any estate be made by M. Stodard, Thomas Martyn and Thomas Vocatour feofees in the said landes unto the said Dormer.

Also it was concluded that the quarterdaye shalbe holden the next Wednesdaye folowyng.

[f. 73v] Randyll.

Mercurii 31ᵐᵒ die Julii.

Eodem die in presencia Magistri, Ricardi Hill, Johannis Kyrkeby, Thome Bedford, gardianorum sive custodum, M. Percyvale, M. Pemberton aldermannorum, West, Lee, Heed, Buk, Povey, nuper magistrorum, Boughton, Grene, Doget et tocius comitive insimul tunc congregate dies quarterii fuit tentus et observatus.

[translation] The same day in the presence of the master, Richard Hill, John Kyrkeby, Thomas Bedford, wardens, Master Percyvale, Master Pemberton, aldermen, West, Lee, Heed, Buck, Povey, late masters,

---

[470] See above, pp. 256–7.
[471] John Stone: see above, n. 38.

Boughton, Grene, Doget and the whole company together assembled, a quarter-day was held and observed.

First the same daye the comon othe[472] of the clothyng atte commaundement of the maister was openly red by the clerk.

Also the composicion of John Chirchman was declared and redd.
Also the last will of John Creke was redd.
Also the last will of Hugh Caundissh redd.
Also the last will of Thomas Reymond redd.

Also the same daye the desire of the Bachelers company put in writyng was graunted and confermed with the consent and aggreament of thole body of the clothing than to gyders assembled. Which writyng was delivered ayen unto the wardeyns of the Bachelers company.

Also it was determyned and concluded the same daye with the consent and will of thole body afforsaid that the M. and wardeyns shuld send for all suche persones that had not paid the money that they were assessed at for the new bieldynges in Frydaye Strete[473] and to know their delayes and all such that denyed their payment they to be compelled by the auctoritee of this place by a certeyn daye to theym to be lymyted and assigned by the said M. and wardeyns.

Also it was condescended that the M. and wardeyns shuld attempte and take knowlege what every persone of the clothyng of his good will and benyvolence wole gyfe toward the new makyng of thest ende of this hall and the celyng of the Guyhald of London which was moved by my lord the Mayre of this citee than.[474]

---

[472] The oath sworn by new liverymen. This along with the oaths sworn by the master, wardens, clerk, beadle and chantry priests survives in a book of oaths compiled in 1491 by the then clerk, William Duryvale: GL, Merchant Taylors' Co., Ancient MS Bk. 1, ff. 1-6.

[473] See Introduction, pp. 17-18. For the assessment, written on a flyleaf which was subsequently bound into the MS, see Appendix I.

[474] This may refer to further work carried out following the construction of 2 glazed louvered openings in Guildhall roof which was funded out of £40 given by William Heryot (mayor 1481-2). Heryot died in 1485 and the work, according to one chronicler, was completed in the 7th year of Henry VII's reign: Barron, *Guildhall*, p. 32; Stow, *Survey*, I, p. 272; *The Chronicle of the Grey Friars of London*, ed. J. G. Nichols (Camden Society, 1852), p. 25.

[f. 74]

Also the same daye with the consent and aggreement of thole body it was decreed and ordeigned that all thoo of the clothyng that paye not for their mete and almes the morow after Midsomer daye orelles by Lammasse daye [1 Aug.] next after accordyng unto theffecte of an ordenaunce therof made in M. Bukkes tyme[475] shalbe clerely dismyssed for ever of all the benefetes and advauntages that might grow or com unto theym herafter by reason of the fraternitee that he or they be of.

Veneris 2do die Augusti.

The same daye the M. with the consent of the wardeyns enjoyned William Batyson to paye a fyne unto thuse of this place bicause of his ungoodly demeanure and unfittyng seyinges that he had and used openly in thall the morowe after Midsomer daye last passed. The said William full presumtuously and obstynatly answered that he wold no such fyne pay with his good will as long as he lyved. Wherfore aswell his demeanure and seiynges as his presumpcion and obstynacie moste be shewed unto the counceyll of the crafte atte their nexte assemblee.

Lune 5to die Augusti

The same daye John Bettes otherwise called Jenyn Bettes brought into this present place the Kynges lettres patentes under his greate seale testifyng that his grace hath admytted the said Jenyn Bettes a verrey denizein of this his royalme as in the same lettres patentez beryng date at Westminster the xxvij day of Aprill in the viijth yere of the reigne of Kyng Henry the vijth [1493] more playnly is conteyned.[476]

[f. 74v]

The same daye M. Gall in the name of Richard Leman,[477] usyng the crafte of bakyng, desired the Maister and wardeyns that the said Leman myght be pardoned and relessed of almaner summaunces, fynes, lottes, scottes, imposicions and all other charges belongyng to this fraternitee excepte vj*s*. viij*d*. for his dyner and almes and iij*d*. for offeryng yerely duryng his lyfe.

---

[475] William Buk was Master in 1488-9.

[476] Actually 28 April 1493: *CPR 1485-94*, p. 430. See above, pp. 256-7.

[477] See above, n. 446.

The same daye Thomas Maryote late apprentice of John Morell not than enrolled and had served ij yeres and di. of his termes was commytted by thauctoritee of this place to serve oute the residue of his termes with James Moncastre.

The same daye the Maister with thavis of the wardeyns gafe licence for their tyme to the forsaid John Bettes to occupie ij foreyns he payng for either of theym that yere vs. summa xs.

The said daye the M. and wardeyns of one assent licenced Piers Barbour to arest John Brigges and John Hopwode his apprentice.

The same daye the said Piers Barbour hath compowned for Robert Potte for his redempcion and admission into this crafte for liijs. iiijd. sterlinges for payment wherof the said Piers hath undertaken in this maner folowing that is to sey on Fryday or Monday next xiijs. iiijd., atte feste of All Seyntes [1 Nov.] than next vjs. viijd., at Candilmas than next [2 Feb. 1494] vjs. viijd., at Pentecoste than next [18 May] vjs. viijd., atte Lammasse [1 Aug.] than next vjs. viijd., atte feste of All Seintes [1 Nov.] than next vjs. viijd., atte feste of Candilmasse than next [2 Feb. 1495] vjs. viijd. in full payment of the said liijs. iiijd. ut patet per obligacionem cum condicione indorsata inde factam expresse.

[f. 75]

Veneris 9ᵐᵒ die Augusti.

The same daye the M. with the consent of the wardeyns enjoyned Thomas West that he shuld not depart oute of this place unto suche tyme that he founde suertee unto William Gerveys for payment of xxxvs. xjd. and if [he] dyd otherwyse than his body shuld be commytted to warde.

APPENDIX I

(A) MISCELLANEOUS ENTRIES FROM THE FLYLEAVES OF VOLUME TWO

[Flyleaf 1][478]

Hic sequntur nomina xxiiij^{or} magis fidedignorum tempore Willelmi Buk magistri.

[translation] Here follow the named of the 24 faithful masters in the time of William Buck, master.[479]

+M. Tego

+M. Stodard

M. Galle

M. Barlowe

M. Materdale

M. Pemberton

M. Keys

M. Lee

M. West

M. Buk

M. West

M. Deplech

M. Stalworth

M. Hede

Stephanus Jenyns

Thomas Randyll

Thomas Martyn

Willelmus Crosby

Johannes Spencer

Walterus Povy

---

[478] The flyleaves of volume 2 contain a number of miscellaneous entries and jottings from the years covered by the surviving minutes. Some of these are incomplete, crossed out and/or illegible and have not been included in this edition.

[479] Buk was Master in 1488-9. This annotations and crossings-out occurred over a number of years following the deaths of men such as Stalworth (1489), Martyn (1491) and Crosby (1496).

~~Thomas Martyn~~
Jacobus Fyttz
Alanus Huberd
Owinus Boughton
Ricardus Adyff
~~Johannes Hardy~~
~~Johannes Lowes~~
~~M. Galle~~
 + ~~Oliverus Warner~~
 + ~~M. Stalworth~~
Willelmus Herte[480]
Jacobus Wilford
Willelmus Grene
Thomas Bromeflete
Johannes Doket
Johannes Russhe

> Hoberd
> Bromeflete
> H. Clough
> John Bernard

> Water Povy   )
> James Wilford   ) auditores pro Thesaurario[481]

Thomas Purvale habet diem solucionis pro aperic[ione] sua videlicet ad Natalem domini *vs*. et ad Pasche *vs*.
  [translation] Thomas Purvale has days of payment for his [shop] opening at Christmas 5*s*. and at Easter 5*s*.

Memorandum that M. West the xij day of Feverer anno v^{to} [1490] hath promised to discharge Henry Alisaundre of all such wrytynges as he hath before tyme of the said Henry. In whosse [eve] handes the same wrytynges ben.

Galymen
Benet de Cena galyman[482] hath licence to holde shop to begynne on Hole Monday.

---

[480] The names of Hert, Wilford, Grene, Bromflete, Doget and Russhe were added subsequently as their first appearances on the court took place from 1490 onwards.
[481] See above, p. 173.
[482] See Glossary.

Item the same Benet hath a man begynyng the ix day of April.
Grevys son late apprentice of Richard Alenson dwellyth in his Faders hous.
Item George ... by saint Johns Chirche in Walbroke.

In the court in the Ryall[483]
John Skotton
William Swannes prentice with the same Skotton

Henry Clough   )
John Doget   )   supervisores pro le Saresyns Hede.

Rowland Walker Thomas Wytney
Edward Newton pinner
Johannes Halle in Grubstrete fletcher

[Flyleaf 1v]

Fynes receyved for quarter dayes and of sumaunces

<u>Dies quarterii xij die Octobris[484]</u>
From Richard Hill warden xij*d*.
Thomas Segge iiij*d*. +[485]
William Burton iiij*d*. +
William Werton iiij*d*. +
Thomas Werton iiij*d*. +
Henry Dod iiij*d*. +
M. Keys iiij*d*. +
x John Povy iiij*d*. +
Richard Tolle iiij*d*. +
David Roche iiij*d*. +
John Hirst iiij*d*. +
x M. Galle iiij*d*. +
Robert Hertyshorn iiij*d*. +
William Grene iiij*d*. +
Henry Clough iiij*d*. +

---

483 'La Riole' was a substantial residence in the parish of St. John Walbrook which was occupied by a number of noblemen and women in the later middle ages. In 1483 it was granted to John, duke of Norfolk, and soon afterwards to Margaret, countess of Richmond and Derby, the mother of the future Henry VII. The identity or functions of the 'court' mentioned in this entry are unclear. Lobel (ed.) *Atlas*, p. 84.
484 Probably 1493, when Hill was upper warden.
485 These annotations probably denote men who had paid their fines.

Rauf Bukberd iiij*d.* +
Thomas Peight iiij*d.* +

vij° die Januarii.[486]

John Bulle, tyler, toke to ferme of the M. the corner tenement in Wodestrete to begynne at Candelmas x yeres for xl*s*. And if he woll have the oder tenement therto adjoynyng he to geve knoweleche therof withyn xiiij dayes at xxx*s*. the yere.

Croftes ij prentices Palmer[487] with William Olyver and with one ayenst the conduit in Cornhill.

Richard Swan hath a prentis with Duncan.

Thomas Egerton had a foren,

Robert Barker had a foren.

William Olyver a foren oute of Suthwerke by vj [wekes?][488]

Willelmus Swanston a foren.

Willelmus Shirbourne hath a prentis called Robys and not bound nor inr[olled].

Richard Peynter for his apprentice in Saint Gyles parish and had a foren called Robert.

Hugh Huchyn in Candelwykestrete a foren.

Memorandum tempore M. Povy.[489]

Willelmus Popes conquestus fuit per apprenticium suum quia non irrotulatur et Popes habet diem essendi hic usque diem veneris proxime.

    [translation] Memorandum in the time of Master Povey.

    William Popes was complained against by his apprentice who was not enrolled, and Popes has until Friday next to come here.

[Fly-leaf 2]

Defalt' xv° die Augusti ad xxiiij°ʳ.

Henry Iryell seythe and disposeth that in the tyme that John Spencer was Maister of this fraternite[490] at a certeyn tyme on after none he cam into the Swan by the grete conduit[491] and there he founde Robert Grevys syttyng with

---

[486] Perhaps 1494.

[487] Altered from 'Crowe'.

[488] Lost in binding.

[489] Walter Povy was Master for 1492–3. For his career see Appendix IV.

[490] 1490–1.

other company and there they dronk togider and whan they had dronken they went oute of the hous and stode withoute the dore. And there they fyll in commoning of a mater bytwene the said Grevys and Ed. Bretowe. The same Grevys soyng than and there that Spencer the Maister of [t]his crafte was a false knave and that he helde with the said Edmond so that he coude have no right of hym. The same Grevys than and there also revylyng the said M. Spencer callyd [hym] false horesson knave and that he wold prove him a knave with moch other ungodely langage in outrageous wyse wherby one then syttyng in the hous heryng the said Grevys have such langage supposyng that the said Grevys had ben displeesed with another he prayed the said Grevys to be his good master and therto the said Grevys seyde than it was not that man that he speke of But it was of another knave and this seyng the said Henry advysed the said Grevys to remembre hym self and so he departed and after that the said Henry herde the [said] Grevys eftesons at another tyme rayle ayenst the said M. Spencer at Sweres hous in the Pultrie[492] ... at another tyme rage ayenst the M. Spencer at ... the pultry.

---

491   The Great Conduit lay at the east end of Cheapside.

492   The location of 'Sweres hous' in the Poultry meant that it was just a short walk from the Swan.

(B) MISCELLANEOUS ENTRIES (mid-1490s)
FROM VOLUME ONE

[The first volume of minutes is known to have originally begun in c.1458, but at some point after 1609 the first 227 folios were lost. Two pages of miscellaneous jottings, mostly relating to the business of the court in the early to mid-1490s were added to the start of the now truncated volume, before they and the surviving minutes were rebound and renumbered. These entries are included here as an appendix as they logically follow on from the formal record of court proceedings contained in volume II.]

Merchant Taylors' Company, Ancient MS Book, 37.

[f. 1v][493]

Money assessed for the new bieldyng in Fridaye strete

First M. Stodard lxs.
Item M. Gall xls.
Item M. West xls. solutum xxs. M. Randill +[494]
Item M. Materdale xiijs. iiijd.
Item Aleyn Hubert xxs. solutum per apprenticium +
solutum +Item James Wylford xls. per Kyrkeby
solutum +Item Owen Boughton xxs. per Kyrkeby
Item James Ffitter xxs. concesit solvere post festum pasche
Item John Bernard xxs. solutum M. +
Item Richard Haydyf xxs. solutum pro ymaginem de auro +
Item John Wotton xxs.
Item James Shyrwode iijs. iiijd. solutum M
Item Richard Gryffyth xxs. + solutum tempore Hert
Item Thomas Martyn vjs. viijd.
Item James Grene xs.
Item George Lovekyn xxs. concesit solvere ante festum pasche proxime
Item Roger Mone xxs. Kyrkeby solutum M Hill +
Item Piers Fforster xxs. solutum Randyll +

---

493 f. 1 blank.
494 This marginal annotation probably indicates those individuals whose contributions had been received. In a number of cases payments were made to prominent liverymen such as Thomas Randall, and these are also noted in the margin.

Item Henry Clough xxs. solutum M. Wylford ±

~~Item Rauf Bukberd xxs. per Kyrkeby~~ solutum ±

Item John Flye

Item Richard Joskyn vjs. viijd.

Item James Assand vjs. viijd.

Item Richard Toll xxs. ±

Item Alexander Bassyngthwayte xs.

Item Richard Leman vjs. viijd. solutum Randyll ±

Item Thomas Werton xiijs. iiijd.

Item Thomas Bedford xs. ±

Item John Bowman xs. solutum Clough tam ipse ~~non~~ computavit societati tempore M. Wylford ±

Item William Batyson xs. ±

Item John Nayler xs. solutum ixs. iiijd. per manus Kyrkeby ±

Item John Horst xs. ±

Item William Bekeham xs. solutum magistro ±

Item John Nicholas vs.

Item John Chicheley vs. solutum Povey ±

Item Robert Hertishorne vjs. viijd.

Item Thomas Pole vjs. viijd.

Item Richard Thomasson xs.

Item Hugh Acton vs. solutum M. ±

Item Paten Patenson vs.

Item William a Lye vs.

Item Richard Fowler xxd. solutum Kyrkeby

Item Thomas Bond vjs. viijd.

Item William Averell xxd. nichill ±

Item Thomas Gall xxd.

Item William Gryndell xxd.

Item Robert Parys vjs. viijd. solutum M. Povey ±

Item William Fox xxd.

Item John Laurence vjs. viijd. ±

Item William Erle iijs. iiijd. ±

Item Robert Johnson iijs. iiijd.

Item John Baskervyle iijs. iiijd.

Item Richard Gyrston iijs. iiijd. solutum M. ±

Item William Orwell vs.

[column 2]

Item John Bode

Item Richard Asshe vjs. viijd.

~~Item John Spereman xxd.~~ receptum per M. Randall

Item John Harryson xx*d*.
Item William Grey ij*s*. iiij*d*.
Item Richard Quykrell v*s*.
Item Rauf Wodeward xx*d*.
Item Richard Lynche ij*s*. iiij*d*.
Item William Werton xiij*s*. iiij*d*.
Item James a Kechyn vj*s*. M. <u>solutum</u>
Item Thomas Speight x*s*. solutum M. ±

Memorandum that on the 19th day of February 11 Hen. VII [1495/6] the said Richard Quykrell paid to Owen Boughton master of the craft in part payment of his loan (*benevolencie*) 20*d*.

[f. 2]

Dettes of divers persones that were assessed to pay for Rydyng[495] and owyng the xxx day of Maye anno ix° [1494]

William Crosby ij*s*. vj*d*.
Henry Iriell ij*s*.
John Rysshe iiij*s*.
William Orwell iiij*s*.
Robert Parys ij*s*. receptum per M. Randyll ±
Robert Greves iiij*s*.
John Nicholas ij*s*.
Richard Frene ij*s*.
William a Lye ij*s*. vj*d*.
Thomas Gall xx*d*.
William Averell viij*d*.
Robert Stephenson ij*s*. iiij*d*.
M. Lee behinde unpaid xij*d*.

[f. 2v]

Memorandum that John Howard at Saynt Andrew Under shafte graunted to pay x*s*. at Cristemas if he were not under preferement by that day.[496]

---

[495] The nature of this occasion is not recorded: it may perhaps have been a royal entry of some kind as the principal civic processions took place following the elections of the mayor and sheriffs in September and October.

[496] Howard has not been identified, although the entry suggests that he may have been a chaplain of some kind, perhaps awaiting an appointment to a benefice.

Memorandum that the ix day of Octobre Cristofre Kyrke receyved a potell oyle.

Pemberton
Materdale
Joskyn
Doket

Setters	Auditours
M. Barlowe	M. Buk
M. Materdale	M. Gale
Alen Hoberd	M. Pemberton
John Hardy	R ...
Thomas Martyn	M. Keys
Thomas Bromfeld	M. West
Thomas Bodley	John Spencer
Richard Joskyn	William Grene
Peter Forster	
Henry Kellowe	
~~John Cok~~	
George Bolton	

arbitratores inter Wilsh' et Burdon

W. Mortymer
Jo. Lowes

Jo. Lye pro iij*li*. videlicet in manibus ...

Walterus Beaufeld in Gracechirchestrete
John Warner.
William Gervey in Saynt Swythunes lane.

Variacio quedam inter Harryson et apprentium suum

Memorandum receyved of John Harryson for ys fredom xs.

M. West
M. Hede
Walter Povey
Thomas Randyll
Richard Dyngley

271

Roger Mone
Richard Cornhill
~~Robert Kelham~~
William Batyson
~~John a Keehyn~~
James Fitz
James Grene
John Povy
Richard Joskyn
Roger Mone

Delyvered to the peauterer the xxiij day of July of the remainder of his vessell
    a charger
    a dosen grete platers
    Item a dosen mydell platers ij molten[497]
    Item viij grete disshes
    ij dosen myddell disshes a dissh molten
    Item ij grete saucers j moltern
    Item vj small saucers ij molten
    et et sic carent xx grete platerz xij midel platers et xvj grete disshes

    For the quarter day
    For the matter concerning Harryson in Cornhill and his apprentice
    10s.
    Item for Swanston in Cornhill
    Item for Greves for his fine 10s.

Item John Wylkokkes concessit solvere S. iijli. xs. debitos al lez Nawlars box.
[translation] Item John Wylkokkes agreed to pay S. £3 10s. owed to 'lez Nawlars box'.[498]

Johannes Mendill [sergeant?]
John Atkynson
John Pykman
James E ...d

Receyved of Archer the xv day of Feverer iijli. xvs. ijd.

M. Percyvale	James Fittz
M. Hert	Thomas Bromeflete

---

[497]   i.e. dishes made of cast metal: *OED.*
[498]   Meaning unclear.

MISCELLANEOUS ENTRIES FROM VOLUME ONE

M. Barlowe

M. Galle

M. Keys

M. Deplache

M. Hede

Ewen Boughton

iiij gardianis

D.

APPENDIX II

ADDITIONAL DOCUMENTS (1467–75) FROM VOLUME ONE

The last two folios of volume I contain copies of documents relating to the company and its members in the late 1460s and early 1470s, evidently written into the back of the volume while the front was used for proceedings of the court. These documents (on folios 21v–22v of the renumbered text) are in a smaller, more formal hand, probably that of Thomas Kirton who was clerk of the company from January 1465.[499]

These earlier records begin with a detailed series of documents relating to the formal transfer of a business from Stephen Piers, a tailor, to his son, John. The main contract was drawn up in February 1467, but additions were made in December 1469 before the master and wardens, and again in April 1470 when the agreement was finalised.[500] The business itself was evidently in a healthy position for the 'divers goods, wares and dettours' belonging to Stephen were valued at £200, and it was perhaps not surprising that the contract contained a requirement for John to make an annual report of its progress. The contract also made provision for a pension of £10, later increased to £13 6s. 8d. p.a., to be paid to Stephen and his wife, Juliana, as well food and clothing for 'one Anne Parys a pore mayden that is deef and dome'. Stephen's career is relatively well-documented in the Tailors' records: he had probably served most of his apprenticeship by 1420 when his master, Robert Hill, died. Instead of transferring to another master, however, Piers managed to obtain the freedom by redemption the same year, a step which involved the payment of the fee of £3 to the guild. Five years later, in 1425–6, he was admitted to the livery of the craft on payment of the usual 20s. fee. In February 1430 he took over the apprenticeship of a John Thomas, whose first master had died and whose second, Henry Goof, had been forced to seek sanctuary at Westminster. Piers enrolled at least another seven apprentices over the next thirty years including Robert Parys, probably a relative of Agnes. He went on to serve as one of the four wardens of the Tailors in 1441–2, but was never elected to the mastership. During his long career he established a close connection with the east of England, possibly as a result of business activities there: between 1435 and 1460, for instance, he was forced to

---

[499] Accounts, II. f. 259.
[500] These were first transcribed and printed in Clode, *Early History*, vol.1, pp. 367–70 although the author omitted the final document, dated 16 Apr. 1470, which finalised the contract.

take action to secure the repayment of debts owed by individuals in Suffolk, Cambridgeshire and Bedfordshire.[501] John Piers was also a succesful tailor: between 1457 and 1473 he enrolled seven apprentices, and by 1464–5 was of sufficient standing to be admitted to join his father as a liveryman of the craft. It is clear, therefore, that Stephen had good reason for hoping that his business would continue to flourish under his son's management. In the event Stephen Piers survived until the spring of 1472/3, although his wife, Juliana, had died at some point during the two years since the contract had been finalised. In his will, dated 16 February and proved on 5 March that year, he asked to be buried next to Juliana in the church of St. Thomas of Acre. He made a number of small bequests to John, and left a bed and bedding to his grandson, also named John. In a final request to his executors he asked that Agnes Parys should receive 'all things leeful to her for herlyf tyme'. John seems to have carried out his father's wishes, for in his own will, proved in June 1485 he required his widow 'to fynde on Ane Pares mete, drynke and all other thynges to her necessary'.[502]

The final document, on folio 22v, concerns the 'White Lion', a brewery situated in Gracechurch Street in the parish of All Hallows Lombard Street. This property, formerly known as 'Le Skut on the Hoop', was left to the company by John Buke (master 1398–9) in his will, dated 26 Januay 1422 and enrolled in the Husting Court in 1427/8. The income from the property (£9 p.a.) was to be used by the Tailors to pay a rent charge to the rector and wardens of All Hallows, Gracechurch Street, and to maintain a perpetual chantry in the church. The chantry was duly established, but in an unusual departure, the Tailors subsequently agreed to pay the priest's stipend of £6 13s. 4d. to the rector and wardens who were then responsible for paying the priest. This was a change of policy for the company, which usually insisted on employing and paying their chantry chaplains themselves. The success of this arrangement was called into question in 1450/1 when it was alleged by the Tailors in a petition to the court of Chancery that the parson of All Hallows had failed in his duty to provide 'a covenable prest dayly ... to synge for his [i.e. Buke's] soule, the soules of Julian, Agnes and Emme his wyves and all christain soules'.[503] By this date the brewery was known as 'The Lion on the hope' and it subsequently underwent another change of name, becoming known as the 'White Lion'. The Tailors continued to receive rent from the property until 1471–2 when, as this document suggests, the property was

---

[501] Accounts, I, ff. 117v, 160v; GL, MS 9171/3, f. 64; *CPMR 1413–1437*, p. 238; *CPR, 1429–36*, p. 432; *1452–61*, pp. 375, 520.

[502] Accounts, II–III; GL MS 9171/6, f. 129v, 9171/7, ff. 23v–24.

[503] *CWCH*, vol. 2, p. 445; PRO, Early Chancery Proceedings, C1/18/186–7, printed in P. Norman, 'Abstracts of documents relating to London from early Chancery proceedings and from the Court of Requests, with explanatory notes', *London Topographical Record*, 6 (1909), pp. 71–2.

conveyed for a period of 'certain years' to the church of All Hallows. Responsibility for the maintenance of Buke's chantry was thus transferred entirely to the rector and wardens, who were, in return, to pay a rent charge of 4s. p.a. to the Tailors. The loss of their income from the White Lion was probably of less significance than the fact that the administration of a chantry of a former master had, for the first time, been ceded to another institution. The decision by the clerk to copy an acquittance relating to the payment of the rent charge into the back of the minute book was doubtless a reflection of the importance of this event. The document is undated although the initials of the master (R.B.) suggest that it may have been drawn up in 1474–5, during the mastership of Richard Bristall, just a few years after the events referred to above.[504] Three of the wardens can probably be identified as Walter Povey (master 1492–3), Walter Stalworth, Ewen (or Owen) Boughton (upper warden 1481–2 and master 1495–6), for whose biographies see Appendix IV.

---

[504] It could also have been drawn up in 1479–80 when Roger Barlowe was master, although this is unlikely given that Ewen Boughton served his second term as warden in 1481–2, giving him only a year's respite from the office.

Merchant Taylors' Company, Ancient MS Book, 37.

VOLUME I

[f. 21v]
Thomas Burgeys magister

Memorandum that I Stephen Piers citezein and tayllour of London have graunted and possessed the xxii^{ti} day of Feverer in the yeer of our lord m cccc lxvii [1467] my trusty and well beloved sone John Piers in the house ther I dwell in Bokeleresbury sett in the paryssh of seint mary Colchirch in London to have & to occupie the said house during my termes that be to come as is commaunded in wrytyng betwene my landlord and me Reservyng unto my selfe and Julyan my wyf allwayes the chaumber that I lye in called the whyte chaumber and an other annexed to the same called the Rede chaumber and that the said John Piers shall acquite me and my said wyf from all maner charges of the said house duryng the said termes as is aforeseid.

Also I will and graunt that my said sone shall have all my servaunts and apprentises them to teche and enforme or do to them to be taught and enfourmed in their occupacions in the best wyse that he can and also them to fynde mete drynk clothyng & all things as is belongyng unto such prentises and I will that the seid apprentises shall obey all maner rules comaunded or taught by my said sone or his wyf & to obey their due correcions and so my said sone to acquite me and my wyf of all maner charges of the said apprentises.

Also I will that my said sone shall fynde and kepe honestly one Anne Parys a pore mayden that is deef and dome mete drynk and clothyng as nedeth.

Also I will that at all due tymes whan that I or my wyf walketh oute that my said sone shall bete me have an honest man chyld to wayte upon me and an honest mayde chyld to wayte upon my wyf at his owne propre cost yef we desire it.

Furthermore to acquite all these charges and other charges hereafter sayng I the said Stephen Piers have graunted yeven and delivered the day and yeer abovesaid unto my said sone diverse goods wares and dettours as it more pleynly specifieth in diverse billes made betwene me and my said sone the which amounteth to the some of ccxx*li*. sterling to have and enjoye the said goodes wares and dettours to by and sell wyth all in the lest wise that he can to his moost profite and encrese of the which the said John Piers shall pay or do to be payed to me and to my said wyf and to either of us that longest leven for our sustenacion in mete drynk & clothyng and all other things to us and either of us necessary x*li*. yeerly to be paid at iiii termes in the yeer that is to sey atte fest of the Nativite of seint John the Baptiste [24 June] next after the date aforeseid ls. atte fest of seint myghell tharchaungel [29 Sept.] than next ensuyng ls. atte fest of the nativite of our lord than next ensuyng ls. atte fest of the annunciacion of our lady [25 Mar.] than next suyng other ls. And so from quarter to quarter and from yeer to yeer duryng my lyf my wyfes lyf and either of us longest lyvyng as is aforeseid and yef so be that my said sone perfourme and kepe these desires aforesaid and therto wit agree in all goodly wise I woll and graunte at this tyme present in the day and yeer abovesaid that I duryng my lyf nor none of my executours in tyme to come nor none other persone in my name shall never interupt nor encumber my said sone John Piers of the said goodes wares and dettours from this day and yeer aforesaid unto the ende of the world.

Also I will that my said sone shall ones in the yeer that is to sey betwene Cristmas & Candlemas [2 Feb.] make a due rekenyng wyth his house that in comfortyng of myself I may know that he goeth forthward & encrese the wych shall be to me grete pleasure.

Also I will that in cas be me lyf to have eny money bestowed in merchaundise of myn awne besyde the goodes wares and dettours aforeseid that my seid sone shall ley it in his shop and so to occcupie it in merchaundising in the best wise he can reservyng to myself that one half of the geyn and to my sone for his labour that other half with goods blessing and myn.

To the which desires and grauntes as is aforeseid I the seid John Piers sone to my right reverend fader & moder Stephen Piers and Julyan his wyf aforeseid aggree and consent to all an singuler that is afore desired or willed by my said fader that is for to say first wher as my said fader hath possessed me in his house as is aforeseid I beryng all the charges of the same and them conveniently discharge I aggree therto accordyng to my said faders desire.

Also wher as my said fader woll that I shall have the rule and charge of his servaunts and prentises them to teche or do them to be taught with sufficient fyndyng and all other things as is aforeseid I aggreee accordyng to my said faders desire.

Also in kepyng and fyndyng of the said Anne Parys I aggree therto accordyng to may faders desire.

Also as touchyng my children to awayte upon my fader and moder at all dewe tymes I aggree therto accordyng to my said faders desire.

Also as touchyng to the pension of xli. the wich shall be payed at iiii termes yeerly by even porcions as is aforeseid I aggree to be bound in an obligacion of ccli. that in cas be that I be behynde of payment after eny day of payment as is aforeseid past ii monethes that than it shall be leefull that the said obligacion to stond in full power and strenketh and yef it so be that the said dayes of paiement be sufficiently content or within ii monethes after eny of the said dayes be content that than the said obligacion to stond in no strenketh ne effect.

Also where as my said fader desireth to have in knowlech ones in the yeer of the rekenyng of my house I aggreee therto that in cas be ther can be due proof made that at every day of rekenyng my goodes wares and dettours be found worth cc*li*. that so long my fader to holde him pleased and agreed and I to rejoise the said wares goods and dettours for evermore without eny interupcion And yef it so be that my said goodes wares and dettours be otherwise found by due processe made note worth cc*li*. as is aforeseid that than it shall be lefull for my fader to enter in to my goodes wares and dettours where so ever they may found and so to kepe my said goodes wares and dettours in his owne possession till I sett hem in very suerte of his duete.

For as moch as Stephen Piers and his sone John Piers bothe afore named hath knowledged aggreed and consented eche of them to the other the day moneth and yeer abovesaid unto all and singuler articles aforeseid and for the more serteinte of trouth and record eche of them to perfourme and kepe the said articles they of them self or com presently unto Tayllours hall before the right honourable and worshipfull maister and wardens in the said day and yeer beyng prayng them that the said articles myght be regestred & entred in to their books of record beryng the said date.

[f. 22]

The Monday the iiii[th] day of Decembre the ix[th] yeer of the reign of kyng Edward the iiii[th] [1469] cam personelly before William Parker maister John Stone John Stodard and John Phelip sumtyme maisters, John Kyffyn Richard Nayler Richard Warner and William Croseby wardeins of the ffraternite of Seint John Baptist of the craft of Tayllours in London at Tayllours hall Stephen Piers and John Piers his sone citezeins and Tayllours of the said citee of London and ther by the meanes of the said maisters and wardeins appeareth ... same folowyng that is to sey that the said Stephen shall kepe all thappointements on his party specified and writen in the leef next heer before and that the the same John Piers shall have and reteign to him selff freely and quitely unto his owne propre use withoute eny ... maner goodes wares dettours and stuff conteigned and specified in the said leef as all other duetees and things that hath been due by the said John Piers unto his said fader and also his moder or which theu or either of hem of hym in eny wise myght desire at eny tyme sithen the begynyng of the world unto the day aforeseid, the said Stephen and Julyan his wif from hensforth beyng good fader and moder their sone and his wif in all things that goodly belongeth.

For the full contentacion of which premisses the said John duryng the lyves of the said Stephen and Julyan his wyf fader and moder to the said John shall pay to the said Stephen xx mark yeerly and immediately after the decese of one of them to him or hir overlyvyng duryng the lyf of him or her overlyvyng x mark yeerly in the said hall at iiii principall termes of the yeer or within ii monethes next suyng everych of the said termes by even porcions.

And that these agrements be kept and perfourmed from hensforth betwene the said partyes they by good advise shall make sufficient writyng for the confermacion and record of the same.

This indenture[505] made betwene Stephen Piers citezein and Tayllour of London and Julyan his wyf on that one partye and John Piers citezein and Tayllour of London sone of the seid Stephen and Julyan and Margarete wyf of the said John on that other partie witnesseth that in the presence of William Parker[506] maister of the ffraternite of Seint John the baptist founded by the craft of Tayllours of the citie of London and of John Kyffyn Richard Nayler Richard Warner and William Croseby wardeins of the same ffraternite at the hall called the Tayllours hall of London the said partyes beth aggreed and accordyd to gider in maner an fourme that foloweth that is to wete that the seid Stephen and Julyan from the day of the date of this indenture fourthward duryng their lyves and of either of them longest lyvyng shall be good and favourable fader and moder in all maner degrees to the said John and Margarete and to teh childern of the same John as nature and reason will reasonably require and that the same Stephen and Julyan frely and quietly shuld suffre the said John to have possessed enjoye and reteign toward himself to his owne propre use and behoef all such goods wares apprentices and dettes as have been geven delivered and sett over by the seid Stephen and Julyan and either of them to the seid John and Margarete before the date of this indenture as well by wrytyng as other wise withoute interupcion impediment or geynseyng of the said Stephen and Julyan or of outher of them or of eny persones or persones for them, and where as the said Stephen hath made the said John his attourney for to recovere certein duetees of certein persones to the use and behoef of the said John as by a letre of attourney by the said Stephen to the said John therof made under the seall of the said Stephen and Thomas Stalbroke alderman of London it may clearly appere, the said Stephen is aggreed and graunted by this indenture that he duryng his lyf shall never revoke the auctorite by him graunted to the said John by the said lettre of attourney ner never geve eny acquietance or other discharge to eny persone named in the same letre of attourney withoute the consent or agreement of the said John, and in full contentacion and plein satisffacion of all the goodes wares apprentises dettes and other the promises aforeseid the said John hath be bound himself by his obligacion to the said Stephen and Julyan in cc*li*.

---

505   This section was not printed in Clode, *Early History*, vol.1, pp. 367–70.
506   Master of the craft 1469–70.

with the condicion endorced upon the same to pay unto them yeerly duryng both their lyves xiii*li.* vj*s.* viij*d.* and whan eny of the said Stephen and Julyan shall fortune to dye than to pay yeerly to him or her that shall fortune to overlyve viii*li.* only and no more duryng the lyf of him or her so overlyvyng as by the said obligacion and condicion it may appere. In witnesse wherof the said parties to these indentures chaungeably have sett their seallis geven the xvjth day of Aprill the yeer of the reign of kyng Edward the iiijth after the conquest the xth [1470].

[f. 22v]

Acquietancia pro parochianis Omnium Sanctorum in Lumbardstrete.

Know all men by [these] presents that we R.B., master, W[alter] P[ovey], H.T, W[alter] S[talworth] and E[wen] B[oughton] wardens of the craft or mistery of tailors and linen-armourers of St. John the Baptist in the city of London have received on the agreed day from J.B.[507] warden and governor of the lands and tenements of the church of All Saints in Lombard Street, four shillings sterling of that annual rent issuing from that tenement called 'Le White Lyon', with the appurtenances, situated in the aforesaid parish formerly belonging to John Buke and now to this mistery, which was demised by the said master and wardens of the same mistery to divers parishioners of the same parish for a certain term of years. It is acknowledged that payment of the which four shillings has been made for the past whole year to this present date and that the warden and other parishioners are quit by these presents, sealed with our seals. Dated the morrow of St Michael the Archangel [29 Sept.] in the year of Our Lord one thousand etc. And in the reign of King etc.[508]

---

[507] Unidentified.
[508] The omission of the year of grace and the regnal year reflects the fact that this was merely a copy of an original document, although it was clearly regarded as important enough to be written into the back of the company's minute book.

APPENDIX III

LISTS OF MASTERS, WARDENS AND OFFICIALS OF THE COMPANY 1486-1493[509]

Masters (elected 24 June)		**Wardens** (elected 24 June)
1485–6	John Percyvale	Not recorded
1486–7	Thomas Cotton	Thomas Randall John Barnard William Grene George Lovekyn
1487–8	John Heed	Not recorded
1488–9	William Buck	Oliver Warner James Wilford Thomas Petyt John Doket
1489–90	Stephen Jenyns	William Grene John Barnard Thomas Bodley Peter Forster
1490–1	John Spencer	Thomas Bromefeld Thomas Howdan Roger Mone Richard Hill
1491–2	William Hert	Henry Clough Nicholas Nynes Henry Kellow Ralph Bukberd

---

[509] Biographies of the masters and wardens can be found in Appendix IV. Details of the careers of the clerks are included in the Introduction, pp. 8–12. Information about all other individuals, where known, has been included in a footnote to the first appearance in the minutes: see Index.

1492–3	Walter Povey	John Doket
		Thomas Petyt
		Richard Dyngley
		John Povey

1493–4	Thomas Randall	Richard Hill
		John Kyrkeby
		Thomas Bedford
		Richard Smyth

Clerks

Mich. 1464 – Aug. 1487	Thomas Kirton
Aug. 1487 – 10 Sept 1492	William Duryvale
Jan. 1493 – aft. 1512	Henry Mayour

Beadles

By Apr. 1486 – July 1493	Thomas Gresyle[510]
July 1493 – bef. 1512	William Erle

Rent Collectors

By Apr. 1486 – bef. 18 June 1490	Simon Lorymer
18 June 1490 – aft. June 1493	Richard Grysten

Chaplains

1. Stipendiary chaplains of the Fraternity of St. John the Baptist, including the chantry chaplains of Thomas Carleton (d. 1389) in St. Paul's cathedral and John Churchman (d. 1412) in St. Martin Outwich.[511]

By Easter 1453 – March 1491	Roger Doket (d. 1491)
By Easter 1469 – ?d.	Richard Wheler (d. 1495)
By Dec. 1487 – aft. June 1493	John Radclyf
Mich. 1492 – aft. June 1493	George Bromehill

---

510 Gresyle had served as rent collector from 1465 until at least 1473.

511 The fraternity had three stipendiary chaplains, all of whom were paid a salary of £6 13s. 4d. p.a. One celebrated Mass in the Tailors' chapel at the Hall, while the others served as the chantry chaplains of Thomas Carleton in St. Paul's and John Churchman in St. Martin's. The three chaplains are not distinguished from one another in the Tailors' accounts or court minutes and it is possible that their resources were pooled for the celebration of these chantries and the other services required by the fraternity of St. John the Baptist.

2. Chaplains of the Chantry of John and William de Oteswich in St. Martin Outwich.[512]

By Dec. 1487 – Mich. 1489	Robert Urton
Mich. 1489 – aft. June 1493	John Burnham

3. Chaplains of the Chantry founded by Peter Mason (d. 1412) in St. Peter Cornhill.

By Easter 1480 – June 1489	John Palmer
June 1489 – aft. June 1493	Robert Cudworth

4. Chaplains of the Chantry founded by Lady Beatrice de Roos (d. 1414) in St. Paul's Cathedral.[513]

21 June 1486 – bef. Dec. 1487	Henry Cheshire
By Dec. 1487 – Mich.1489	William Camell
Mich. 1489 – Mich. 1491	Robert Cardemaker
Mich. 1491 – aft. June 1493	Thomas Roos

512 As well as celebrating John Churchman's chantry in St. Martin's, the Tailors were also obliged to pay half the stipend of £6 13*s*. 4*d*. of another priest who was to celebrate Mass daily for the souls of John and William de Oteswich who substantially rebuilt the church in the 14th century. The other half was paid by the parish. *CPR 1405–8*, p. 56; Davies, thesis, pp. 54–5.

513 The chaplain was presented by the descendants of the founder. Thomas Roos was almost certainly a relative.

APPENDIX IV

BIOGRAPHIES OF THE MASTERS, WARDENS AND MEMBERS OF THE COURT OF ASSISTANTS 1486–1493

NB. References to these men in the court minutes can be found in the Index.

ADYFF (Haydyff), Richard. Presented first apprentice 1458–9. Admitted to the livery 1460–61. Chosen as warden 1473–4 but apparently never elected master of the craft. Almost certainly related to George A, rector of St. Dunstan in the West, who had himself been admitted as an 'honorary' member of the Tailors' fraternity in 1443–4. His will dated 28 July 1494 and proved 26 Feb. 1494/5. Asked to be buried before the chancel in the church of St. John the Evangelist in Watling Street. Accounts, I, f. 373; II, ff. 153, 193v; Hopkinson, *Ancient Records*, p. 113; G. Hennessey, *Novum Repertorium Ecclesiasticum Parochiale Londinense* (London, 1898), p. 137; PRO, PROB 11/10, ff. 152v–153.

BARLOWE, Roger. Apprenticeship not recorded. Admitted to the livery of the Tailors' company 1458–9. One recorded apprentice, John Warten, enrolled 1473–4. One of four men who entered into a bond of £126 13s. 4d. in June 1481 for the patrimony of the sons of a fellow tailor, Robert Middleton. Chosen as master of the Tailors 1479–80 and was frequently present at meetings of the court 1486–93. Supplied cloth to the Great Wardrobe for the coronation of Richard III, 1483, and continued to supply to the Great Wardrobe of Henry VII until at least 1493 when he was owed £80 for goods he had provided. Involved in property transactions with prominent aldermen and merchants, including George Cely, Thomas Betson and William Martyn. Acquired property himself in Lombard Street in the parish of St. Mary Wolnoth. A common councilman by 1485 and was chosen as auditor of the city 21 Sept. 1484–6 (with Hugh PEMBERTON, q.v.). Made will 1492 (property) and testament 1493 (goods). Asked to be buried in the chapel of BVM and St. Nicholas in St. Mary Wolchurch and bequeathed a tenement in the parish of St. Michael Cornhill to the fraternity of Our Lady there. Bequests to the Tailors' Fraternity of St. John the Baptist, churches in Tring and Olney, Bucks., the Fraternity of Parish Clerks in London, and to various members of his family. The residue of his estate was left to his widow, Beatrice. His son, John, was appointed to oversee the wills. Died 1499. *Coro. Richard III* ed. Sutton and Hammond, pp. 307–8, *CWCH*, ii. 602; PRO,

PROB 11/9, f. 192; Accounts, II, f. 152; *Cal. Letter Bk. L*, pp. 178, 191, 215, 225, 230; CLRO, hr 201/7, 9; 214/22–3, 25, 37–8.

BARNARD (Bernard), John. Possibly the JB who was apprenticed in 1455–6 to Ralph Titlow. Enrolled an apprentice of his own 1466–7. Admitted to the livery 1470–1. In Feb. 1489 JB, with John HARDY (q.v.) was a surety before the chamberlain for the delivery of patrimony to the children of John Gardyner, whose death in 1486 may have led to Barnard's election as one of the wardens of the Tailors' company. Chosen as warden for a second time June 1489 but never elected to the mastership. Perhaps the JB who exported cloth through the port of London with Stephen JENYNS (q.v.) in Jan. 1506. Accounts, II, ff. 61, 294v; III, f. 22; *Cal. Letter Bk. L*, p. 268; Hopkinson, *Ancient Records*, p. 114; PRO, E122/79/12, mm. 1–1d.

BEDFORD, Thomas. Enrolled an apprentice in 1466–7 and admitted to the livery 1469–70. Served as warden of the company 1493–4. Accounts, II, f. 293; III, f. 6.

BODLEY, Thomas. A member of same family as the founder of the Bodleian Library. Apprenticed in 1461–2 to John Frecok, obtained the freedom and was admitted to the livery of the craft in 1471–72. Chosen as warden of the company in June 1489. Drew up his will on 27 Nov. 1491 in which he asked to be buried in his parish church of St. Botolph Billingsgate. He established a 2 year chantry in the same church and required his executors to appoint Thomas Driffeld, a former bursar of Eton College, as his priest at 11 marks p.a. He also left 12*d*. to the almsmen and women of Saffron Walden in Essex. The will was proved on 1 Aug. 1492. Accounts, I, f. 35v; PRO, PROB 11/9, ff. 211–212v. His widow, Joan, went on to marry Thomas Bradbury, a mercer who was elected mayor in 1509. For further details of Bodley's family and his property see A. F. Sutton, 'Lady Joan Bradbury (d. 1530)', in *Medieval London Widows* eds. Barron and Sutton, pp. 210–13.

BOUGHTON, Owen or Ewen. Possibly related to fellow tailor Andrew B. who was admitted to the livery in 1470–71. Likely that he was admitted to the livery in the 1470s, but little recorded of him prior to his service as warden of the company 1474–5 and 1481–2. Subsequently chosen as master for the year 1495–6. Made his will Feb. 1504/5 and requested burial in the chancel of All Hallows Bread Street. Wife Eleanor and daughters Joan and Agnes to share his goods and chattels. Bequeathed to the 'maister [and] wardeyns of the comynaltie of taillours my lytell stondyng cup coverd of silver gilt'. This, along with a similar cup given by his widow, was recorded in an inventory of the company's plate taken in 1512. Established a chantry for two years and an obit for 20 years in All Hallows. Will proved 30 May 1505. Accounts, III, f. 6;

Hopkinson, *Ancient Records*, pp. 113–14; PRO, PROB 11/14, ff. 249–249v; Clode, *Memorials*, pp. 89, 91.

BROMEFELD (Bromflete, Brounfeld), Thomas. Probably the TB who enrolled apprentices 1460–1, and who was admitted to the livery 1466–7. First known appearance on the court of assistants not until 7 Feb. 1488. In Feb. 1473 he and John SWAN (q.v.) were wardens of the fraternity of Our Lady and St. Dunstan in the church of St. Dunstan in the West. Elected warden of the Tailors' company for 1490–1, and master for 1498–9. Made will 'seke and feble in body' on 26 July 1500 and asked for burial in the church of St. Dunstan in the West. Left 40s. to the Tailors' fraternity and 6s. 8d. to the bachelors' company. Residue of estate to Jane his wife and Owen and John his sons. Nicholas NYNES (q.v.) appointed one of the overseers of the will which was proved 22 June 1502. Accounts, II, ff. 192v, 296v. *Cal. Letter Bk. L*, p. 110; Hopkinson, *Ancient Records*, pp. 114–5; PRO, PROB 11/13, ff. 101–101v.

BUCK (Buke), William. Possibly a descendant of John Buke, master of the Tailors in 1398–9, who left property in Gracechurch Street to the company. Apprenticed to John Wyche 1453–4. Admission to livery prob. early 1470s (accounts damaged). Chosen as master of the Tailors' company for 1488–9. From at least 1479 until his death was a major supplier of cloth to the household of William Worsley, dean of St. Paul's. Made will 24 Feb. 1500/1, asking for burial in the chapel of St. George in St. Mary Aldermanbury. Extensive arrangements for funeral services etc. His 4 sons to receive £100 in cash and items of silver plate when of age, and his widow, Margaret, was left £80 to assist with their upbringing. The will proved 7 May 1501. His inquisition *post mortem*, not carried out until July 1532, stated that he died on 28 May 1502 – probably an error for 1501 – and that he held a capital messuage and four other tenements in the parish of St. Mary Aldermanbury worth £20 p.a. By this date three of his four sons had died. Contributed three out of nine panels of a tapestry recording the life of St. John the Baptist which were listed in an inventory of 1512. The others were supplied by the company and by Stephen JENYNS (q.v.) who, at some point before 1508, had married Buck's widow, Margaret. Accounts, II, f. 3; Clode, *Memorials*, pp. 84–5; British Library, Royal MS 2 B. XIII; *The Household Accounts of William Worsley, Dean of St. Paul's 1479-97* eds. S. Hovland and H. Kleineke (Stamford, forthcoming); PRO, PROB 11/12, ff. 82v–84; *Abstracts of Inquisitions Post Mortem Relating to the City of London in the Tudor Period*, ed. G. S. Fry, 3 vols (London, 1896–1908), vol. 1, pp. 35–6, 47–8.

BUKBERD, Ralph. Apprenticed 1474–5, but his master not known (accounts damaged). Chosen as warden of the Tailors for 1491–2 and 1497–8 but did not serve as master. Exported cloth through the port of London Dec. 1502.

Possibly the 'John' Buckberd who was appointed as customs collector in the port of London Feb. 1506-7. Accounts, III, f. 73v; Hopkinson, *Ancient Records*, pp. 114-5; PRO, E122/80/2, m. 17; *CFR 1485-1509*, p. 376.

CLOUGH, Henry. Enrolled at least 11 apprentices between 1463 and 1480 and admitted to the livery of the craft 1465-6. The previous year the company had employed John PERCYVALE (q.v.) then a serjeant-at-mace of the mayor, to assist in the release of HC from Newgate prison for 'verbis inhonestis' uttered against members of the Skinners' company. In May 1486 he and John STODARD (q.v.) among those who entered into a bond before the chamberlain for the patrimony of the daughters of a fellow tailor, Richard Elys. Served as warden of the Tailors' company 1491-2. Drew up will 1512 asking for burial in the cloister of the priory church of St. John Clerkenwell. Lands in London and Acton. Probate 25 May 1512. Accounts, II, ff. 261, 278; *Cal. Letter Bk. L*, p. 231; Hopkinson, *Ancient Records*, p. 114; PRO, PROB 11/17, ff 62v-63, 194v.

COTTON, Thomas. Admitted to the livery 1466-67. In June 1485, with Hugh PEMBERTON and Stephen JENYNS (q.q.v.), entered into a bond with the chamberlain for the delivery of £920 to the children of Richard Nayler (master of the Tailors 1475-6). Served as master of the craft 1486-7 (see above), but the minutes show no further appearances at the court after the end of his mastership. Accounts, II, f.296v; *Cal. Letter Bk. L*, p. 221.

CROSBY, William. A WC was apprenticed to Walter Hertilpole in 1437-8 and presented an apprentice in 1444-5. Not clear whether it was this same man who enrolled further apprentices in 1458-9, 1462-3, 1465-6, and 1470-1 and who was chosen as warden of the craft for 1469-70. This WC attended just five court meetings 1486-93, the last being on 7 May 1489. Made his will 3 Oct. 1495 requesting burial in his parish church of St. Antonin. Six persons of the craft of tailors to bear body to the church. Will proved 9 Jan. 1495/6. Accounts, I, ff. 293, 386v, II, ff. 151, 227v, 275v; III, f. 20; Hopkinson, *Ancient Records*, p. 113; GL, MS 9171/8, ff. 117-117v.

DOGET (Doket), John. Apprenticed to John Stone (master of the Tailors 1449-50 and sheriff of London 1464-5) in 1465-6. Chosen as warden of the Tailors for 1488-9 and 1492-3, elected master for 1500-1. Served as sheriff of the city Sept. 1509-10: petition to mayor Feb. 1535 named Doget and Nicholas NYNES (q.v.) as among the former sheriffs who had been 'reduced to extreme poverty' by the financial demands of the office. Drew up will 13 Feb. 1512/13 asking for burial in the church of St. John the Evangelist, Watling Street, next to Stone's tomb. Bequeathed 5 marks and lands in Berkshire to the Merchant Taylors' Company, and gave further lands in the county, worth £4 p.a., to Brasenose College, Oxford, for the establishment of a scholarship in his name; the scholar was to be chosen by the Merchant Taylors. He was still alive in August 1513 when his son, John the younger, appointed him as supervisor of his own will. The latter was proved on 9 Sept. and the elder John's will was probably proved in November the same year. An inventory compiled by the Merchant Taylors in 1512 mentioned 'an almery with iii dores of the cost of Mr. Doget behynde the parlour dore'. Possibly related to Roger Doket, one of the chaplains employed by the Tailors during the period covered by the court minutes. Accounts, II, f. 275v; *Cal. Letters and Papers Hen. VIII*, vol. 8, p. 78; Clode, *Early History*, vol. 1, p. 103; PRO, PROB 11/17, ff. 205v–206, 217–217v.

DUPLAGE (Depleche etc.), Robert. Route to the freedom not recorded but had become a freeman by 1453 when he presented the first of at least 16 apprentices enrolled by him before 1474. Admitted to the livery 1454-5 and chosen as master of the Tailors for 1481-2. Supplier of drapery to the Great Wardrobe by 1480 and supplied scarlet and woollen cloth for the coronations of both Richard III and Henry VII. Involved in several lengthy legal disputes included one concerning a debt claimed from Sir Gilbert Debenham in 1468, which was eventually settled in Feb. 1485. A resident of Cordwainer Street ward in 1483-4 when he was listed as employing a German servant named Robert Aleyn. Does not appear to have been appointed to any significant office in the city government, although in 1476 and 1487 he acted as a surety for the patrimonies of the children of fellow citizens. Possibly this man who, with John Roger, was made bailiff of Sandwich 1484. Accounts, II–III, *passim*; *CCR 1476-85*, p. 397; J. L. Bolton (ed.) *The Alien Communities of London in the Fifteenth Century: The subsidy rolls of 1440 and 1483-4* (Stamford, 1998), p. 90; *Cal. Letter Bk. L*, pp. 138, 245. Further details in *Coro. Richard III* ed. Hammond and Sutton, pp. 336–7.

DYNGLEY, Richard. No record of apprenticeship or admission to the livery (gaps in the records from 1470 onwards), although a long career is suggested by the enrolment of an apprentice by a man of this name as early as 1456-7. Chosen as warden of the Tailors 1492-3. Drew up will 8 Mar. 1497/8 requesting burial in the church of St. Matthew Friday Street, near the body of his first wife. Established a one year chantry and an obit to be celebrated for 20 years in the church. Bequests included a small sum to be given to the almsmen of the Tailors' company. Accounts, II, f. 100; GL, MS 9171/8, ff. 174–5.

FITTE (Fytte), James. Admitted to the livery 1458-59, and presented apprentice 1466-7. Lived in Westminster where, in 1460, he was warden of the Assumption guild in St. Margaret's church. Appointed on several occasions as a surety for the delivery of patrimonies before the chamberlain of the city. Paid for a stained glass window in St. Margaret's Westminster in return for celebration of his obit, 1498/9. Died 1500/1. Accounts, II, f. 152; G. Rosser, *Medieval Westminster* (Oxford, 1989), p. 378. *Cal. Letter Bk. L*, pp. 211, 268.

FORSTER, Peter. Possibly related to William F. (master of the Tailors' company in 1448-9, died 1453). Nothing recorded of Peter's career within the craft until 1480-1 when he enrolled William Dawson as his apprentice. Chosen as warden of the Tailors for 1489-90. Accounts, III, f. 135v; Hopkinson, *Ancient Records*, p. 114.

GALLE, William. Apprenticed to William Blakeman in 1442-3 and obtained the freedom by 1453-4 when he was admitted to the livery of the Tailors. Chosen as master of the company in June 1471 and was probably the longest serving member of the court by the time of his death. Auditor of accounts of London Bridge Sept. 1471-3 and warden of the bridge 1474-87. In Feb. 1481 chosen as one of the collectors of a subsidy in the ward of Farringdon Without. Collector of customs in the port of London 1494-6 when he and fellow collector failed to account for receipts. By his will, proved on 20 Apr. 1497, he established a 7 year chantry in the church of St. Dunstan in the West where he asked to be buried. Left 100s. 'in werkes of pitee' to the poor of the Tailors' fraternity of St. John the Baptist 'wherof I am a brother' and an additional 40s. to the Bachelors. Brother of Henry Galle (d. 1466) who lived in the same parish and who was the first husband of Thomasine Bonaventure, later the wife of John PERCYVALE (q.v.). Accounts, I, f. 357, II, f. 5v; Clode, *Memorials*, pp. 69-71; *Cal. Letter Bk. L*, pp. 97, 107, 123, 235; Cobb (ed.), *Overseas Trade*, p. xxix; PRO, PROB 11/11, f. 75; Davies, 'Dame Thomasine Percyvale', p. 190 and n. 193.

GRENE, William. Presented first apprentice 1467-8, but admission to livery not recorded. Chosen as one of the four wardens of the craft in June 1486 and 1489, joined the court of assistants in February 1488 and served as master in 1507-8. Listed in the alien subsidy roll of 1483-4 as a resident of Cordwainer Street ward and an employer of two German servants. Married Ellen, widow of Stephen Trappys, shortly after the latter's death in Oct. 1485 and on 24 May 1486 came before the court to deliver 'xli. sterlynges accordyng to the Bequest of the said Stephyn Trappys toward the ledyng of Taylours halle' (see Text). In November 1488 the wardship of Trappys's daughters was awarded to Grene and a number of other men, including John LEE (q.v.). Exported cloth through the port of London Aug. 1491. Accounts, II, f. 312; Clode, *Early History*, II, p. 339; Bolton (ed.), *Alien Communities*, p. 90; *Cal. Letter Bk. L*, pp. 243, 267, 271; PRO, E122/78/9, m. 17.

HARDY (or Hardyng), John. Apprenticed to William Person (master of the company 1462–3), probably in the late 1460s and while still an apprentice was bequeathed 40s. in the latter's will, proved in July 1473. Presented apprentice of his own 1476–7. Married three times, his second wife being Person's widow, Joan. Made will 7 Nov. 1489, requesting burial before the high altar of St. Dunstan in the West. Established 3 year chantry in church, and left substantial rents and the sum of £24 to the fraternity of St. Mary and St. Dunstan to buy property. Left 40s. to the Tailors' company. Executors incl. John BARNARD (q.v.), and the supervisor of the will was Stephen JENYNS (q.v.). The will proved 15 Jan. 1489/90. (Sir) William Fitzwilliam (master 1499–1500, sheriff 1506–7) was one of those who, in Oct. 1492, entered into a bond before the chamberlain for the patrimony of Hardy's son, John. PRO, PROB 11/ 8, ff. 238–240; GL, MS 9171/6, ff. 132–133; *Cal. Letter Bk. L*, pp. 268, 293.

HEED (Hede), John. Obtained the freedom by redemption 1463–4, on payment of £3 to the Tailors. Admitted to the livery the following year and enrolled his first apprentice in 1465–6. Not elected to any city offices but chosen on three occasions as a surety for the delivery of patrimonies to the heirs of citizens. Chosen as master of the craft for 1487–8, although most of court minutes relating to his term are missing Outspoken and controversial figure within the company and in the summer of 1492 was imprisoned by the mayor for refusing to submit to the will of the court (see Introduction and above, pp. 207–10). Made will Apr. 1494 in which he asked for burial in church of St. Katherine Cree. Marble tomb to have images of JH and three wives. Established chantry for 6 years in St. Katherine's – salary of priest to be negotiated annually. master and wardens of the Tailors to receive 'a convenant recreacion ... in mete and drinke' for attending his obit. Bequest for maintenance of highway at Staindrop, Co. Durham, suggests that he may have been born there. Executors incl. Nicholas NYNES (q.v.). No probate recorded. Accounts, II, ff. 239, 255v, 275v; *Cal. Letter Bk. L*, pp. 211, 216, 294; GL, MS 9171/8, ff. 73–73v.

HERT (Hart etc.), William. Obtained the freedom by redemption in 1462–3, the same year in which he was admitted to the livery of the Tailors' company. He subsequently enrolled apprentices on at least four occasions during the 1460s. Probably chosen as warden in the late 1470s or early 1480s, although his earliest known appearance at a meeting of the court of assistants was on 5 Jan. 1488/9. His mastership (1491–2) is one of those covered by the surviving court minutes. Auditor of the accounts of the wardens of London Bridge in Sept. 1492–4. By late May 1493 was a 'seke man' (see Text). Will dated 6 Sept. 1493: described himself as 'gentilman and late maister of the fraternite of taylours', and asked to be buried next to his son in the church of the White

Friars. Among the bequests of goods to family members were items left to two other sons, both of whom were described as 'scoler of Cambrigge'. As well as property in London he also owned a house in Bishop's Stortford and two houses in Colchester. No date of probate given. Accounts, II, ff. 226v, 228; *Cal. Letter Bk.* L, pp. 289, 297; PRO, PROB 11/10, ff. 6–6v.

HILL, Richard. Nothing recorded of his apprenticeship, but the minutes record his admission to the livery of the craft on 26 May 1486 with James WILFORD. In 1486 and 1489 entered into bonds before the chamberlain for the patrimonies of the children of a draper and a grocer. Chosen as warden of the craft for 1490–1 and 1493–4. Possible that he served as master in 1504–5, 1505–6 or 1508–9. *Cal. Letter Bk.* L, pp. 236, 268; Hopkinson, *Ancient Records,* p. 114, 120.

HOBERD (Hobard, Hubert), Alan. Apprenticed 1455–6 to Roger TEGO (q.v.), and acted on the latter's behalf in dealings with Sir John Howard (later duke of Norfolk) in Mar. 1466. Had set up business in Fleet Street by Oct. 1468 when his servant supplied Howard with 'a pare bregandynes'. Admission to Tailors' livery not recorded but prob. early 1470s (records damaged). Presented Thomas Hoberd (possibly his son) and Thomas Polt as his apprentices 1474–5. By Mar. 1476 had married Alice, daughter of William Luke, a London brewer. Exported cloth through the port of London 1480–1 and supplied cloth worth £9 15s. 4d. for the coronation of Henry VII. Inventory of plate belonging to the Merchant Taylors' Company taken in 1512 recorded 12 silver spoons bequeathed by Hoberd. Accounts, II, f. 63; III, f. 73; A. Crawford (ed.) *The Household Books of John Howard, Duke of Norfolk 1462-1471* (Gloucester, 1992), pt. I, pp. 332, 577; *Calendar of Plea and Memoranda Rolls of the City of London, 1323-1482,* 6 vols, ed. A. H. Thomas and P. E. Jones (Cambridge, 1926–61), vol. 6 (1458–1482), p. 79, n. 1; Cobb (ed.), *Overseas Trade,* p. 115; ; L. G. Wickham Legg (ed.) *English Coronation Records* (London, 1901), p. 199.

HOWDAN, Thomas. Presented first apprentices 1466–7, and admitted to the livery of the craft 1472–3. Warden of the Tailors 1490–1, 1494–5. Described as 'late master' of the company in an inventory carried out in 1512, and so possibly served as master in 1504–5. Before death drew up an indenture with the company in which he agreed to convey £333 6s. 8d. in money and plate to the master and wardens for the payment of a stipend of £7 10s. 11d. p.a. to a chantry priest in St. Mary Abchurch. His will dated 12 Feb. 1512/13 and proved on 14 Mar. the same year. Burial to be in the chapel of St. Thomas in St. Mary Abchurch. Left the Merchant Taylors' Company his best standing cup and made arrangements for his chantry to be administered by the company. The clerk of the company, Henry Mayour, was appointed as an executor and among his tasks was the recovery of a debt of £140 owed by William Heron. A third of this sum was to be used to repair or replace vestments, books and other goods employed for his chantry. Shortly after his death his executors were involved in a dispute with the company after it was found that Howdan had failed to deliver the money and plate as promised but had left them with his executors 'enclosed to gyder in an a bagge'. The company accused the executors of using the money for 'the augmentacion of the porcion of his said wyfe'. The matter seems to have been resolved and his widow, Isabella, left the company a rent charge on tenements in Bradstreet on her death in 1515–16. Accounts, II, f.293; III, f. 47v; Hopkinson, *Ancient Records*, pp. 114–5, 120; *Cal. Letter Bk. L*, p. 321; Clode, *Memorials*, pp. 91, 228, 285; idem, *Early History*, vol.1, pp. 372–3; C. J. Kitching (ed.) *London and Middlesex Chantry Certificate, 1548* (London Record Society, 16, 1980), pp. 87–8; PRO, PROB 11/12, ff. 224–225v; *CWCH*, vol.2, p. 624.

JENYNS, (Sir) Stephen. From Wolverhampton, Staffs. Son of William J. of Tenby, Pembrokeshire and Ellen, daughter and coheiress of William Land of Wolverhampton. Apprenticed 1462–3 to Thomas Pye. In June 1485 he and Hugh PEMBERTON (q.v.) entered into a bond before the chamberlain for the delivery of patrimony of £920 to the children of Richard Nayler (master of the Tailors 1475–6). Probably served as warden of the Tailors' company (dates unknown) and was chosen as master for 1498–90. Regularly attended meetings of the court 1486–93. Prominent from the 1480s as a cloth merchant, exporting cloth through the port of London on numerous occasions, and became a merchant of the Calais staple. Sheriff 1498–9 and alderman for the wards of Castle Baynard (1499–1505), Dowgate (1505–8), and Lime Street (1508–23). Chosen as mayor for 1508–9, and led the city's delegations to the funeral of Henry VII and to the coronation of Henry VIII, following which event he was knighted. During his term of office he presented an illuminated copy of the Gospel readings for use at Mass, together with a matching volume of Epistles to his parish church of St. Mary Aldermanbury. By this date he had married Margaret, wife of his predecessor as master, William BUCK (q.v.). An assistant of the Fraternity of the Holy Name of Jesus in St. Paul's cathedral by 1514. Founded Wolverhampton Grammar School, having obtained letters patent Sept. 1512 and Apr. 1513 which allowed the Merchant Taylors' Co. to hold lands worth £20 p.a. for this purpose and authorised SJ to convey the manor of Rushock, Worcs. to the company. School prob. administered by Jenyns until his death in 1523, then entrusted to his son-in-law, and fellow merchant taylor, John Nicholls. On the latter's death in 1531 the governance of the school placed in the hands of the Merchant Taylors' Company where it remained until 1766. Further lands in London had been placed in the hands of feoffees who incl. Richard HILL and James WILFORD (q.q.v.), and these were conveyed to the company via the will of

John Bennett (d. 1528) and these used to fund Jenyns's chantry and obit. Other achievements included substantial building works in the church of St. Andrew Undershaft carried out c.1520. Accounts, II, f. 227v; *Cal. Letter Bk. L*, p. 221; Cobb (ed.), *Overseas Trade*, pp. 88–9, 110, 112, 114; E122/78/9, mm. 15–17; 79/12, mm. 1–2d, 4, 8d; 80/2, mm. 18, 19d; 80/3, mm. 17, 18v, 23, 24; 203/6, f. 4v, 19v; BL, Royal MS 2 B. xii, xiii; Bodleian Library, Oxford, MS Tanner 221, f. 29; G. P. Mander, *The History of the Wolverhampton Grammar School* (Wolverhampton, 1913), pp. 1–31; *Calendar of Letters and Papers of the Reign of Henry VIII*, vol. 1 (pt. i), pp. 212, 647, 826; Clode, *Early History*, vol.2, pp. 22–38; GL, Merchant Taylors' Co., Ancient MS Bk. 8, pp. 90–3; *CWCH*, vol. 2, pp. 642–3.

KELLOW, Henry. Nothing recorded of his apprenticeship or admission to the livery of the craft although he presented an apprentice in 1477–8. Kellow was a prominent parishioner of the parish of St. Mary at Hill who served as churchwarden in 1488–89 and 1489–90. He was allocated a prime position in an unusual diagrammatic representation of the parish hierarchy included with the churchwardens' accounts. Listed as a resident of Billingsgate ward in the 1483–4 alien subsidy roll as the employer of two German servants. Chosen as warden of the Tailors for 1491–2. Made his will in December 1493 requesting burial in St. Mary's between the pew of William Remyngton (an alderman who was one of his executors) and the rood loft 'so that pewes may be sette over my sepulchre'. Left nothing in his will to the Tailors apart from requiring his executors to settle any debts he owed to the company. C. Burgess, 'Shaping the Parish: St. Mary at Hill, London in the Fifteenth Century', in J. Blair and B. Golding (eds), *The Cloister and the World: Studies in Medieval History in Honour of Barbara Harvey* (Oxford, 1996), pp. 248n, 251, 255, 2661–5, 285–6; H. Littlehales (ed.), *The Medieval Records of a London City Church, St. Mary at Hill, 1420–559*, Early English Text Society, orig. ser. 125, 128 (1904–5), pp. 114, 126, 134, 144, 154, 196; Bolton (ed.), *Alien Communities*, p. 53; PRO, PROB 11/10, ff. 173v–174v.

KEYES (Kayse, Cays etc.), Gilbert. Obtained the freedom, perhaps by redemption, by 1441–2 when he presented his first apprentice. In 1445 he was one of 94 members of the yeomen tailors' fraternity who were fined for failing to turn up to greet Margaret of Anjou on her arrival in London. Probably admitted to the livery 1445–53 (gap in records). Served as warden of the Company 1464–5, and master in 1474–5. Auditor of the accounts of the wardens of London Bridge Sept. 1474–6. Exported cloth through the port of London 1480–1. Drew up will Feb. 1499 asking for burial in St. Thomas of Acre, although a parishioner of St. Matthew Friday Street. Probate inventory (damaged) of his goods taken that year. Accounts, I, ff. 341v, 387v; *Cal. Letter*

Bk. L, pp. 123, 133; Cobb (ed.), *Overseas Trade*, pp. 134, 154; PRO, PROB 2/162; 11/12, f. 44.

KIRKEBY (Kyrkeby), John. Admitted to the freedom of the city by redemption May 1472, and paid the Tailors £3 for this. Entry to livery not recorded. Supplied cloth to the Great Wardrobe for the coronation of Richard III. Chosen as warden of the Tailors for 1493-4 and 1496-7; elected master 1501-2, and served as one of the sheriffs of the City for 1507-8. In Mar. 1491 entrusted with the delivery of patrimony to the son of Walter STALWORTH (q.v.). An executor of two associates from the Great Wardrobe including the keeper from 1480-1505, Peter Courteys. Made will 4 June 1511 requesting burial in the church of the Black Friars in London. Lived in Ironmonger Lane where he leased a property from St. Thomas of Acon. Bequests to churches in Lichfield including St. Michael's where he established a chantry. Probate granted 29 June 1511. Gave six large silver bowls (397 oz) to the Tailors in return for his obit for 80 years in the Black Friars and £100 for an obit in St. Mary Colechurch. Accounts, III, f. 33v; CLRO, Recognizance Roll 25, m.2; *Cal. Letter Bk. L*, p. 279; Clode, *Memorials*, p. 108; idem, *Early History*, vol. 1, p. 97. See also *Coro. Richard III* ed. Hammond and Sutton, p. 365.

LEE, John. Obtained freedom by 1459-60 when he presented his first apprentice. Admitted to the livery of the Tailors' company 1460-1, and enrolled a further eight apprentices 1461-72. Chosen as master of the company for 1483-4. Connected with Sir John Paston and with the latter's younger brother, John III, who stayed at Lee's house in Ludgate in 1479. No surviving will but still alive 31 July 1493 when present at quarter-day meeting. Accounts, II, f. 171v, 193v, 207, 227v, 276v, 293v; III, f. 34; N. Davis (ed.) *The Paston Letters*, 2 vols (Oxford, 1971), vol. 1, pp. 590, 592, 615, 617-8; Davies, thesis, p. 38.

LEWES, John. No record of apprenticeship or admission to the livery. Enrolled first apprentice 1462-3. Entered into bonds 1470, 1473 and 1474 with the chamberlain to ensure the delivery of patrimonies to the children of London citizens. His will dated 14 Oct. 1488 and proved 15 Jan. 1488/9: burial to be in the church of St. Dunstan in the West. His executors included Nicholas NYNES (q.v.). Accounts, II, f. 227v; *Cal. Letter Bk. L*, pp. 88, 112, 114; PRO, PROB 11/8, ff. 242v-243.

LOVEKYN, George. Born in Paris and received letters of denization in 1476. As early as 1470, however, he was making robes for Edward IV and in September 1475 was appointed as serjeant tailor in the Great Wardrobe. He made Richard III'S coronation robes and those of Henry VII whom he served as king's tailor until his death in 1504. Although he was chosen as warden in

1486-7 Lovekyn had relatively few dealings with the Tailors' company during his career. For a detailed biography see Anne F. Sutton, 'George Lovekyn, Tailor to Three Kings of England, 1470-1504', *Costume*, 15 (1981), pp. 1-12.

MARCHALL, William. Apprenticed 1436-7 to Ralph Sutton, admitted to the livery of the craft in 1453-54 and served as warden in 1463-4. He enrolled at least seven apprentices, including one of his sons, another William, between 1453 and 1475. Entry in the minutes for 26 May 1486 excused him from service as master of the craft, perhaps on the grounds of ill health. Had drawn up his will on 4 Oct. 1485 but survived for another 5½ years until his death in the spring or early summer of 1491. Left sums of cash to his 6 daughters and bequests to 5 London fraternities. Among his other bequests was the sum of 20*d*. to be given to men 'being in the lyvery of the crafte of taylours to bere my body at my decese to the churche and ley my body in my grave'. Accounts, II-III, *passim*; PRO, Prob. 11/8, ff. 333-335.

MARTYN, Thomas. Perhaps a son of the John Martyn who was warden of the craft in 1456-7. Apprenticed in 1458-9 to John Sharpe '*extra Algate*'. A man of this name, described as 'of Southwark' admitted to the freedom by redemption 1465-6. Admission to livery of the craft not recorded, but prob. mid 1470s (damage to records). Not elected to any office in the city or the craft and attended no more court meetings after 18 July 1491, suggesting that he died later that year. Hopkinson, *Ancient Records*, p. 112; Accounts, II, ff. 151v, 274v.

MATERDALE, John. Master of the Tailors' Company in 1480-1. Apprenticed 1440-1 to John Spencer (perhaps the father of the master of 1490-1). Entered the livery in 1463-64. A party to various bonds concerning the inheritances of the children of fellow citizens. Churchwarden of St. Michael Bassishaw in 1481, and chosen as auditor of the accounts of the wardens of London Bridge Sept.1482, 1483. Drew up his will 22 Sept. 1497 asking for burial in St. Michael's. His executors were his widow, Katherine, and fellow court members Stephen JENYNS and John SPENCER (q.q.v.). Accounts, I, f. 329v; II, f. 241v; *Cal. Letter Bk. L*, pp. 126, 155, 189, 195, 210; PRO, PROB 11/11, ff. 219-219v.

MONE (Moone), Roger. Obtained the freedom by redemption in 1473-4 and entered the livery of the craft four years later. Took on several apprentices during his career and became a prominent member of the company, being chosen as one of the wardens in June 1490 and again in 1497. Like a number of his fellow liverymen he supplied cloth to the Great Wardrobe. Exported wool and skins to Calais through the port of London 1496, described as a merchant of the staple. He drew up his will on 17 Feb. 1499 in which he

BIOGRAPHIES

asked for burial in the little churchyard of St. Paul's. His bequests included 40s. to the Tailors' fraternity of St. John the Baptist, 2s. to those tailors who carried his body to the church, and sums of money to fund two temporary chantries. His 'cousin' Thomas Speight, tailor (master 1509-10) was left a blue gown. His lands in London and Essex were left to his two sons, with the reversion bequeathed to the Tailors. Executors included William BUCK (q.v.) and James WILFORD (q.v.). The will was proved 28 March 1500/1. Accounts, III, ff. 58v, 115; Hopkinson, *Ancient Records*, p. 114; *Coro. Richard III* ed. Sutton and Hammond, p. 375; PRO, E122/203/6, ff. 17, 36, 36v, 42; PROB 11/12, ff. 1-2.

NYNES, Nicholas. Admitted to the livery of the craft 1466-67. Chosen as warden of the craft for 1491-2 and as master for 1496-7. Enrolled his son, Simon, as his apprentice 22 Nov. 1490 (see Text). Served as one of the auditors of the accounts of London Bridge Sept. 1495-7, 1499-1501 and was alderman for Bishopsgate ward 8 June 1501-3 and Farringdon Without 1503-4. Elected sheriff for 1502-3: petition to mayor Feb. 1535 named Nynes and John DOGET (q.v.) as among the former sheriffs who had been 'reduced to extreme poverty' by the financial demands of the office. Accounts, II, f.296v; Hopkinson, *Ancient Records*, p. 114; *Cal. Letter Bk. L*, pp. 303, 309; Beaven, *Aldermen*, II, p. 18; *Cal. Letters and Papers Hen. VIII*, vol. 8, p. 78.

PEMBERTON, Hugh. Apprenticed in 1457-8 to Richard Nayler (master of the Company in 1475-6, alderman 1482-3), following whose death in 1485 he, along with Stephen JENYNS (q.v.), entered into a bond with the chamberlain of the city on behalf of Nayler's children. Had obtained the freedom by 1466-67 when admitted to the livery of his craft and enrolled six apprentices between 1466 and 1476. Was active as a general merchant: exported cloth through the port of London in Sept. 1472, was involved in the importation of calf skins from Genoa in 1479, and in 1483 took delivery of a large consignment of silk from a Venetian merchant. Several members of his family were also active in London in the early 1470s, including John Pemberton, a chancery clerk who was MP for Southwark in 1450, and Peter Pemberton who was from Eltham in Kent. HP was chosen as master of the Tailors for the year 1482-3 and as one of the auditors of the accounts of the wardens of London Bridge Sept. 1484-6, 1499-1500. In the summer of 1485 was a member of the committee appointed to co-ordinate the city's defence against Henry Tudor, and was among those chosen to ride to meet him after the battle of Bosworth. Supplied cloth worth more than £75 for the new King's coronation. Chosen by the commonalty as an MP to attend the Parliament summoned to meet 9 Nov. 1487. Served as sheriff of London from Feb.-Sept. 1490 on the death in office of Robert Revell. Alderman for Farringdon Without 1491-4 and for Aldgate 1494-1500. Will dated 7 Sept. 1500 and proved 28 Jan. 1501. Burial in choir of St. Martin Outwich with 5 masses of the Five Wounds to be said for five days afterwards. His wife Katherine survived him and in July 1503 herself exported cloth through the port of London. She died in 1508 and was buried alongside her husband in St. Martin's where she established a chantry for herself and Hugh. Their two sons, Matthew and Rowland were also buried in the church. Accounts, II, ff. 125, 296v; PRO, E122/194/20, m.10d; 80/3, m.26; *CCR 1476-85*, pp. 140, 305, 391. *CPMR 1458-82*, p. 168; Hopkinson, *Ancient Records*, p. 113; *Cal. Letter Bk. L*, pp. 215, 221, 225, 277; CLRO, Journal 9, ff. 83v, 84; Wickham Legg (ed.) *English Coronation Records*, p. 199; Beaven, *Aldermen*, vol. 2, p. 18; Dean and Chapter, Canterbury, Register F, f. 214v; PRO, PROB 11/16, ff. 15v–17, 42v, 43v.

PERCYVALE, Sir John. From Macclesfield in Cheshire. Began his career as serjeant-at-mace in the mayor's household, a post he held from 1457 until bef. Sept. 1467. Had already built up links with the Tailors by 1468-9 when admitted to the livery of the craft. Prob. around this time that he married Thomasine Barnaby (née Bonaventure), the widow of two tailors, Henry Galle (d. 1466) and Thomas Barnaby (d. 1467), whose businesses he inherited. Enrolled his first apprentices 1469-70 and became active as a general merchant, trading in a variety of commodities including wine and iron. No record of service as warden of the Tailors but was master for 1485-6. Alderman for Vintry ward 1485 and then for Langbourn, where he acquired his main residence, from 1496-d. Sheriff Sept. 1486-7. Knighted by Henry VII 1487. Auditor of accts. of London Bridge Sept. 1493-5. Was the losing candidate for the mayoralty on four occasions (1489, 1491, 1496, 1497), but eventually elected Sept. 1498, apparently with the support of the King, becoming the first member of the company to achieve that office. His earlier failures blamed by the Tailors upon their rivals, the Drapers, but the author of the *Great Chronicle* (a draper) put them down to the 'hote apetyte which he hadd yerely to that offyce'. Probably closely concerned in the acquisition of the controversial charter granted to the Tailors in Jan. 1503, widely viewed in the city as infringing the rights of the other companies. Will dated 21 Feb. and testament 4 March 1502/3. Numerous bequests included valuable items of plate left to 'the hole body of my felawship of taillours' as well as 12 messuages in Lombard Street which were to be used by the company to fund the salaries of two chantry priests in St. Mary Wolnoth. By deed of 25 Feb. 1503 founded Macclesfield Grammar school, having been 'much stirred' by consultations with his friend Thomas Savage, then archbishop of York. Died later that year, his heir being Richard P. of Ipswich (d. 1529). Following his death his widow, Thomasine, took over his business and began making arrangements for her own grammar school, to be founded in the parish of her birth, Week St. Mary in Cornwall. The school had been established under its first master by the time of her death in 1512. She made further bequests to the Merchant Taylors' Company including tenements in St. Martin in the Vintry which were to be used to augment the chantries established by her late husband. For a fuller account of the lives of John and Thomasine Percyvale, and the foundation of their schools, see Davies, 'Dame Thomasine Percyvale', pp. 185–207; Clode, *Early History*, vol. 2, pp. 8–21. For their wills see PRO, PROB 11/13, ff. 191v–193v; 11/17, ff. 218–221v; *CWCH*, vol. 2, pp. 605, 618.

PETYT, Thomas. Originally from Hever in Kent, but nothing recorded of his apprenticeship (if any). He enrolled an apprentice in 1480–1 but the date of his admission to the livery is unknown. Warden 1488–9, 1492–3 and master of the company 1497–8. Exported cloth through the port of London 1480–1, 1490–1. He died while still master of the Tailors at some point before the end of March 1498 whereupon his predecessor, Nicholas NYNES (q.v.), served out the remaining months until the election of Thomas BROMEFELD (q.v.) in June. He had in fact drawn up his will in February the previous year, well before his election. Its extensive provisions included cash bequests to his children and to Agnes, his third wife, who was to have governance of his daughter Jane, his lands called 'the Burgoyne' in Southwark, and estates at Hever and Westerham in Kent while his sons Thomas and John were minors. The will also disposed of shops and a warehouse, and numerous bequests were made to servants and apprentices. One of the souls to benefit from an obit to be established in his parish church of St. Magnus the Martyr was that of fellow tailor and near neighbour, Henry KELLOW (q.v.). His household goods included 'a boke of parchemyn writen with gold lettres called Speculum Vite Christi' and a suit of mail which he had inherited from his father. The Tailors themselves were to receive 100s. and 2 standing cups, one of which had belonged to Kellow. These were duly recorded in an inventory of the Company's plate taken in March 1512. The will was proved on 25 Mar. 1498. Accounts, III, f. 136; Hopkinson, *Ancient Records*, pp. 114–5; Cobb (ed.), *Overseas Trade*, pp. 116, 132, 155; PRO, E122/78/9, mm. 9d, 17; Clode, *Memorials*, pp. 74–5, 89; PRO, Prob. 11/11, ff. 160–162.

PHILIP (Phelip), John. Possibly the JP who was apprenticed 1441–2 to Luke Philibowe and who had obtained the freedom by 1453–4 when he presented an apprentice of his own. This man subsequently went on to serve as master of the craft in 1466–7 and for part of 1476–7 following the death in office of Richard Warner. With William GALLE and John STODARD (q.q.v.) was a surety for the sum of £100 on behalf of the children of a fellow tailor, Thomas Burgeys (master 1467) in July 1471. In July 1477 chosen with six others by the Common Council to sell superfluous brick and lime originally bought to repair the city wall. Enrolled 12 apprentices 1453–70. Prob. died. in the summer of 1486 as his last recorded appearance at the court was 24 May that year. Accounts, I, f. 341v; II, f. 4; Hopkinson, *Ancient Records*, pp. 112, 113; *Cal. Letter Bk. L*, pp. 94, 149.

POVEY, John. Brother of Walter P. (q.v.). Apprenticed to William Person (master of the Tailors' company 1462-3) in 1462-3. Prob. admitted to the livery in the 1470s (records damaged). Chosen as warden in June 1492, when his brother was master, and again in June 1495. Made his will 19 July 1499 asking for burial in the church of St. Mary Aldermary where he established a 7 year chantry. Left £26 13s. 4d. to the Tailors for an obit to be celebrated for 40 years. His son William and daughter Joan were left bequests of £100 each. His executors included his 'beloved brother' Walter, and his 'cosyn' John Tresawell who became master of the company in June 1511. The will was witnessed by Henry Mayour, the clerk of the company, who on this occasion was described as 'notary papall'. The will was proved 1 Aug. 1499. Accounts, II, f. 226v; Hopkinson, *Ancient Records*, pp. 112, 114; PRO, PROB 11/11, ff. 300-300v.

POVEY, Walter. Brother of John P. (q.v.). Apprenticed 1457-8 to Robert Colwich (master 1460-1 and city chamberlain 1463-74). Admitted to the livery 1469-70. Exported 92 cloths through the port of London in 1480-1, and a supplier of cloth to the Great Wardrobe 1480, 1483 and for the coronations of Richard III and Henry VII. On the latter occasion provided 4989 staves of ray cloth worth £124 16s. 6d. Supplied scarlet and ray cloth worth more than £97 for the coronation of Elizabeth of York, 1487, when he was one of the common councilmen chosen to attend on the Chief Butler. Auditor of accounts of London Bridge Sept. 1488-90. Perhaps the 'Walter Peby' who was listed in the alien subsidy roll of 1483 as the employer of a German servant. Warden of the Tailors' company 1474-5 and master 1492-3. A merchant adventurer by 1502. Drew up will on 28 Oct. the same year 'sore seke of body'. Requested burial in St. Mary Aldermary 'afore the Roode there in the myddle of the said churche atte the hedde of the buriall of master Raufe Hollande late Alderman deceased'. Holand (d. 1452) had been Colwich's master and was perhaps seen by WP as a kind of 'occupational grandfather'. Left his children 100 marks each to be taken out of the sale of goods from his shops. No date for probate. Was the executor of his brother's will. Accounts, II, f. 124v; III, f.6; Cobb (ed.), *Overseas Trade*, pp. 126, 129, 151, 155; *Coro. Richard III* ed. Hammond and Sutton, p. 386; Wickham Legg (ed.) *English Coronation Records*, p. 199; *Cal. Letter Bk. L*, pp. 261, 270; Bolton (ed.), *Alien Communities*, p. 91; *Acts of Court* ed. Lyell and Watney, pp. 250-1; Dean and Chapter of Canterbury, Register F, f. 200; Hopkinson, *Ancient Records*, p. 114.

RANDALL, Thomas. Apprenticed 1467–8 to Richard WEST (q.v.). He subsequently married West's daughter and on 7 Apr. 1486 enrolled his son, William, as his apprentice. In his 1496 will West bequeathed him a psalter 'lymmed with gold'. No record of his admission to the livery or of any apprentices presented before 1486. Exported cloth through the port of London 1480–1, 1490–1, 1495–6, 1503 and became a merchant of the Calais Staple. Chosen as warden of the tailors June 1486, and as master for 1493–4. Still a member of the court 1499, but had apparently retired to Hackney by Jan. 1508/9 when he made his will in which he bequeathed property in the parish of St. Lawrence Pountney in London. The will was proved 28 Mar. 1515. Accounts, II, f. 312; Cobb (ed.), *Overseas Trade*, p. 99; PRO, E122/78/9, mm. 15d, 16d–17; 203/6, ff. 28v, 30, 32, 32v, 35, 35v; 80/2, m. 27; PROB 11/11, f. 48v; 11/18, ff. 119–119v; Clode, *Memorials*, p. 75.

RUSSH, John. Little is recorded of this individual who only made four appearances as a member of the court from Feb. to May 1491. He is probably to be identified as the JR of London whose will was proved in the Prerogative Court of Canterbury on 16 May 1498 and who asked to be buried in the church of St. Mary Barking. PRO, PROB 11/11, ff. 174v–175.

SMYTH, Richard. Apprenticeship and admission to the livery not recorded. Enrolled apprentices in 1476–7 and 1477–8. Chosen as warden of the Tailors 1493–4 and 1496–7; elected master 1502–3 and served as one of the sheriffs of the city 1508–9. Drew up will 22 Mar. 1524 requesting burial in the church of St. John the Evangelist, Watling Street. Bequests incl. torches to the churches at Stapleford Tawney and Vernon Tawny, Essex. Will proved 1 June 1527. Inquisition *post mortem* recorded that he died 27 Mar. 1526/7, leaving property worth £29 p.a. in St. John's parish to the Tailors for the establishment of a chantry and an obit there. Accounts, III, ff. 101, 112v; PRO, PROB 11/22, ff. 154v–155; *Abstracts of Inquisitions Post Mortem Relating to the City of London in the Tudor Period*, ed. G. S. Fry, 3 vols (London, 1896–1908), vol. 1, pp. 45–6.

SPENCER, John. Possibly the son of the JS who was warden of the craft in 1451–2. Apprenticed in 1453–4 to William MARCHALL (q.v.), and obtained the freedom by 1462–3 when he enrolled Thomas Barley as his apprentice. Admitted to the livery of the craft 1466–67. Received pardon of his outlawry June 1467 for debts of £120 and £10 owed to a Hereford merchant and a 'senglewoman' of London respectively. Chosen as master of the Tailors for 1490–1. Retired to Streatham where he died 1510 leaving 40s. to the company. Hopkinson, *Ancient Records*, pp. 112, 114; Accounts, II, f. 3, 227, 296v; *CPR 1467-77*, p. 4; GL, Merchant Taylors' Co., Ancient Deeds, LIV.

STALWORTH, Walter. Admitted to the livery 1464–65, and warden 1474–5. Little else recorded of him prior to 1486 and he made only eight subsequent appearances at the court, the last being on 1 Sept. 1488. Made his will 31 July 1487 requesting burial in the church of the Austin Friars. His son William, also a tailor, was to receive £200 as well as his tenements in the parish of St. Margaret's Westminster on attaining the age of 26. The will was proved 24 Jan. 1488/9. In Mar. 1491 patrimony was delivered to William in the city chamber. Accounts, II, f.255v; *Cal. Letter Bk. L*, p. 279; PRO, PROB 11/8, ff. 142–3.

STODARD, John. Master of the Company in 1465–6, and perhaps again in 1484–5. He was apprenticed to William Latoner in 1440–1 and by 1453 had obtained the freedom and entered the livery. Over the next 20 years he presented at least 16 apprentices. Chosen auditor of the Bridge House accounts Sept. 1476, 1477. Regularly attended meetings of the court until his death, which probably took place in the summer of 1490. Hopkinson, *Ancient Records*, p. 112; Accounts, I, f. 329v; II, f. 3; *Cal. Letter Bk. L*, pp. 94, 144, 151, 231.

SWAN, John. Admitted to the livery 1462–63, but not known whether he obtained the freedom by apprenticeship or by another route. Presented apprentices in 1465–6 and 1466–7. Warden of the Tailors 1465–6 and master 1470–1. Warden of the fraternity of St. Mary and St. Dunstan, in the church of St. Dunstan in the West with Thomas BROMEFELD (q.v.), 1473. Auditor of the accounts of the wardens of London Bridge Sept. 1481–1 and served as alderman for Tower ward 1483–92, and as sheriff Sept. 1485–6. Among those chosen by common council to attend the chief butler at coronation of Richard III, July 1483. Died May 1492 and buried in chapel of Our Lady in White Friars. Bequests suggest possible Yorkshire origins. Survived by wife Rose who delivered the sum of 1,075 marks to the Tailors for the establishment of chantries and other services for John's soul (see above, pp. 257, 259). She died in early 1497 and her will contained further bequests to the company, including 10 marks per annum for a chantry priest in the church of St. Benet Fink for 10 years. Accounts, II, f. 228; *Cal. Letter Bk. L*, pp. 110, 181, 208; Beaven, *Aldermen*, vol. 2, p. 18; *CPR 1461-7*, p. 463; PRO, PROB 11/9, ff. 130–1, 11/11, ff. 169v–171v.

TEGO (or Tygoo), Roger. Apprenticed 1436–7 to John Kyng (master of the Company 1433–4), and had obtained the freedom by 1444–5 when he presented his first apprentice. Admission to livery not recorded but probably between 1445 and 1453 (records missing). Enrolled 12 apprentices 1453–74, including Alan HOBERD (q.v.). Chosen as master of the Tailors' Company for 1463–4. Auditor of accounts of wardens of London bridge Sept. 1468–70.

A regular supplier of cloth and clothing to Sir John Howard (later duke of Norfolk) in the 1460s: the Howard household books also record payments to his wife and servants. Last recorded appearance at the court of assistants was 24 June 1490 and prob. died soon afterwards. An inventory of plate carried out in January the following year lists 'a stondyng gilt cup, covered, chaced with a Tyger in the botom, of the gifte of master Tego'. Accounts, I, ff. 279, 386; II, ff. 3, 63, 100, 151v, 171v, 207v, 275, 294v, 328v, III, f. 60; *Cal. Letter Bk. L*, pp. 80, 86, 162; Crawford (ed.) *Household Books*, pt. II, pp. 150, 215, 246–7, 286, 406, 415, 463, 483, 484, 487, 490; Clode, *Memorials*, p. 83.

WARNER, Oliver. Apprenticed 1456-7 to William Gowman. Possibly related to several other Warners who were members of the company in the 1450s and 1460s. Warden of the company 1488-9, attended first court meeting 24 Mar. 1490, but died later that year. Will dated 16 Sept. 1490 and proved 8 Oct. Left robes to two brothers and the residue of his estate to his widow, Joan. Burial in St. Katherine Cree. Accounts, II, f. 99; Hopkinson, *Ancient Records*, pp. 113–4; PRO, PROB 11/8, ff. 205v–206.

WEST, Richard. He was apprenticed to John Prynce (master 1456-7) in 1441-2, duly obtained the freedom, and was eventually admitted to the livery in 1463-64. His first known apprentice (1464-5) was a relative, John West, while another was Thomas RANDALL (q.v.). In December 1469 he embarked upon a partnership with a Nicholas Mille to whom he supplied £400 worth of cloth which Mille was to trade with for 12 years on his behalf. The partnership broke up after Mille claimed that West was trying to take more profit than he was entitled to. Probably master of the Tailors' Company in 1478-9 (for which no records survive) judging from his position ahead of Roger BARLOWE, (master in 1479-80, q.v.) in subsequent attendance lists. Chosen to assess residents of Dowgate ward for their part of a 'benevolence' of 5,000 marks raised in 1481 to help the King against the Scots. Became involved in a dispute (c.1475-1485) with William Lucas, the anchorite at All Hallows London Wall, who was the former guardian of one of West's apprentices. WL claimed that West had ill-treated the apprentice and had made false allegations of the apprentice's own misbehaviour in order to justify his refusal to pay back a loan. because of the apprentice's own misbehaviour. In his will, proved in March 1496/7, he described himself as 'late citizein and tailloure of London now of Blakemore in the countie of Essex', suggesting that he had recently retired there. Among his bequests was a psalter to Randall, by then his son-in-law. West's own son, William, was apprenticed to Randall on 7 Apr. 1486. Accounts, I, f. 341v; II, f. 241v; *Cal. Letter Bk. L*, pp. 175–6; PRO, C1/59/165; 66/66–9; PROB 11/11, ff. 43v–44.

WILFORD, James. From Rye in Sussex. Apprenticeship not recorded but admission to the livery of the Tailors noted in the minutes for 26 May 1486 (see Text). Chosen as warden of the company for 1488-9 and became master in June 1494. He served as sheriff of London 1499-1500, auditor of the accounts of London Bridge 1506-8, and was alderman for Aldgate ward 1500-11. Active as a cloth merchant from the 1490s onwards. First wife was Elizabeth, daughter of a John Bettenham of Pluckley in Kent. Subsequently married Joan and Margaret (not identified). One of his six sons, also William, was apprenticed to him on 18 Aug. 1488 and in Sept. 1506 the two men exported cloth through the port of London on the same ship. William himself served as master of the Merchant Taylors' Company for 1518-19, and several other descendants were also prominent members of the company in the 16th century. By an agreement of 26 May 1514 gave the company £433 6s. 8d., in return for which the Merchant Taylors agreed to celebrate his obit, fund an annual Good Friday sermon in St. Bartholomew the Less, and pay him an annuity of £9 13s. 4d. This agreement incorporated into his will of 26 Apr. 1526 in which he requested burial in St. Bartholomew's and made detailed arrangements for the services to be celebrated for his soul and for various charitable bequests, including the employment of the residue of the annuity on repairs to the highway he had 'caused to be made' between Northiam in Sussex and Riverhill (nr. Biddenden) in Kent. Left the manors of Hartridge and Hockridge in Kent to his eldest son, Thomas. His executors included Michael English, a mercer and alderman, who married Wilford's daughter. The couple were left the sum of 400 marks. Beaven, *Aldermen*, II. 20; Hopkinson, *Ancient Records*, pp. 114-6; Clode, *Memorials*, pp. 124, 283, 524; idem, *Early History*, vol.2, pp. 16, 30, 40-1. For his wills see *CWCH*, vol.2, p. 633 and PRO, PROB 11/22, ff. 102v-105v (transcribed in *Archaeologia Cantiana*, 48, pp. 30-32).

GLOSSARY OF TERMS

1. WORDS AND PHRASES

Aliens, *alientes* (Lat.) – immigrants from the continent. Sometimes referred to together with other immigrants to London as 'foreigns' (see below).

Bachelors' Company – association, also known as the fraternity of yeomen tailors, which was founded for the majority of freemen who were not members of the fraternity of St. John the Baptist (see below). Feast day celebrated on the Decollation of St. John the Baptist (29 August).

Bocher, botcher – a repairer or seller of second-hand clothing (*OED*). For much of the fifteenth century the Tailors tried to restrict aliens and other immigrants to this sector of the craft in an attempt to lessen the threat they posed to freemen of the craft who made new clothes. See Davies, 'Artisans, Guilds and Government', p. 146.

Chantry – an arrangement whereby a priest would celebrate a daily Mass, typically at an altar in a parish church, for the benefit of the souls of particular individuals, normally including that of the founder. Chantries were usually founded through donations of real property or money, which would be used to pay the stipend of the priest for a specified number of years or, less frequently, in perpetuity. The London livery companies were frequently used by individuals to implement such arrangements, and bequests of property for such purposes were common in the fourteenth and fifteenth centuries. See also 'obit' below.

Foreigns, foreyns, *forinsecos* (Lat.) – a term used to include all immigrants to London whether from the continent, Wales, Scotland, Ireland or from elsewhere in England.

Fraternity of St. John the Baptist – exclusive association for the wealthier tailors who were known as 'liverymen' after the robes worn on ceremonial occasions. Granted seven royal charters between 1327 and 1503, the last of which allowed it to change its name to the Merchant Taylors' Company. As a legally constituted body it held property on behalf on the craft, had a common box for funds, and could sue and be sued in law courts. Its master and wardens were responsible for administering the affairs of the fraternity but also exercised a wider

305

jurisdiction over the craft as a whole which they regulated on behalf of the City government.

Free sewer – a term used for tailors who had completed their apprenticeships but who had not yet opened shops of their own. A number of these men were employed as covenanted servants by more established freemen.

Galleyman, galyman – a term used in London and in other ports such as Southampton to describe traders and their servants who, after arriving by ship from the continent, were permitted to sell their goods in designated shops. Several ordinances concerning galleymen were passed by London's government in the late fifteenth century restricting their activities. Many appear to have been tailors and, as the court minutes suggest, the company itself actively sought to extract fines from those who wished to set up businesses in the capital. Further references in the Tailors' account books to fines levied during 'le temps des galeys' and 'le galeytyme' suggest that such workers often arrived in ships at particular times of the year. See Davies, thesis, pp. 169–70.

Mistery – a synonym for 'craft', this word was used both in connection with an individual's occupation and in a collective sense, e.g. the mistery of tailors. From the Latin *misterium* and the French *mestier*.

Obit; *obitus* (Lat.) – a Mass held annually, usually on the anniversary of the founder's decease and intended to benefit his or her soul and the souls of other named individuals. Less costly than a 'chantry' (see above), it was a popular choice for many individuals. Livery companies such as the Tailors were frequently used to administer such arrangements for their members and for other individuals with whom they had established a connection.

Occupy, to; *occupo* (Lat) – two related meanings occur in the minutes, both connected with the world of work. The first of these indicated that someone practised a particular trade (e.g. 'he occupied the craft of tailor'), while the second meaning was used in connection with employment (e.g. 'he employed X as his apprentice'). Both the Latin and English forms are used frequently in the minutes.

Opener, 'opner' etc. – a freeman who had paid the customary fine in order to obtain a license to open a shop.

Quit-rent, *quietus redditus* (Lat.) – a rent, usually a small amount, paid by freeholders or copyholders in lieu of services once owed to the original holders, often institutions such as religious houses.

Shaper, to shape; *apto* (Lat.) – this verb and its Latin equivalent were frequently used in connection with the work of tailors, whose primary skill lay in being able to 'shape' cloth according to the latest fashions: *OED*; Davies, thesis, p. 244.

Sir, *dominus* (Lat.), – this title was frequently used in the Middle Ages to refer to lay chaplains, such as those who were employed as chantry priests by the Tailors. The term has been retained in the text but omitted elsewhere to distinguish such men from knights who, in the text, are normally referred to by the addition of the words '*miles*' or 'knight'.

Set over, to – used in the minutes to denote the transfer of an apprentice to another master after the latter had died, left the City or had been found guilty of breaching regulations concerning apprenticeship.

Yeomen tailors – see 'Bachelors' company', above.

2. DAYS OF THE WEEK

[die] Dominica	Sunday
[die] Lune	Monday
[die] Martis	Tuesday
[die] Mercurii	Wednesday
[die] Jovis	Thursday
[die] Veneris	Friday
[die] Sabbati	Saturday

3. FEAST DAYS AND FESTIVALS USED IN THE MINUTES

All Hallows/All Saints' day (1 November)
Annunciation of the Blessed Virgin Mary (25 March)
Assumption of the Blessed Virgin Mary (15 August)
Candlemas (2 February)
Conception of the Blessed Virgin Mary (8 Dec.)
Decollation of St. John the Baptist (29 August)
Midsummer day (24 June)
Nativity of the Blessed Virgin Mary (8 September)
Nativity of St. John the Baptist (24 June)
Purification of the Blessed Virgin Mary (2 February)
St. Andrew (30 November)
St. Bartholomew (24 August)
St. George the Martyr (23 April)

St. Katherine the Virgin (25 November)
St. Martin (11 November)
St. Michael the Archangel (29 September)
SS Philip and James (1 May)
St. Peter's Chains/Lammas day (1 August)
SS Simon and Jude (28 October)

INDEX

This index aims to be comprehensive for all place- and personal-names, and for most subjects covered by the court minutes. To save space, and avoid excessive duplication, most of the subjects are to be found under the headings 'London' and 'Merchant Taylors' Company' although cross-references have been provided to other important subjects located elsewhere. In a number of cases, notably entries for court members, indexed entries may appear more than once on the cited page. References to notes where both the main text and a footnote are relevant appear in the form '74 + n. 86'; and in the form '74: n. 86' where only the note is relevant. Where other references follow a note reference, a semi-colon is used to divide them.

Page references in **bold** type indicate where biographical material on particular individuals may be found.

Individuals whose surnames are in UPPER CASE served as masters, wardens or as members of the court of assistants in the period 1486–1493. Their biographies can be found in Appendix IV.

Unless otherwise indicated, all individuals indexed are London tailors or their apprentices.

elected warden of Bachelors' Co., 204

Catelyn, Robert, 148
  apprentice of, 183
Catero, Peter de, galleyman, 116
Catterick Bridge, co. Yorks.
  tailor of, 94
Cavendish, Hugh, **60 + n. 53**; 71, 73, 84, 107, 134, 162, 220, 260
Cawdry, John
  apprentice of, 129
Cays, *see* Keyes
Cely, George, merchant, 285
Cena, Benedict de, galleyman, 114, 116 + n. 188; 122, 181, 264
Chamberleyn, Thomas
  dispute involving, 85
Chambre, John a, 98
Champernoun, Hugh, **57: n. 40**; 95, 118, 127, 150, 186, 200, 217
Chancery, royal, 123 + n. 204
Chantries, *see* Merchant Taylors' Company: chantries
Chantry commissioners, 22: n. 56
Chapel Royal, 42: n. 103
Chapman, John
  dispute involving, 195
Charfull, William
  dispute involving, 134
Charles VIII of France, 43
Charnall, Adam, of Moulton, co. Lincs., yeoman, 55
  John, son of, 55
Chawny, William, of Boston, co. Lincs., baker, 189
  Thomas, son of, 189, 202
Chelsea, co. Middx., 42
Chesham, Andrew, 153
Chesshire, Henry, chaplain, 21, 66, 284
Cheyne, Thomas, 136
  apprentice of, 139
Chicheley, John, 223, 269
Chicheley, Thomas, 250
Chigwell, co. Essex, 159: n. 272
Churchman, John, grocer, 20, 22–3, 73, 90 + n. 129; 95, 126–7, 138, 150, 176, 186, 200, 217, 219, 234 + n. 428; 260, 283

Chybold, Thomas, 173
Clarke, Geoffrey, of Cambridge, vintner, 62
  John, son of, 62
Clarke (Clerk), John
  apprentices of, 70, 121, 125
  disputes involving, 140, 145, 177
Clay, Robert, 64
Clay, Roger, 49, 223
  apprentices of, 153, 169
Clerk, Richard, 169
Clerk, Thomas, 143
Clerk, William, 112
Clode, Charles, company historian, 8
Clopton, Hugh, mercer and alderman
  mayoralty of, 209: n. 368
Cloth, 102, 213, 300, 303
  disputes over, 125, 141
  yard-stick used to measure, 198 + n. 346
Clothing, 96, 141–2, 145, 190, 202, 213, 242
  second-hand market, *see* London, trades and occupations: botchers
CLOUGH, Henry, 128, 163, 173, 177, 190, 192, 197, 203, 213, 223, 264–5, 269, 282, **288**
  dispute involving, 171
  elected warden, 183
Clyfton, Edmund, 106
Cockermouth, co. Cumb., 72
  yeoman of, 159
Cok, George, 176
Cok (Cokke, Cook), John, 111, 120, 133, 181, 223, 226, 247
  apprentices of, 91, 117
  Henry, son of, 247
Cok (Cokke), William, 186
  apprentices of, 95, 117, 151, 230
Cok, William, saddler, 235–6
Cokbene, William, 104
Cokson, John, of Derby, tailor, 105
  Richard, son of, 105
Colchester, co. Essex, 292
Colette, John, 54
Colman, John, 103
Colson (Colston), Robert, 226, 245
  apprentices of, 105, 108, 179

Howard, Sir John (later duke of
    Norfolk), 265: n. 483; 292, 303
HOWDAN, Thomas, 11, 92, 125, 142,
    163-4, 167, 172, 187, 223, 282,
    292-3
    apprentice of, 103
    elected warden, 165
Howe, *see* Hore
Howlet, *see* Hewelet
Hoxton, co. Middx., coiner of, 62
Hubanke, John
    apprentice of, 78
Hubert, *see* Hoberd
Huchyns, Hugh, 226, 266
Hugh, Hugh, of Carnarvon, Wales, 51
    William, son of, 51, 138
Humfrey, John, 48-49
Humfrey, Thomas, 48
Humfrey, Thomas, of Braham/Brame,
    Co. Cambs.
    John, son of, 50
Hyde, Robert, 226
Hymeson, Rowland, 162, 190
    dispute involving, 27, 189-90
Hynde, John
    apprentices of, 140, 151
Hynseley, William, 116

Imbroke, Thomas, procurator of the
    Arches, 238
Ingle (Yngill), Robert, 106
    apprentice of, 172
    elected warden of Bachelors' Co.,
    138
Inns of Court
    Lincoln's Inn, 9: n. 21
Iryell, Henry, 223, 239, 266, 270
Iryell, Richard, 112
Irysely, William, 55, 67
Iryssh, John
    dispute involving, 141
Islington, co. Middx., 62 + n. 57
Jackson, Richard, 100
Jackson, Robert, 124-5, 138
Jakes, Richard, chaplain, 93
Jawderell, William, 22, **75** + **n. 88**; 120,
    219
    Alice, wife of, 75, 219

Jenkyns, David, 85
JENYNS, Stephen, 13-14, 26, 28, 35,
    51, 67, 74, 81, 91-92, 97, 103, 111,
    114, 117-18, 127, 131-5, 144, 156,
    159: n. 273; 165-8, 170, 173, 179,
    183-5, 188, 191, 194-6, 200, 202,
    204-5, 208-10, 217, 221, 231, 243-4,
    247, 251, 253-5, 259, 263, 282, 286,
    288, 291, **293-4**, 296-7
    alderman, 293
    apprentice of, 62
    disputes involving, 131, 239
    election as master, 135
    Margaret, wife of, widow of William
    Buck, 287
    mayoralty, 35, 293
John, David, 70-71
John, Lodewic, 117
    apprentice of, 119
John, Nicholas, 140, 144-5
    apprentices of, 144, 157
Johnson, David
    apprentices of, 114, 154
Johnson, John, 173, 224, 232
Johnson (Johnston), Robert, 141, 223,
    227, 269
    apprentice of, 95
    dispute involving, 97
Joskyn, Richard, 83, 95, 222-3, 269,
    271-2
Jowderell, *see* Jawderell
Joynour, William, 162, 226
    apprentices of, 104, 176
Judson, John, 157

Kechyn, James a, 270
Kechyn, John a, 181, 222, 272
    apprentices of, 99, 175
Kelham, Robert, 96-97, 133-4, 151-2,
    171, 192, 222, 272
    apprentice of, 104
KELLOW, Henry, 133, 190, 197, 223,
    271, 282, **294**, 299
    apprentices of, 133, 180
    elected warden, 183
Kellow, Robert, 227
Kelly, John, 142
Kelly, Richard, 72